Fourth Edition

THE BEDFORD HANDBOOK FOR WRITERS

Diana Hacker

BEDFORD BOOKS of ST. MARTIN'S PRESS | BOSTON

For Bedford Books
Publisher: Charles H. Christensen
Associate Publisher/General Manager: Joan E. Feinberg
Managing Editor: Elizabeth M. Schaaf
Development Editor: Katherine A. Retan
Production Editor: Anne Benaquist
Copyeditor: Barbara G. Flanagan
Text design and typography: Claire Seng-Niemoeller
Cover design: Hannus Design Associates

The Bedford Handbook for Writers, Fourth Edition, was formerly titled
Rules for Writers.

For information, write: St. Martin's Press, Inc.
175 Fifth Avenue, New York, NY 10010
Editorial Offices: Bedford Books of St. Martin's Press
29 Winchester Street, Boston, MA 02116

ISBN: 0–312–09600–3 (Instructor's Annotated Edition)
      0–312–07530–8 (hardcover Student Edition)
      0–312–07529–4 (paperback Student Edition)

ACKNOWLEDGMENTS

Nelson W. Aldrich, Jr., from *Old Money: The Mythology of America's Upper
   Class.* Copyright © 1988 by Nelson W. Aldrich, Jr. Reprinted by permission
   of Alfred A. Knopf, Inc.
The American Heritage Dictionary of the English Language, from the entry "regard." Copyright © 1992 by Houghton Mifflin Company. Reprinted by permission from *The American Heritage Dictionary of the English Language.*
Natalie Angier, from "The Anatomy of Joy," *The New York Times Magazine.* Copyright © 1992 by The New York Times Company. Reprinted by
   permission.
Russell Baker, from *Growing Up.* Copyright © 1982 by Russell Baker. Published
   by Congden & Weed.

*Acknowledgments and copyrights are continued at the back of the book on
pages 720–21, which constitute an extension of the copyright page.*

Preface for Instructors

When I began writing this book, I had been teaching long enough to know just what I wanted in a handbook. At Prince George's Community College, my colleagues and I teach five composition classes a semester, each with twenty-five students of varying abilities, so there is all too little time for individualized grammar lessons. I wanted a handbook so clear and accessible that our students could learn from it on their own. I had in mind a book that would give students what they seem to prefer—straightforward, unambiguous rules—but without suggesting that rules are absolutes or that writing well is simply a matter of following the rules.

Further, because our students have such a range of abilities, I hoped for a book that would be useful for all of them, offering a little help or a lot of help depending on their needs. Finally, I envisioned a handbook that would support the philosophy of composition that we work so hard to convey in the classroom. Writing is a process, we tell our students, and revision is central to that process. Revision is not a punishment for failing to get things right the first time. Nor is it a perfunctory clean-up exercise. It occurs right on the pages of a rough draft, often messily, with cross-outs and insertions, and it requires an active mind, a mind willing to look at a draft from the point of view of the reader, to spot problems, and to choose solutions.

With these aims in mind, then, I began writing this book. And it was with them in mind that I rewrote it again and again, with each draft edging closer to my vision. Now, nine years after its initial publication and after much classroom testing, I have revised the book once again. Here are its principal features.

Hand-edited sentences. Most of the examples appear as they would in a rough draft, with handwritten revisions made in color over typeset faulty sentences. Unlike the usual technique of printing separate incorrect and correct versions of a sentence, hand-edited sentences highlight the revision, allowing students to grasp both the error and its correction at a glance. Further, hand-edited sentences mimic the process of revision as it should appear in the students' own drafts.

Award-winning design. At the 1985 New England Book Show, the judges presented the first edition of this book (then titled *Rules for Writers*) with a Special Merit Award, remarking that it was a pleasure to see a reference book "designed with taste, clarity, and simplicity." Because the design highlights rules and examples, the book is easy to skim; readers who want more help will find it in full explanations following rules and in small-print comments pegged to examples.

Quick reference charts. Many of the handbook's full-page charts take students back to their own writing, helping them review their drafts for common problems such as comma splices and subject-verb agreement. Other charts summarize important material: guidelines for peer reviewers, a checklist for global revision, strategies for avoiding sexist language, and so on.

New to this edition are eighteen "Looking at Yourself as a Writer" charts. When writers experience a problem repeatedly, often their difficulties can be traced to root causes: false or half-learned rules, fossilized habits, confused motivations, or needless fears. For example, a writer may be addicted to comma splices for cognitive or emotional reasons that cannot be addressed simply by learning rules and working exercises. Other writers may have difficulty asserting a thesis because of cultural conflicts or a lack of confidence. In the "Looking at Yourself as a Writer" charts, I hope to encourage the kind of self-reflection that leads to those occasional moments of recognition and flashes of insight that help us all grow as writers.

An organization reflecting the writing process. *The Bedford Handbook for Writers* moves from the whole paper and paragraphs through sentence rhetoric and diction to grammar, punctuation, and mechanics. This organization puts the stages of the writing process in context, thereby showing students when—as well as how—to revise and edit their drafts.

A problem-solving approach to errors. Where relevant, *The Bedford Handbook for Writers* attends to the linguistic and social causes of errors and to the effect of errors on readers. The examples of errors in the text are realistic, most having been drawn from student essays and local newspapers. The text treats these errors as problems to be solved, often in light of rhetorical considerations, not as violations of a moral code. Instead of preaching at students, it shows them why problems occur, how to recognize them, and how to solve them.

Extensive coverage of ESL problems. Part VI focuses exclusively on common problems facing speakers of English as a second language. Section 29, expanded in this edition, discusses ESL problems with verbs; section 30 explains when to use the articles *a, an,* and *the*; and section 31 alerts ESL students to a variety of other potential trouble spots and includes new material on prepositions.

New ESL boxes throughout the book alert students to possible ESL problems; a quick-reference chart of these boxes appears at the back of the book. In addition, more ESL material has been added to the following ancillaries: *Supplemental Exercises, Diagnostic Resources, Bedford Basics,* and *Background Readings.*

Special attention to dialect differences. Section 27, "Choose standard English verb forms," helps students with such matters as omitted *-s* and *-ed* endings and omitted verbs, problems often caused by dialect differences. Section 17d, on nonstandard English, contains cross-references to practical advice that appears elsewhere in the book.

Straightforward advice on composing and revising. Instead of philosophizing about the writing process, Part I of *The Bedford Handbook for Writers* shows students, through a multiplicity of examples on a variety of topics, how to find a process that will work for them. The emphasis, throughout, is on flexibility.

Part I now includes three student essays, two of them new, all accompanied by drafts or outtakes from different stages of the writing process.

Six chapters on the research paper. The "Research Guide," now Part IX, has been substantially revised. The section on using the library has been brought up to date, with more emphasis on computerized library resources. A new section on critical reading precedes the section on taking notes. Coverage of MLA and APA documentation systems is more thorough, and many of the models have been updated. Finally, a new APA paper has been added.

The "Research Guide" continues to focus on matters most troublesome to students: choosing and narrowing a topic, finding sources, integrating quotations, and avoiding plagiarism both at the note-taking and the drafting stages of the writing process. Full-page charts show students how to handle quotations, summaries, and paraphrases without plagiarizing.

A chapter on writing about literature. Chapter 53 takes students through the process of writing about literature: from forming an interpretation and planning the essay to drafting and revising it. Two sample essays are included: one on Langston Hughes's "Ballad of the Landlord" (without secondary sources) and one on Eudora Welty's "Why I Live at the P.O." (with secondary sources).

A chapter on writing arguments. Using a process approach, Chapter 52 shows students how to construct an argument that will have some hope of persuading readers who do not already agree with their views. The logical fallacies and common mistakes in inductive and deductive reasoning appear at the end of the chapter.

A unique section on document design. Both in the business world and in the academic world, writers are becoming increasingly interested in document design—the use of visual cues to help readers. Section 54, "Principles of document design," provides guidelines on selecting format options and using headings, displayed lists, and other visuals to make documents more effective. Section 55 (formerly 46) now includes both MLA and APA guidelines for preparing academic manuscripts. Section 56 (formerly 58) gives advice on business letters, résumés, and memos.

Extensive exercises, some with answers. At least one exercise set accompanies nearly every section of the book. Most sets begin with five lettered sentences with answers in the back of the book so students can test their understanding independently. The sets then continue with ten numbered sentences whose answers appear only in the *Instructor's Annotated Edition*, so that instructors may use the exercises in class or assign them as homework.

To help students learn to use the handbook independently as a reference, I have included three tutorials in "How to Use this Book" (formerly "Introduction for Students") and two exercises in section 4, "Revising and editing sentences."

A user-friendly index. The index of *The Bedford Handbook for Writers* helps students find what they are looking for even if they don't know grammatical terminology. When facing a choice between *I* and *me*, for example, students may not know to look up "Case" or even "Pronoun, case of." They are more likely to look up "*I*" or "*me*," so *The Bedford Handbook for Writers* includes index entries for "*I* versus *me*" and "*me* versus *I*." Similar user-friendly entries appear throughout the index of the fourth edition.

A wide array of ancillaries. To make *The Bedford Handbook for Writers* more useful for both students and instructors, the publisher has expanded the package of resources accompanying the handbook. All are free of charge to instructors, and a few are available for student purchase as well.

PRACTICAL RESOURCES FOR INSTRUCTORS
Instructor's Annotated Edition

Diagnostic Resources to Accompany The Bedford Handbook for Writers (with ESL versions)

Transparencies to Accompany The Bedford Handbook for Writers

PROFESSIONAL RESOURCES FOR INSTRUCTORS
Background Readings for Instructors Using The Bedford Handbook for Writers

The Bedford Guide for Writing Tutors

The Bedford Bibliography for Teachers of Writing, Third Edition

RESOURCES FOR STUDENTS
Bedford Basics: A Workbook for Writers, Second Edition (with Answer Key)

Answers to Exercises in The Bedford Handbook for Writers

Supplemental Exercises for The Bedford Handbook for Writers (with Answer Key)

Resources for Research and Documentation across the Curriculum to Accompany The Bedford Handbook for Writers

Research Workbook for The Bedford Handbook for Writers

Preparing for the CLAST with The Bedford Handbook for Writers

Preparing for the TASP with The Bedford Handbook for Writers

SOFTWARE
Grammar Hotline for The Bedford Handbook for Writers (IBM and Mac versions)

Exercise Tutor for The Bedford Handbook for Writers (IBM and Mac versions)

Writer's Prologue (IBM and Mac versions)

MicroGrade: A Teacher's Gradebook (IBM and Mac versions)

Acknowledgments

No author can possibly anticipate the many ways in which a variety of students might respond to a text: Where might students be confused? How much explanation is enough? What is too intimidating? Do the examples appeal to a range of students? Are they free of stereotypes? To help me answer such questions, nearly two hundred professors from more than one hundred colleges and universities contributed useful insights based on their varied experiences in the classroom.

For their many helpful suggestions, I would like to thank an unusually perceptive group of reviewers:

Gwen Anderson, Delaware County Community College
Marian Arkin, City University of New York, LaGuardia
 Community College
Christopher Baker, Lamar University
Eileen Barrett, California State University, Hayward
Mary Jo Berger, Randolph-Macon College
Cynthia Biggers, Parkland College
Lisa Birnbaum, University of Tampa
Wendy Bishop, Florida State University
Patricia Bizzell, College of the Holy Cross
Judy Boschult, Phoenix College
Steve Brahlek, Palm Beach Community College
Phyllis Burke, Hartnell College
Edna Burow, California State University, Northridge
Marilyn Carlson, Augustana College
Minnie Collins, Seattle Central Community College
Karis Crawford, University of Michigan
Avon Crismore, Indiana University–Purdue University
 at Fort Wayne
Frank DeBernardo, University of Maryland, College Park
George Diamond, Moravian College
Rocco Ditello, Broward Community College
Jane Dugan, Cleveland State University
Mitch Evich, Northeastern University
Richard Fabrizio, Pace University
Clara Fendley, Scottsdale Community College

Kathryn Flannery, Indiana University
Jack Folsom, Montana State University
Tahita Fulkerson, Tarrant County Junior College
Barbara Gable, University of California, Riverside
Barbara Gaffney, University of New Orleans
Susan Galloway, St. Mary's University
Iris Hart, Santa Fe Community College
Mary Kathrine Homer, Panola College
Rebecca Moore Howard, Colgate University
Beverly Huttinger, Broward Community College
Barbara Helfgott Hyett, Boston University
Barbara Jensen, Modesto Junior College
Leila Kapai, University of the District of Columbia
Brian Kennedy, Cedarville College
Paul Kleinpoppen, Florida Community College at Jacksonville
Mary Lauburg, Saint Louis Community College at Florissant
    Valley
Jennifer Low, University of Virginia
Kate Mangelsdorf, University of Texas at El Paso
John McCann, State University of New York, Stony Brook
Tim McLaughlin, Bunker Hill Community College
Kate Mele, Roger Williams University
Mark Miller, Pikes Peak Community College
Susan Miller, Santa Fe Community College
Terry Miller, Indian River Community College
William Mullinix, Prince George's Community College
Barbara Nightingale, Broward Community College
Marlene Pomper, Passaic County Community College
William Rakauskas, University of Scranton
Tom Recchio, University of Connecticut
James Robinson, University of Hawaii, Kapiolani Community
    College
Susan Roth, Prince George's Community College
Mary Jane Schenck, University of Tampa
Anne Shadrake, Virginia Marti College
Marsha Sinagra, Nova University
David Smith, Central Missouri State University
Joyce Stauffer, Indiana University–Purdue University
    at Fort Wayne
Bonnie K. Stevens, Augustana College

Kimberly Sullivan, Clark College
David Taylor, Moravian College
Kathleen Tickner, Brevard Community College
Richard Tracz, Oakton Community College
Julie Warmke-Robitaille, Santa Fe Community College
Molly Wingate, Colorado College
Kristin Woolever, Northeastern University
Noël Yount, Pearl River Public Library

For helping me to see the strengths and deficiencies of the third edition, thanks go to the many instructors who took the time to answer a detailed questionnaire:

Jeffrey Allen, University of Illinois at Chicago; Philip Auslander, Georgia Institute of Technology; George H. Bailey, Northern Essex Community College; Robert J. Barthell, Southeast Community College; Suzanne L. Bergman, Indiana University–Purdue University at Fort Wayne; Jane Borrelli, State University of New York, Albany; Thad Bower, University of California, Los Angeles; R. T. Burcaw, Moravian College; Edna Burow, California State University, Northridge; Mary E. Carey, University of Houston, Clear Lake; Marilyn A. Carlson, Augustana College; Lorrayne Carroll, University of Southern Maine; Ted Ciuba, Merced College; Sandra Clark, Bethel College; Lisa Cochran, University of Illinois at Chicago; Sharon E. Cogdill, University of Massachusetts, Lowell; Minnie A. Collins, Seattle Central Community College; Karis Crawford, University of Michigan; Tiffani Crawford, Bakersfield College; Richard W. Crowell, Boston University; M. Francine Danis, Our Lady of the Lake University; Jane Dugan, Cleveland State University; Donald E. Dunham, Broome Community College; Tyson L. Dutton, Clark College; Kathy Eisele, Onondaga Community College; Richard Fabrizio, Pace University; Diane H. Feigenson, Fairfield University; Susan Fisher, Towson State University; Rebecca Fjelland, Mankato State University; Sally Fox, North Seattle Community College; Polly Fry, University of Minnesota; Barbara Gable, University of California, Riverside; Donald Gallo, Central Connecticut State University; Susan Galloway, St. Mary's University; Luis R. Gamez, Fordham University; Diane Wellins Gaus, Bryant College; Pere Gifra, University of Illinois at Urbana-Champaign;

Evelyn V. Goke, Suomi College; Nancy Goldstein, Brandeis University; Michelle Erica Green, De Paul University; Marland D. Griffith, Rockingham Community College; John G. Hanna, University of Southern Maine; M. Janet Harris, Cornell University; V. J. Harrold, Delta College; Chris Hennessey, Babson College; Martha L. Henning, Portland Community College; Cynthia Herman, George Mason University; Edwin L. Hetfield, Jr., Onondaga Community College; Vranna Sue Hinck, University of Texas at Dallas; Ellen Horowitz, Adelphi University; Rebecca M. Howard, Colgate University; Patrick B. Hunter, California State University, Northridge; Mike Hurley, Bridgewater State College; Barbara Helfgott Hyett, Boston University; Anne Jackets, Everett Community College; Eleanor D. James, Montgomery County Community College; Patricia Johnson, San Diego State University; Jean-Marie Kauth, University of Michigan; Paul J. Killorin, Portland Community College; Rosemarie King, Millikin University (IL); Michael Kleeberg, Ball State University; David Kramer, City University of New York, York College; Janet L. Kurtz, Lancaster Bible College; Russ Larson, Eastern Michigan University; Chuck Lewis, University of Minnesota; Barbara Lightner, Indiana University–Purdue University at Fort Wayne; Rae Longest, University of Houston, Clear Lake; Jennifer Low, University of Virginia; Richard Maas, Central Missouri State University; Joyce Magnotto, Prince George's Community College; Barbara Marx, Northern Virginia Community College; Jeremy Mattson, Michigan State University; D. P. McDonough, Central Connecticut State University; Elliot McEldowney, Tufts University; Mark S. Miller, Pikes Peak Community College; Terry Miller, Indian River Community College; William Nichols, Denison University; Brian O'Driscoll, Portland Community College; Carol Osborne, University of Virginia; Tom Palombi, University of Virginia; Roswell Park, State University of New York College at Buffalo; William Peirce, Prince George's Community College; Gary Phillips, Clark College; Mark Pizzato, University of Wisconsin, Milwaukee; Carolyn Plumb, University of Washington; Leigh Pomeroy, Mankato State University; William Rakauskas, University of Scranton; Randal Ries, University of Illinois at Chicago; Robert E. Ryan, Clark College; Arlyne Samuels, City University of New York, Queensborough Community College; Carmen Schmersahl, Mount Saint Mary's College; Jo C. Searles,

Pennsylvania State University, Altoona Campus; Eugene Senff, Everett Community College; W. A. Senior, Broward Community College; Anne Shadrake, Virginia Marti College; Margaret Shirley, University of New Hampshire; Susan Stan, University of Minnesota; Marija Stankus-Saulaitis, University of Connecticut at Torrington; Joyce Stauffer, Indiana University–Purdue University at Fort Wayne; Bonnie K. Stevens, Augustana College; J. T. Stewart, Seattle Central Community College; Brendan Strasser, Kutztown University of Pennsylvania; Patricia Swift, Broward Community College; Leslie Tannenbaum, Ohio State University; David W. Taylor, Moravian College; Kathleen Tickner, Brevard Community College; Beth Walsh, Cleveland State University; Jianping Wang, University of Minnesota; Dana Cairns Watson, University of California, Los Angeles; Robert M. White, Rutgers University, Newark Campus; Ann Williams, University of New Hampshire; Daniel Wright, Concordia College; Sarah Wright, University of Virginia; Eldon Young, Cypress College; Betty R. Youngkin, University of Dayton; Bin Zhu, Boston University

Writing a handbook is truly a collaborative effort. Barbara Flanagan, Lloyd Shaw, William Peirce, Susan Roth, and Ruth Thomas helped me improve the research paper chapters; William Peirce assisted with the chapter on argument; Julia Sullivan contributed to the chapter on writing about literature; and Owen Shows, Mitch Evich, and Glenn Blalock helped with the exercises. My thanks go to all of them.

I am grateful as well to the authors of the book's ancillaries: to Leigh Ryan for her insightful *Guide for Writing Tutors*; to Glenn Blalock for his carefully edited *Background Readings*; to Wanda Van Goor, Mitch Evich, and Owen Shows for their varied *Diagnostic Resources*; to Wanda Van Goor for her lively exercises in *Bedford Basics*; to Deanne Harper for her innovative *Research Workbook*; to Barbara Fister for her excellent *Resources for Research and Documentation across the Curriculum*; and to Barbara Sloan and Carolyn Christensen West and to Ellen Shull and Paula Tran for their useful guides *Preparing for the CLAST* and *Preparing for the TASP*.

I am indebted to the students whose essays appear in this edition—Jim Dixon, Gary Laporte, Margaret Peel, Karen Shaw, Marie Visosky, and Diane Williford—not only for permission to use their work but for permission to adapt it for pedagogical purposes as well. My thanks also go to the following students for permission to use their paragraphs: Celeste Barrus, Jane Betz, Jim Drew, Connie Hailey, William G. Hill, Matthew J. Holicek, Patricia Klein, Linda Lavelle, David Queen, Julie Reardon, Margaret Stack, and John Clyde Thatcher.

Several talented editors have made invaluable contributions to the book. Kathy Retan has been a superb developmental editor: intelligent, tactful, patient, good-humored. Her fresh insights, based on her own recent classroom experience, were especially helpful as I wrestled with the "Looking at Yourself as a Writer" charts and the new section on document design. Copyeditor Barbara Flanagan has once again brought grace and consistency to the final manuscript; her keen eye has saved me from many a blunder. Proofreader Maggie Carr caught many a problem as well.

Book editor Anne Benaquist has expertly steered the book through production with the help of Jonathan Burns; and managing editor Elizabeth Schaaf has once again orchestrated the production of the book and its ancillaries with unflappable calm. DeNee Reiton Skipper has handled the page make-up with expertise. And award-winning designer Claire Seng-Niemoeller once again deserves credit for designing the charts and the clean, uncluttered pages that highlight the book's hand-edited sentences.

Also appreciated are the editors and coordinators of the book's many ancillaries. Ellen Kuhl shared thoughtful insights about the workbook, and Lori Chong skillfully managed its production. Beth Castrodale worked enthusiastically with the authors of eight ancillaries: *Guide for Writing Tutors, Background Readings, Resources for Research and Documentation across the Curriculum, Diagnostic Resources, Supple-*

mental Exercises, Preparing for the CLAST, Preparing for the TASP, and the *Annotated Instructor's Edition.* Kathy Retan edited the *Research Workbook,* and Meredith Weenick investigated software; in addition, Meredith, Andrea Goldman, and Kim Chabot handled other matters too numerous to mention. Ann Sweeney deserves a medal for shepherding most of these ancillaries through production, often under impossible deadlines.

Special thanks are due to publishers Chuck Christensen and Joan Feinberg. Ten years ago Chuck took a chance on an unknown community college professor with an inexplicable urge to write a handbook. I am deeply grateful to him for giving me this opportunity. In retrospect, I suppose Chuck knew that almost anyone could learn to write a handbook under the guidance of Joan Feinberg. Certainly a better teacher-editor could not have been found. Joan has consistently set a standard of excellence, and over the years she has nudged me toward it, always with intelligence, grace, and good humor. It would be impossible to overstate my gratitude.

Finally, a note of thanks goes to my parents, Clair and Georgiana Tarvin, and to Joseph and Marian Hacker, Robert Hacker, Greg Tarvin, Betty Renshaw, Bill Fry, Bill Mullinix, Joyce Magnotto, Christine McMahon, Anne King, Wanda Van Goor, Melinda Kramer, Joyce McDonald, Tom Henderson, the Dougherty family, and Robbie and Austin Nichols for their support and encouragement; and to the many students over the years who have taught me that errors, a natural by-product of the writing process, are simply problems waiting to be solved.

Diana Hacker

Prince George's Community College

How to Use This Book

Though it is small enough to hold in your hand, *The Bedford Handbook for Writers* will answer most of the questions you are likely to ask as you plan, draft, and revise a piece of writing: How do I choose and narrow a topic? What can I do if I get stuck? How do I know when to begin a new paragraph? Should I write *none was* or *none were*? When does a comma belong before *and*? What is the difference between *accept* and *except*?

How to find information with an instructor's help

When you are revising an essay that has been marked by your instructor, tracking down information is simple. If your instructor marks problems with a number such as *16* or a number and letter such as *12e*, you can turn directly to the appropriate section of the handbook. Just flip through the colored tabs on the upper corners of the pages until you find the number in question. The number *16*, for example, leads you to the rule "Tighten wordy sentences," and *12e* takes you to the subrule "Repair dangling modifiers." If your instructor uses an abbreviation such as *w* or *dm* instead of a number, consult the list of abbreviations and symbols inside the back cover of the book, where you will find the name of the problems *(wordy; dangling modifier)* and the number of the section to consult.

How to find information on your own

With a bit of practice, you will be able to find information in this book without an instructor's help—usually by turning to the brief table of contents inside the front cover, the index at the back of the book, the Glossary of Usage beginning on page 689, or one of the book's directories or lists.

THE BRIEF TABLE OF CONTENTS   Although you may occasionally want to turn to the full table of contents, the brief contents inside the front cover is usually a faster way into the book. As a quick glance at this table of contents will show you, *The Bedford Handbook for Writers* is organized to reflect the writing process. Advice about composing and revising comes first, followed by strategies for crafting sentences and choosing words and then editing them for grammar, punctuation, and mechanics. (Special help for speakers of English as a second language appears after the material on editing for grammar.) The book continues with several special reference sections: on research, writing arguments, writing about literature, document design, and grammar basics. It ends with a Glossary of Usage (an alphabetical list of commonly misused words) and the index.

Once you have become familiar with the plan of the book, the brief table of contents will often lead you quickly to the information you need. The following tutorial is designed to familiarize you with the plan of the book.

TUTORIAL 0-1 Using the brief table of contents

Use the brief table of contents (inside the front cover) to answer the following questions.

1. *The Bedford Handbook for Writers* contains seven student essays. Where can the first of them be found?
2. One part of the handbook is designed for speakers of English as a second (or third or fourth) language (ESL). What page does this part begin on? (Part titles are printed in rust.)
3. In what subsection of section 32 will you find a rule on using commas for introductory elements?
4. Where can you find advice regarding the use of appropriate language?
5. Which part of the handbook will help you learn to edit your writing for common grammatical problems?
6. Which part of the handbook gives a review of grammar basics: parts of speech, sentence patterns, and so on?
7. Which section of the handbook tells you how to document sources using the Modern Language Association (MLA) system?
8. Where will you find rules on capitalization?
9. On what page does the Glossary of Usage (an alphabetized list of commonly misused words) begin?
10. Where will you find advice on planning an essay?

ANSWERS TO TUTORIAL 0-1

1. At the end of Part I
2. Page 317 (Part VI)
3. Subsection 32b
4. Section 17
5. Part V: Editing for Grammar
6. Part XII: Grammar Basics
7. Section 50
8. Section 45
9. Page 689
10. Section 1

THE INDEX When the brief table of contents does not lead you quickly to the information you need, try the index at the back of the book. The index, arranged alphabetically, often takes you to the exact page you're looking for. You don't need to be a grammar expert to use it. The following tutorial shows you how the index works.

TUTORIAL 0–2 Using the index

Assume that you have written the following sentences and want to know the answers to the questions in brackets. Use the index to locate the information you need, and edit the sentences if necessary.

1. When in Aruba, Marlena bought several shell paintings for Donelle and me. [Should I use *me* or *I*?]
2. My favorite newscasters are those which reveal their point of view. [Is it okay to use *which* to refer to *newscasters*?]
3. The lower atmosphere consists of the troposphere, the stratosphere, and the mesosphere. [Should I put a colon after *of*?]
4. Anyone taking the school bus to the volleyball game must bring in a permission slip signed by their parents. [Is it okay to use *their* to refer to *Anyone*?]
5. Each of the documents has been carefully proofread by two readers. [Should I use *has* or *have*?] Hint: Look up *Each.*
6. Shortly after being seated, a waiter approached our table with a smile. [Does this sentence begin with a dangling modifier?]
7. Parents should monitor the television their children see, however, many parents give up because they would need to preview too many programs. [Should I use a comma or a semicolon before *however*?]
8. We only looked at two houses before buying the house of our dreams. [Is *only* in the right place?]
9. We had intended to go surfing but spent most of our vacation lying on the beach. [Should I use *lying* or *laying*?]
10. In Saudi Arabia it is considered ill mannered for you to accept a gift. [Is it okay to use *you* when I mean "anyone in general"?]

ANSWERS TO TUTORIAL 0–2

1. Looking up "*I* versus *me*" or "*me* versus *I*" will lead you to section 24, which explains why *me* is correct.

2. The index entry for *which* leads you to section 23e. The rule explains that *who* or *whom* (not *which*) should be used to refer to people: *those who reveal their point of view.*

3. The index entry "Colon" leads you to section 35. The final subsection, 35d, explains that a colon should not be used after a preposition such as *of.*

4. The index entry "*anybody, anyone*" mentions that the word is singular, so you might not need to look further to realize that the plural *their* is incorrect. The second page reference leads you to section 22a, which cautions against using a plural pronoun to refer to a singular word such as *anyone.* It also suggests non-sexist strategies for revision, such as *Anyone taking the school bus to the volleyball game must bring in a permission slip signed by his or her parents* or *Students taking the school bus to the volleyball game must bring in a permission slip signed by their parents.*

5. Looking up "*each*" leads you to section 21d and a quick answer: *Each* is singular, so the verb *has* is correct. Looking up "*has* versus *have*" takes you first to section 27c, where you will discover a cross-reference to section 21.

6. You can look up "Dangling modifiers" or "Modifier(s), dangling" to find section 12e, which tells you that *Shortly after being seated* is a dangling modifier because the subject of the sentence does not name the people being seated.

7. Looking up "*however*" leads you to section 32f, which explains that a conjunctive adverb like *however* is preceded by a semicolon and usually followed by a comma when it separates two independent clauses. This index also leads you to sections 20b and 34b, which explain the same thing. (The original sentence is a comma splice.)

8. The index entry "*only*" leads you to section 12a, which explains that limiting modifiers such as *only* should be placed before the words they modify. This sentence should read *We looked at only two houses before buying the house of our dreams.*

9. Index entries for both "*lie, lay*" and "*lay, lie*" will take you to section 27b and to the Glossary of Usage, which explain why *lying* (meaning "resting or reclining") is correct.

10. Looking up "*you*, indefinite use of" leads you to section 23d, which explains that *you* should not be used to mean "anyone in general." You can revise the sentence by using *a person* in place

of *you*, or you can restructure the sentence completely: *In Saudi Arabia accepting a gift is considered ill mannered.*

THE GLOSSARY OF USAGE   The Glossary of Usage beginning on page 689 explains the difference between commonly confused words, such as *advise* and *advice* or *among* and *between.* It also lists colloquialisms and jargon that are inappropriate in formal written English. For an exercise on using the Glossary of Usage, see page 59.

DIRECTORIES AND LISTS   Certain frequently consulted items appear in directories or lists. The directory to the Modern Language Association (MLA) documentation models is on pages 490–91, which are printed with a vertical band of color. Directories to documentation models for alternative systems appear on pages 542 and 543. At the end of the book, after the index, you will find a quick-reference list of the charts in *The Bedford Handbook for Writers.* You will also find a list of the handbook's ESL notes, useful for speakers of English as a second language. Inside the back cover are a list of correction symbols and an index of grammatical terms.

The following tutorial gives you practice consulting the handbook as a reference.

TUTORIAL 0–3   Finding answers in real-life situations

If you have done tutorials 0–1 and 0–2, you have used the brief table of contents and the index of this book (and you know where to find the Glossary of Usage). Now imagine that you are in the following real-life situations. For each situation, decide which reference aid is most likely to lead you quickly to the information you need: the brief table of contents, the index, or the Glossary of Usage. If the first reference aid you try leads to a dead end, try another.

1. You are Ray Farley, a community college student who has been out of high school for ten years. You recall learning to punctuate items in a series by putting a comma between all items except

the last two. In your college readings, however, you have noticed that most writers use a comma between all items. You're curious about the current rule. What does the handbook tell you?

2. You are Maria Sanchez, an honor student working in your university's writing center. Mike Lee has come to you for help. He is taking a writing-intensive course with a psychology professor who marks down an essay a full letter grade for each sentence fragment, comma splice, or fused sentence. What sections of the handbook will help Mike learn to revise his own writing for these problems?

3. You are John Pell, engaged to Jane Dalton. In a note to Jane's parents, you have written "Thank you for giving Jane and myself such a generous contribution toward our honeymoon trip to Hawaii." You wonder if you should write "Jane and I" or "Jane and me" instead. What does the handbook tell you?

4. You are Diane Jacobs, an English major. You have drafted and revised a five-page analytical essay about a literary work (without documentation), and you are ready to type the final copy. It is midnight. You have no idea how to format the essay, but you recall your professor saying something about MLA guidelines. Where in the handbook will you find MLA guidelines on manuscript format? Which of the book's seven student essays will you consult as a model?

5. You are Joe Thompson, a first-year college student. Your girlfriend, Samantha, who has completed two years of college, seems to enjoy correcting your English. Just yesterday she corrected your sentence "I felt badly about her death" to "I felt bad about her death." You're sure you've heard many educated persons, including professors, say "I felt badly." Upon consulting the handbook, what do you discover?

6. You are Selena Young, an African American woman who works for HUD in a supervisory capacity. Two of your employees, Jake Gilliam, an African American man, and Susan Green, a white woman, have writing problems involving -s endings on verbs. You suspect that these problems stem from nonstandard dialects spoken at home.

   Susan and Jake are in danger of losing their jobs because your boss thinks that anyone who writes "the landlords agrees" or "the tenant refuse" is beyond hope. You disagree. Susan and

Jake are more intelligent than your boss supposes, and they have asked for your help. Where in the handbook can they find the rules they need? Is there a chart they can consult when in doubt?

ANSWERS TO TUTORIAL 0–3

1. Using the brief table of contents (inside the front cover) Ray Farley can locate Part VII, Editing for Punctuation, which begins with section 32, The comma. Section 32c explains that although usage varies, most experts advise using a comma between all items in the series—because omitting the comma can lead to ambiguities or misreadings. (The index would work as well but would be slower.)

2. Writing center tutor Maria Sanchez would probably use the brief table of contents to find section 19 on fragments and section 20 on comma splices and fused sentences. (Since these are common problems, she might even have the numbers memorized.) Students who didn't know to look under "Editing for Grammar" in the table of contents could use the index instead. The index also gives the page numbers of useful charts on reviewing one's own writing for fragments, comma splices, and fused sentences.

3. Unless John Pell is a grammar expert, he would have difficulty finding the appropriate section in the brief table of contents. Few people know that the issue of "*I* versus *me* versus *myself*" appears under "Case of personal pronouns" (section 24). Pell could look up "*I*," "*me*," or "*myself*" in the index, however, and find page 270, which explains that "Thank you for giving Jane and me such a generous contribution" is correct. An entry for *myself* also appears in the Glossary of Usage, with a cross-reference to section 24.

4. Diane Jacobs could use the brief table of contents to locate section 55, "Academic formats." A quick look at section 55 would tell her that 55a deals with MLA guidelines on format. The index could also lead her to section 55; she could look up "Format," "Manuscript Formats," or "MLA style." To locate the sample student essay (without documentation), which appears at the end of section 53, Jacobs would probably scan the brief table of contents.

5. By consulting the index or the Glossary of Usage, Joe Thompson would find page 692, where he would learn that "I felt bad" is correct. If Thompson wanted a fuller understanding of why it is correct, he could follow up the cross-reference to section 26.

6. Not everyone knows that grammarians classify problems with -s endings on verbs under "Subject-verb agreement," so Selena Young would probably look up "-s" in the index. The subentry "as verb ending" would lead her to sections 21 and 27c. By browsing through section 21, she would discover a chart on page 253 that would be useful for her employees.

How to use this book for self-study

In a composition class, most of your time should be spent writing. Therefore it is unlikely that you will want to study all of the chapters in this book in detail. Instead you should focus on the problems that tend to crop up in your own writing. Your instructor (or your college's writing center) will be glad to help you design an individualized program of self-study.

The Bedford Handbook for Writers has been designed so that you can learn from it on your own. By providing answers to some exercise sentences, it allows you to test your understanding of the material. Most exercise sets begin with five sentences lettered a–e and conclude with ten sentences numbered 1–10. Answers to the five lettered sentences appear in an appendix at the end of the book.

Diana Hacker

Contents

Part II

Part III

Part IV

Part V

Part VI

Part VII

Part VIII

Part IX

Part XI

Part XII

PART I

Composing and Revising

Since it's not possible to think about everything all at once, most writers work on a piece of writing in stages. They begin by generating ideas and sketching a plan. When they feel ready to attempt an initial draft, they rough it out imperfectly, concentrating more on content than on style, grammar, and mechanics. If possible, they then get away from the draft for a while.

For most writers, revising is seldom a one-step process. The larger elements of writing receive attention first — the focus, organization, paragraphing, content, and overall strategy. Improvements in sentence structure, word choice, grammar, punctuation, and mechanics usually come later.

Of course, the writing process will not always occur for you quite as simply as just described. While drafting, for example, you may discover an interesting new approach to your topic that demands a revised plan. Or while revising you may need to generate more ideas and draft new material. Although you should generally move from planning to drafting to revising, be prepared to circle back to earlier stages whenever the need arises.

1

Generate ideas and sketch a plan.

Before attempting a first draft, spend some time generating ideas. Mull over your subject while listening to music or driving to work, jot down inspirations on scratch paper, and explore your insights with anyone willing to listen. At this stage you should be collecting information and experimenting with ways of focusing and organizing it to best reach your readers.

1a Assess the writing situation.

Begin by taking a look at the writing situation in which you find yourself. The key elements of the writing situation include your subject, the sources of information available to you, your purpose, your audience, and constraints such as length, document design, and deadlines.

It is unlikely that you will make final decisions about all of these matters until later in the writing process — after a first draft, for example. Nevertheless, you can save yourself time by thinking about as many of them as possible in advance. For a quick checklist, see pages 14–15.

Subject

Frequently your subject will be given to you. In a psychology class, for example, you might be asked to explain Bruno Bettelheim's Freudian analysis of fairy tales. Or in a course on the history of filmmaking, you might be assigned an essay on the political impact of D. W. Griffith's silent film *The Birth of a Nation.* In the business world, your assignment might be to draft a quarterly sales report or craft a diplomatic letter to a customer who has complained about your firm's computer software.

Sometimes you will be free to choose your own subject. Then you will be wise to select a subject that you already know something about or one that you can reasonably investigate in the time you have. Students in composition classes have written successfully on all of the subjects listed here, most of which were later narrowed into topics suitable for essays of 500–750 words. By browsing through the lists, perhaps you can pick up some ideas of your own.

> *Education:* computers in the classroom, an inspiring teacher, sex education in junior high school, magnet schools, a learning

disability such as dyslexia, programmed instruction, parochial schools, teacher certification, a local program to combat adult illiteracy, creative means of funding a college education

Careers and the workplace: working in an emergency room, the image versus the reality of a job such as lifeguarding, a police officer's workday, advantages of flextime for workers and employers, company-sponsored day care, mandatory drug testing by employers, sex or racial discrimination on the job, the psychological effects of unemployment, the rewards of a part-time job such as camp counseling

Families: an experience with adoption, a portrait of a family member who has aged well, the challenges facing single parents, living with an alcoholic, a portrait of an ideal parent, growing up in a large family, the problems of split custody, an experience with child abuse, the depiction of male-female relationships in a popular TV series, expectations versus the reality of marriage, overcoming sibling rivalry, the advantages or disadvantages of being a twin

Health: a vegetarian diet, weight loss through hypnotism, a fitness program for the elderly, reasons not to smoke, the rights of smokers or nonsmokers, overcoming an addiction, lithium as a treatment for depression, the side effects of a particular treatment for cancer, life as a diabetic, the benefits of an aerobic exercise such as swimming, caring for a person with AIDS

Sports and hobbies: an unusual sport such as free-fall parachuting, surviving a wilderness program, bodybuilding, a sport from another culture, the philosophy of karate, the language of sports announcers, pros and cons of banning boxing, coaching a Little League team, cutting the costs of an expensive sport such as skiing, a portrait of a favorite sports figure, sports for the handicapped, the discipline required for a sport such as gymnastics, the rewards of a hobby such as woodworking

The arts: working behind the scenes at a theater, censorship of rock and roll lyrics, photography as an art form, the Japanese tea ceremony, the influence of African art on Picasso, the appeal of a local art museum, a portrait of a favorite musician or artist, performing as a musician, a high school for the arts, the colorization of black-and-white films, science fiction as a serious form of literature, a humorous description of romance novels or hard-boiled detective thrillers

Social justice: an experience with racism or sexism, affirmative action, reverse discrimination, making public transportation accessible for the physically handicapped, an experience as a juror, a local program to aid the homeless, discrimination against homosexuals, pros and cons of a national drinking age of twenty-one

Death and dying: working on a suicide hotline, the death of a loved one, a brush with death, caring for terminally ill patients, the Buddhist view of death, explaining death to a child, passive euthanasia, death with dignity, an out-of-body experience

Violence and crime: an experience with a gun, a wartime experience, violence on television news programs, visiting a friend in prison, alternative sentencing for first offenders, victims' rights, a successful program to eliminate violence in a public high school, violence between parents and children or between husband and wife

Nature and ecology: safety of nuclear power plants, solar energy, wind energy, air pollution in our national parks, grizzly bears in Yellowstone, communication among dolphins, organic gardening, backpacking in the Rockies, marine ecology, an experimental farming technique, cleaning up Boston Harbor, the preservation of beaches in Delaware

Many of these subjects are too broad. Part of your challenge as a writer will be whittling broad subjects down to manageable topics. If you are limited to a few pages, for example, you could not possibly do justice to a subject as broad as "sports for the handicapped." You would be wise to restrict your paper to a topic more manageable in the space allowed —perhaps a description of the Saturday morning athletic program your college offers for handicapped children. The chart on page 7 suggests specific ways to narrow a subject to a topic.

Sources of information

Where will your facts, details, and examples come from? Can your topic be illustrated by personal experience, or will you need to search out relevant information through direct observation, interviews, questionnaires, or reading?

PERSONAL EXPERIENCE You can develop many topics wholly through personal experience, depending of course on your own life experiences. The students who wrote about lifeguarding, learning disabilities, weight loss through hypnotism, and free-fall parachuting all spoke with the voice of experience, as did those who wrote about flextime, coaching a Little League team, and company-sponsored day care. When narrowing their subjects, those students chose to limit themselves to information they had at hand. For example, instead of writing about company-sponsored day care in general—a subject that would have required a great deal of research— one student limited her discussion to the successful day-care center at the company for which she worked.

DIRECT OBSERVATION Direct observation is an excellent means of collecting information about a wide range of subjects, such as parent-child relationships on the television program *The Simpsons*, the language of sports announcers, or the appeal of a local art museum. For such subjects, do not rely on your memory alone; your information will be fresher and more detailed if you actively collect it, with a notebook or tape recorder in hand. As writer Stuart Chase advises young journalists assigned to report on their city's water system, "You will write a better article if you heave yourself out of a comfortable chair and go down in tunnel 3 and get soaked."

Ways to narrow a subject to a topic

SUBDIVIDING YOUR SUBJECT

Many subjects can be subdivided. Instead of writing about cen-sorship of popular songs, for example, you might select a sub-division of this general subject: censorship of rap music. Or instead of writing about homelessness in general, you might focus on homeless families in a particular shelter.

RESTRICTING YOUR PURPOSE

Often you can narrow your subject by restricting your purpose. For example, if your subject is drug testing in the workplace, you might at first hope to persuade readers that it should be banned in all situations. Upon further reflection, however, you might realize that this goal is more than you could hope to ac-complish, given your word limit. By adopting a more limited purpose—to show that drug testing is unreliable, to argue that its use by private employers should be banned, or to demon-strate that it violates an innocent person's right to privacy— you would have a better chance of success.

RESTRICTING YOUR AUDIENCE

Another way to narrow your subject is to write for a particular audience. For example, instead of writing to a general audience on a subject such as teenage pregnancy, you might address persons with a special interest in the subject: young people, parents, or counselors working for Planned Parenthood.

CONSIDERING THE INFORMATION AVAILABLE TO YOU

One of the most natural ways to narrow a subject is to look at the information you have collected. If you have gathered a great deal of information on one aspect of your subject (for example, discrimination against persons with AIDS) and less informa-tion on other aspects (such as the causes of AIDS or promising treatments for AIDS), you may have found your topic.

INTERVIEWS AND QUESTIONNAIRES   Interviews and questionnaires can supply you with detailed and interesting information on a variety of subjects. A nursing student interested in the care of terminally ill patients might interview nurses at a hospice; a political science major might speak with a local judge to learn about alternative sentencing for first offenders; a future teacher might conduct a survey on the classroom use of computers in local schools. It is a good idea to tape interviews to preserve any lively quotations that you might want to weave into your essay. (See page 459.) Keep questionnaires simple and specify a deadline to ensure that you get a reasonable number of responses.

READING   Reading will be your primary source of information for many college assignments, which will generally be of two kinds: analytical assignments that call for a close reading of one book, essay, or literary work or research assignments that send you to the library to consult a variety of sources on a particular topic. For analytical essays, you can usually assume that your reader is familiar with the work and has a copy of it at hand. You select details from the work not to inform readers but to support an interpretation. When you quote from the work, page references are often sufficient. For research papers, on the other hand, you cannot assume that your reader is familiar with your sources or has them close at hand. This means that you must formally document all quoted and summarized or paraphrased material (see 50 and 51). When in doubt about the need for formal documentation, consult your instructor.

Purpose

Your purpose will often be dictated by the specific writing situation that faces you. Perhaps you have been asked to take minutes for a club meeting, to draft a letter requesting payment from a client, or to describe the results of a biology experiment. Even though your overall purpose is fairly obvious in such situations, a close look at that purpose can help you make a variety of necessary decisions. How detailed should the minutes be? Is your purpose to summarize the meeting or to establish a careful record of discussion in case future controversies arise? How firmly should your letter request payment? Do you need the money at all costs, or do you hope to get it without risking loss of the client's business? How technical is the biology report expected to be?

In many writing situations, part of your challenge will be discovering a purpose. Consider, for example, the topic of magnet schools — schools that draw students from different neighborhoods because of features such as advanced science classes or late-afternoon day care. Your purpose could be to inform parents of the options available in your county. Or you might argue that the county's magnet schools are not promoting racial integration as had been planned. Or you might propose that the board of education create a magnet high school for the arts on your college campus.

Although no precise guidelines will lead you to a purpose, you can begin by asking yourself which one or more of the following aims you hope to accomplish.

PURPOSES FOR WRITING

to inform	to evaluate
to persuade	to recommend
to call readers to action	to request
to change attitudes	to propose
to analyze	to provoke thought
to argue	to express feelings
to theorize	to entertain
to summarize	to give aesthetic pleasure

It is surprising how often writers misjudge their own purposes: informing, for example, when they should be recommending; summarizing when they should be analyzing; or expressing feelings about problems instead of proposing solutions. Before beginning any writing task, therefore, pause to ask, "Why am I communicating with my readers?" And this question will lead you to another important question: "Just who are those readers?"

Audience

Audience analysis can often lead you to an effective strategy for reaching your readers. One writer, whose purpose was to persuade teenagers not to smoke, jotted down the following observations about her audience:

> dislike lectures, especially from older people
> have little sense of their own mortality
> are concerned about physical appearance and image
> want to be socially accepted
> have limited budgets

This analysis led the writer to focus more on the social aspects of smoking (she pointed out, for instance, that kissing a smoker is like licking an ashtray) than on the health risks. Her audience analysis also warned her against adopting a preachy tone that her readers might find offensive. Instead of lecturing to her audience, she decided to draw examples from her own experience as a hooked smoker: burning holes in her best sweater, driving in zero-degree weather late at night in search of an open tavern to buy cigarettes, rummaging through ashtrays for stale butts, and so on. The result was an essay that reached its readers instead of alienating them.

The following checklist will help you decide how to approach your audience.

AUDIENCE CHECKLIST

How well informed are your readers about the subject?

What do you want them to learn about the subject?

How interested and attentive are they likely to be?

Will they resist any of your ideas?

What is your relationship to them: Employee to supervisor? Citizen to citizen? Expert to novice? Scholar to scholar?

How much time are they willing to spend reading?

How sophisticated are they as readers? Do they have large vocabularies? Can they follow long and complex sentences?

Of course, in some writing situations the audience will not be neatly defined for you. Nevertheless, many of the choices that you make as you write will tell readers who you think they are (novices or experts, for example), so it is best to be consistent — even if this means creating an audience that is in some sense a fiction.

Writers in the business world often find themselves writing for multiple audiences. A letter to a client, for instance, might be distributed to sales representatives as well. Readers of a report may include persons with and without technical expertise or readers who want details and those who prefer a quick overview. To satisfy the demands of multiple audiences, business writers have developed a variety of strategies: attaching cover letters to more detailed reports, adding boldface headings, placing summaries in the left margin, and so on.

In the academic world, considerations of audience can be more complex than they seem at first. Your professor will read your essay, of course, but most professors play multiple roles while reading. Their first and most obvious roles are as coach and judge; less obvious is their role as an intelligent and objective reader, the kind of person who might reasonably be informed, convinced, entertained, or called to action by what you have to say.

Some professors create writing assignments that specify an audience, such as a hypothetical supervisor, readers of a local newspaper, or fellow academics in a particular field of study. Other professors expect you to imagine an audience appropriate to your purpose and your subject. Still others prefer that you write for a general audience of educated readers — nonspecialists who can be expected to read with an intelligent, critical eye. When in doubt about an appropriate audience for a particular assignment, check with your professor.

Length, document design, and deadlines

Writers seldom have complete control over length, document design, and deadlines. Journalists usually write within strict word limits set by their editors, businesspeople routinely aim for conciseness, and most college assignments specify an approximate length.

Certain document designs may also be required by your writing situation. Specific formats are used in the business world for documents such as letters, memos, reports, budget analyses, and personnel records. In the academic world, you may need to learn precise conventions for lab reports, critiques, research papers, and so on. For most undergraduate essays, a standard format is acceptable (see 55). The conventions used for research papers are discussed in 50 and 51.

In some writing situations, you will be free to create your own document design, complete with headings, displayed lists, and perhaps even visuals, such as charts and graphs. Quite sophisticated results are now possible on computers, and both writers and readers are becoming increasingly interested in designs that improve readability. For a discussion of the principles of document design, see 54.

A final constraint is the deadline. The deadline tells you what is possible and helps you plan your time. For complex writing projects, such as research papers, you'll need to manage your time quite carefully. By working backward from the deadline, you can create a schedule of target dates for completing various parts of the process. See page 440 for an example.

EXERCISE 1–1

Choose one of the subject areas mentioned on pages 3–5 and add at least five subjects to those already on the list. If other members of your class have also done this exercise, pool the results.

EXERCISE 1–2

Narrow five of the following subjects into topics that would be manageable for an essay of two to five pages.

1. Working behind the scenes at a theater
2. A sport from another culture
3. Violence between parents and children
4. The advantages or disadvantages of being a twin
5. An experience with adoption
6. The side effects of a particular treatment for cancer
7. Computers in the classroom
8. Parochial schools
9. Performing as a musician
10. An experience with racism or sexism

EXERCISE 1–3

Which of the following subjects might be illustrated wholly by personal experience? For the others, suggest possible sources of information: direct observation, interviews, questionnaires, or reading.

1. The problems of split custody
2. Working in an emergency room
3. Backpacking in the Rockies
4. The influence of African art on Picasso
5. Violence on television news programs
6. The discipline required for a sport such as gymnastics
7. Photography as an art form
8. Affirmative action
9. A local program to aid the homeless
10. Visiting a friend in prison

Checklist for assessing the writing situation

At the beginning of the writing process, you may not be able to answer all of the questions on this checklist. That's fine. Just be prepared to think about them later.

NOTE: It is not necessary to think about the elements of a writing situation in the exact order listed in this chart.

SUBJECT

— Has a subject (or a range of possible subjects) been given to you, or are you free to choose your own?

— Is your subject worth writing about? Can you think of any readers who might be interested in reading about it?

— How broadly can you cover the subject? Do you need to narrow it to a more specific topic (because of length restrictions, for instance)?

— How detailed should your coverage be?

SOURCES OF INFORMATION

— Where will your information come from: Personal experience? Direct observation? Interviews? Questionnaires? Reading?

— If your information comes from reading, what sort of documentation is required?

PURPOSE

— Why are you writing: To inform readers? To persuade them? To entertain them? To call them to action? Some combination of these?

AUDIENCE

— How well informed are your readers about the subject?

— What do you want them to learn about the subject?

— How interested and attentive are they likely to be?

— Will they resist any of your ideas?

— What is your relationship to them: Employee to supervisor? Citizen to citizen? Expert to novice? Scholar to scholar?

— How much time are they willing to spend reading?

— How sophisticated are they as readers? Do they have large vocabularies? Can they follow long and complex sentences?

LENGTH

— Are you working with any length specifications? If not, what length seems appropriate, given your subject, your purpose, and your audience?

DOCUMENT DESIGN

— Must you use a particular design for your document? If so, do you have guidelines or examples that you can consult?

DEADLINE

— What is your deadline? How much time will you need to allow for the various stages of writing, including typing and proofreading the final draft?

EXERCISE 1-4

Suggest a purpose and audience for five of the following subjects.

1. A vegetarian diet
2. Cutting the costs of an expensive sport such as skiing
3. The challenges facing single parents
4. Advantages of flextime for workers and employers
5. Growing up in a large family
6. Pros and cons of a national drinking age of twenty-one
7. Science fiction as a serious form of literature
8. An usual sport such as free-fall parachuting
9. A police officer's workday
10. Working on a suicide hotline

EXERCISE 1-5

For each of the following paired items, choose the sentence or passage that is more effective, given the writer's purpose and audience. Be prepared to explain your choices.

1. Here are two notices sent out by dentists to remind patients to call for an appointment. Which notice is more effective?

   a. Things to do today:
      1. Floss.
      2. Call your dentist.
      It's time again for your regular dental checkup, so please call today for an appointment.

   b. It is the custom of this office to notify patients on record for periodical examination of the mouth. This service is rendered to safeguard previous work and to ensure future good health and appearance. May I suggest you call.

2. If you were writing an instruction booklet for machinists at a tractor manufacturer, which version of the following sentence would you choose?

   a. Move the control lever to the reverse position after the machine stops.

   b. After the machine stops, move the control lever to the reverse position.

3. In an essay about a short story, which sentence announces a clearer interpretation?

   a. In "The Lottery," Shirley Jackson uses symbolism to reveal the emptiness of rituals and traditions and the dark side of human nature.

   b. Shirley Jackson's "The Lottery" uses subtle symbolism along with incongruities to exemplify the loss of significance of some rituals and traditions and flaws of human nature.

4. In a business letter promoting the writer's company to an audience aware of the company's former problems, which version of the following sentence is more effective?

   a. At this point in time ours is a revitalized and emergent company no longer attached to outmoded marketing concepts, no longer subject to inbred managerial alliances, and never again dependent on reactionary governmental influences.

   b. We have revitalized our company with new marketing ideas, a forward-looking management, and a wider base of clients.

5. Which of the following sentences would be more effective in a campus newspaper article criticizing the food in the cafeteria's vending machines?

   a. First and foremost, the hamburgers that are sold in the cafeteria's machines are dry in texture and cold to the taste.

   b. When I turned to the machine, I decided to try a sizzling hamburger, lean and juicy. Instead, out came a small dry patty so cold that the fat was congealed in tiny globs on top of the meat.

1b Experiment with ways to explore your subject.

Instead of just plunging into a first draft, experiment with one or more techniques for exploring your subject, perhaps one of these:

listing	freewriting
clustering or branching	keeping a journal
asking questions	talking

For writing based on reading, two other techniques will also prove useful: note taking and annotating (see 48 and 53).

Whatever technique you turn to, the goal is the same: to generate a wealth of ideas. At this early stage of the writing process, you should aim for quantity, not necessarily quality, of ideas. If an idea proves to be off the point, trivial, or too far-fetched, you can always throw it out later.

Listing

You might begin by simply listing ideas, putting them down in the order in which they occur to you — a technique sometimes known as "brainstorming." Here, for example, is a list one student writer jotted down:

Lifeguarding — an ideal summer job?

my love of swimming and lying in the sun

hired by Powdermill Village, an apartment complex

first, though, there was a test

two weeks of training — grueling physical punishment plus book work

I passed. The work was over — or so I thought.

greeted by manager; handed a broom, hose, bottle of disinfectant

scrubbing bathrooms, cleaning the pool, clearing the deck of dirt and leaves

little kids breaking every pool rule in the book — running on deck, hanging on buoyed ropes, trying to drown each other

spent most of my time blowing the whistle

working the evening shift no better — adults smuggling in gin and tonics, sexual advances from married men

by end of day, a headache and broom-handled hands

The ideas appear here in the order in which they first occurred to the writer. Later she felt free to rearrange them, to cluster them under general categories, to delete some, and to add others. In other words, she treated her initial list as a source of ideas and a springboard to new ideas, not as an outline.

Clustering or branching

Unlike listing, the techniques of clustering and branching highlight relationships among ideas. To cluster ideas, write your topic in the center of a sheet of paper, draw a circle around it, and surround that with related ideas connected to it with lines. If some of the satellite ideas lead to more specific clusters, write them down as well. The writer of the following diagram was exploring ideas for an essay on home uses for computers.

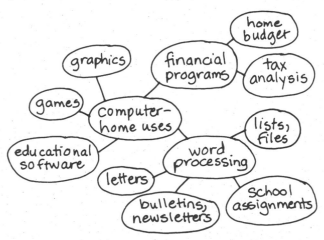

To use the branching technique, put the main idea at the top of a page and then list major supporting ideas beneath it, leaving plenty of space between ideas. To the right of each major idea, branch out to minor ideas, drawing lines to indicate the connections. If minor ideas lead to even more specific ideas, continue branching. Here, for example, is a branching diagram for an essay describing an innovative magnet high school called "School without Walls."

School without walls — an attractive option

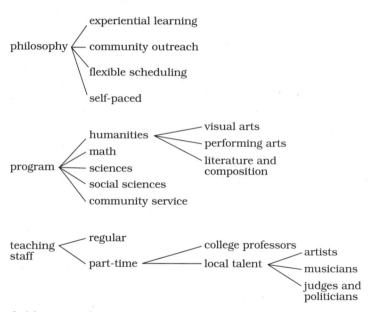

Asking questions

By asking relevant questions, you can generate many ideas —and you can make sure that you have adequately surveyed your subject. When gathering material for a story, journalists routinely ask themselves Who? What? When? Where? Why? and How? In addition to helping journalists get started, these questions ensure that they will not overlook an important fact: the date of a prospective summit meeting, for example, or the exact location of a neighborhood burglary.

Whenever you are writing about events, whether current or historical, the journalist's questions are one way to get started. One student, whose subject was the negative reaction in 1915 to D. W. Griffith's silent film *The Birth of a Nation*, began exploring her topic with this set of questions:

Who objected to the film?

What were the objections?

When were protests first voiced?

Where were protests most strongly expressed?

Why did protesters object to the film?

How did protesters make their views known?

In the academic world, scholars often generate ideas with questions related to a specific discipline: one set of questions for analyzing short stories, another for evaluating experiments in social psychology, still another for reporting field experiences in anthropology. If you are writing in a particular discipline, try to discover the questions that scholars typically explore. These are frequently presented in textbooks as checklists. See 53a for an example.

Freewriting

In its purest form, freewriting is simply nonstop writing. You set aside ten minutes or so and write whatever comes to you, without pausing to think about word choice, spelling, or even meaning. If you get stuck, you can write about being stuck, but you should keep your pencil moving. The point is to loosen up, relax, and see what happens. Even if nothing much happens, you have lost only ten minutes. It's more likely, though, that something interesting will emerge on paper—perhaps an eloquent sentence, an honest expression of feeling, or a line of thought worth exploring.

To explore ideas on a particular topic, consider using a technique known as *focused freewriting*. Again, you write quickly and freely—without regard for word choice, spelling, punctuation, or even paragraphing—but this time you focus on a subject and pay some attention to meaning. The following passage was written freely by a student who was recalling childhood visits to his grandparents' farm.

> Memories. Memories of Canton, Mississippi. We called it The Farm, like it was the only farm in the world. There was lots to keep us busy, 90 acres of untamed pastures. One of the first things that comes to mind is playing in the haybarn, climbing through the hay stacked high to the rafters. We would burrough a path between the bails tunnelling our way to the top. This was alot of fun until someone disturbed one of the many wasp nests making everyone scatter. Cruising the pastures, we enjoyed testing sound travel. We would spread out from each other and still talk at a normal tone audibly. I remember once getting over 100 yards away from my brother—although we would have to talk slowly and clearly, we could understand each other. Another game for the pasture was to lie on the ground, be very quiet, slow our breathing, and wait for the buzzards. We could never figure out how they knew we weren't dead.
> — David Queen, student

Despite the awkward beginning, the misspellings, and some problems with punctuation, this freewriting has potential. Its writer later polished some of the sentences and included them in an essay.

Keeping a journal

A journal is a collection of personal, exploratory writings. An entry in a journal can be any length—from a single sentence to several pages—and it is likely to be informal and experimental.

In a journal, meant for your eyes only, you can take risks. In one entry, for example, you might do some freewriting or focused freewriting. In another, you might pose a series of interesting questions, whether or not you have the answers. In still another, you might play around with language for the sheer fun of it: writing "purple prose," for instance, or parodying the style of a favorite author or songwriter.

Keeping a journal can be an enriching experience in its own right, since it allows you to explore issues of concern to you without worrying about what someone else thinks. A journal can also serve as a sourcebook of ideas to draw on in future essays; on rare occasions, in fact, a journal entry may emerge as a polished essay of interest to readers other than yourself. Some writers find that they do their best work when writing for themselves, deliberately ignoring the constraints of a formal writing situation.

Should you decide to keep a journal, here are some prompts to help you get started.

SOME IDEAS FOR JOURNAL WRITINGS

— Record some stories from your family's history.

— Describe some of your more interesting dreams.

— Write about a moral dilemma that you (or a friend or relative) once faced or that you now face.

— Describe a turning point in your life.

— Write a history of your involvement with a hobby or an art form; or write about current projects.

— Record your first impressions of a course you are taking this semester.

— Keep a running log of your involvement in a class that features interesting group discussions.

— Write an imaginary dialogue between two major historical figures you have read about, or a scientist and a philosopher, or characters in different novels.

— Comment on an interesting idea encountered in one of your college classes — a historical interpretation, a psychological theory, a new biological breakthrough.

— Parody the style of a favorite author or songwriter. Or mimic the style of a genre with which you are familiar (such as romances, hard-boiled detective novels, or sports writing).

Talking

The early stages of the writing process need not be lonely. Many writers begin a writing project by brainstorming ideas in a group, debating a point with friends, or engaging in conversation with a professor. Others turn to themselves for company—by talking nonstop into a tape recorder.

Talking can be a good way to get to know your audience. If you're planning to write a narrative, for instance, you can test its dramatic effect on a group of friends. Or if you hope to advance a certain argument, you can try it out on listeners who hold a different view.

As you have no doubt discovered, conversation can deepen and refine your ideas before you even begin to set them down on paper. Our first thoughts are not necessarily our wisest thoughts; by talking and listening to others we can all stretch our potential as thinkers and as writers.

EXERCISE 1–6

Generate a list of at least fifteen items for one of the subjects listed on pages 3–5.

EXERCISE 1–7

Using the technique of clustering or branching, explore one of the subjects listed on pages 3–5.

1c Settle on a tentative focus.

As you explore your subject, you will begin to see possible ways to focus your material. At this point, try to settle on a tentative central idea.

For many types of writing, your central idea can be asserted in one sentence, a generalization preparing readers for the supporting details that will follow. Such a sentence, which will ordinarily appear in the opening paragraphs of your finished essay, is called a *thesis.* A successful thesis — like the following, all taken from articles in *Smithsonian*—points both the writer and the reader in a definite direction.

> Much maligned and the subject of unwarranted fears, most bats are harmless and highly beneficial.

> Geometric forms known as fractals may have a profound effect on how we view the world, not only in art and film but in many branches of science and technology, from astronomy to economics to predicting the weather.

> Aside from his more famous identities as colonel of the Rough Riders and President of the United States, Theodore Roosevelt was a lifelong professional man of letters.

The thesis sentence usually contains a key word or controlling idea that limits its focus. The preceding sentences, for example, prepare for essays that focus on the *beneficial* aspects of bats, the *effect* of fractals on how we view the world, and Roosevelt's identity as a writer, or *man of letters.*

It's a good idea to formulate a thesis early in the writing process, perhaps by jotting it on scratch paper, by putting it at the head of a rough outline, or by attempting to write an introductory paragraph that includes the thesis. Your tentative thesis will probably be less graceful than the thesis you include in the final version of your essay. Here, for example, is one student's early effort:

> Although they both play percussion instruments, drummers and percussionists are very different.

The thesis that appeared in the final draft of the student's paper was more polished.

> Two types of musicians play percussion instruments — drummers and percussionists — and they are as different as Quiet Riot and the New York Philharmonic.

Don't worry too soon about the exact wording of your thesis, however, because your main point may change as your drafts evolve. (See 2b and 3b.)

For some types of writing, it may be difficult or impossible to express the central idea in a thesis sentence; or it may be unwise or unnecessary to put a thesis sentence in the paper itself. A personal narrative, for example, may have a focus too subtle to be distilled in a single sentence, and such a sentence might ruin the story. Strictly informative writing, like that found in many business memos, may be difficult to summarize in a thesis. In such instances, do not try to force the central idea into a thesis sentence. Instead, think in terms of an overriding purpose, which may or may not be stated directly in the paper itself.

1d Sketch a tentative plan.

Once you have generated some ideas and formulated a tentative thesis, you may want to sketch an informal outline. Informal outlines can take many forms. Perhaps the most common is simply the thesis followed by a list of major supporting ideas.

> Hawaii is losing its cultural identity.
>
> — pure-blooded Hawaiians increasingly rare
> — native language diluted
> — natives forced off ancestral lands
> — little emphasis on native culture in schools
> — customs exaggerated and distorted by tourism

Clustering or branching diagrams, often used to generate ideas, can also serve as rough outlines (see pages 19 and 20). And if you began by jotting down a list of ideas (see page 18), you may be able to turn the list into a rough outline by crossing out some ideas, adding others, and numbering the ideas to create a logical order.

Another type of informal outline, the tree diagram, pictures more complex relations among ideas. Here, for example, is a tree diagram on the subject of the disposal of nuclear waste.

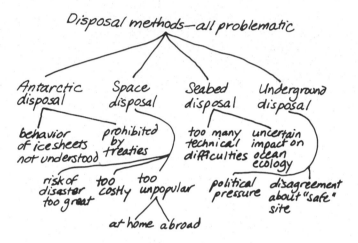

When to use a formal outline

Early in the writing process, rough outlines have certain advantages over their more formal counterparts: They can be produced more quickly, they are more obviously tentative, and they can be revised more easily should the need arise. However, a formal outline may be useful later in the writing process, after you have written a rough draft, especially if your subject matter is complex.

The student who sketched the tree diagram about the disposal of nuclear waste later wrote a sentence outline that improved and clarified the structure of his rough draft. Notice that the student's thesis is an important part of the outline.

Everything else in the outline supports it, either directly or indirectly.

> Thesis: Although various methods for limiting or disposing of nuclear wastes have been proposed, each has serious drawbacks.

  I. The process of limiting nuclear waste through partitioning and transmutation has serious drawbacks.
   A. The process is complex and costly.
   B. Nuclear workers' exposure to radiation would increase.

  II. Antarctic ice sheet disposal is problematic for scientific and legal reasons.
   A. Our understanding of the behavior of ice sheets is too limited.
   B. An international treaty prohibits disposal in Antarctica.

  III. Space disposal is unthinkable.
   A. The risk of an accident and resulting worldwide disaster is great.
   B. The cost is prohibitive.
   C. The method would be unpopular at home and abroad.

  IV. Seabed disposal is unwise because we do not know enough about the procedure or its impact.
   A. Scientists have not yet solved technical difficulties.
   B. We do not fully understand the impact of such disposal on the ocean's ecology.

  V. Deep underground disposal endangers public safety and creates political problems.
   A. Geologists disagree about the safest disposal sites, and no sites are completely safe.
   B. There is much political pressure against the plan from citizens who do not want their states to become nuclear dumps.

In constructing a formal outline, keep the following guidelines in mind.

1. Put the thesis at the top.

2. Make items at the same level of generality as parallel as possible (see 9).
3. Use sentences unless phrases are clear.
4. Use the conventional system of numbers and letters for the levels of generality.

   I.
      A.
      B.
         1.
         2.
            a.
            b.
               (1)
               (2)
                  (a)
                  (b)
   II.

5. Always use at least two subdivisions for a category, since nothing can be divided into fewer than two parts.
6. Limit the number of major sections in the outline; if the list of roman numerals begins to look like a laundry list, find some way of clustering the items into a few major categories with more subcategories.
7. Be flexible; in other words, be prepared to change your outline as your drafts evolve.

2

Rough out an initial draft.

As long as you treat an initial draft as a rough draft, you can focus your attention on ideas and organization, knowing that problems with sentence structure and word choice can always be dealt with later.

2a Let it be rough and keep it moving.

Before beginning a first draft, gather together your prewriting materials — lists, diagrams, outlines, freewriting, and so on. In addition to helping you get started, such notes and blueprints will encourage you to keep moving. With your earlier thoughts close by, you won't need to pause so frequently, staring at a blank page in search of ideas. Writing tends to flow better when it is drafted relatively quickly, without many stops and starts. The trick, of course, is to relax — to overcome the fear that grips many of us as we face that blank page.

At one time or another, we all experience writer's block. But if writer's block is a chronic problem for you, consider whether you're being too hard on yourself. Do you demand that your sentences all be stylish and perfectly grammatical right from the start? Do you expect your ideas to emerge full-blown, like Athena from the head of Zeus?

Professional writers are not so tough on themselves. Jacques Barzun, for example, lets his rough-draft sentences be "as stupid" as they wish. Joan Didion acknowledges that she discovers ideas *as she writes;* for her, writing is a way of learning, not just a means of revealing already known truths. As Didion puts it, "I write entirely to find out what I'm thinking, what I'm looking at, what I see and what it means."

2b For most types of writing, draft an introduction that includes a thesis.

The introduction announces the main point; the body develops it, usually in several paragraphs; the conclusion drives it home. You can begin drafting, however, at any point. If you find it difficult to introduce a paper that you have not yet written, you can write the body first and save the introduction for later.

For most writing tasks, your introduction will be a paragraph of 50 to 150 words. Perhaps the most common strategy is to open the paragraph with a few sentences that engage the reader and to conclude it with a statement of the essay's main point. The sentence stating the main point is called a *thesis*. (See 1c.) In the following examples, the thesis has been italicized.

> To the Australian aborigines, the Dreamtime was the time of creation. It was then that the creatures of the earth, including man, came into being. There are many legends about that mystical period, but unfortunately, the koala does not fare too well in any of them. *Slow-witted though it is in life, the koala is generally depicted in myth and folklore as a trickster and a thief.* — Roger Caras, "What's a Koala?"

> When I was sixteen, I married and moved to a small town to live. My new husband nervously showed me the house he had rented. It was after dark when we arrived there, and I remember wondering why he seemed so apprehensive about my reaction to the house. I thought the place seemed shabby but potentially cozy and quite livable inside. The morning sun revealed the reason for his anxiety by exposing the squalor outdoors. Up to that point, my contact with any reality but that of my own middle-class childhood had come from books. *The next four years in a small Iowa town taught me that reading about poverty is a lot different from living with it.*
> — Julie Reardon, student

Ideally, the sentences leading to the thesis should hook the reader, perhaps with one of the following:

a startling statistic or unusual fact

a vivid example

a description

a paradoxical statement

a quotation or bit of dialogue

a question

an analogy

a joke or an anecdote

Such hooks are particularly important when you cannot assume your reader's interest in the subject. Hooks are less necessary in scholarly essays and other writing aimed at readers with a professional interest in the subject.

Although the thesis frequently appears at the end of the introduction, it can just as easily appear at the beginning. Much work-related writing, in which a straightforward approach is most effective, commonly begins with the thesis.

> *Flextime scheduling, which has proved its effectiveness at the Library of Congress, should be introduced on a trial basis at the main branch of the Montgomery County Public Library.* By offering flexible work hours, the library can boost employee morale, cut down on absenteeism, and expand its hours of operation.   — David Warren, student

In narrative and descriptive writing, it is not always necessary to have an explicitly stated thesis. (See 1c.) However, an introduction without a thesis should clearly suggest the purpose and direction of the essay to follow. For example, even though a thesis has not been directly stated in the following introduction, readers understand that they are about to hear a gripping story about danger at sea.

> At the Coast Guard Training Center in Alameda, California, our instructors stressed that we still had much to learn about the sea's moods and temperaments. Our training, they said, was only inadequate preparation for what could happen to us in open water. "The ocean humbles even the most experienced skipper!" warned one teacher ominously. He often spoke of the *Edmund Fitzgerald,* an ore carrier which had foundered in a winter storm on Lake Superior. Even though the ship was over seven hundred feet from stem to stern and equipped with the latest technology, she went down in less than a sweep of the radar's antenna. But it made no difference

to me. After all, those men on the *Fitzgerald* were only civilians; I was a Coast Guardsman. After fifteen weeks at the Center, after long hours delving into the art of navigation and piloting, I could deal with any emergency. Steering—"wheeling" as we called it—was my forte. Several times in fact, in less-than-perfect conditions, I had brought ships through narrow entrances in the breakwall. I could handle any ship of any tonnage. There was nothing that I couldn't do.

—Jonathan Schilk, student

Characteristics of an effective thesis

An effective thesis should be a generalization, not a fact; it should be limited, not too broad; and it should be sharply focused, not too vague.

Because a thesis must prepare readers for facts and details, it cannot itself be a fact. It must always be a generalization demanding proof or further development.

> **TOO FACTUAL**   The first polygraph was developed by Dr. John A. Larson in 1921.

> **REVISED**   Because the polygraph has not been proved reliable, even under the most controlled conditions, its use by private employers should be banned.

Although a thesis must be a generalization, it must not be *too* general. You will need to narrow the focus of any thesis that you cannot adequately develop in the space allowed. Unless you were writing a book or a very long research paper, the following thesis would be too broad.

> **TOO BROAD**   Many drugs are now being used successfully to treat mental illnesses.

You would need to restrict the thesis, perhaps like this:

> **REVISED**   Despite its risks and side effects, lithium is an effective treatment for depression.

Finally, a thesis should be sharply focused, not too vague. Beware of any thesis containing a fuzzy, hard-to-define word such as *interesting, good,* or *disgusting.*

> **TOO VAGUE**   Many of the songs played on station WXQP are disgusting.

The word *disgusting* is needlessly vague. To sharpen the focus of this thesis, the writer should be more specific.

> **REVISED**   Of the songs played on station WXQP, all too many depict sex crudely, sanction the beating or rape of women, or foster gang violence.

In the process of making a too-vague thesis more precise, you may find yourself outlining the major sections of your paper, as in the preceding example. This technique, known as *blueprinting*, helps readers know exactly what to expect as they read on. It also helps you, the writer, control the shape of your essay.

LOOKING AT YOURSELF AS A WRITER
The thesis sentence

In much college writing, you will need to focus on a thesis in your introduction and to prove the thesis in the body of your essay. Although the thesis is usually only one sentence long, it can be surprisingly hard to write. When you have trouble formulating a good thesis, consider possible causes and cures for your difficulties.

CAUSE   You are trying to write the thesis sentence by itself.
CURE   Try drafting the whole introduction, placing the thesis sentence in context (usually at the end of the introduction).

CAUSE Once you have written a thesis, you tend to cling to it, even if the body of the essay doesn't exactly support it.

CURE View your initial thesis as tentative. As you draft an essay, you may discover a main idea that is more interesting than the one you began with. As writer E. M. Forster put it, "How do I know what I think until I see what I say?"

CAUSE You underestimate the importance of a clear thesis statement because you are unfamiliar with the academic world in which you are trying to write.

CURE Develop an appreciation for the goals of academic writing: to seek the truth, to argue a point, to propose solutions, to deepen insights, to clarify a theory, to challenge conventional wisdom. To reach any of these goals, you will need to articulate a thesis.

CAUSE You feel that a thesis sentence will not be significant unless it makes a grand, sweeping statement about life. But you lack the evidence to back up such a sweeping statement.

CURE Aim to do less, and you will accomplish more. As Darcy O'Brien advises writers, "Do not be grand. Try to get the ordinary into your writing. . . . Middletown today, not Mankind through the ages."

CAUSE You fear that a thesis sentence will sound too blunt. Perhaps this is because you come from a culture that values a more indirect approach. Or maybe you are a person who feels uncomfortable being assertive or maybe you lack the confidence to be assertive.

CURE: Try to be flexible — to adapt to the needs of readers in your particular writing situation. You might also experiment with strategies for softening the tone of a thesis sentence without sacrificing clarity. With practice, writers can learn to assert a main idea simply and directly without sounding too blunt.

2c   Fill out the body.

Before drafting the body of an essay, take a careful look at your introduction, focusing especially on your thesis sentence. What does the thesis promise readers? Try to keep this focus in mind.

It's a good idea to have a plan in mind as well. If your thesis sentence outlines a plan (see 2b) or if you have sketched a preliminary outline, try to block out your paragraphs accordingly. If you do not have a plan, you would be wise to pause for a moment and sketch one (see 1d). Of course it is also possible to begin without a plan—assuming you are prepared to treat your first attempt as a "discovery draft" that will almost certainly be tossed (or radically rewritten) once you discover what you really want to say.

2d   Attempt a conclusion.

The conclusion should echo the main idea, without dully repeating it. Often the concluding paragraph can be relatively short. By the end of the essay, readers should already understand your main point; your conclusion simply drives it home and perhaps suggests its significance.

In addition to echoing your main idea, a conclusion might summarize the essay's key points, pose a question for future study, offer advice, or propose a course of action. To end an essay detailing the social skills required of a bartender, one writer concludes with some advice:

> If someone were to approach me one day looking for the secret to running a good bar, I suppose I would offer the following advice: Get your customers to pour out their ideas at a greater rate than you pour out the liquor. You will both win in the end.   —Kathleen Lewis, student

To make the conclusion memorable, consider including a detail, example, or image from the introduction to bring readers full circle; a quotation or bit of dialogue; an anecdote; or a humorous, witty, or ironic comment. To end a narrative describing a cash register holdup, one student uses an anecdote that includes some dialogue:

> It took me a long time to get over that incident. Countless times I found myself gasping as someone "pointed" a dollar bill at me. On one such occasion, a jovial little man buying a toy gun for his son came up to me and said in a Humphrey Bogart impression, "Give me all your money, Sweetheart." I didn't laugh. Instead, my heart skipped a beat, for I had heard those words before.
> — Diana Crawford, student

Whatever concluding strategy you choose, avoid introducing wholly new ideas at the end of an essay. Also avoid apologies and other limp, indeterminate endings. The essay should end crisply, preferably on a positive note.

Do not become discouraged if the perfect conclusion eludes you at the rough-draft stage of the writing process. Because the conclusion is so closely tied to the rest of the essay in both content and tone, you may well decide to rework it (or even replace it) as your drafts evolve.

EXERCISE 2–1

The following are paired introductions written by students. One is a rough-draft version, and the other is a revision. Decide which introduction in each pair is the revision, and be prepared to discuss how it has been improved. Feel free to make further suggestions for improvement.

NOTE: Judith Burgin is introducing an essay that explains an insight, John Curley is introducing a descriptive essay, and Terry L. Burns is introducing a narrative. (For the writing assignments these students were working with, see pages 64, 74, and 78.)

1a.   Most TV sports announcers irritate me. I enjoy televised professional sports, especially football, but I cannot understand the low quality of sports broadcasting provided by the networks. I could forgive the numerous technical errors and the consistently mispronounced names if the running commentary were tolerable.   —Judith Burgin

b.   Howard Cosell is not the only offender. Most television sports announcers set my teeth on edge. I enjoy televised professional sports, especially football, but cannot understand the low quality of sports broadcasting provided by the networks. The numerous technical errors and mispronounced names would be forgivable if the running commentary were tolerable. Every Sunday during football season, overstatements abound, clichés cascade, and the nonstop chatter leaves nothing to the viewer's own interpretation.   —Judith Burgin

2a.   Each time I've tried to describe the beauty I have discovered under the rolling waves of the sea, my friends have countered with their moviegoing experience from *Jaws* and its toothy sequel, *Jaws 2*, which portray divers as fools treading water where angels fear to go. In *Jaws 2*, you may recall, the bride of Jaws snacked on two scuba divers, a fast-moving water skier, a helicopter pilot, and the resident diving instructor before the local sailboat regatta became the main course. In my travels over the past ten years, I have experienced a far more peaceful world underwater: from coral gardens along the Pacific shores of Thailand, to an underwater wedding in Australia, to oil tankers sunk by Nazis along the New Jersey coast, to the pastel hues of the Caribbean Sea. A description of the ultimate might be appropriate enticement to urge you to join me undersea.   —John Curley

b.   Each time I've tried to describe the beauty I have discovered under the sea, my friends have countered with scenes from *Jaws* and its toothy sequel, *Jaws 2*. In *Jaws 2*, you may recall, the bride of Jaws snacked on two scuba divers, a fast-moving water skier, a helicopter pilot, and the resident diving instructor before the local sailboat regatta became the main course. Had you traveled with me, however, over the past ten years, you would have experienced a far more peaceful world underwater: from coral gardens along the Pacific shores of Thailand, to an underwater wedding in Australia, to oil tankers sunk by Nazis along the New Jersey coast, to the pastel hues of the Caribbean Sea.   —John Curley

3a.   Crickets chirped in the grass surrounding the compound as four men, dressed only in white government-issue under-wear, made their way through the dark barracks. Airman Goodrich woke as the rough military blanket settled over his head and chest. He tried to move, but the four men held the blanket securely, pinning him to his bunk. His feet kicked as a fifth man rose from his neighboring bunk and began to pum-mel him to unconsciousness. Goodrich's screams shattered the night, yet no one moved a muscle to help. Though the snoring, which was incessant at night, had stopped abruptly and com-pletely, everyone pretended to sleep. When the screaming and pleading had finally died away, Goodrich was motionless. The moonlight poured through the windows, casting unearthly shadows across his body.   —Terry L. Burns

 b.   Screams shattered the sleep of one hundred men in the dark barracks as Airman Goodrich pleaded for help. Everyone knew what was happening. Three men were holding a blanket over Goodrich's upper torso and head as the fourth pummeled him into unconsciousness, yet no one moved a muscle to help. Everyone pretended to be asleep, though the snoring, which was incessant at night, had stopped abruptly and completely. When the screaming finally stopped, the room was deadly si-lent. The only sounds to be heard were the chirping of the crickets in the grass surrounding the compound and the omi-nous buzz of the locust in the trees. Goodrich lay still on his bunk, the moonlight pouring through the windows, casting eerie shadows across his body.   —Terry L. Burns

3

Make global revisions: Think big.

Revising is not just a matter of moving words around and correcting grammar. It involves much larger changes, global improvements that can be quite dramatic. Whole paragraphs might be dropped, others added. Material once stretched over two or three paragraphs might be condensed into one. Entire sections could be rearranged. Even the content may change dramatically, for the process of writing stimulates thought.

Major revising can be difficult, sometimes even painful. You might discover, for example, that an essay's first three paragraphs are nothing but padding, that its central argument tilts the wrong way, and that you sound like a stuffed shirt throughout. But the sheer fact that you can see such problems in your writing is a sign of hope. Those opening paragraphs can be dropped, the argument's slant realigned, the voice made more human.

3a Get some distance, perhaps with the help of reviewers.

Many of us resist global revisions because we find it difficult to distance ourselves from a draft. We tend to review our work from our own, not from our audience's, perspective.

To distance yourself from a draft, begin by putting it aside for a while, preferably overnight or even longer. When you return to it, try to play the role of your audience as you read. Mark any places where your readers are likely to be confused, misled, or annoyed; look too for sentences and paragraphs that are not likely to persuade.

If at all possible, enlist the help of reviewers — persons willing to play the role of audience for you. Possible reviewers include peers, such as family members, friends, and other students; and professionals, such as professors, trained writing center tutors, and practicing writers. Ask your reviewers to focus on the larger issues of writing, not on the fine points. If they are at first preoccupied by fine points such as grammar and spelling — and many peer reviewers often are — remind them that you are not ready to think about such matters. For the moment, you are interested in their response to the essay as a whole.

Many professors set aside class time for peer review sessions in which students respond to each other's drafts in written comments, discussions, or both. For guidelines on being a peer reviewer, see the chart on pages 42–43.

3b Approach global revision in cycles.

The process of global revision can be overwhelming, so it is best to approach it in cycles, with each cycle encompassing a particular purpose for revising. Five common cycles of global revision are discussed in this section:

— Strengthening the content

— Sharpening the focus

— Improving the organization

— Clarifying the point of view

— Refining the tone

You can handle these cycles in nearly any order, and you may be able to skip or combine some of them.

If you have asked someone to review your draft, you have already begun to see which of these cycles most need your attention. And by giving some thought to your overall purpose

Guidelines for peer reviewers

READING THE ESSAY

As you read, you may want to pencil a few marks in the margin: perhaps a check mark (√) for sentences or passages that seem especially effective, a question mark (?) for spots that confused you, a plus mark (+) for places where you'd like to hear more details. Don't get carried away, however. Remember that you are not "grading" a finished essay; you are helping a fellow writer get distance from a rough draft. Above all, do not mark errors in grammar, punctuation, and spelling. The writer can deal with such matters later.

WRITING COMMENTS

Although some professors may ask you to write comments on the draft of an essay, most prefer that you respond on a separate sheet of paper. Here are some ideas for written responses:

1. In a sentence, describe the writer's apparent purpose and audience.
2. In a sentence, explain what the introduction promises readers; in other words, explain what you, as a reader, expect to hear in the rest of the essay.
3. List the two or three passages that best fulfill the promise of the introduction.
4. List a few things that you would like to hear more about.
5. Try to sketch a very simple outline of the draft. (If this is difficult, the writer may need to work on organization.)
6. Write down two or three sentences from the draft that you found particularly interesting or well written.

DISCUSSING YOUR IDEAS WITH THE WRITER

If you have the opportunity to discuss your ideas with the writer, here are some guidelines to keep in mind:

1. Try to open your conversation with descriptive, rather than evaluative, comments. For example, if the writer's subject is physical handicaps, you might begin by saying, "I think your point is that many adults are insensitive and patronizing when they encounter persons with physical handicaps."

2. When you turn to evaluative comments, make the first ones positive. For example, you might mention that you found the writer's second paragraph a powerful example of insensitivity toward handicapped persons.

3. An effective peer review session is a dialogue, not a monologue. Try to get the writer talking by asking questions—about the draft-in-progress and about the subject. As writers talk about their subject with an interested listener, they often recall useful details and vivid examples that might be included in the essay.

4. If you have suggestions for improvement, try to tie them to the writer's goals. For instance, you might advise the writer to put the most dramatic example of insensitivity toward the handicapped last, where it will have maximum impact on readers. Or you might suggest that a descriptive passage would gain power if abstractions were replaced with concrete details.

5. Throughout the review session, look on yourself as a coach, not a judge, as a proposer of possibilities, not a dictator of revisions. It is the writer, after all, who will have to grapple with the task of improving the essay.

6. At the end of the review session, you might want to express interest in reading the writer's next revision or final draft. Such interest — if it is sincere — can be a powerful motivation for a writer.

and audience, you'll discern even more clearly where your essay does—and does not—need major reworking.

Strengthening the content

In reviewing the content of a draft, consider whether any text (sentences, paragraphs, or longer passages) should be added or deleted, keeping in mind your readers' needs. Then, if your purpose is to argue a point, consider how persuasively you have proved your point to an intelligent, discerning audience. When necessary, rethink your argument.

ADDING TEXT   If any paragraphs or sections of the essay are developed too skimpily to be clear and convincing (a common flaw in rough drafts), you will need to add specific facts, details, and examples. This necessity will take you back to the beginning of the writing process: listing specifics, perhaps clustering them, and then roughing out new sentences and paragraphs. Many writers deliberately overwrite a first draft, filling it out with more details than they will probably need, to avoid having to produce new material later. The process of cutting and rearranging is almost always easier than beginning again from scratch.

DELETING TEXT   Look for sentences and paragraphs that can be cut without serious loss of meaning. Perhaps you have repeated yourself or strayed from your point. Maybe you have given undue emphasis to minor ideas. Cuts may also be necessitated by word limits, such as those imposed by a college assignment or by the realities of the business world, where readers are often pressed for time.

RETHINKING YOUR ARGUMENT   A first draft presents you with an opportunity for rethinking your argument. You can often deepen your ideas on a subject by asking yourself some hard questions. Is your claim more sweeping than the evidence allows? Have you left out an important step in the argument? Have you dealt with the arguments of the opposition? Is your thinking flawed by logical fallacies? The more challenging your subject, the more likely you will find yourself adjusting your early thoughts. (For more about argumentative writing, see 52.)

Sharpening the focus

A draft is clearly focused when it fixes the reader's attention on one central idea and does not stray from that idea. You can sharpen the focus of a draft by clarifying the introduction (especially the thesis) and by deleting any text that is off the point.

CLARIFYING THE INTRODUCTION First you will want to make sure that your introduction looks and reads like an introduction. Can readers tell where the introduction stops and the body of the essay begins? Have you perhaps included material in the introduction that really belongs in the body of the essay? Is your introduction long-winded?

Next check to see whether the introduction focuses clearly on the main point of the essay. Does it let readers know what to expect as they read on? Does it make the significance of the subject clear so that readers will want to read on?

The most important sentence in the introduction is the thesis. (See 2b.) If your essay lacks a thesis, make sure that you have a good reason for not including one. If your thesis is poorly focused or if it doesn't accurately state the real point of the essay, you'll need to revise it.

DELETING TEXT THAT IS OFF THE POINT Compare the essay's introduction, particularly its thesis statement, with the body of the essay. Does the body of the essay fulfill the promise of the introduction? If not, one or the other must be adjusted. Either rebuild the introduction to fit the body of the paper or keep the introduction and delete any sentences or paragraphs that stray from its point.

Improving the organization

A draft is well organized when its major divisions are logical and easy for readers to follow. To improve the organization of your draft, consider taking one or more of the following actions: adding or sharpening topic sentences, moving blocks of text, reparagraphing, and inserting headings.

ADDING OR SHARPENING TOPIC SENTENCES   Topic sentences, as you probably know, state the main ideas of the paragraphs in the body of an essay. (See 5a.) Topic sentences act as signposts for readers, announcing ideas to come.

You can review the organization of a draft by reading only the topic sentences. Do they clearly support the essay's main idea? Do they make a reasonable sentence outline of the paper? If your draft lacks topic sentences, make sure you have a good reason for omitting these important signposts.

MOVING BLOCKS OF TEXT   Improving the organization of a draft can be as simple as moving a few sentences from one paragraph to another or switching the order of paragraphs. Often, however, the process is more complex. As you move blocks of text, you may need to supply transitions to make them fit smoothly in the new positions; you may also need to rework topic sentences to make your new organization clear.

Before moving text, consider sketching a revised outline. Divisions in the outline might become topic sentences in the restructured essay. (See 1d.)

REPARAGRAPHING AND INSERTING HEADINGS   Occasionally you can clarify the organization of a draft simply by combining choppy paragraphs or by dividing those that are too long for easy reading. (See 6d.)

In long documents, such as research papers or business reports, you may be able to clarify your organization by inserting headings. Possible headings include phrases, declarative or imperative sentences, and questions. To draw attention to headings, consider centering them, putting them in boldface, underlining them, using all capital letters, or some combination of these. (See also pp. 619–623.)

Clarifying the point of view

If the point of view of a draft shifts confusingly or if it seems not quite appropriate for your purpose, audience, and subject, consider adjusting it.

There are three basic points of view to choose from: the first person (*I* or *we*), the second person (*you*), and the third person (*he/she/it/one* or *they*). Each point of view is appropriate in at least some contexts, and you may need to experiment before discovering which one best suits your needs.

THE THIRD-PERSON POINT OF VIEW Much academic and professional writing is best presented from the third-person point of view (*he/she/it/one* or *they*), which puts the subject in the foreground. The *I* point of view is usually inappropriate in such contexts because, by focusing attention on the writer, it pushes the subject into the background. Consider, for example, one student's first-draft description of the behavior of a species of frog that he had observed in the field.

> Each frog that *I* was able to locate in trees remained in its given tree during the entirety of *my* observation period. However, *I* noticed that there was considerable movement within the home tree.

Here the *I* point of view is distracting, as the student himself noticed when he began to revise his report. His revision focuses more on the frogs, less on himself.

> Each frog located in a tree remained in that tree throughout
> the observation period. The frogs moved about considerably,
> however, within their home trees.

Just as the first-person pronoun *I* can draw too much
attention to the writer, the second-person pronoun *you* can
focus unnecessarily on the reader. One biology manual, for
example, in an exercise meant to focus on the skeletal system,
shifts the attention instead to the reader:

> Give at least two functions of the backbone from *your* reading.

This exercise would be clearer and more direct if presented
without the distraction of the *you* point of view.

> What are two functions of the backbone?

Although the third-person point of view is often a better
choice than the *I* or *you* point of view, it is by no means
trouble-free. Writers who choose it can run into problems
when they want to use singular pronouns in an indefinite
sense. For example, when Miss Piggy says that a reason for
jogging is "to improve *one's* emotional health and make *one*
feel better about *oneself,*" one wishes she wouldn't use quite
so many *one*'s, doesn't one? The trouble is that American
English, unlike British English, does not allow this pronoun
to echo unself-consciously throughout a sentence. The repetitions sound stuffy.

Some years ago Americans would have said "to improve
a person's emotional health and to make *him* feel better about
himself," with the understanding that *him* really meant *him
or her.* Today, however, this use of *him* is offensive to many
readers and is best avoided. On the other hand, "to make *him
or her* feel better about *himself or herself*" is distinctly awkward. So what is poor Miss Piggy to say?

Her only hope, it turns out, is a flexible and inventive mind. She might switch to the plural: *Joggers run to improve their emotional health and to make them feel better about themselves.* Or she could restructure the sentence altogether: *Jogging improves a person's emotional health and self-image.* (See 17f and 22a.)

THE SECOND-PERSON POINT OF VIEW   The *you* point of view, which puts the reader in the foreground, is appropriate if the writer is advising readers directly, as in giving tips on raising children or instructions on flower arranging. All imperative sentences, such as the advice for writers in this book, are written from the *you* point of view, although the word itself is frequently omitted and understood. "Sketch a plan" means "*You* should sketch a plan"; everyone knows this, so the *you* is not expressed.

In the course of giving advice or instructions, the actual word *you* may be appropriate and even desired. In advising gardeners about walkways, for example, newspaper columnist Henry Mitchell feels free to use the words *you* and *your* as the need arises:

> If *your* main walk is less than four feet wide, and if it is white concrete, then widen it, no matter what has to be sacrificed . . . and resurface it with brick, stone, or something less glaring and dull. Three flowers against a good-looking pavement will do more for *you* than thirty flowers against white concrete. [Italics added.]

Mitchell might have written this passage from the third-person point of view instead ("If *the gardener's* walk is less than four feet wide . . ."), but the effect would have seemed oddly indirect. Even at the risk of sounding a bit bossy, Mitchell has wisely selected the imperative stance instead.

Notice that Mitchell's *you* means "you, the reader." It does not mean "you, anyone in general." Indefinite uses of *you,* such as the following example, are inappropriate in formal writing (see 23d).

> Young Japanese women wired together electronic products on a piece-rate system: The more *you* wired, the more *you* were paid.

Here the writer should have stayed with the third-person point of view instead.

> The more *they* wired, the more *they* were paid.

THE FIRST-PERSON POINT OF VIEW If much of a writer's material comes from personal experience, the *I* point of view will prove most natural. It is difficult to imagine, for example, how James Thurber could have avoided the word *I* in describing his early university days:

> *I* passed all the other courses that *I* took at *my* university, but *I* could never pass botany. This was because all botany students had to spend several hours a week in a laboratory looking through a microscope at plant cells, and *I* could never see through a microscope. *I* never once saw a cell through a microscope. This used to enrage my instructor. [Italics added.]
> — "University Days"

Thurber's *I* point of view puts the writer in the foreground, and since the writer is in fact the subject, this makes sense.

Writers who are aware that the first-person point of view is sometimes viewed as inappropriate in academic writing often overgeneralize the rule. Concluding that the word *I* is never appropriate, they go to extreme lengths to avoid it.

> Mama read with such color and detail that *one* could fancy *oneself* as the hero of the story.

Since the paper in which this sentence appeared was a personal reminiscence, the entire paper sounded more natural once the writer allowed himself to use the word *I:*

> Mama read with such color and detail that *I* could fancy *myself* as the hero of the story.

Refining the tone

The tone of a piece of writing expresses the writer's feelings about the subject and audience, so it is important to get it right. If the tone seems too flippant — or too stuffy, bossy, patronizing, or hostile — obviously it should be modified.

Any piece of writing drafted in anger or frustration will almost certainly need to be toned down. The following rough draft, for example, was written by a secretary in response to criticisms of a newsletter sent out by the organization for which she worked:

> Dear Mr. Martin:
>
> I know our newsletter is crudely laid out, the reason being that I type it from rough drafts under a tight enough deadline that only major errors of judgment get retyped. Perhaps we'd do better if we had a word processor.
>
> I think you were wrong to dismiss the offending story as bragging about *Nuclear War: What's in It for You?* The book was nominated for the prize, a fact worthy of mention despite the fact that it did not win.
>
> In any case, I am glad to hear that you liked the open letter to the president. Would that the *Philadelphia Inquirer* had liked it as well.
>
> Sincerely,
>
> Robbie Nichols

Cycles of global revision

STRENGTHENING THE CONTENT

Look for opportunities

- — to add specific facts, details, and examples
- — to delete repetitious or ineffective text
- — to rethink your argument

SHARPENING THE FOCUS

Look for opportunities

- — to clarify the introduction (especially the thesis)
- — to delete text that is off the point

IMPROVING THE ORGANIZATION

Look for opportunities

- — to add or sharpen topic sentences
- — to move blocks of text
- — to reparagraph and perhaps add headings

CLARIFYING THE POINT OF VIEW

Look for opportunities

- — to make the point of view more consistent
- — to use a more appropriate point of view
- — to avoid the problem of sexist English

REFINING THE TONE

Look for opportunities

- — to approach your audience more diplomatically
- — to use language more appropriate for your subject and your audience

As she reached the last paragraph of the rough draft, the writer saw the need to be more diplomatic. Later, in a calmer mood, she revised the letter like this:

Dear Mr. Martin:

We are glad to hear that you liked Roger Molander's "An Open Letter to the President." Would that the *Philadelphia Inquirer* had liked it as well.

I do think you were wrong to dismiss the sentence about *Nuclear War: What's in It for You?* as "bragging." It is a fairly direct sentence, and there may well be those among the faithful who wouldn't otherwise have known about its nomination for the prize.

Your comments about the physical layout of the story were, in fact, echoed by the staff here. The layout could not be changed, however, because it was typed under a tight deadline that allowed retyping only in cases of major errors of judgment.

Thank you for writing. Even though our newsletter has a limited circulation, we hope that Roger's open letter will elicit serious thought about the president's March 23 address on weapons in space.

Sincerely,

Robbie Nichols

4

Revise and edit sentences; proofread the final draft.

When you revise sentences, you focus on effectiveness; when you edit, you check for correctness. As with global revision, sentence revision may be approached in cycles, with each cycle focusing on a different purpose for making changes. The

Cycles of sentence-level revision

The numbers in this chart refer to sections in this handbook.

STRENGTHENING SENTENCES

Look for opportunities

— to use more active verbs (14a)
— to prune excess words (16)

CLARIFYING SENTENCES

Look for opportunities

— to balance parallel ideas (9)
— to supply missing words (10)
— to untangle mixed constructions (11)
— to repair misplaced or dangling modifiers (12)
— to eliminate confusing shifts (13)

INTRODUCING VARIETY

Look for opportunities

— to combine choppy sentences (8a)
— to restructure weak compounds (8b)
— to vary sentence openings (15a)

REFINING THE STYLE

Look for opportunities

— to choose language more appropriate for the subject and
audience (17)
— to choose more exact words (18)

An editing checklist

At first this checklist may seem overwhelming, but as your instructor responds to your writing and as you become familiar with the rules in this handbook, you'll begin to see which problems, if any, tend to cause you trouble. You can then devise a personal checklist of errors to look for as you edit. (The numbers in the chart refer to sections in this handbook.)

GRAMMAR

Sentence fragments (19)
Comma splices and fused sentences (20)
Subject-verb agreement (21)
Pronoun-antecedent agreement (22)
Pronoun reference (23)
Case of nouns and pronouns (24)
Case of *who* and *whom* (25)
Adjectives and adverbs (26)
Standard English verb forms (27)
Verb tense, mood, and voice (28)
ESL problems (29, 30, 31)

PUNCTUATION

The comma and unnecessary commas (32, 33)
The semicolon (34)
The colon (35)
The apostrophe (36)
Quotation marks (37)
End punctuation (38)
Other punctuation marks (39)

MECHANICS

Abbreviations and numbers (40, 41)
Italics (underlining) (42)
Spelling and the hyphen (43, 44)
Capital letters (45)

main purposes for revising sentences—to strengthen, clarify, vary, and refine them—are detailed in the chart on page 54. A checklist on editing for grammar, punctuation, and mechanics appears on page 55.

To save yourself time, you should ordinarily revise and edit sentences right on the pages of an earlier draft, like this:

> *deciding*
> Finally ~~we decided~~ that perhaps our dream needed ~~some~~
> prompting, ~~and~~ we visited a fertility doctor and began the expen-
> *some*
> sive, time–consuming round of procedures that held out ~~the~~ prom-
> *our dream's fulfillment. Our efforts, however, were* *As*
> ise of ~~fulfilling our dream.   All this was~~ to no avail./. ~~and as~~ we
> *could no longer*
> approached the sixth year of our marriage, we ~~had reached the~~
> ~~point where we couldn't~~ even discuss our childlessness without be-
> coming very depressed.   We questioned why this had happened to
> *such a*
> us./•Why had we been singled out for ~~this~~ major disappointment?

The original paragraph was flawed by wordiness and an excessive reliance on structures connected with *and.* Such problems can be addressed through any number of acceptable revisions. The first sentence, for example, could have been changed like this:

> Finally we decided that perhaps our dream needed ~~some~~
> *After visiting*
> prompting./. ~~and we visited~~ a fertility doctor , *we* ~~and~~ began the expen-
> *promised hope*
> sive, time—consuming round of procedures that ~~held out the prom-~~
> ~~ise~~ of fulfilling our dream.

Though some writers might argue about the effectiveness of these improvements compared with the previous revision, most would agree that both versions are better than the original.

Some of the paragraph's improvements involve less choice and are not so open to debate. The hyphen in *time-consuming* is necessary; a noun must be substituted for the pronoun *this*, which was being used more loosely than grammar allows; and the question mark in the next to last sentence must be changed to a period.

Proofreading

After revising and editing, you are ready to prepare the final manuscript. (See 55 for guidelines.) At this point, make sure to allow yourself enough time for proofreading—the final and most important step in manuscript preparation.

Proofreading is a special kind of reading: a slow and methodical search for misspellings, typographical mistakes, and omitted words or word endings. Such errors can be difficult to spot in your own work because you may read what you intended to write, not what is actually on the page. To fight this tendency, try proofreading out loud, articulating each word as it is actually written. You might also try proofreading your essay backward, a strategy that takes your attention away from the meanings you intended and forces you to think about small surface features instead.

Although proofreading may be dull, it is crucial. Errors strewn throughout an essay are distracting and annoying. If the writer doesn't care about this piece of writing, thinks the reader, why should I? A carefully proofread essay, on the other hand, sends a positive message: It shows that you value your writing and respect your readers.

EXERCISE 4–1

On a piece of scratch paper, jot down notes describing how you typically approach a writing task. Then, on another sheet of paper, list ways in which you might improve your handling of the writing process. Be prepared to discuss your notes in class. The following questions are meant to prompt your thoughts; don't feel that your notes must address them all.

1. What do you do, if anything, before you begin a first draft? For example, do you jot down notes on scratch paper, talk about your ideas with a friend, or come up with insights late at night and then sleep on them?
2. How do you organize your ideas — in your head or on paper? Do you use outlines or diagrams and, if so, how formal are they?
3. Where and when are you most comfortable writing?
4. Do you type rough drafts, write them in longhand, or use a word processor? Are you addicted to any sort of paper and pen? Do you single-space or double-space a draft? Do you write on both sides of the paper?
5. Do you use a dictionary, a thesaurus, or a reference such as *The Bedford Handbook for Writers*? If so, when do you usually consult these references — while writing the first draft or later?
6. How do you "get distance" from a draft? Do you get advice from an objective reader and then rewrite if necessary? Or do you usually handle revision all on your own? Which of your friends and relatives can be trusted to offer helpful advice? Have you ever asked for feedback from an instructor or a writing center tutor?
7. Do you make major revisions in a rough draft — revisions that go beyond the level of the sentence? For example, do you consider adding, deleting, or moving whole paragraphs? If so, how do you handle such changes — by making them on a word processor, by cutting and taping, by using circles and arrows, or by recopying the whole draft?
8. What sorts of sentence-level revisions do you make?
9. How do you handle proofreading?
10. How much time do you usually spend on a writing assignment? Do you spread your work over several days or wait until the last minute? What proportion of your time is devoted to each stage of the writing process: planning, writing, and revision?

EXERCISE 4–2

This exercise gives you practice finding information in *The Bedford Handbook for Writers*. Each of the following "rules" violates the principle it expresses. Find the handbook section that explains the principle (by using the chart inside the front cover or the index at the back) and then correct the error. Example:

Each pronoun agrees with ~~their~~ *its* antecedent.

1. A verb have to agree with its subject.
2. A writer must be careful not to shift your point of view.
3. Don't use no double negatives.
4. When dangling, watch your modifiers.
5. Discriminate careful between adjectives and adverbs.
6. In the writing center, they say that vague pronoun reference is unacceptable.
7. Don't write a comma splice, you must connect the clauses with a comma and a coordinating conjunction or with a semicolon.
8. About sentence fragments. You should avoid them.
9. In most contexts, the passive voice should be avoided.
10. Watch out for *-ed* endings that have been drop.
11. The distinction between *which* and *that* is a matter which some writers take very seriously.
12. In choosing the proper case, follow the example of we teachers, whom are the experts.
13. Its important to use apostrophe's correctly.
14. Watch out for irregular verbs that have came to you in the wrong form.
15. Last but not least, avoid clichés like the plague.

EXERCISE 4–3

This exercise gives you practice consulting the Glossary of Usage in *The Bedford Handbook for Writers* (pp. 689–704). Look up the italicized words to see if they are used correctly here. Then edit any sentences containing incorrect usage. Example:

The pediatrician gave my daughter *an* injection for her allergy.

1. The *amount* of horses a Comanche warrior had in his possession indicated the wealth of his family.

2. This afternoon I plan to *lie* out in the sun and begin working on a tan.
3. We will *contact* you by phone as soon as the tickets arrive.
4. Changing attitudes *toward* alcohol have *effected* the beer industry.
5. Jenny *should of* known better than to attempt that dive.
6. Everyone in our office is *enthused* about this project.
7. George and Pat are selling *there* house because now that *their* children are grown, *their* planning to move to Arizona.
8. Most sleds are pulled by no *fewer* than two dogs and no more than ten.
9. It is *man's* nature to think wisely and act foolishly.
10. Dr. Newman and *myself* have agreed to arrange the retirement party.

COMPOSING AND REVISING ON A WORD PROCESSOR

A word processor, as you probably know, is a computer equipped with software that allows writers to compose and revise text with ease. Although a word processor cannot think for you, it can be a useful tool at all stages of the writing process: planning, drafting, and revising.

Planning

You can list or "brainstorm" ideas as easily on a word processor as with pencil and paper, especially if you are a fast typist. Later you can delete ideas, add others, and rearrange the order, all with a few keystrokes. And as you begin to perceive relationships among ideas, you may be able to turn your list into an informal outline.

You can create outlines quite easily on a word processor. Some software packages will generate a formal outline structure for you — not the words, of course, but the conventional system of numbers and letters at appropriate indent levels.

If you like to begin a writing task by asking yourself questions, consider keeping sets of questions on file in your computer. A college student, for example, might use one set of questions for writing about literature, another for science reports, another for case studies in sociology or psychology, and so on. In some disciplines, software is available with sets of questions developed by experts in the field. Check with a professor or with your school's writing center to learn about such computer programs.

Software has also been developed to speed the process of academic research. Instead of taking notes on note cards, you can type notes on the computer, code them to reflect the divisions of your outline, and later print the notes in sorted batches. To rearrange the notes, you simply change their codes.

Although the computer can be a useful tool for planning, its advantages over pencil and paper should not be overstated. Not all planning techniques can be done on a word processor, and a computer will not always be available when an idea strikes. Many writers find that they plan just as easily with pencil and paper; they turn to the computer primarily for drafting and revising.

Drafting

Whether to write a first draft on a word processor is a matter of personal preference. Some writers prefer the sensation of a pencil or pen moving on paper; others like to get their fingers moving on a keyboard.

One advantage of drafting at a keyboard, if you are a good typist, is speed: Your thoughts are not likely to race ahead of your fingers, as they sometimes do when you are drafting by hand. Another advantage is legibility. As you draft, you will find yourself reviewing from time to time what you have already written. Typed copy — whether on a screen or printed out on paper — is more legible than most handwriting.

A third advantage is flexibility. Because changes are so easy to make, a word processor encourages experimentation. If you get stuck while writing the opening paragraph, for example, you can skip ahead, knowing that it will be easy to insert the introduction later. Or you can switch screens and use an empty screen for brainstorming. Or if you have a creative but unusual idea for the introduction, you can try it out, confident that if it doesn't work, you can make it disappear in seconds.

If you decide to type an initial draft on a word processor, it's a good idea to print out hard copy as you go along so that you can easily review what you have written. (Otherwise you will need to scroll from screen to screen.) Be sure to save your draft in the computer's memory periodically as you are working and before turning off the computer.

Revising

The word processor is an excellent tool for revision. As mentioned earlier, revising is nearly always a two-step process. Global revisions, those that affect blocks of text longer than a sentence, generally should be handled first. They include changes in focus, organization, paragraphing, and content. Sentence-level revisions — improvements in sentence structure, word choice, grammar, punctuation, and mechanics — can come later.

GLOBAL REVISIONS Let's assume that you have typed and saved your rough draft on a computer equipped with word processing software. You have printed a copy of the draft, reviewed it for global revisions, and indicated on it where you need to add, delete, and move chunks of text.

Once you have called up the text onto the computer's screen, you move the cursor to the place where you want to add, delete, or move text. Most word processing packages allow you to add text simply by typing it in and to delete text by hitting a delete key. Moving blocks of text is a bit more complicated, usually requiring several keystrokes, but with practice it too is relatively simple.

Because the computer saves time, it encourages you to experiment with global revisions. Should you combine two paragraphs? Would your conclusion make a good introduction? Might several paragraphs be rearranged for greater impact? Will boldface headings improve readability? With little risk, you can explore the possibilities. When a revision misfires, it is easy to restore your original draft.

SENTENCE-LEVEL REVISIONS Some writers handle sentence-level revisions directly at the computer, but most prefer to print out a hard copy of the draft, mark it up, and then return to the computer. Once you've indicated changes on the hard copy, you can enter them into the computer in a matter of minutes.

Software can provide help with sentence-level revisions. Many word processing programs have spelling checkers that will catch most but not all spelling errors, and some have thesauruses to help with word choice. Other programs, called *text analyzers* or *style checkers*, will flag a variety of possible problems: wordiness, jargon, weak verbs, long sentences, and so on. Be aware, however, that a text analyzer can only point out *possible* problems. It can tell you that a sentence is long, for example, but you must decide whether your long sentence is effective.

To proofread your final text, either read the words on the screen or, if this is too hard on your eyes, print a new copy and proofread the hard copy. Enter any necessary corrections into the computer, print a final copy, and you are done. To preserve the final draft, be sure to save it before you turn off the computer.

EXPOSITORY STUDENT ESSAY: EXPLAINING AN INSIGHT

Gary Laporte, who wrote "Sports on TV — A Win or a Loss?" (pp. 72–73), was responding to the following assignment.

ASSIGNMENT: EXPLAINING AN INSIGHT

When you explain an insight on a topic, you offer readers a fresh or interesting way of looking at it. In other words, you give them a way of understanding something that they may have understood differently before.

You might challenge a conventional view that has not been validated by your own experience: the view, for example, that growing up in a small town is idyllic or that work as a flight attendant is glamorous. You might explain an insight about a group with which you are familiar: Harley-Davidson bikers, farmers, the physically challenged, people from another culture. You might give readers a new way of looking at some aspect of the media: maybe by ridiculing the language of sports announcers, revealing stereotypes in a television series, explaining why *Star Trek* has had such lasting appeal, or showing that the history of rap music is more complex than most people think. Or you might give readers an insight into one of your special interests, such as photography, mountain climbing, or one of the martial arts.

Your insight should appear in a thesis sentence early in the essay, most likely at the end of the introductory paragraph (see pages 30–32 of *The Bedford Handbook*). For this assignment, your information should come from personal knowledge, interviews, or direct observation. Aim for an essay from 500 to 1,000 words long — from two to four typed pages, double-spaced.

Laporte's writing process

Laporte thought about the assignment for several days, but he was unable to come up with a subject. He was still pondering the question when he watched a basketball playoff game on television. Besides interviewing the stars of each team, the sportscaster spoke with a ten-year-old fan whose ambition was to become a famous athlete. Why famous? thought Laporte. Why not a *good* athlete? Don't people who see games on TV understand that winning depends on good play and teamwork, not on competing with one another for fame and the camera's attention?

Laporte decided that television sports might make a good essay subject since he knew something about it. He jotted down ideas during breaks in the game and came up with the following list:

Cooperation should be focus, not competition

TV creates stars — cameras follow them, commentators interview them

TV doesn't show whole game, only most dramatic shots, slow-motion replays

More people admire sports stars than admire the president of U.S.

Sports stars make more money than president, also do commercials for money

Money becomes purpose of sport

Sports should represent American values — teamwork, shared enthusiasm — easier to see in live games where spectators participate

Cheering, choosing what to watch, buying beer & hot dogs, catching fly balls.

Later, Laporte reread his list and concluded that his focus should be the effect of television on both athletes and spectators. With this focus in mind, he formulated a tentative thesis and sketched a rough outline.

Although it is convenient, TV creates a distance between the sport and its fans and between the athletes and the team.

— television's convenience to fans
  — no need to travel and spend money
  — ability to see more games
— television's damage to sports
  — creates distance between the sport and fans
  — creates distance between the athletes and the team

Working from his list and outline, Laporte wrote a rough draft. He wrote quickly, focusing more on his ideas than on grammar, punctuation, and spelling. As you read his rough draft, which follows, consider what changes (aside from grammar, punctuation, and spelling) you would recommend.

LAPORTE'S ROUGH DRAFT

Sports on TV--A Win or a Loss?

Team sports are as much a part of American life as Mom and apple pie, and they have a good tendency to bring people together. They encourage team members to cooperate with one another, they also create shared enthusiasm among fans. Thanks to television, this togetherness now seems available to nearly all of us at the flick of a switch. We do not have to buy tickets, and travel to a stadium, to see the World Series or the Super Bowl, these games are on television. We can enjoy the game in the comfort of our own living room. After Thanksgiving or Christmas dinner, the whole family may gather around the TV set to watch football together. It would appear that television has done us a great service. But is this really the case?

It is necessary to look at the differences between live and televised sports. We can see more games than if we had to attend each one in person, and we can follow greater varieties of sports. On the other hand, television creates a distance between the sport and the fans and between athletes and the teams they play for.

The gap between a game and those who watch it on television has two major aspects. One is that the armchair audience sees only what the camera shows. The advantage of this is that we get a clear look at important plays; also, if we miss a play, we can fall back on the commentator's explanation or the instant replay, which often shows us exactly what happened in slow motion. The disadvantage is that we have no choice about what to watch. If a viewer would rather follow someone in the backfield than the quarterback or would rather look at a batter warming up than a commercial, they are out of luck. The other aspect of observing a game on television is that we miss all the sights, sounds, and smells that link live viewers with the players and one another. When a fly ball comes over the fence, the television audience cannot try to catch it. The roar of cheers after a touchdown is less exciting from the living room sofa than when you are sitting in the bleachers. Someone watching a televised game may feel silly cheering at all, since there is no chance those tiny figures on the screen will hear it.

TV creates a gap between athletes and their teams, in addition. Traditionally, sports have been viewed as arenas where teamwork is essential, and the goals of the group overshadow personal ambition. TV cameras, however, find it more dramatic and more convenient to focus on individual achievements than something as intangible as teamwork. Interviews with sports stars are often part of a televised game. Athletes make more money than the president of the United States, and they appear in the media more often, and they are universally admired. In addition, sports stars have the extra added benefit of endorsing products on TV commercials for large bonus payments.

Teams sports are a major part of American life. All the more so since television has brought them into most of our homes. The challenge for sports fans is to support their favorite teams in ways to encourage the best values represented by sports. One way is to continue to attend live games rather than watch games on television.

Before beginning to revise this draft, Laporte brought it to class for a peer review session. Three of Laporte's class-mates read the draft and responded to it, using the chart on pages 42–43 as a guideline for their discussion. Here are some of their comments and suggestions:

I like your details describing the distance between the spectator and the sport (in the third paragraph). You make me experience what you mean.

Why did you put your thesis at the end of the second paragraph? Wouldn't it be more effective in the introduction?

You talk about advantages to televised sports in the first and second paragraphs. Maybe this should all be in one place.

You do a good job of acknowledging that TV does have its advantages.

Your language seems too stiff in places. Does your audience really require such a formal approach?

Two of your paragraphs are pretty long. Maybe you could tighten up the third paragraph, which seems wordy. The fourth paragraph probably needs to be divided.

You haven't convinced me that television separates the players from their team. An example or two would help.

You're tending to shift from the *we* point of view to the *they* point of view and back again. I'd use the *we* point of view because it is more personal. And after all, most of us are fans.

You seem to have two introductory paragraphs. Shouldn't you get to the point faster?

I like the way you pull the essay together in the concluding paragraph.

Notice that Laporte and his classmates were focusing on global matters, not on sentence-level revisions. Because the draft needed a fair amount of work, it made little sense to tinker with its sentences, some of which would be thrown out anyway. For an example of Laporte's global revisions, see page 70.

Once Laporte had written the second draft, he felt ready to devote his full attention to matters of style and correctness. He tightened wordy sentences, combined sentences for better flow, chose his words more carefully, and brought consistency to his style. Finally, with his handbook and dictionary close by, he corrected errors in grammar, punctuation, and spelling. For an example of Laporte's sentence-level revisions, see page 71.

Laporte's final draft appears on pages 72–73.

EXAMPLE OF GLOBAL REVISIONS

Sports on TV--A Win or a Loss?

Team sports are as much a part of Americain life as Mom and apple pie, and they have a good tendency to bring people together.
They encourage team members to cooperate with one another,
they also create shared enthusiasm among fans.   Thanks to television, this togetherness now seems available to nearly all of us
at the flick of a switch. We do not have to buy tickets, and travel
to a stadium, to see the World Series or the Super Bowl, these
games are on television.   We can enjoy the game in the comfort of
our own living room. After Thanksgiving or Christmas dinner, the
whole family may gather around the TV set to watch football together. It would appear that television has done us a great service.   But is this really the case? *Although television does
make sports more accessible, it also creates a
distance between the sport and the fans and
between athletes and the teams they play for.*
*The advantage of television is that it provides
sports fans with greater convenience.*

[insert]

*We can see more games than if we had to attend
each one in person, and we can follow a greater
variety of sports.*

EXAMPLE OF SENTENCE-LEVEL REVISIONS

Sports ~~on TV~~ Televised --A Win or a Loss?

Team sports ~~are~~ tend as much a part of America/n life as Mom and apple pie, ~~and they have a good tendency~~ to bring ~~people~~ us together, and They encourage team members to cooperate with one another, ^ they ~~also~~ create shared enthusiasm among fans. ~~Thanks to~~ Because of television, this togetherness now seems available ~~to nearly all of us~~ at the ~~flick of a switch.~~ twist of a dial. ~~It would appear that television has done us a great service.~~ But is this really the case? Although television ~~does make~~ makes sports more accessible, it also creates a distance between the sport and the fans and between athletes and ~~the~~ their teams . ^ ^ ~~they play for.~~

The advantage of television is that it provides sports fans with greater convenience. We do not have to buy tickets/ and travel to a stadium/ to see the World Series or the Super Bowl/ but ~~these games are on television.~~ We can enjoy any ~~the~~ game in the comfort of our own living ~~room~~ rooms. We can see more games than if we had to attend each one in person, and we can follow a greater ~~varieties~~ variety of sports.

LAPORTE'S FINAL DRAFT

Televised Sports--A Win or a Loss?

Team sports, as much a part of American life as Mom and apple pie, tend to bring us together. They encourage team members to cooperate with one another, and they create shared enthusiasm among fans. Because of television, this togetherness now seems available at the twist of a dial. But is this really the case? Although television makes sports more accessible, it also creates a distance between the sport and the spectator and between athletes and their teams.

The advantage of television is that it provides sports fans with greater convenience. We do not have to buy tickets and travel to a stadium to see the World Series or the Super Bowl but can enjoy any game in the comfort of our own living rooms. We can see more games than if we had to attend each one in person, and we can follow a greater variety of sports.

The price paid for this convenience, however, is high. Television changes the role of the fans who watch the game, making their participation more passive and distant. As television spectators, we see only what the camera shows. Yes, we do get a clearer look at important plays, and if we miss a detail, the commentator's explanation or the instant replay will fill us in. But we have no choice about what to watch. We cannot decide to follow the wide receiver rather than the quarterback or to watch a batter warming up rather than a commercial. Moreover, we miss all the sights, sounds, and smells that link live viewers with the players and with one another. When a fly ball comes over the fence, we cannot try to catch it. The roar of cheers after a touchdown is less exciting from the living room sofa than from the bleachers. We may feel silly cheering at all, since there is no chance those tiny figures on the screen will hear us.

The distance television has created between viewers and players does little more than reduce excitement and perhaps cheapen the experience of watching a game, but the unwholesome gap television creates between athletes and their teams threatens the foundation of team sports. Teamwork has always been paramount in team sports; the goals of the group have always overshadowed personal ambition. Television cameras, however, find it more dramatic to focus on individuals rather than on something as intangible as teamwork. In addition, the economics of television advertising and of team sports as big business create a situation in which players compete with one another for astronomical salaries and the chance to endorse products on television commercials.

Not surprisingly, the competition fostered by television causes players to try to make themselves look good, sometimes at the expense of the team. For example, a basketball player might take--and miss--a difficult shot instead of passing the ball to a teammate left unguarded closer to the basket. Or a star hockey player might work behind the scenes to keep a promising rookie from replacing him.

Team sports are a major part of American life, all the more so since television has brought them into our homes. The challenge for sports fans is to support their favorite teams in ways that encourage the best values represented by sports. One way to do this is to attend more live games rather than watch games on television. Attendance at live games may give the teams, the players, and the television networks the message that teamwork, not individual achievement and financial success, is what matters most about sports.

DESCRIPTIVE STUDENT ESSAY: PROFILING A PERSON OR A PLACE

Diane Williford, who wrote "Grandpa" (pp. 76–78), was responding to the following assignment.

ASSIGNMENT: PROFILING A PERSON OR A PLACE

A profile describes a person or a place — not just in general, but with a particular focus. You might focus on a person's interesting job, hobby, or lifestyle. You might write about someone who has made a major contribution to his or her community, church, place of employment, or organization; someone who has overcome a problem such as anorexia or a learning disability; or someone who played a significant role in your growing up. You could profile someone you do not admire: an abusive parent, for example, or a childhood friend who joined a violent gang.

If you'd rather profile a place, consider taking readers into an unfamiliar or exotic world — a scuba diving expedition, a spelunking adventure, a boat trip through the Everglades. Encourage readers to visit a favorite museum, historic district, or park (or discourage them from visiting a place you found disappointing). Introduce readers to a foreign country or an ethnic neighborhood with which you are familiar.

Unless you have a good reason for omitting it, include a thesis sentence in your introductory paragraph, probably at its end (see pages 30–35 of *The Bedford Handbook for Writers*). For this assignment, your information should come from personal knowledge, interviews, or direct observation. Aim for an essay from 500 to 1,000 words long — two to four typed pages, double-spaced.

Williford's writing process

Through the process of freewriting, Diane Williford discovered the person she wanted to write about: her grandfather.

WILLIFORD'S FREEWRITING

Someone who played a significant role in my growing up.
Mother--no.

Father--no.

Grandmother: Taught me to be independent, to fight, to be a good mother (children always come first). No emotions, no time for children. Making money to take care of the family.

Grandfather: Always gave me time, never tried to influence me, taught me to think for myself, spoiled me.

I was raised by my grandmother in a small town in Virginia. She didn't believe in spoiling children, she believed children should be seen only when necessary, heard not at all, and given only the basics--food and clothes, a roof, a good spanking. My grandmother wasn't the type to talk a lot to children unless she wanted to show you something. If you didn't do it right the first time, she made you start all over again until you got it right, and the only right was her right.

Grandpa was the quiet one, he was a big black man--strong and proud. Since he and grandmother had divorced before I came along, I didn't see him except on weekends. But he always made them special. I can't say if he was as smart as my grandmother was, she owned her own business, he worked for a living. But he always tried to answer my questions and he had time to listen to me.

A lot of what I know about my grandfather's past, I learned from other people. I know he fled from North Carolina in the middle of the night with his family, because he had married a near-white woman and the police and Klan were always stopping him and harassing him. I know he once shot a man dead who kept robbing his house. I know he broke a bone in his leg and never reported it to his job because jobs were scarce and he was scared he would lose it and not be able to take care of his family.

Of the two grandparents, I guess I remember my grandfather most fondly. He's old now and lives in a nursing home. He's still special, he's still my grandpa.

In addition to doing freewriting, Diane Williford recalled memories of her grandfather by telling her sons about him and by placing a long-distance phone call to Grandpa himself.

When she sat down to write a rough draft, Williford found that the words came quite easily. The draft expressed pretty much what she wanted to say, but Williford saw room for improvements. She revised the introduction, completely rewrote the conclusion, and deleted a weak paragraph in the middle of the essay. Then she polished sentences to make them tighter and more emphatic and corrected a few problems with grammar and punctuation. Here is her final draft.

WILLIFORD'S FINAL DRAFT

Grandpa

I don't have a lot of fantastic memories of childhood. There were no spectacular family adventures, no unique family projects that taught some sort of moral lesson, no out-of-the-ordinary holidays. We ate family meals together, but most of the time the children and adults lived in different worlds. The kids went to school, did homework, and played; the adults worked. I was lucky, though. When I wanted a little of both worlds, I could always turn to Grandpa.

I remember vividly the weekends at his house. Sitting on his lap, going to wrestling matches, walking down the street or through a park--these were things I did with Grandpa. I wasn't just a kid to him: I was his granddaughter, and I was special. He was special too.

Thomas D. Williford was a giant of a man. He stood six feet two inches and weighed over 250 pounds. He moved with purpose and carried himself with respect. Tom was a proud man, a good man, and all who knew him said so. Even if you didn't know him, you would notice his inner strength, his patience, his self-esteem.

   Grandpa wasn't a scholar. In fact, he didn't even make it through grade school. He was born at the turn of the century, and educating black men wasn't a necessity then. He went to work when he was sixteen, and for the next forty years he worked in a coal factory. Then he worked in a steel mill for another twenty years. He stopped working only because the steel mill closed and he was too old to find another job.

   When I was with Grandpa, I could be a child and yet see things through grown-up eyes. "You see that tree, Cookie," he would say. "That tree was here before those houses. God put that tree there; man put the houses. Which is more beautiful?" If I climbed a tree, he didn't say, "Get down." He said, "Climb it right so you won't fall."

   "You appreciate what you work for," he used to say. He taught that lesson well. He never let me win any game; he taught me to win by learning to lose. If he couldn't answer a question, he was honest about it, but he would also say, "Why don't you find out and let me know too." He listened to me and he heard my feelings, not just my words.

   There was a tougher side to Grandpa, and I suppose this, too, made him special. There was the black man who fled with his near-white wife and children from North Carolina to avoid harassment and threats from the Ku Klux Klan. There was the quiet man whose home was robbed three times by the same drunk, who reported it three times to the police with no results, and who finally waited for the man to do it a fourth time--and shot him dead as he climbed through the bedroom window in the middle of the night. And there was the man who fractured his leg at work, never reported it because he couldn't afford not to work, and years later still endures the pain of the ill-mended fracture.

Grandpa is almost ninety-five and now resides in a nursing home in Windsor, North Carolina. The leg he fractured forty years ago is too weak to carry his weight. His eyes are going bad. But to me he's still the big, strong man who used to take his grandchild in his arms and rock her, the man who taught a small child to see all the things around her with open eyes, the man who taught a child to try until she wins and becomes the best. He's still special and, thanks to him, so am I.

NARRATIVE STUDENT ESSAY: RE-CREATING AN EXPERIENCE

Marie Visosky, who wrote "Orphaned at Five" (pp. 81–82), was responding to the following assignment.

ASSIGNMENT: RECREATING AN EXPERIENCE

A narrative essay recreates an experience for a central purpose: usually to reveal an insight about the action or people involved. You might write about an experience in which you encountered people from a culture different from your own. You might write about a turning point in your life — perhaps a time when you were forced suddenly to grow up, a time when you faced a difficult challenge, or a time when you reassessed your values. You might describe an experience in which you learned to do something new: coaching a Little League team, designing stage sets for a play, forming a musical group. Or you might recount an adventure that tested you in some way. If you have experienced work in an emergency room, on an ambulance or fire truck, or as a police officer, you might describe in vivid detail one day or evening at work to give readers an inside view of this stressful job.

A narrative should have a central focus, but it is not always necessary to express the focus in a thesis sentence early in the essay (see pp. 30–32 of *The Bedford Handbook for Writers*); at times you will want to get right to the action. A narrative should of course be based on personal experience. Aim for an essay from 500 to 1,000 words long—two to four typed pages, double-spaced.

Visosky's writing process

When Marie Visosky read the narrative writing assignment, she knew immediately what she would write about. On a Thanksgiving Day when she was only five years old, she learned that both of her parents had been killed in an automobile crash. Although the memories were painful, Visosky wanted to show what the experience was like for a child too young to understand what was happening to her.

Because Visosky knew so much about her topic and because organizing the essay chronologically was easy, her first draft didn't need much global revision. She condensed the introduction and made a few cuts to tighten the narrative. Once she had completed her second draft, she turned her attention to revising and editing sentences for greater effectiveness. Here are the sentence-level changes Visosky made in the first four paragraphs of her second draft.

VISOSKY'S SENTENCE-LEVEL REVISIONS

Celery sticks ~~made great~~ *served as slugger* bats; olives ~~were just the right size~~ *substituted for baseballs* ~~ball~~ to be smashed across the kitchen. Cousins Sonny and Guido were pitcher and catcher, and my sister Dorrie was a combination of infield and outfield. I came up to bat for the first time just as Gramps called for us to come into the living room.

~~There was a~~ *A* policeman ~~standing~~ *stood* in the doorway. Nonnie and Aunt Sandy were crying. All morning we had been told to stop touching the Thanksgiving dinner or ~~we'd get into a lot of trouble.~~ *we would be punished.* Who expected to go to jail because of olives!

Gramps pulled Dorrie and me onto his lap and hugged us close. "Your momma and daddy were going to get Uncle Vince and a truck hit their car. God took them to heaven." He started to cry. I wished he would let us down. His sweater ~~was prickly~~, *prickly smelled of tobacco,* and his mouth was purple from wine.

Dorrie and I went home with Aunt Sandy. My stomach was hurting and making noises, *tiger /* ~~Everybody~~ *but everyone* was crying so I was afraid to say I was hungry.

VISOSKY'S FINAL DRAFT

Orphaned at Five

Celery sticks served as slugger bats; olives substituted for baseballs to be smashed across the kitchen. Cousins Sonny and Guido were pitcher and catcher, and my sister Dorrie was a combination of infield and outfield. I came up to bat for the first time just as Gramps called for us to come into the living room.

A policeman stood in the doorway. Nonnie and Aunt Sandy were crying. All morning we had been told to stop touching the Thanksgiving dinner or we would be punished. Who expected to go to jail because of olives!

Gramps pulled Dorrie and me onto his lap and hugged us close. "Your momma and daddy were going to get Uncle Vince and a truck hit their car. God took them to heaven." He started to cry. I wished he would let us down. His prickly sweater smelled of tobacco, and his mouth was purple from wine.

Dorrie and I went home with Aunt Sandy. My stomach was hurting and making tiger noises, but everyone was crying so I was afraid to say I was hungry.

In the morning we went to a dark room where Mother and Daddy were lying in coffins. It smelled so sweet in that room, and the red-glassed candles burning everywhere made it sticky hot. Mother wore a lacy pink dress. A pink satin blanket covered her feet. Daddy looked so white, as if he wore makeup like Mother. Folded newspapers were hidden inside his trouser legs.

At night we all knelt down on the blue carpet and prayed a long, long time with Father Minnorra from Our Lady of the Angels Church. My knees were sore and I shifted my weight from one leg to the other. Aunt Sandy touched my shoulder and said, "Marie, stop that rocking. Kneel up."

The morning of the funeral was very bright. The curtains were opened in the coffin room. Aunt Sandy held my hand. She wore a black hat with a big black feather. Her eyes had big red circles around them, and her mouth was bright red. She reminded me of the clown in my circus coloring book.

Aunt Sandy kissed Daddy and lifted me to do the same. I touched his cheek. His skin was stiff. I kissed his forehead. We moved to Mother. Aunt Sandy lifted me again. I kissed Mother, then stood on the kneeler. I moved down and lifted the pink satin cover. Mother's shoes were pink. I moved back toward her head. Touching, touching as I went. Her hair was soft. Her lips were not soft. I pressed her mouth. It was tight. I pushed my fingers into her mouth. I saw and felt cotton. Aunt Sandy pulled me away.

A man in striped pants pulled down the backs of the coffins. Nonnie was crying. Gramps was blowing his nose. Someone took Dorrie and me to a big car. We sat on two little pull-down seats behind the driver.

At the cemetery everyone was crying and praying. Aunt Sandy fainted when the two men with ropes lowered the coffins into the graves. Father Minnorra gave Dorrie and me each a white flower. Mine was turning brown and its petals were falling. I gave the flower to Gramps so I could put my cold hands in my coat pockets.

PART II

Constructing Paragraphs

Except for special-purpose paragraphs, such as introductions and conclusions (see 2b and 2d), paragraphs are clusters of information supporting an essay's main point (or advancing a story's action). Aim for paragraphs that are clearly focused, well developed, organized, coherent, and neither too long nor too short for easy reading.

5

Focus on a main point.

A paragraph should be unified around a main point. The point should be clear to readers, and all sentences in the paragraph must relate to it.

5a State the main point in a topic sentence.

As readers move into a paragraph, they need to know where they are—in relation to the whole essay—and what to expect in the sentences to come. A good topic sentence, a one-sentence summary of the paragraph's main point, acts as a signpost pointing in two directions: backward toward the thesis of the essay and forward toward the body of the paragraph.

Like a thesis statement (see 1c), a topic sentence is more general than the material supporting it. Usually the topic sentence comes first.

> *Nearly all living creatures manage some form of communication.* The dance patterns of bees in their hive help to point the way to distant flower fields or announce successful foraging. Male stickleback fish regularly swim upside-down to indicate outrage in a courtship contest. Male deer and lemurs mark territorial ownership by rubbing their own body secre-

tions on boundary stones or trees. Everyone has seen a frightened dog put his tail between his legs and run in panic. We,
too, use gestures, expressions, postures, and movement to give
our words point. [Italics added.]

— Olivia Vlahos, *Human Beginnings*

Sometimes the topic sentence is introduced by a transitional sentence linking it to earlier material. In the following
paragraph, the topic sentence (italicized) has been delayed to
allow for a transition.

But flowers are not the only source of spectacle in the
wilderness. *An opportunity for late color is provided by the
berries of wildflowers, shrubs, and trees.* Baneberry presents
its tiny white flowers in spring but in late summer bursts
forth with clusters of red berries. Bunchberry, a ground-cover
plant, puts out red berries in the fall, and the red berries of
wintergreen last from autumn well into winter. In California,
the bright red, fist-sized clusters of Christmas berries can be
seen growing beside highways for up to six months of the year.
[Italics added.]

—James Crockett et al., *Wildflower Gardening*

Occasionally the topic sentence may be withheld until the
end of the paragraph—but only if the earlier sentences hang
together so well that the reader perceives their direction, if not
their exact point. The opening sentences of the following paragraph state facts, making them supporting material rather
than topic sentences, but they strongly suggest a central idea.
The topic sentence at the end is hardly a surprise.

Tobacco chewing starts as soon as people begin stirring.
Those who have fresh supplies soak the new leaves in water
and add ashes from the hearth to the wad. Men, women, and
children chew tobacco and all are addicted to it. Once there
was a shortage of tobacco in Kaobawa's village and I was
plagued for a week by early morning visitors who requested
permission to collect my cigarette butts in order to make a wad

of chewing tobacco. Normally, if anyone is short of tobacco, he can request a share of someone else's already chewed wad, or simply borrow the entire wad when its owner puts it down somewhere. *Tobacco is so important to them that their word for "poverty" translates as "being without tobacco."* [Italics added.]
—Napoleon A. Chagnon, *Yanomamo: The Fierce People*

Although it is generally wise to use topic sentences, at times they are unnecessary. A topic sentence may not be needed if a paragraph continues developing an idea clearly introduced in a previous paragraph, if the details of the paragraph unmistakably suggest its main point, or if the paragraph appears in a narrative of events where generalizations might interrupt the flow of the story.

5b Do not stray from the point.

Sentences that do not support the topic sentence destroy the unity of a paragraph. If the paragraph is otherwise well focused, such offending sentences can simply be deleted or perhaps moved elsewhere. In the following paragraph describing the inadequate facilities in a high school, the information about the typing instructor (in italics) is clearly off the point.

As the result of tax cuts, the educational facilities of Lincoln High School have reached an all-time low. Some of the books date back to 1970 and have long since shed their covers. The lack of lab equipment makes it necessary for four to five students to work at one table, with most watching rather than performing experiments. The few typewriters in working order have not been cleaned in so long that most letters come out blotchy and hard to read. There is only one self-correcting typewriter and no prospect of the school's ordering a word processor or computer anytime soon. *Also, the typing instructor left to have a baby at the beginning of the semester, and most of the students don't like the substitute.* As for the furniture, many of the upright chairs have become recliners, and the desk legs are so unbalanced that they play seesaw on the floor.

Sometimes the cure for a disunified paragraph is not as simple as deleting or moving material. Writers often wander into uncharted territory because they cannot think of enough evidence to support a topic sentence. Feeling that it is too soon to break into a new paragraph, they move on to new ideas for which they have not prepared the reader. When this happens, the writer is faced with a choice: Either find more evidence to support the topic sentence or adjust the topic sentence to mesh with the evidence that is available.

LOOKING AT YOURSELF AS A WRITER
Topic sentences

Professors and business supervisors often complain about the writing that is submitted to them, and one of their loudest complaints concerns topic sentences. Why, they wonder, do so many students and employees have trouble stating the point of a paragraph in its first sentence?

If you have experienced this difficulty, ask yourself why. Here are some common causes and cures.

CAUSE   You haven't decided how to organize your draft, so you don't know what key idea to express in the topic sentence for each paragraph.

CURE   Jot down an informal outline and build a topic sentence for each key point in the outline. It's best to do this before drafting, but you can do it later as well.

CAUSE   You are focusing on details and forget the reader's need to see how the details fit into the overall structure of the essay. The forward flow of writing tempts nearly all of us to blur the structure while we are drafting.

CURE   As you revise a draft, pay special attention to organization, inserting (or sharpening) topic sentences as needed.

Topic Sentences (Continued)

CAUSE You are trying to link the opening sentence of a new paragraph to the last sentence of the previous paragraph.

CURE When you move into a new paragraph, don't worry about subtle links between sentences. Pay attention instead to links between larger chunks of text — the move from one topic to another.

CAUSE You are aware that some professional writers, especially journalists and informal essayists, do not always use clear topic sentences.

CURE Develop a flexible approach to writing. In some contexts, topic sentences may not be so important. In the academic world, however, topic sentences are often necessary for clarifying the lines of an argument or reporting the research in a field. In the business world, topic sentences (along with headings) are essential, since readers often scan for information.

EXERCISE 5-1

Underline the topic sentence in the following paragraph and eliminate any material that does not clarify or develop the central idea.

A recent plan of the mayor's threatens to destroy one of the oldest and most successfully integrated neighborhoods in our city, replacing it with luxury condominiums and a shopping mall. This neighborhood, Thompson's Fields, was settled by a mixture of immigrants from Ireland, Italy, Poland, and Austria in the early part of the twentieth century. Over the years black and Hispanic families have also moved in and have become part of the community. When the mayor designated a five-block area along the neighborhood's main street as the location for a redevelopment program, the community decided to take the mayor to court. The mayor has hired the best urban planners and architects in the country to design and build three large skyscrapers along with parking facilities for the area. One woman has even moved to the city from California to work on the project. If the court accepts the case, the lawyer for the residents will be Ann Tyson, who grew up in Thompson's Fields. The residents have seen a great deal of change over the years, but they refuse to stand by while their homes are razed for some gentrification project that they will never enjoy.

6

Develop the main point.

Topic sentences are generalizations in need of support, so once you have written a topic sentence, ask yourself, "How do I know that this is true?" Your answer will suggest how to develop the paragraph.

6a Flesh out skimpy paragraphs.

Though an occasional short paragraph is fine, particularly if it functions as a transition or emphasizes a point, a series of brief paragraphs suggests inadequate development. How much development is enough? That varies, depending on the writer's purpose and audience.

For example, when she wrote a paragraph attempting to convince readers that it is impossible to lose fat quickly, health columnist Jane Brody knew that she would have to present a great deal of evidence because many dieters want to believe the opposite. She did *not* write:

> When you think about it, it's impossible to lose — as many diets suggest — 10 pounds of *fat* in ten days, even on a total fast. Even a moderately active person cannot lose so much weight so fast. A less active person hasn't a prayer.

This three-sentence paragraph is too skimpy to be convincing. But the paragraph that Brody wrote contains enough evidence to convince even skeptical readers:

> When you think about it, it's impossible to lose — as many diets suggest — 10 pounds of *fat* in ten days, even on a total fast. A pound of body fat represents 3,500 calories. To lose 1 pound of fat, you must expend 3,500 more calories than you consume. Let's say you weigh 170 pounds and, as a moderately active person, you burn 2,500 calories a day. If your diet contains only 1,500 calories, you'd have an energy deficit of 1,000 calories a day. In a week's time that would add up to a 7,000-calorie deficit, or 2 pounds of real fat. In ten days, the accumulated deficit would represent nearly 3 pounds of lost body fat. Even if you ate nothing at all for ten days and maintained your usual level of activity, your caloric deficit would add up to 25,000 calories. . . . At 3,500 calories per pound of fat, that's still only 7 pounds of lost fat.
>
> — Jane Brody, *Jane Brody's Nutrition Book*

6b Choose a suitable pattern of development.

Although paragraphs may be patterned in an almost infinite number of ways, certain patterns of development occur frequently, either alone or in combination: examples and illustrations, narration, description, process, comparison and contrast, analogy, cause and effect, classification and division, and definition. There is nothing magical about these methods of development. They simply reflect some of the ways in which we think.

Examples and illustrations

Examples, perhaps the most common pattern of development, are appropriate whenever the reader might be tempted to ask, "For example?" Though examples are just selected instances, not a complete catalog, they are enough to suggest the truth of many topic sentences, as in the following paragraph.

> Normally my parents abided scrupulously by "The Budget," but several times a year Dad would dip into his battered, black strongbox and splurge on some irrational, totally satisfying luxury. Once he bought over a hundred comic books at a flea market, doled out to us thereafter at the tantalizing rate of two a week. He always got a whole flat of pansies, Mom's favorite flower, for us to give her on Mother's Day. One day a boy stopped at our house selling fifty cent raffle tickets on a sailboat and Dad bought every ticket the boy had left — three books' worth. — Connie Hailey, student

Illustrations are extended examples, frequently presented in story form. Because they require several sentences apiece, they are used more sparingly than examples. When well selected, however, they can be a vivid and effective means of developing a point. The writer of the following paragraph uses illustrations to demonstrate that Harriet Tubman, famous conductor on the underground railway for escaping slaves, was a genius at knowing how and when to retreat.

> Part of Harriet Tubman's strategy of conducting was, as in all battle-field operations, the knowledge of how and when to retreat. Numerous allusions have been made to her moves when she suspected that she was in danger. When she feared the party was closely pursued, she would take it for a time on a train southward bound. No one seeing Negroes going in this direction would for an instant suppose them to be fugitives. Once on her return she was at a railway station. She saw some men reading a poster and she heard one of them reading it aloud. It was a description of her, offering a reward for her capture. She took a southbound train to avert suspicion. At another time when Harriet heard men talking about her, she pretended to read a book which she carried. One man remarked, "This cannot be the woman. The one we want can't read or write." Harriet devoutly hoped the book was right side up. — Earl Conrad, *Harriet Tubman*

Narration

A paragraph of narration tells a story or part of a story. Narrative paragraphs are usually arranged in chronological order, but they may also contain flashbacks, interruptions that take the story back to an earlier time. The following paragraph, from Jane Goodall's *In the Shadow of Man*, recounts one of the author's experiences in the African wild.

> One evening when I was wading in the shallows of the lake to pass a rocky outcrop, I suddenly stopped dead as I saw the sinuous black body of a snake in the water. It was all of six feet long, and from the slight hood and the dark stripes at the back of the neck I knew it to be a Storm's water cobra — a deadly reptile for the bite of which there was, at that time, no serum. As I stared at it an incoming wave gently deposited part of its body on one of my feet. I remained motionless, not even breathing, until the wave rolled back into the lake, drawing the snake with it. Then I leaped out of the water as fast as I could, my heart hammering.
>
> — Jane Goodall, *In the Shadow of Man*

Description

A descriptive paragraph sketches a portrait of a person, place, or thing by using concrete and specific details that appeal to one or more of our senses — sight, sound, smell, taste, and touch. Consider, for example, the following description of the grasshopper invasions that devastated the midwestern landscape in the late 1860s.

> They came like dive bombers out of the west. They came by the millions with the rustle of their wings roaring overhead. They came in waves, like the rolls of the sea, descending with a terrifying speed, breaking now and again like a mighty surf. They came with the force of a williwaw and they formed a huge, ominous, dark brown cloud that eclipsed the sun. They dipped and touched earth, hitting objects and people like hailstones.

But they were not hail. These were live demons. They popped, snapped, crackled, and roared. They were dark brown, an inch or longer in length, plump in the middle and tapered at the ends. They had transparent wings, slender legs, and two black eyes that flashed with a fierce intelligence.

— Eugene Boe, "Pioneers to Eternity"

Process

A process paragraph is patterned in time order, usually chronologically. A writer may choose this pattern either to describe a process or to show readers how to perform a process. The following paragraph describes the physiological processes that accompany laughter.

One state of joy that scientists have been able to capture in the laboratory is laughter. Sustained hilarity, it turns out, is among the more agreeable forms of aerobics. The muscles of the abdomen, neck, and shoulders rapidly tighten and relax; heart rate and blood pressure increase; inhalation and expiration become more spasmodic and deeper. When laughter subsides, blood pressure and pulse are likely to fall to lower, often more salubrious levels than before the merriment began. "One hundred laughs is equivalent to 10 minutes of rowing," says Dr. Fry [researcher at Stanford University Medical School]. — Natalie Angier, "The Anatomy of Joy"

Here is a paragraph that shows readers how to perform a process — that of opening an oyster.

An oyster has an irregular shape. The valves are rough and their lips hard to find. Crooked and wrinkled, the hairline crack between the valves can't be widened with the blade of a knife; the point must enter first. Furthermore, a big Chincoteague doesn't fit the left hand. One must hold the animal slanting against the edge of the kitchen sink and poke around, seeking the slot by touch as much as by sight. It takes painful practice. When the knifepoint finds a purchase, push carefully and quickly before the oyster realizes what's afoot and

gets a firmer grip on itself. Push in the wrong place—it's easy
to mistake a growth line for the groove—and the knife takes
on a life of its own. It can skid and open up your hand. This
delicate work requires patient agility to find the groove, push
the knife in, then slit the muscle and open the critter without
losing too much juice. (Restaurants serve oysters on their flat
shell. It's better to throw that one away and lay the delicacies
on a bed of crushed ice in the roundest half-shell which holds
its delicious liquor. Sprinkle each one with lemon juice—a
healthy oyster will wriggle the slightest bit at this to prove it's
alive—lift the dishlike shell to the lips, and drink the oyster
down. It's a delicious, addicting experience.)

> —Philip Kopper, "How to Open an Oyster"

Comparison and contrast

To compare two subjects is to draw attention to their similarities, although the word *compare* also has a broader meaning
that includes a consideration of differences. To contrast is to
focus only on differences.

Whether a comparison-and-contrast paragraph stresses
similarities or differences, it may be patterned in one of two
ways. The two subjects may be presented one at a time, block
style, as in the following paragraph of contrast.

So Grant and Lee were in complete contrast, representing
two diametrically opposed elements in American life. Grant
was the modern man emerging; beyond him, ready to come on
the stage, was the great age of steel and machinery, of crowded
cities and a restless burgeoning vitality. Lee might have ridden
down from the old age of chivalry, lance in hand, silken banner
fluttering over his head. Each man was the perfect champion of
his cause, drawing both his strengths and weaknesses from
the people he led.

> —Bruce Catton, "Grant and Lee: A Study in Contrasts"

Or a paragraph may proceed point by point, treating the two
subjects together, one aspect at a time. The following paragraph uses the point-by-point method to contrast the writer's

academic experiences in an American high school and an Irish convent.

> Strangely enough, instead of being academically inferior to my American high school, the Irish convent was superior. In my class at home, *Love Story* was considered pretty heavy reading, so imagine my surprise at finding Irish students who could recite passages from *War and Peace.* In high school we complained about having to study *Romeo and Juliet* in one semester, whereas in Ireland we simultaneously studied *Macbeth* and Dickens's *Hard Times,* in addition to writing a composition a day in English class. In high school, I didn't even begin algebra until the ninth grade, while at the convent seventh graders (or their Irish equivalent) were doing calculus and trigonometry.   — Margaret Stack, student

Analogy

Analogies draw comparisons between items that appear to have little in common. Writers turn to analogies for a variety of reasons: to make the unfamiliar seem familiar, to provide a concrete understanding of an abstract topic, to argue a point, or to provoke fresh thoughts or changed feelings about a subject. In the paragraph below, physician Lewis Thomas draws an analogy between the behavior of ants and that of humans. Thomas's analogy helps us to understand the social behavior of ants and forces us to question the superiority of our own human societies.

> Ants are so much like human beings as to be an embarrassment. They farm fungi, raise aphids as livestock, launch armies into wars, use chemical sprays to alarm and confuse enemies, capture slaves. The families of weaver ants engage in child labor, holding their larvae like shuttles to spin out the thread that sews the leaves together for their fungus gardens. They exchange information ceaselessly. They do everything but watch television.
> — Lewis Thomas, "On Societies as Organisms"

Although analogies can be a powerful tool for illuminating a subject, they should be used with caution in arguments. Just because two things may be alike in one respect, we cannot conclude that they are alike in all respects. (See *false analogy*, page 584.)

Cause and effect

When causes and effects are a matter of argument, they are too complex to be reduced to a simple pattern (see page 585). However, if a writer wishes merely to describe a cause-and-effect relationship that is generally accepted, then the effect may be stated in the topic sentence, with the causes listed in the body of the paragraph.

> The fantastic water clarity of the Mount Gambier sinkholes results from several factors. The holes are fed from aquifers holding rainwater that fell decades — even centuries — ago, and that has been filtered through miles of limestone. The high level of calcium that limestone adds causes the silty detritus from dead plants and animals to cling together and settle quickly to the bottom. Abundant bottom vegetation in the shallow sinkholes also helps bind the silt. And the rapid turnover of water prohibits stagnation.
>
> — Hillary Hauser,
> "Exploring a Sunken Realm in Australia"

Or the paragraph may move from cause to effects, as in this paragraph from a student's essay on the effects of her family's formal manners on her friends.

> My family's formality often made visitors uncomfortable. Before coming to my house for dinner, my friends used to beg me to teach them to say grace the way we did, because they worried about not fitting in. During the meal they would watch anxiously to see which fork I used, and sometimes they could only stammer when my father asked them questions about world events. It wasn't long before I came to wonder if the

purpose of good table manners was really to give guests indigestion. Friends who came to my house for dinner often didn't come again; more often, I went to their houses.

—Jane Betz, student

Classification and division

Classification is the grouping of items into categories according to some consistent principle. Philosopher Francis Bacon was using classification when he wrote that "some books are to be tasted, others to be swallowed, and some few to be chewed and digested." Bacon's principle for classifying books is the degree to which they are worthy of our attention, but books of course can be classified according to other principles. For example, an elementary school teacher might classify children's books according to their level of difficulty, or a librarian might group them by subject matter. The principle of classification that a writer chooses ultimately depends on the purpose of the classification.

In the following paragraph, essayist E. B. White groups the people of New York City into three categories, according to their reasons for being there.

There are roughly three New Yorks. There is, first, the New York of the man or woman who was born here, who takes the city for granted and accepts its size and its turbulence as natural and inevitable. Second, there is the New York of the commuter — the city that is devoured by locusts each day and spat out each night. Third, there is the New York of the person who was born somewhere else and came to New York in quest of something. Of these three trembling cities the greatest is the last — the city of final destination, the city that is a goal. It is this third city that accounts for New York's high-strung disposition, its poetical deportment, its dedication to the arts, and its incomparable achievements. Commuters give the city its tidal restlessness, natives give it solidity and continuity, but the settlers give it passion. And whether it is a farmer arriving from Italy to set up a small grocery store in a slum, or a young

girl arriving from a small town in Mississippi to escape the
indignity of being observed by her neighbors, or a boy arriving
from the Corn Belt with a manuscript in his suitcase and a
pain in his heart, it makes no difference: each embraces New
York with the intense excitement of first love, each absorbs
New York with the fresh eyes of an adventurer, each generates
heat and light to dwarf the Consolidated Edison Company.
                                    — E. B. White, "Here Is New York"

Division takes one item and divides it into parts. As with
classification, division should be made according to some consistent principle. Dividing a tree into roots, trunk, branches,
and leaves makes sense; listing its components as branches,
wood, water, and sap does not, for the categories overlap.

The following paragraph describes the parts of a lemon
and their uses.

Absolutely every part of a lemon is useful in some way,
from its seeds to its outermost peel. Lemon-pip oil,
unsaturated and aromatic, is important in the soap industry
and in special diets. The pulp left over from squeezed lemons
is evaporated and concentrated into "citrus molasses" which
is sold as a base for making vinegar and as an ingredient in
bland syrups and alcohol. The remains of the "rag" or pulp is
also sold as cattle feed. Most of the pectin used to thicken and
solidify jams, jellies, and marmalades comes from the white
pith of citrus fruits. Among these, lemon and lime pectin has
the highest "jelly grade" or capacity to thicken liquids. It is
widely used in medicines taken to combat diarrhea. The
flavedo, or outer yellow layer of lemon peel, is invaluable for its
intense taste and scent. (The word *zest*, which originally meant
"skin or peel," then specifically "citrus peel," is now in common
use as signifying "lively enjoyment.")
                                    — Margaret Visser, *Much Depends on Dinner*

Definition

A definition puts a word or concept into a general class and
then provides enough details to distinguish it from others in
the same class. For example, in one of its senses the term *grit*

names the class of things that birds eat, but it is restricted to those items — such as small pebbles, eggshell, and ashes — that help the bird grind food.

Many definitions may be presented in a sentence or two, but abstract or difficult concepts may require a paragraph or even a full essay of definition. In the following paragraph, the writer defines envy as a special kind of desire.

> Envy is so integral and so painful a part of what animates human behavior in market societies that many people have forgotten the full meaning of the word, simplifying it into one of the synonyms of desire. It is that, which may be why it flourishes in market societies: democracies of desire, they might be called, with money for ballots, stuffing permitted. But envy is more or less than desire. It begins with the almost frantic sense of emptiness inside oneself, as if the pump of one's heart were sucking on air. One has to be blind to perceive the emptiness, of course, but that's just what envy is, a selective blindness. *Invidia,* Latin for envy, translates as "nonsight," and Dante had the envious plodding along under cloaks of lead, their eyes sewn shut with leaden wire. What they are blind to is what they have, God-given and humanly nurtured, in themselves.
>
> —Nelson W. Aldrich, Jr., *Old Money*

Extended definitions frequently make use of other patterns of development, such as examples, illustrations, or comparison and contrast. Here, for example, is a paragraph that uses a number of illustrations to define the typical teenage victim in a "slasher" film.

> Since teenagers are the target audience for slasher films, the victims in the films are almost always independent, fun-loving, just-out-of-high school partygoers. The girls all love to take late-night strolls alone through the woods or to skinny-dip at midnight in a murky lake. The boys, eager to impress the girls, prove their manhood by descending alone into musty cellars to restart broken generators or by chasing psychotic killers into haylofts and attics. Entering dark and gloomy

houses, young men and women alike decide suddenly that now's a good time to save a few bucks on the family's electric bill—so they leave the lights off. After hearing a noise within the house, they always foolishly decide to investigate, thinking it's one of their many missing friends or pets. Disregarding the "safety in numbers" theory, they branch off in separate directions, never to see each other again. Or the teenagers fall into the common slasher-movie habit of walking backward, which naturally leads them right into you-know-who. Confronted by the ax-wielding maniac, the senseless youths lose their will to survive, close their eyes, and scream.

— Matthew J. Holicek, student

EXERCISE 6–1

Write a paragraph modeled on one of the patterns discussed in this section. Some possible topics — most of which you'll need to restrict — are listed here.

Examples or illustrations: sexism in a comic strip, ways to include protein in a vegetarian diet, the benefits of a particular summer job, community services provided by your college, violence on the six o'clock news, educational software for children

Narration: the active lifestyle of a grandparent, life with an alcoholic, working in an emergency room, the benefits (or problems) of intercultural dating, growing up in a large family, the rewards of working in a nursing home, an experience that taught you a lesson, a turning point in your life

Description: your childhood home, an ethnic neighborhood, a rock concert, a favorite painting in an art gallery, a garden, a classic car, a hideous building or monument, a style of dress, a family heirloom (such as a crazy quilt or a collection of Christmas tree ornaments), a favorite park or retreat

Process: how to repair something, how to develop a successful job interview style, how to meet someone of the opposite sex, how to practice safe scuba diving, how to build a set for a play, how to survive in the wilderness, how to train a dog, how to quit smoking, how to make bread

Comparison and contrast: two neighborhoods, teachers, political candidates, colleges, products; country living versus city living; the stereotype of a job versus the reality; a change in attitude toward your family's religion or ethnic background

Analogy: between a family reunion and a circus, between training for a rigorous sport and boot camp, between settling an argument and being a courtroom judge, between a dogfight and a boxing match, between raising a child and tending a garden

Cause and effect: the effects of water pollution on a particular area, the effects of divorce on a child, the effects of an illegal drug, why a particular film or television show is popular, why an area of the country has high unemployment, why early training is essential for success as a ballet dancer, violinist, or athlete

Classification: types of clothing worn on your college campus, types of people who go to college mixers, types of dieters, types of television weather reports, types of rock bands, types of teachers

Definition: a computer addict, an ideal parent or teacher, an authoritarian personality, an intellectual, a sexist, anorexia nervosa, a typical heroine in a Harlequin romance, a typical blind date

6c Consider possible ways of arranging information.

In addition to choosing a pattern of development (or a combination of patterns), you may need to make decisions about arrangement. If you are developing a paragraph with examples, for instance, you'll need to decide how to order the examples. Or if you are contrasting two items point by point, you'll need to decide which points to discuss first, second, and so on. Often considerations of purpose and audience will help you make these choices.

Three of the most common ways of arranging information are treated in this section: time order, spatial order, and order of climax. Other possible arrangements include order of complexity (from simple to complex), order of familiarity (from most familiar to least familiar), and order of audience appeal (from "safe" ideas to those that may challenge the audience's views).

Order of time

Time order, usually chronological, is appropriate for a variety of purposes such as narrating a personal experience, telling an anecdote, describing an experiment, or explaining a process. The following paragraph, arranged in chronological order, appears in *Blue Highways,* an account of the author's travels on the back roads of America.

> Orion Saddle Road, after I was committed to it, narrowed to a single rutted lane affording no place to turn around; if I met somebody, one of us would have to back down. The higher I went, the more that idea unnerved me — the road was bad enough driving forward. The compass swung from point to point, and within five minutes it had touched each of the three hundred sixty degrees. The clutch started pushing back, and ruts and craters and rocks threw the steering wheel into nasty jerks that wrenched to the spine. I understood why, the day before, I'd thought there could be no road over the Chiricahuas; there wasn't. No wonder desperadoes hid in this inaccessibility.   — William Least Heat Moon

Time order need not be chronological. For example, you might decide to arrange events in the order in which they were revealed to you, not in the order in which they happened. Or you might choose to begin with a dramatic moment and then flash back to the events that led up to it.

Order of space

For descriptions of a location or a scene, a spatial arrangement will seem natural. Imagine yourself holding a video camera and you'll begin to see the possibilities. Might you pan the scene from afar and then zoom to a close-up? Would you rather sweep the camera from side to side — or from top to bottom? Or should you try for a more impressionistic effect, focusing the camera on first one and then another significant feature of the scene?

The writer of the following paragraph describes the contents of a long, narrow pool hall by taking us from the front to the back.

> The pool tables were in a line side by side from the front to the back of the long, narrow building. The first one was the biggest, and the best snooker players used it. Beyond it were the other tables used by lesser players, except for the last one. This was the bank's pool table, used only by the best players in the county. —William G. Hill, student

Order of climax

When ideas are presented in the order of climax, they build toward a conclusion. Consider the following paragraph describing the effects on workers of long-term blue-collar employment. All of the examples have an emotional impact, but the final one — even though it might at first seem trivial — is the most powerful. It shows us just how degrading blue-collar work can become.

> I met people who taught me about human behavior. I saw people take amphetamines to keep up with ever-rising production rates. I saw good friends, and even relatives, physically attack each other over job assignments that would mean a few cents' difference. I observed women cheating on their husbands and men cheating on their wives. I watched women hand over their entire paycheck to a bookie. I saw pregnant women, their feet too swollen for shoes, come to work in slippers. I saw women with colds stuff pieces of tissue up their nostrils so they wouldn't have to keep stopping to blow their nose. —Linda Lavelle, student

Because the order of climax saves the most dramatic examples for the end, it is appropriate only when readers are likely to persist until the end. In much business writing, for example, you cannot assume that readers will read more than the first couple of sentences of a paragraph. In such cases, you will be wise to open with your most powerful examples, even at the risk of allowing the paragraph to fizzle at the end.

6d If necessary, adjust paragraph length.

Most readers feel comfortable reading paragraphs that range between 100 and 200 words. Shorter paragraphs force too much starting and stopping, and longer ones strain the reader's attention span. There are exceptions to this guideline, however. Paragraphs longer than 200 words frequently appear in scholarly writing, where they suggest seriousness and depth. Paragraphs shorter than 100 words occur in newspapers because of narrow columns; in informal essays to quicken the pace; and in business letters, where readers routinely skim for main ideas.

In an essay, the first and last paragraphs will ordinarily be the introduction and conclusion. These special-purpose paragraphs are likely to be shorter than the paragraphs in the body of the essay. Typically, the body paragraphs will mimic the essay's organization: one paragraph per point in short essays, a group of paragraphs per point in longer ones. Some ideas require more development than others, however, so it is best to be flexible. If an idea stretches to a length unreasonable for a paragraph, you should divide it, even if you have presented comparable points in the essay in single paragraphs.

Paragraph breaks are not always made for strictly logical reasons. Writers use them for the following reasons as well.

REASONS FOR BEGINNING A NEW PARAGRAPH

— to mark off the introduction and the conclusion

— to signal a shift to a new idea

— to indicate an important shift in time or place

— to emphasize a point (by placing it at the beginning or the end, not in the middle, of a paragraph)

— to highlight a contrast

— to signal a change of speakers (in dialogue)

— to provide readers with a needed pause

— to break up text that looks too dense

Beware of using too many short, choppy paragraphs, however. Readers want to see how your ideas connect, and they become irritated when you break their momentum by forcing them to pause every few sentences. Here are some reasons you might have for combining some of the paragraphs in a rough draft.

REASONS FOR COMBINING PARAGRAPHS

— to clarify the essay's organization

— to connect closely related ideas

— to maintain momentum

— to bind together text that looks too choppy

7

Improve coherence.

When sentences and paragraphs flow from one to another without discernible bumps, gaps, or shifts, they are said to be coherent. Coherence can be improved by strengthening the various ties between old information and new: in other words, between sentences that have been read and those that are about to be read. A number of techniques for strengthening those ties are detailed in this section.

7a Link ideas clearly.

In the first draft of a paragraph or essay, writers do not always link their ideas as clearly as possible. To check a draft for clear connections among ideas, try to look at it from the point of view of a reader. Think in terms of the reader's expectations.

What readers look for in a paragraph

As you know, readers usually expect to learn a paragraph's main point in a topic sentence early in the paragraph. Then, as they move into the body of the paragraph, they expect to encounter specific details, facts, or examples that support the topic sentence—either directly or indirectly. Consider the following example, in which all of the sentences following the topic sentence directly support it.

> A passenger list of the early years of the Orient Express would read like a *Who's Who of the World*, from art to politics. Sarah Bernhardt and her Italian counterpart Eleonora Duse used the train to thrill the stages of Europe. For musicians there were Toscanini and Mahler. Dancers Nijinsky and Pavlova were there, while lesser performers like Harry Houdini and the girls of the Ziegfeld Follies also rode the rails. Violinists were allowed to practice on the train, and occasionally one might see trapeze artists hanging like bats from the baggage racks. — Barnaby Conrad III, "Train of Kings"

If a sentence does not directly support the topic sentence, readers expect it to support another sentence in the paragraph and therefore to support the topic sentence indirectly. Composition scholar Francis Christensen has invented a useful system for numbering the sentences in a paragraph to depict the hierarchic connections among sentences that readers look for. The topic sentence, being most general, receives the number 1, and any sentences that directly support it receive the number 2. Sentences that support level 2 sentences receive the number 3, and so on. Here, for example, is Christensen's numbering system as applied to a paragraph by columnist Ellen Goodman.

1. In the years since Kitty Genovese's murder, social scientists have learned a great deal about bystander behavior.
   2. They've learned that the willingness to intervene depends on a number of subtle factors beyond fear.
      3. It turns out that people are less likely to help if they are in a crowd of bystanders than if they are the only one.
         4. Their sense of responsibility is diffused.
         4. If the others aren't helping, they begin to reinterpret what they are seeing.
      3. People are also more passive in urban neighborhoods or crowded city spots where they suffer from "excessive overload" or simply turn off.
      3. They rarely get involved if they believe that the victim knows the assailant.
         4. This is especially true if the crime being witnessed is . . . a rape or attempted rape.

Because the sentences in this paragraph are arranged in a clear hierarchy, readers can easily follow the writer's train of thought.

To check one of your own paragraphs for clear connections among ideas, look to see if the hierarchic chain has been broken at any point. The topic sentence should announce the main idea, and the rest of the sentences should support it either directly or indirectly. When a sentence supports the topic sentence indirectly, it must support an earlier sentence that is clearly linked (directly or indirectly) to the topic sentence. If you can't find such a sentence, you'll need to add one or rethink the entire chain of ideas.

What readers look for in an essay

Like the sentences within paragraphs, the paragraphs within an essay should be arranged in a clear hierarchy. Readers expect to learn the essay's main point in the first paragraph, often in a thesis statement (see 1c). And by scanning the topic sentence of each paragraph in the body of the essay, readers hope to understand how each paragraph connects with what has come before. As a rule, a topic sentence should tell readers whether the information they are about to read supports the thesis statement directly or supports a key idea in the essay, which in turn supports the thesis.

Consider the following thesis statement and topic sentences, taken from an essay by student Thu Hong Nguyen. Each of Nguyen's topic sentences supports the thesis statement directly.

THESIS STATEMENT IN OPENING PARAGRAPH
From the moment she is mature enough to understand commands, to the day she is married off, to the time when she bears her own children, a Vietnamese woman tries to establish a good name as a diligent daughter, a submissive wife, and an altruistic mother.

TOPIC SENTENCE IN FIRST BODY PARAGRAPH
In order to be approved of by everyone, a Vietnamese daughter must work diligently to help her parents.

TOPIC SENTENCE IN SECOND BODY PARAGRAPH
Once she enters an arranged marriage, a good Vietnamese woman must submit to her husband.

TOPIC SENTENCE IN THIRD BODY PARAGRAPH
Finally, to be recognized favorably, a Vietnamese woman must sacrifice herself for the benefit of the children it is her duty to bear.

Topic sentences do not always have to interlock with the thesis quite so tightly as in Nguyen's essay. Nevertheless, by scanning the opening sentence or two of each paragraph, readers should have at least a rough sense of the connections of ideas within the whole essay.

7b Repeat key words.

Repetition of key words is an important technique for gaining coherence, because if too much information seems new, a paragraph will be hard to read. To prevent repetitions from becoming dull, you can use variations of a key word (*hike, hiker, hiking*), pronouns referring to the word (*hikers . . . they*), or synonyms (*walk, trek, wander, tramp, climb*).

In the following paragraph describing plots among indentured servants in seventeenth-century America, the well-known historian Richard Hofstadter binds sentences together by repeating the key word *plots* and echoing it with variations (all in italics).

> *Plots* hatched by several servants to run away together occurred mostly in the plantation colonies, and the few recorded servant *uprisings* were entirely limited to those colonies. Virginia had been forced from its very earliest years to take stringent steps against *mutinous plots,* and severe punishments for *such behavior* were recorded. Most servant *plots* occurred in the seventeenth century: a contemplated *uprising* was nipped in the bud in York County in 1661; apparently led by some left-wing offshoots of the *Great Rebellion,* servants *plotted* an *insurrection* in Gloucester County in 1663, and four leaders were condemned and executed; some discontented servants apparently joined *Bacon's Rebellion* in the 1670's. In the 1680's the planters became newly apprehensive of discontent among the servants "owing to their great necessities and want of clothes," and it was feared that they would *rise up* and *plunder* the storehouses and ships; in 1682 there were plant-cutting *riots* in which servants and laborers, as well as some planters, took part. [Italics added.]
> — Richard Hofstadter, *America at 1750*

7c Use parallel structures for parallel ideas.

Parallel grammatical structures are frequently used within sentences to underscore the similarity of ideas (see 9). They may also be used to bind together a series of sentences expressing similar information. In the following passage describing folk beliefs, anthropologist Margaret Mead presents similar information in parallel grammatical form.

> Actually, almost every day, even in the most sophisticated home, something is likely to happen that evokes the memory of some old folk belief. The salt spills. A knife falls to the floor. Your nose tickles. Then perhaps, with a slightly embarrassed smile, the person who spilled the salt tosses a pinch over his left shoulder. Or someone recites the old rhyme, "Knife falls, gentleman calls." Or as you rub your nose you think, That means a letter. I wonder who's writing?
> — Margaret Mead, "New Superstitions for Old"

A less skilled writer might have varied the structure, perhaps like this: *The salt gets spilled. Mother drops a knife on the floor. Your nose begins to tickle.* But these sentences are less effective; Mead's parallel structures help tie the paragraph together.

7d Maintain consistency.

Coherence suffers whenever a draft shifts confusingly from one point of view to another or from one verb tense to another. (See 13.) In addition, coherence can suffer when new information is introduced with the subject of each sentence. As a rule, a sentence's subject should echo a subject or object in the previous sentence.

The following rough-draft paragraph is needlessly hard to

read because so few of the sentences' subjects are tied to earlier subjects or objects. The subjects appear in italics.

> *One* goes about trapping in this manner. At the very outset *one* acquires a "trapping" state of mind. A *library* of books must be read, and preferably *someone* with experience should educate the novice. *Preparing* for the first expedition takes several steps. The *purchase* of traps is first. A *pair* of rubber gloves, waterproof *boots*, and the grubbiest *clothes* capable of withstanding human use come next to outfit the trapper for his adventure. The *decision* has to be made on just what kind of animals to seek, what sort of bait to use, and where to place the traps. Finally, the *trapper* needs a heavy stick, in case it is necessary to club the animal and drown him.

Although the writer repeats a number of key words, such as *trapping*, the paragraph seems disconnected because new information is introduced with the subject of each sentence.

To improve the paragraph, the writer used the first-person pronoun as the subject of every sentence. The revision is much easier to read.

> *I* went about trapping in this manner. To acquire a "trapping" state of mind, *I* read a library of books and talked at length with an experienced trapper, my father. Then *I* purchased the traps and outfitted myself by collecting a pair of rubber gloves, waterproof boots, and the grubbiest clothes capable of withstanding human use. Next *I* decided just what kinds of animals to seek, what sort of bait to use, and where to place my traps. Finally, *I* found a heavy stick, in case it would be necessary to club the animal and drown it.
>
> —John Clyde Thatcher, student

Notice that Thatcher combined some of his original sentences. By doing so, he was able to avoid excessive repetitions of the pronoun *I*. Notice, too, that he varied his sentence openings (most sentences do not begin with *I*) so that readers are not likely to find the repetitions tiresome.

7e   Provide transitions.

Certain words and phrases signal connections between ideas, connections that might otherwise be missed. Included in the following list are coordinating conjunctions, such as *and, but,* and *or*; subordinating conjunctions, such as *although* and *if*; conjunctive adverbs, such as *however* and *therefore*; and transitional phrases, such as *in addition* and *for example.*

TO SHOW ADDITION
and, also, besides, further, furthermore, in addition, moreover, next, too, first, second

TO GIVE EXAMPLES
for example, for instance, to illustrate, in fact, specifically

TO COMPARE
also, in the same manner, similarly, likewise

TO CONTRAST
but, however, on the other hand, in contrast, nevertheless, still, even though, on the contrary, yet, although

TO SUMMARIZE OR CONCLUDE
in other words, in short, in summary, in conclusion, to sum up, that is, therefore

TO SHOW TIME
after, as, before, next, during, later, finally, meanwhile, then, when, while, immediately

TO SHOW PLACE OR DIRECTION
above, below, beyond, farther on, nearby, opposite, close, to the left

TO INDICATE LOGICAL RELATIONSHIP
if, so, therefore, consequently, thus, as a result, for this reason, since

Skilled writers use transitional expressions with care, making sure, for example, not to use *consequently* when *also* would be more precise. They are also careful to select transitions with an appropriate tone, perhaps preferring *so* to *thus* in an informal piece, *in summary* to *in short* for a scholarly essay.

In the following paragraph, taken from an argument that dinosaurs had the " 'right-sized' brains for reptiles of their body size," biologist Stephen Jay Gould uses transitions (italicized) with skill.

> I don't wish to deny that the flattened, minuscule head of the large bodied "Stegosaurus" houses little brain from our subjective, top-heavy perspective, *but* I do wish to assert that we should not expect more of the beast. *First of all,* large animals have relatively smaller brains than related, small animals. The correlation of brain size with body size among kindred animals (all reptiles, all mammals, *for example*) is remarkably regular. *As* we move from small to large animals, from mice to elephants *or* small lizards to Komodo dragons, brain size increases, *but* not so fast as body size. *In other words,* bodies grow faster than brains, *and* large animals have low ratios of brain weight to body weight. *In fact,* brains grow only about two-thirds as fast as bodies. *Since* we have no reason to believe that large animals are consistently stupider than their smaller relatives, we must conclude that large animals require relatively less brain to do as well as smaller animals. *If* we do not recognize this relationship, we are likely to underestimate the mental power of very large animals, dinosaurs in particular. [Italics added.]
>
> — Stephen Jay Gould, "Were Dinosaurs Dumb?"

EXERCISE 7-1

Use Francis Christensen's numerical system (see 7a) to indicate the relations among sentences in the following paragraph.

> Once children have learned to read, they go beyond their textbooks and explore the popular books written just for them. In order to see how these books portray men and women, I decided to visit the St. Peter Public Library. One book I found,

The Very Worst Thing, tells of the adventures of a little boy on his first day in a new school. He arrives at school wearing the new sweater his mother has knit for him and is greeted by his teacher, Miss Pruce, and his male principal. At recess, the girls jump rope and toss a ball back and forth while the boys choose football teams and establish a tree house club. For show-and-tell that day, Henry, his new friend, brings a snake and some mice; Alice shows her foreign dolls; and Elizabeth demonstrates how to make fudge with Rice Krispies. In another book, *Come Back, Amelia Bedelia,* Amelia is fired from her job of baking for Mrs. Rogers, so she tries to find work as a beautician, a seamstress, a file clerk, and an office girl for a doctor. After trying all of these jobs unsuccessfully, she goes back to Mrs. Rogers and gets back her old job by making cream puffs. The rest of the books I looked at contained similar sex-role stereotypes — boys wear jeans and T-shirts, set up lemonade stands, and play broomball, while girls wear dresses, play dress-up, and jump rope. Men are businessmen, soldiers, veterinarians, and truck drivers. Women are housewives, teachers, and witches who make love potions for girls wanting husbands.   — Patricia Klein, student

EXERCISE 7–2

If you were to divide the paragraph in Exercise 7–1 into two paragraphs, at what point would you make the break? Why?

EXERCISE 7–3

Looking again at the paragraph in Exercise 7–1, find examples of the following techniques for gaining coherence: repetition of key words, parallel structures, and transitions.

PART III

Crafting Sentences

8

Coordinate equal ideas; subordinate minor ideas.

When combining two or more ideas in one sentence, you have two choices: coordination or subordination. Choose coordination to indicate that the ideas are equal or nearly equal in importance. Choose subordination to indicate that one idea is less important than another.

Coordination

Coordination draws attention equally to two or more ideas. To coordinate single words or phrases, join them with a coordinating conjunction or with a pair of correlative conjunctions (see 57g). To coordinate independent clauses — word groups that could stand alone as a sentence — join them with a comma and a coordinating conjunction or with a semicolon:

, and	, but	, or	, nor
, for	, so	, yet	;

The semicolon is often accompanied by a conjunctive adverb such as *moreover, furthermore, therefore,* or *however* or by a transitional phrase such as *for example, in other words,* or *as a matter of fact.* (See the chart on page 118 for a more complete list.)

Assume, for example, that your intention is to draw equal attention to the following two ideas.

Grandmother lost her sight. Her hearing sharpened.

To coordinate these ideas, you can join them with a comma and the coordinating conjunction *but* or with a semicolon and the conjunctive adverb *however.*

Grandmother lost her sight, but her hearing sharpened.

Grandmother lost her sight; however, her hearing sharpened.

It is important to choose a coordinating conjunction or conjunctive adverb appropriate to your meaning. In the preceding example, the two ideas contrast with one another, calling for *but* or *however.*

Subordination

To give unequal emphasis to two or more ideas, express the major idea in an independent clause and place any minor ideas in subordinate clauses or phrases. (For specific subordination strategies, see the chart on page 119.)

Deciding which idea to emphasize is not a matter of right and wrong but is determined by the meaning you intend. Consider the two ideas about Grandmother's sight and hearing.

Grandmother lost her sight. Her hearing sharpened.

If your purpose were to stress your grandmother's acute hearing rather than her blindness, you would subordinate the idea concerning her blindness.

As she lost her sight, Grandmother's hearing sharpened.

The less important idea appears in an adverb clause modifying the verb *sharpened.*

To focus on your grandmother's growing blindness, you would subordinate the idea concerning her hearing.

Though her hearing sharpened, Grandmother gradually lost her sight.

Here the less important idea appears in an adverb clause modifying the verb *lost.*

Using coordination to combine sentences of equal importance

1. Consider using a comma and a coordinating conjunction. (See 32a.)

   , and   , but   , or   , nor
   , for   , so   , yet

   ▶ In Orthodox Jewish funeral ceremonies, the shroud is a
   simple linen vestment, ~~The~~ *and the* coffin is plain wood with
   no adornment.

2. Consider using a semicolon and a conjunctive adverb or transitional phrase. (See 34b.)

also	in addition	now
as a result	in fact	of course
besides	in other words	on the other hand
consequently	in the first place	otherwise
finally	meanwhile	still
for example	moreover	then
for instance	nevertheless	therefore
furthermore	next	thus
however		

   ▶ Tom Baxter has been irritating me lately; *therefore,* I avoid him
   whenever possible.

3. Consider using a semicolon alone. (See 34a.)

   ▶ Nicklaus is like fine wine; *he* ~~He~~ gets better with time.

Using subordination to combine sentences of unequal importance

1. Consider putting the less important idea in a subordinate clause beginning with one of the following words. (See 59b.)

after	before	that	which
although	even though	unless	while
as	if	until	who
as if	since	when	whom
because	so that	where	whose

   ▶ ~~My~~ *When my* son asked his great-grandmother if she had been a slave/, ~~She~~ *she* became very angry.

   ▶ My sister owes much of her recovery to a bodybuilding program/ *that she* ~~She~~ began ~~the program~~ three years ago.

2. Consider putting the less important idea in a phrase. (See 59a, 59c, 59d, and 59e.)

   ▶ Karate, ~~is~~ a discipline based on the philosophy of nonviolence./, ~~It~~ teaches the art of self-defense.

   ▶ ~~Alvin was~~ *E*ncouraged by his professor to apply for the job/, ~~He~~ *Alvin* filed an application on Monday morning.

   ▶ I reached for the knife out of habit/, ~~My eyes scanned~~ *my eyes scanning* the long shiny blade for a price sticker. In a low, steady voice, my customer said, "This is a holdup."

8a Combine choppy sentences.

Short sentences demand attention, so you should use them primarily for emphasis. Too many short sentences, one after the other, make for a choppy style.

If an idea is not important enough to deserve its own sentence, try combining it with a sentence close by. Put any minor ideas in subordinate structures such as phrases or subordinate clauses.

CHOPPY	The huts vary in height. They measure from ten to fifteen feet in diameter. They contain no modern conveniences.
IMPROVED	The huts, which vary in height and measure from ten to fifteen feet in diameter, contain no modern conveniences.

Three sentences have become one, with minor ideas expressed in an adjective clause beginning with *which*.

▶ Agnes was another student I worked with. She was a hyperactive child.

The revision emphasizes that Agnes was a hyperactive child and de-emphasizes the rest of the information, which appears in an appositive phrase.

▶ *Although the* The Market Inn, is located at 2nd and E streets. It doesn't look very impressive from the outside. The food, however, is excellent.

Minor ideas are expressed in a subordinate clause (*Although . . . outside*), which in turn contains a participial phrase (*located . . . streets*) modifying *Market Inn*.

Although subordination is ordinarily the most effective technique for combining short, choppy sentences, coordination is appropriate when the ideas are equal in importance.

▶ The hospital decides when patients will sleep and wake/, It
                                                and
   dictates what and when they will eat/, It tells them when they

   may be with family and friends.

Equivalent ideas are expressed in a coordinate series.

ESL NOTE: When combining sentences, do not repeat the subject of the sentence; also do not repeat an object or adverb in an adjective clause. See 31b and 31c.

▶ The apartment that we moved into it needed many repairs.

▶ Tanya climbed into the tree house that the boys were

   playing in it.

LOOKING AT YOURSELF AS A WRITER
Choppy sentences

Combining choppy sentences is a natural part of revision for most writers, but if your writing style is unusually choppy, ask yourself why. Here are three common causes and cures.

CAUSE   You are afraid of writing run-on sentences, so you play it safe by keeping your sentences short.

CURE   You are right to be concerned about run-on sentences, but try not to worry about them while drafting. Often you can fix a run-on sentence by subordinating minor ideas — the same strategy that usually works for combining choppy sentences. (See 20d.)

Choppy sentences (continued)

CAUSE You aren't sure how to punctuate sentences that contain subordinate clauses and phrases, so you keep your sentences simple.

CURE Take a few risks when drafting. You can get help with punctuation later—from your instructor or your school's writing center or by consulting Part VII of *The Bedford Handbook*.

CAUSE You are not yet comfortable with the subordination strategies that are necessary for a smooth writing style.

CURE When combining choppy sentences in your drafts, consult the chart on page 119, which gives examples of subordination strategies.

EXERCISE 8–1

In the following paragraphs, combine choppy sentences by subordinating minor ideas or by coordinating ideas of equal importance. More than one effective revision is possible.

Some scientists favor continued research to advance the technology of genetic engineering. They argue that they are only refining the process of selective breeding that has benefited society for many years. For centuries, they claim, scientists have recognized variations in plant and animal species from generation to generation. In the early nineteenth century, scientists explained those variations as part of an evolutionary process. They called this process natural selection. Later scientists found ways to duplicate this process of natural selection. They did not want to leave the process to chance. They developed the technique of selective breeding.

Dairy farmers use selective breeding. They do it to increase production from their herds. They choose the best milk-producing cows for breeding. These cows have certain genetic traits. These traits make them top producers. Breeding them selectively increases the chance that the offspring will inherit those same genetic traits. Then they will be top producers too. For the same reasons, farmers identify the cows that are low producers. They choose not to use them for breeding.

Scientists argue that genetic engineering is not much different from selective breeding. They claim that it can produce similar positive results. Society, they say, should support their research. Society can only benefit, as it has in the past.

8b Avoid ineffective or excessive coordination.

Coordinate structures are appropriate only when you intend to draw the reader's attention equally to two or more ideas: *Professor Naake praises loudly, and she criticizes softly.* If one idea is more important than another — or if a coordinating conjunction does not clearly signal the relation between the ideas—you should subordinate the lesser idea.

INEFFECTIVE	Closets were taxed as rooms, and most colonists stored their clothes in chests or clothes presses.
IMPROVED	Because closets were taxed as rooms, most colonists stored their clothes in chests or clothes presses.

The revision subordinates the less important idea by putting it in a subordinate clause. Notice that the subordinating conjunction *Because* signals the relation between the ideas more clearly than the coordinating conjunction *and*.

Because it is so easy to string ideas together with *and*, writers often rely too heavily on coordination in their rough drafts. The cure for excessive coordination is simple: Look for opportunities to tuck minor ideas into subordinate clauses or phrases.

▶ *When*
Jason walked over to his new Miata, ~~and~~ he saw that its
windshield had been smashed.

The minor idea has become a subordinate clause beginning with
When.

▶ My uncle *noticing*
~~noticed~~ my frightened look. ~~and~~ told me that
Grandma had to feel my face because she was blind.

The less important idea has become a participial phrase modifying the noun *uncle.*

▶ *After four hours,*
~~Four hours went by, and~~ a rescue truck finally arrived, but by
that time we had been evacuated in a helicopter.

Three independent clauses were excessive. The least important
idea has become a prepositional phrase.

EXERCISE 8–2

Combine or restructure the following sentences by subordinating minor ideas or by coordinating ideas of equal importance. You must
decide which ideas are minor because the sentences are given out of
context. Revisions of lettered sentences appear in the back of the
book. Example:

The crew team finally returned to shore, *where they* ~~and~~ had a party
on the beach ~~and celebrated~~ *to celebrate* the start of the season.

a. My grandfather has dramatic mood swings, and he was diagnosed as manic-depressive.
b. The losing team was made up of superstars. These superstars
acted as isolated individuals on the court.

c. We keep our use of insecticides, herbicides, and fungicides to a minimum. We are concerned about the environment.

d. The aides help the younger children with reading and math. These are the children's weakest subjects.

e. My first sky dive was from an altitude of 12,500 feet, and it was the most frightening experience of my life.

1. Bay Street is located in the heart of downtown Nassau. It houses the Straw Market.

2. I noticed that the sky was glowing orange and red. I bent down to crawl into the bunker.

3. Sister Consilio was enveloped in a black robe with only her face and hands visible. She was an imposing figure.

4. Cocaine is an addictive drug and it can seriously harm you both physically and mentally, if death doesn't get you first.

5. These particles are known as "stealth liposomes," and they can hide in the body for a long time without detection.

6. At the airport I was met by my host mother, Madame Kimmel. She was a very excitable woman who knew absolutely no English.

7. He walked up to the pitcher's mound. He dug his toe into the ground. He swung his arm around backward and forward. Then he threw the ball and struck the batter out.

8. The Chesapeake and Ohio Canal is a 184-mile waterway constructed in the 1800s. It was a major source of transportation for goods during the Civil War era.

9. The lift chairs were going around very fast. They were bumping the skiers into their seats.

10. The first football card set was released by the Goudey Gum Company in 1933. The set featured only three football players. They were Red Grange, Bronko Nagurski, and Knute Rockne.

8c Do not subordinate major ideas.

If a sentence buries its major idea in a subordinate construction, readers may not give the idea enough attention. Express the major idea in an independent clause and subordinate any minor ideas.

▶ Lanie, who ∧ now walks with the help of braces,/. had polio as a child.

(handwritten insertions: "had polio as a child," and strikethrough of "had polio as a child.")

The writer wanted to focus on Lanie's ability to walk, but the original sentence buried this information in an adjective clause. The revision puts the major idea in an independent clause and tucks the less important idea into an adjective clause (*who had polio as a child*).

▶ As ∧ I was driving home from my new job, heading down Ranchitos Road, when my car suddenly overheated.

(handwritten insertion: "As" and strikethrough of "when")

The writer wanted to emphasize that the car was overheating, not the fact of driving home. The revision expresses the major idea in an independent clause, the less important idea in an adverb clause (*As I was driving home from my new job*).

8d Do not subordinate excessively.

In attempting to avoid short, choppy sentences, writers sometimes move to the opposite extreme, putting more subordinate ideas into a sentence than its structure can bear. If a sentence collapses of its own weight, occasionally it can be restructured. More often, however, such sentences must be divided.

▶ Our job is to stay between the stacker and the tie machine watching to see if the newspapers jam/. in which case we pull the bundles off and stack them on a skid, because otherwise they would back up in the stacker.

(handwritten insertion: "If they do," and strikethrough of "in which case")

EXERCISE 8-3

In each of the following sentences, the idea that the writer wished to emphasize is buried in a subordinate construction. Restructure each sentence so that the independent clause expresses the major idea and lesser ideas are subordinated. Revisions of lettered sentences appear in the back of the book. Example:

> *Though*
> Catherine has weathered many hardships, ~~though~~ she has
> ∧
> rarely become discouraged. [*Emphasize that Catherine has*
>
> *rarely become discouraged.*]

a. We experienced a routine morning at the clinic until an infant in cardiac arrest arrived by ambulance. [*Emphasize the arrival of the infant.*]

b. My 1969 Camaro, which is no longer street legal, is an original SS396. [*Emphasize the fact that the car is no longer street legal.*]

c. I presented the idea of job sharing to my supervisors, who to my surprise were delighted with the idea. [*Emphasize the supervisors' response to the idea.*]

d. Although native Hawaiians try to preserve their ancestors' sacred customs, outsiders have forced changes on them. [*Emphasize the Hawaiians' attempt to preserve their customs.*]

e. Sophia's country kitchen, which overlooks a field where horses and cattle graze among old tombstones, was formerly a lean-to porch. [*Emphasize that the kitchen overlooks the field.*]

1. My grandfather, who raised his daughters the old-fashioned way, was born eighty-six years ago in Puerto Rico. [*Emphasize how the grandfather raised his daughters.*]

2. I was losing consciousness when my will to live kicked in. [*Emphasize the will to live.*]

3. Louis's team worked with the foreign mission by building new churches and restoring those damaged by hurricanes. [*Emphasize the building and restoring.*]

4. The rotor hit, gouging a hole about an eighth of an inch deep in my helmet. [*Emphasize the fact that the rotor gouged a hole in the helmet.*]

5. Although Sarah felt that we lacked decent transportation, our family owned a Jeep, a pickup truck, and a sports car. [*Emphasize Sarah's feeling that the family lacked decent transportation.*]

9

Balance parallel ideas.

If two or more ideas are parallel, they are easier to digest when expressed in parallel grammatical form. Single words should be balanced with single words, phrases with phrases, clauses with clauses.

A kiss can be a comma, a question mark, or an exclamation

point. — Mistinguett

This novel is not to be tossed lightly aside, but to be hurled

with great force. — Dorothy Parker

In matters of principle, stand like a rock; in matters of taste,

swim with the current. — Thomas Jefferson

Writers often use parallelism to create emphasis. (See 14c.)

9a Balance parallel ideas in a series.

Readers expect items in a series to appear in parallel grammatical form. When one or more of the items violates readers' expectations, a sentence will be needlessly awkward.

▶ Abused children commonly exhibit one or more of the

  following symptoms: withdrawal, rebelliousness,
                                              depression.
  restlessness, and ~~they were depressed~~.
                    ⋀

The revision presents all of the items as nouns.

▶ Esperanza is responsible for stocking merchandise, writing
                                     selling
  orders for delivery, and ~~sales of~~ computers.
                          ⋀

The revision uses *-ing* forms for all items in the series.

▶ After assuring us that he was sober, Sam drove down the
                                              went through
  middle of the road, ran one red light, and two stop signs.
                                          ⋀

The revision adds a verb to make the three items parallel: *drove
. . . , ran . . . , went through. . . .*

NOTE: In headings and lists, aim for as much parallelism as
the content allows. See 54b and 54c.

9b Balance parallel ideas presented as pairs.

When pairing ideas, underscore their connection by expressing them in similar grammatical form. Paired ideas are usually connected in one of three ways: (1) with a coordinating
conjunction such as *and, but,* or *or*; (2) with a pair of correlative conjunctions such as *either . . . or* or *not only . . . but
also*; or (3) with a word introducing a comparison, usually
than or *as.*

Parallel ideas linked with coordinating conjunctions

Coordinating conjunctions (*and, but, or, nor, for, so,* and *yet*)
link ideas of equal importance. When those ideas are closely

parallel in content, they should be expressed in parallel grammatical form.

▶ At Lincoln High School, vandalism can result in suspension
   expulsion
   or even ~~being expelled~~ from school.
                 ∧

   The revision balances the nouns *expulsion* and *suspension.*

▶ Many states are reducing property taxes for homeowners and
   extending
   ~~extend~~ financial aid in the form of tax credits to renters.
   ∧
   The revision balances the verb *reducing* with the verb *extending.*

NOTE: If a clause beginning with *and who* or *and which* is not paired with an earlier *who* or *which*, delete the conjunction *and.*

▶ Austin is a young man of many talents ~~and~~ who recently

   graduated from the University of Chicago.

Parallel ideas linked with correlative conjunctions

Correlative conjunctions come in pairs: *either . . . or, neither . . . nor, not only . . . but also, both . . . and, whether . . . or.* Make sure that the grammatical structure following the second half of the pair is the same as that following the first half.

▶ The shutters were not only too long but also ~~were~~ too wide.

   The words *too long* follow *not only*, so *too wide* should follow *but also.* Repeating *were* creates an unbalanced effect.

                                                      to
▶ I was advised either to change my flight or ̭ take the train.
                                              ∧
   To change my flight, which follows *either*, should be balanced with *to take the train*, which follows *or.*

Comparisons linked with than *or* as

In comparisons linked with *than* or *as,* the elements being compared should be expressed in parallel grammatical structure.

▶ It is easier to speak in abstractions than ~~grounding~~ *to ground* one's

   thoughts in reality.

▶ Mother could not persuade me that giving is as much a joy as
   ~~to receive.~~ *receiving.*

To speak in abstractions is balanced with *to ground one's thoughts in reality. Giving* is balanced with *receiving.*

NOTE: Comparisons should also be logical and complete. See 10c.

9c Repeat function words to clarify parallels.

Function words such as prepositions (*by, to*) and subordinating conjunctions (*that, because*) signal the grammatical nature of the word groups to follow. Although they can sometimes be omitted, include them whenever they signal parallel structures that might otherwise be missed by readers.

▶ Many smokers try switching to a brand they find distasteful
   or *to* a low tar and nicotine cigarette.

In the original sentence the prepositional phrase was too complex for easy reading. The repetition of the preposition *to* prevents readers from losing their way.

▶ The ophthalmologist told me that Julie was extremely
         that
farsighted but corrective lenses would help considerably.
                    ^

A second subordinating conjunction helps readers sort out the
two parallel ideas: *that* Julie was extremely farsighted and *that*
corrective lenses would help.

NOTE: If it is possible to streamline the sentence, repetition of
the function word may not be necessary.

▶ The board reported that its investments had done well in the

first quarter but ~~that they~~ had since dropped in value.

Instead of linking two subordinate clauses beginning with *that*,
the revision balances the two parts of a compound predicate —
had done well in the first quarter and *had since dropped in value.*

EXERCISE 9–1

Edit the following sentences to correct faulty parallelism. Revisions
of lettered sentences appear in the back of the book. Example:

We began the search by calling the Department of Social
                        requesting
Services and ~~requested~~ a list of licensed day-care centers in
              ^
our area.

a. The system has capabilities such as communicating with other
   computers, processing records, and mathematical functions.
b. The personnel officer told me that I would answer the phone,
   welcome visitors, distribute mail, and some typing.
c. Nolan helped by cutting the grass, trimming shrubs, mulching
   flowerbeds, and leaf clean-up.

LOOKING AT YOURSELF AS A WRITER
Parallelism

Nearly all writers encounter occasional problems with parallelism. Here are some common causes and cures.

CAUSE You don't realize how awkward faulty parallelism can sound to readers.

CURE Read aloud some sentences containing faulty parallelism (sentences in 9 or in Exercise 9–1, for example) to hear how awkward they sound. You can use the same read-aloud strategy for your own drafts.

CAUSE You worry so much about sentence variety that you introduce it in inappropriate contexts.

CURE Learn to appreciate the power of parallelism. In your reading, notice how skilled writers use parallelism to emphasize connections among ideas. Shakespeare has Hamlet say "to die, to sleep, perchance to dream" (not "to die, to sleep, perchance some dreaming").

CAUSE You can't think of the right word or you're not sure how to spell the word that's needed to complete your parallel ideas.

CURE Check a thesaurus or a dictionary.

d. How ideal it seems to raise a family here in Winnebago instead of the air-polluted suburbs.

e. Michiko told the judge that she had been pulled out of a line of fast-moving traffic and of her perfect driving record.

1. The summer of our engagement, we saw a few plays, attended family outings, and a few parties.

2. At the arts and crafts table, the children make potholders, key rings, weave baskets, paint, and assemble model cars.
3. The examiners observed us to see if we could stomach the grotesque accidents and how to cope with them.
4. During basic training, I was not only told what to do but also what to think.
5. Activities on Wednesday afternoons include fishing trips, dance lessons, and computers.
6. Bill finds it harder to be fair to himself than being fair to others.
7. More plants fail from improper watering than any other cause.
8. Your adviser familiarizes you with the school and how to select classes appropriate for your curriculum.
9. To administer the poison, the tribe's sorcerers put it in their victims' food, throw it into their huts, or it can be dropped into their mouths or nostrils while they sleep.
10. The babysitter was expected to feed two children, entertain them, take phone messages, and some cleaning in the kitchen.

EXERCISE 9–2

Describe the parallel structure in the following passages and discuss how the use of parallelism contributes to the effectiveness of each. (Also see 14c, which discusses parallel structure.)

1. All respect we may have had for politicians, preachers, lawyers, governors, Presidents, senators, congressmen was utterly destroyed as we watched them temporizing and compromising over right and wrong, over legality and illegality, over constitutionality and unconstitutionality. — Eldridge Cleaver
2. One of the devastating weaknesses of university learning, of the store of knowledge and opinion that has been handed down through academic training, has been its almost total erasure of women's experience and thought from the curriculum, and its exclusion of women as members of the academic community.
— Adrienne Rich
3. Knowing others is wisdom; knowing the self is enlightenment. Mastering others requires force; mastering the self needs strength. — Lao-tzu

4. How can I love the man who raped my mother, killed my father, enslaved my ancestors, dropped atomic bombs on Japan, killed off the Indians, and keeps me cooped up in the slums?
— Malcolm X

5. I don't want to achieve immortality through my work. I want to achieve it through not dying. — Woody Allen

10

Add needed words.

Do not omit words necessary for grammatical or logical completeness. Readers need to see at a glance how the parts of a sentence are connected.

> **ESL NOTE:** Languages sometimes differ in the need for certain words. In particular, be alert for missing verbs, articles, subjects, or expletives. See 29e, 30, and 31a.

10a Add words needed to complete compound structures.

In compound structures, words are often omitted for economy: *Tom is a man who means what he says and [who] says what he means.* Such omissions are perfectly acceptable as long as the omitted words are common to both parts of the compound structure.

If the shorter version defies grammar or idiom because an omitted word is not common to both parts of the compound structure, the word must be put back in.

▶ Some of the regulars are acquaintances whom we see at work

who

or live in our community.

The word *who* must be included because *whom live in our community* is not grammatically correct.

accepted

▶ I never have and never will accept a bribe.

Have . . . accept is not grammatically correct.

in

▶ Many of these tribes still believe and live by ancient laws.

Believe . . . by is not idiomatic in English.

NOTE: Even when the omitted word is common to both parts of the compound structure, occasionally it must be inserted to avoid ambiguity. The sentence *My favorite English professor and mentor influenced my choice of a career* suggests that the professor and mentor are the same person. If they are not, *my* must be repeated: *My favorite English professor and my mentor influenced my choice of a career.*

10b Add the word *that* if there is any danger of misreading without it.

If there is no danger of misreading, the word *that* may be omitted when it introduces a subordinate clause. *The value of a principle is the number of things [that] it will explain.* Occasionally, however, a sentence might be misread without *that.*

that

▶ As Luis began to prepare dinner, he discovered the oven

wasn't working properly.

Luis didn't discover the oven; he discovered that the oven wasn't working properly.

▶ Many civilians believe the air force has a vigorous exercise

    that
    ∧

program.

The word *that* tells readers to expect a clause, not just *the air force*, as the direct object of *believe*.

10c Add words needed to make comparisons logical and complete.

Comparisons should be made between items that are alike. To compare unlike items is illogical and distracting.

                                        that of
▶ Christopher had an attention span longer than the other

                                          ∧

children.

It is illogical to compare an attention span and children. Since repeating the words *attention span* would be awkward, inserting *that of* corrects the problem.

                                      those in
▶ Henry preferred the hotels in Pittsburgh to Philadelphia.

                                            ∧

Hotels must be compared with hotels.

Sometimes the word *other* must be inserted to make a comparison logical.

              other
▶ Chicago is larger than any city in Illinois.

                      ∧

Since Chicago is not larger than itself, the original comparison was not logical.

Sometimes the word *as* must be inserted to make a comparison grammatically complete.

▶ Ben is as talented, if not more talented than, the other actors.
                    ᵃˢ

The construction *as talented* is not complete without a second *as*: *as talented as . . . the other actors.*

Finally, comparisons should be complete enough to ensure clarity. The reader should understand what is being compared.

INCOMPLETE	Brand X is a lighter beer.
COMPLETE	Brand X is a lighter beer than Brand Y.

Also, there should be no ambiguity. In the following sentence, two interpretations are possible.

AMBIGUOUS	Kelly helped me more than my roommate.
CLEAR	Kelly helped me more than *he helped* my roommate.
CLEAR	Kelly helped me more than my roommate *did*.

10d Add the articles *a, an,* and *the* where necessary for grammatical completeness.

Articles are sometimes omitted in recipes and other instructions that are meant to be followed while they are being read. Such omissions are inappropriate, however, in nearly all other forms of writing, whether formal or informal.

▶ Blood can be drawn only by doctor or by authorized person
                          a   *an*
who has been trained in procedure.
                   the

ESL NOTE: Articles can cause special problems for speakers of English as a second language. See 30.

EXERCISE 10-1

Add any words needed for grammatical or logical completeness in the following sentences. Revisions of lettered sentences appear in the back of the book. Example:

that

The officer at the desk feared the prisoner in the

∧

interrogation room would escape.

a. Dip paintbrush into paint remover and spread thick coat on small section of door.
b. Some say that Ella Fitzgerald's renditions of Cole Porter's songs are better than any singer.
c. SETI (the Search for Extraterrestrial Intelligence) has and will continue to excite interest among space buffs.
d. Samantha got along better with the chimpanzees than Albert.
e. We were glad to see Yellowstone National Park was recovering from the devastating forest fire.

1. Their starting salaries are higher than other professionals with more seniority.
2. For many years Americans had trust and affection for Walter Cronkite.
3. In my opinion, her dependence on tranquilizers is no healthier than the alcoholic or the addict.
4. Our nursing graduates are as skilled, if not more skilled than, those of any other state college.
5. Jupiter is larger than any planet in our solar system.
6. State officials were more concerned with the damage than what caused it.
7. Great-Uncle John's car resembled other bootleggers: it had a smoke screen device useful in case of pursuit by the sheriff.

8. Darryl was both gratified and apprehensive about his scholarship to UCLA.
9. From the family room window we saw our favorite tree, which we had climbed so often as children, was gone.
10. It was obvious that the students liked the new teacher more than the principal.

11

Untangle mixed constructions.

A mixed construction contains parts that do not sensibly fit together. The mismatch may be a matter of grammar or of logic.

11a Untangle the grammatical structure.

Once you head into a sentence, your choices are limited by the range of grammatical patterns in English. (See 58 and 59.) You cannot begin with one grammatical plan and switch without warning to another.

MIXED	For most drivers who have a blood alcohol content of .05 percent double their risk of causing an accident.
REVISED	For most drivers who have a blood alcohol content of .05 percent, the risk of causing an accident is doubled.
REVISED	Most drivers who have a blood alcohol content of .05 percent double their risk of causing an accident.

The writer began with a long prepositional phrase that was destined to be a modifier but then tried to press it into service as the subject of the sentence. This cannot be done. If the sentence is to begin with the prepositional phrase, the writer must finish the sentence with a subject and verb (*risk . . . is doubled*). The writer who wishes to stay with the original verb (*double*) must head into the sentence another way: *Most drivers. . . .*

▶ ~~When an employee is~~ *Being* promoted without warning can be alarming.

The adverb clause *When an employee is promoted without warning* cannot serve as the subject of the sentence. The revision replaces the adverb clause with a gerund phrase, a word group that can function as the subject. (See 59b and 59c.)

▶ Although I feel that Mr. Dawe is an excellent calculus instructor, ~~but~~ a few minor changes in his method would benefit both him and the class.

The *although* clause is subordinate, so it cannot be linked to an independent clause with the coordinating conjunction *but.*

Occasionally a mixed construction is so tangled that it defies grammatical analysis. When this happens, back away from the sentence, rethink what you want to say, and then say it again as clearly as you can.

MIXED In the whole-word method children learn to recognize entire words rather than by the phonics method in which they learn to sound out letters and groups of letters.

REVISED   The whole-word method teaches children to recognize entire words; the phonics method teaches them to sound out letters and groups of letters.

ESL NOTE: English does not allow double subjects; nor does it allow an object or adverb to be repeated in an adjective clause. See 31b and 31c.

▶ The squirrel that came down our chimney ~~it~~ did much

damage.

▶ Hearing screams, Serena ran over to the pool that her

daughter was swimming in. ~~it.~~

11b Straighten out the logical connections.

The subject and the predicate should make sense together; when they don't, the error is known as *faulty predication.*

▶ The ~~growth in the~~ number of applications is increasing

rapidly.

It is not the growth that is increasing but the number of applications.

                    double personal exemption for the
▶ Under the revised plan, the elderly, / ~~who now receive a double~~

~~personal exemption,~~ will be abolished.

The exemption, not the elderly, will be abolished.

An appositive and the noun to which it refers should be logically equivalent. When they are not, the error is known as *faulty apposition*.

▶ ~~The tax accountant,~~ *Tax accounting,* a very lucrative field, requires

intelligence, patience, and attention to detail.

The tax accountant is a person, not a field.

11c   Avoid *is when, is where,* and *reason . . . is because* constructions.

In formal English many readers object to *is when, is where,* and *reason . . . is because* constructions on either grammatical or logical grounds. Grammatically, the verb *is* (as well as *are, was,* and *were*) should be followed by a noun that renames the subject or by an adjective that describes it, not by an adverb clause beginning with *when, where,* or *because.* (See 58b and 59b.) Logically, the words *when, where,* and *because* suggest relations of time, place, and cause—relations that do not always make sense with *is, was,* or *were.*

▶ Anorexia nervosa is ~~where people,~~ *a disorder suffered by people who,* believing they are too fat,

diet to the point of starvation.

Anorexia nervosa is a disorder, not a place.

▶ ~~The reason~~ I missed the exam ~~is~~ because my motorcycle

broke down.

The writer might have changed *because* to *that* (*The reason I missed the exam is that my motorcycle broke down*), but the revision above is more concise.

LOOKING AT YOURSELF AS A WRITER
Mixed constructions

An occasional mixed construction is nothing to worry about; just revise oddly structured sentences when you encounter them. But if many of your sentences are spinning out of control, try to discover why. Here are some common causes of mixed constructions, each of which suggests its own cure.

CAUSE   You don't know what you want to say about your subject, so you wind up in a tangle of words.

CURE   Spend more time on prewriting activities (see 1b). Begin drafting only when you have some promising ideas to work with.

CAUSE   You are attempting to write in a style more sophisticated than you can handle.

CURE   Write in a simpler, more direct style. Readers appreciate plain English more than you may think. (See 17a and 17b.)

CAUSE   While drafting, you are overly conscious of style — of how you "sound" on paper.

CURE   Focus on your meaning and often the style will take care of itself. Besides, you can always improve the sound of your sentences later.

CAUSE   You tend to cling to a particular sentence opening, even though you can't find the right words to finish the sentence.

CURE   Experiment with alternatives; maybe you should open the sentence another way. When handwriting, make cross-outs and insertions; when working on a computer, delete and insert text until you get the sentence you want.

EXERCISE 11–1

Edit the following sentences to untangle mixed constructions. Revisions of lettered sentences appear in the back of the book. Example:

    L
~~By l~~oosening the soil around your jade plant will help the air

and nutrients penetrate to the roots.

a. My instant reaction was filled with anger and disappointment.
b. I brought a problem into the house that my mother wasn't sure how to handle it.
c. It is through the misery of others that has made old Harvey rich.
d. A cloverleaf is when traffic on limited-access freeways can change direction.
e. Bowman established the format in which future football card companies would emulate for years to come.

1. The more experienced pilots in the system Zeke assigned two aircraft to them.
2. Depending on the number and strength of drinks, the amount of time that has passed since the last drink, and one's body weight determines the concentration of alcohol in the blood.
3. Reluctantly we decided that Tiffany's welfare would not be safe living with her mother.
4. By pushing the button for the insert mode opens the computer's memory.
5. The reason the Eskimos were forced to eat their dogs was because the caribou, on which they depended for food, migrated out of reach.
6. The shelter George stayed in required the men to leave at nine in the morning, in which they had to take their belongings with them.
7. Mei-Ling had to train herself on a mainframe computer that was designed for data entry but it was not intended for word processing.
8. In this box contains the key to your future.
9. Who would have thought that a department store salesperson could be a life-threatening job?
10. Using surgical gloves is a precaution now worn by dentists to prevent contact with the patients' blood and saliva.

12

Repair misplaced and dangling modifiers.

Modifiers, whether they are single words, phrases, or clauses, should point clearly to the words they modify. As a rule, related words should be kept together.

12a Put limiting modifiers in front of the words they modify.

Limiting modifiers such as *only, even, almost, nearly,* and *just* should appear in front of a verb only if they modify the verb: *At first, I couldn't even touch my toes, much less grasp them.* If they limit the meaning of some other word in the sentence, they should be placed in front of that word.

▶ You will ~~only~~ need to plant *only* one package of seeds.

▶ Our team didn't ~~even~~ score *even* once.

▶ Bob ~~almost~~ ate *almost* the whole chicken.

> *Only* limits the meaning of *one,* not *need. Even* modifies *once,* not *score; almost* modifies *the whole chicken,* not *ate.*

12b Place phrases and clauses so that readers can see at a glance what they modify.

Although phrases and clauses can appear at some distance from the words they modify, make sure your meaning is clear.

When phrases or clauses are oddly placed, absurd misreadings can result.

> **MISPLACED** The king returned to the clinic where he had undergone heart surgery in 1992 in a limousine sent by the White House.

> **REVISED** Traveling in a limousine sent by the White House, the king returned to the clinic where he had undergone heart surgery in 1992.

The revision corrects the false impression that the king underwent heart surgery in a limousine.

▶ ~~There~~ are many pictures of comedians ~~on the walls~~ *On the walls* who have performed at Gavin's.

The walls didn't perform at Gavin's; the comedians did. The writer at first revised the sentence like this: *There are many pictures of comedians who have performed at Gavin's on the walls.* But this creates another absurd effect. The comedians weren't performing on the walls.

▶ The robber was described as a six-foot-tall *150-pound,* man with a heavy mustache. ~~weighing 150 pounds.~~

The robber, not the mustache, weighed 150 pounds. The revision makes this clear.

Occasionally the placement of a modifier leads to an ambiguity, in which case two revisions will be possible, depending on the writer's intended meaning.

> **AMBIGUOUS** We promised when the play was over that we would take Charles to an ice cream parlor.

> **CLEAR** When the play was over, we promised Charles that we would take him to an ice cream parlor.

CLEAR	We promised Charles that we would take him to an ice cream parlor when the play was over.

The first revision suggests that the promising occurred when the play was over, the second that the taking would occur when the play was over.

12c Move awkwardly placed modifiers.

As a rule, a sentence should flow from subject to verb to object, without lengthy detours along the way. When a long adverbial element separates a subject from its verb, a verb from its object, or a helping verb from its main verb, the result is usually awkward.

▶ ~~Kilmer,~~ *A* ~~after~~ doctors told him that he would never walk
   Kilmer
   again, initiated an intensive program of rehabilitation.
   ∧

There is no reason to separate the subject *Kilmer* from the verb *initiated* with a long adverb clause.

▶ ~~Oscar Lewis spent,~~ *I* in researching *The Children of Sanchez,*
   Oscar Lewis spent
   ∧ hundreds of hours living with the Sanchez family in a slum of

Mexico City.

The *in* phrase needlessly separates the verb *spent* from its object, *hundreds of hours.*

▶ ~~Many students have,~~ *B* by the time they reach their senior
   many students have
   year, completed all the requirements for their major.
   ∧

The helping verb *have* should be closer to its main verb, *completed.*

EXCEPTION: Occasionally a writer may choose to delay a verb or an object to create suspense. In the following passage, for example, Robert Mueller inserts the *after* phrase between the subject *women* and the verb *walk* to heighten the dramatic effect.

> I asked a Burmese why women, after centuries of following their men, now walk ahead. He said there were many unexploded land mines since the war. — Robert Mueller

---

ESL NOTE: English does not allow an adverb to appear between a verb and its object. See 31d.

▶ Yolanda lifted ~~easily~~ the fifty-pound weight/ *easily.*

12d Do not split infinitives needlessly.

An infinitive consists of *to* plus a verb: *to think, to breathe, to dance.* When a modifier appears between *to* and the verb, an infinitive is said to be "split": *to carefully balance.* If a split infinitive is obviously awkward, it should be revised.

▶ ~~The~~ *If possible, the* patient should try to, ~~if possible,~~ avoid going up and down stairs.

Usage varies when a split infinitive is less awkward than the preceding one. To be on the safe side, however, you should not split such infinitives, especially in formal writing.

▶ The candidate decided to ~~formally~~ launch her campaign/ *formally.*

When a split infinitive is more natural and less awkward than alternative phrasing, most readers find it acceptable: *We decided to actually enforce the law* is a perfectly natural construction in English. *We decided actually to enforce the law* is not.

EXERCISE 12–1

Edit the following sentences to correct misplaced or awkwardly placed modifiers. Revisions of lettered sentences appear in the back of the book. Example:

Answering questions *in a telephone survey* can be annoying. ~~in a telephone survey~~

a. He only wanted to buy three roses, not a dozen.
b. Within the next few years, orthodontists will be using the technique Kurtz developed as standard practice.
c. Celia received a flier about a workshop on making a kimono from a Japanese nun.
d. Jurors are encouraged to carefully and thoroughly sift through the evidence.
e. Each state would set a program into motion of recycling all reusable products.

1. We hope Monica will realize that providing only for her children's material needs is harmful before it is too late.
2. The orderly confessed that he had given a lethal injection to the patient after ten hours of grilling by the police.
3. Several recent studies have encouraged heart patients to more carefully watch their cholesterol levels.
4. Mike, as the next wave rolled in, dropped in easily and made a smooth turn, but the wave closed out.
5. He promised never to remarry at her deathbed.
6. The recordings were all done at the studio of the late Jimi Hendrix named Electric Ladyland.
7. The old Marlboro ads depicted a man on a horse smoking a cigarette.
8. Lasers only destroy the target, leaving the surrounding healthy tissue intact and undamaged.

9. The Secret Service was falsely accused of mishandling the attempted assassination by the media.
10. The adoption agency informed us that we would be able to at long last get a child.

12e Repair dangling modifiers.

A dangling modifier fails to refer logically to any word in the sentence. Dangling modifiers are usually introductory word groups (such as verbal phrases) that suggest but do not name an actor. When a sentence opens with such a modifier, readers expect the subject of the following clause to name the actor. If it doesn't, the modifier dangles.

DANGLING   Deciding to join the navy, the recruiter enthusiastically pumped Joe's hand. [*Participial phrase*]

DANGLING   Upon seeing the barricade, our car screeched to a halt. [*Preposition followed by a gerund phrase*]

DANGLING   To please the children, some fireworks were set off a day early. [*Infinitive phrase*]

DANGLING   Though only sixteen, UCLA accepted Martha's application. [*Elliptical clause with an understood subject and verb*]

These dangling modifiers falsely suggest that the recruiter decided to join the navy, that the car saw the barricade, that the fireworks intended to please the children, and that UCLA is only sixteen years old.

To repair a dangling modifier, you must restructure the sentence in one of two ways: (1) change the subject of the sentence so that it names the actor implied by the introductory modifier or (2) turn the modifier into a word group that includes the actor.

> **DANGLING** When watching a classic film such as *Gone With the Wind*, commercials are especially irritating.

> **REPAIRED** When watching a classic film such as *Gone With the Wind*, I find commercials especially irritating.

> **REPAIRED** When I'm watching a classic film such as *Gone With the Wind*, commercials are especially irritating.

A dangling modifier cannot be repaired simply by moving it: *Commercials are especially irritating when watching. . . .* Readers still don't know who is doing the watching.

▶ ~~Opening~~ *When the driver opened* the window to let out a huge bumblebee, the car accidentally swerved into the lane of oncoming cars.

The car didn't open the window; the driver did. The writer has revised the sentence by putting the driver in the opening modifier.

▶ After completing seminary training, ~~women's~~ *women have often been denied* access to the pulpit. ~~has often been denied.~~

The women (not their access to the pulpit) complete the training. The writer has revised the sentence by making *women* (not *women's access*) the subject.

EXERCISE 12–2

Edit the following sentences to correct dangling modifiers. Most sentences can be revised in more than one way. Revisions of lettered sentences appear in the back of the book. Example:

LOOKING AT YOURSELF AS A WRITER
Dangling modifiers

Most writers encounter occasional problems with dangling modifiers. Here are a few of the most common causes and cures.

CAUSE   You are trying to avoid using the word *I*, so you write a sentence like this: *At the age of twenty, my father let me drive his restored Mustang.*

CURE   Don't be afraid to use the word *I* in a personal narrative or in other writing that is clearly about you: *When I turned twenty, my father let me drive his restored Mustang.*

CAUSE   You are writing in the passive voice, with the subject of your sentence receiving the action instead of doing it, like this: *To finance the rescue effort, thousands of dollars were donated.*

CURE   Write in the active voice unless you have a good reason for choosing the passive: *To finance the rescue effort, citizens donated thousands of dollars.* (See 14a and 28c.)

CAUSE   To achieve sentence variety, you are putting certain modifiers up front in a sentence — without noticing that they dangle.

CURE   Keep the modifier up front, for variety, but add an actor to it. Or change the subject of the sentence so that it names the actor.

CAUSE   You think your sentence is clear even though the modifier dangles.

CURE   In fact, you may be right. Be aware, though, that some readers — especially English professors — find dangling modifiers distracting.

Reviewing your writing for dangling modifiers

First look for the most common trouble spots:

SENTENCES OPENING WITH A VERBAL

There are three kinds of verbals (see also 59c):

> *-ing* verb forms such as *walking* (present participles)
>
> *-ed, -d, -en, -n,* or *-t* verb forms such as *planted, eaten, taught* (past participles)
>
> *to* verb forms such as *to become* (infinitives)

▶ Excited about winning the championship, a raucous ~~we held~~

  celebration ~~was held~~ in the locker room.

SENTENCES OPENING WITH A WORD GROUP CONTAINING A VERBAL

▶ After ~~swimming~~ *I swam* across the lake, the lifeguard scolded

  me for risking my life.

SENTENCES OPENING WITH AN ELLIPTICAL CLAUSE (A CLAUSE WITH OMITTED WORDS)

▶ Although *I was* only four years old, my father insisted that I

  learn to read.

Dangling modifiers (continued)

Next test your sentences for dangling modifiers:

Does an opening phrase suggest an action without naming the actor?

NO ➡ No problem

YES

Does the subject of the independent clause name the actor?

YES ➡ No problem

NO

Revise the dangling modifier.

If you find a dangling modifier, revise the sentence in one of two ways:

1. Change the subject of the independent clause so that it names the actor implied by the modifier.
2. Turn the modifier into a word group that includes the actor.

a student must complete

To acquire a degree in almost any field, two science courses.
∧   ∧

~~must be completed.~~

a. Reaching the heart, a bypass was performed on the severely blocked arteries.
b. Nestled in the cockpit, the pounding of the engine was muffled only slightly by my helmet.
c. While dining at night, the lights along the Baja coastline created a romantic atmosphere perfect for our first anniversary.
d. While still a beginner at tennis, the coaches recruited my sister to train for the Olympics.
e. After returning to Jamaica, Marcus Garvey's "Back to Africa" movement slowly died.

1. When flashing, do not speed through a yellow light.
2. Exhausted from battling the tide and the undertow, a welcome respite appeared in the swimmer's view — the beach!
3. Upon entering the lawyer's office, a young man sitting next to the door holding a shotgun caught my attention.
4. As president of the missionary circle, one of Grandmother's duties is to raise money for the church.
5. When investigating burglaries and thefts, it was easy for me to sympathize with the victims because I had been a victim myself two years ago.
6. Spending four hours on the operating table, a tumor as large as a golf ball was removed from the patient's stomach.
7. As a child growing up in Nigeria, my mother taught me to treat all elders with respect.
8. At the age of twelve, my social studies teacher entered me in a public speaking contest.
9. Although too expensive for her budget, Juanita bought the lavender skirt.
10. While looking at the map, a police officer approached and asked if she could help.

13

Eliminate distracting shifts.

13a Make the point of view consistent in person and number.

The point of view of an essay is the perspective from which it is written: first-person singular (*I*), first-person plural (*we*), second-person singular or plural (*you*), third-person singular (*he, she, it, one*), or third-person plural (*they*). Writers who are having difficulty settling on an appropriate point of view sometimes shift confusingly from one to another. The solution is to choose a suitable perspective and then stay with it. (See page 47.)

▶ One week our class met in a junkyard to practice rescuing a

victim trapped in a wrecked car. We learned to dismantle the

car with the essential tools. ~~You~~ *We* were graded on ~~your~~ *our* speed

and ~~your~~ *our* skill in extricating the victim.

The writer should have stayed with the *we* point of view. *You* is inappropriate because the writer is not addressing readers directly. *You* should not be used in a vague sense meaning "anyone." (See 23d.)

▶ ~~Everyone~~ *You* should purchase a lift ticket unless you plan to

spend most of your time walking or crawling up a steep hill.

Here *you* is an appropriate choice because the writer is giving advice directly to readers.

▶ *Police officers are*
~~A police officer is~~ often criticized for always being there when
they aren't needed and never being there when they are.

The writer shifted from the third-person singular (*police officer*)
to the third-person plural (*they*), probably in an effort to avoid
the wordy *he or she* construction: *A police officer is often criticized
for always being there when he or she is not needed and never
being there when he or she is.* The most effective revision, the
writer decided, was to draft the sentence in the plural. (See 22a
and 17f.)

13b Maintain consistent verb tenses.

Consistent verb tenses clearly establish the time of the actions being described. When a passage begins in one tense
and then shifts without warning and for no reason to another,
readers are distracted and confused.

▶ *rose   fell*
My hopes ~~rise~~ and ~~fall~~ as Joseph's heart started and stopped.
inserted   *Flowed*
The doctors ~~insert~~ a large tube into his chest, and blood ~~flows~~
from the incision onto the floor. The tube drained some blood
from his lung, but it was all in vain. At 8:35 P.M. Joseph was
declared dead.

The writer had tried to make his narrative vivid by casting it in
the present tense, but he found this choice too difficult to sus-
tain. A better approach, he decided, was to draft the whole narrative in the past tense.

Writers often encounter difficulty with verb tenses when
writing about literature. Because fictional events occur outside the time frames of real life, the past and the present

tenses may seem equally appropriate. The literary convention, however, is to describe fictional events consistently in the present tense.

▶ The scarlet letter is a punishment sternly placed upon

Hester's breast by the community, and yet it ~~was~~ *is* an

extremely fanciful and imaginative product of Hester's own

needlework.

13c Make verbs consistent in mood and voice.

Unnecessary shifts in the mood of a verb can be as distracting as needless shifts in tense. There are three moods in English: the *indicative,* used for facts, opinions, and questions; the *imperative,* used for orders or advice; and the *subjunctive,* used in certain contexts to express wishes or conditions contrary to fact (see 28b).

The following passage shifts confusingly from the indicative to the imperative mood.

▶ The officers advised us against allowing anyone into our

homes without proper identification. ~~Also,~~ *They also suggested that we* alert neighbors to

vacation schedules.

Since the writer's purpose was to report the officers' advice, the revision puts both sentences in the indicative.

A verb may be in either the active voice (with the subject doing the action) or the passive voice (with the subject receiving the action). (See 28c.) If a writer shifts without warning from one to the other, readers may be left wondering why.

▶ When the tickets are ready, the travel agent notifies the
         lists each ticket
  client/, ~~Each ticket is then listed~~ on a daily register form ,and
files   ^
  a copy of the itinerary . ~~is filed.~~
  ^   ^

The passage began in the active voice (*agent notifies*) and then
switched to the passive (*ticket is listed, copy is filed*). Because the
active voice is clearer and more direct, the writer put all the verbs
in the active voice.

13d Avoid sudden shifts from indirect to direct
questions or quotations.

An indirect question reports a question without asking it: *We
asked whether we could take a swim.* A direct question asks
directly: *Can we take a swim?* Sudden shifts from indirect to
direct questions are awkward. In addition, sentences containing such shifts are impossible to punctuate because indirect
questions must end with a period and direct questions must
end with a question mark. (See 38b.)

▶ I wonder whether the sister knew of the murder and, if so, ~~did~~
whether she reported
~~she report~~ it to the police.
^

The revision poses both questions indirectly. The writer could
also ask both questions directly: *Did the sister know of the murder and, if so, did she report it to the police?*

An indirect quotation reports someone's words without
quoting word for word: *Annabelle said that she is a Virgo.* A
direct quotation presents the exact words of a speaker or
writer, set off with quotation marks: *Annabelle said, "I am a
Virgo."* Unannounced shifts from indirect to direct quotations
are distracting and confusing, especially when the writer fails

to insert the necessary quotation marks, as in the following example.

> Mother said that she would be late for dinner and ~~please do~~ *asked me not to*
> ~~not~~ leave for choir practice until Dad ~~comes~~ home. *came*

The revision reports all of the mother's words. The writer could also quote directly: *Mother said, "I will be late for dinner. Please do not leave for choir practice until Dad comes home."*

LOOKING AT YOURSELF AS A WRITER
Shifts

Shifts in a rough draft alert you to choices you must make as a writer. Once you have made those choices — by deciding on an appropriate point of view or tense, for example—eliminating shifts in the final draft will be a simple matter.

Shifts in point of view

CAUSE   You are trying to avoid the word *I* or the word *you* in a context where these pronouns may be appropriate.

CURE   Consider drafting your essay from the *I* or the *you* point of view. For appropriate uses of these points of view, see pages 47–51.

CAUSE   You are trying to avoid sexist language without resorting to the wordy *he or she* construction.

CURE   Consider writing in the plural. (See 22a.)

CAUSE   You have selected the pronoun *one* in an attempt to include both men and women, but repeating *one* seems awkward, so you shift to another pronoun such as *their* or *you.*

Shifts (continued)

CURE You are right that repetitions of *one* sound awkward, at least to American ears: *One* must watch *one's* pronouns. Try another point of view instead: *Writers* must watch *their* pronouns. *You* must watch *your* pronouns.

Shifts in tense

CAUSE To make the action of a narrative more immediate, you are casting it in the present tense, but at times you shift to the past.

CURE Read your narrative to yourself twice — once using all present-tense verbs and once using all past-tense verbs. Then choose the tense that you feel sounds better. If you are still in doubt, ask another writer for advice.

CAUSE You are writing about literature and you're not sure whether to use the present or the past tense.

CURE Choose the present tense, since that is the literary convention.

Shifts from indirect to direct questions or quotations

CAUSE By inserting direct questions or quotations, you hope to make your style more vivid, but you end up mixing direct and indirect questions or quotations.

CURE You are right that adding direct questions or quotations can make your writing more lively. Consider revising your sentence to use the direct approach consistently.

CAUSE In spoken English you hear such shifts all the time, and they don't seem to bother anyone.

CURE Be aware that the standards for written English are stricter than those for spoken English.

EXERCISE 13–1

Edit the following sentences to eliminate distracting shifts. Revisions of lettered sentences appear in the back of the book. Example:

> For most people quitting smoking is not easy once ~~you~~ *they* are
>
> hooked.

a. The young man who burglarized our house was sentenced to probation for one year, a small price to pay for robbing one of their personal possessions as well as of their trust in other human beings.

b. After the count of three, Mikah and I placed the injured woman on the scoop stretcher. Then her vital signs were taken by me.

c. A minister often has a hard time because they have to please so many different people.

d. We drove for eight hours until we reached the South Dakota Badlands. You could hardly believe the eeriness of the landscape at dusk.

e. The question is whether ferrets bred in captivity have the instinct to prey on prairie dogs or is this a learned skill.

1. Police officers always follow strict codes of safety. For example, always point the barrel of the gun upward when the gun is not in use.

2. There was no way that I could fight the current and win. Just as I was losing hope, a stranger jumps off a passing boat and swims toward me.

3. One young aide, Kay, was very unprofessional. Curse words were used when trying to quiet the children.

4. The polygraph examiner will ask if you have ever stolen goods on the job, if you have ever taken drugs, and have you ever killed or threatened to kill anyone.

5. A single parent often has only their ingenuity to rely on.

6. When the director travels, you will make the hotel and airline reservations and you will arrange for a rental car. A detailed itinerary must also be prepared.

7. As I was pulling in the decoys, you could see and hear the geese heading back to the bay.

8. Rescue workers put water on her face and lifted her head gently onto a pillow. Finally, she opens her eyes.

9. With a little self-discipline and a desire to improve oneself, you too can enjoy the benefits of running.

10. We always follow a strict routine at the campground. First we erected the tent, rolled out the sleeping bags, and set up the kitchen; then we all head for the swimming pool.

14

Emphasize your point.

Within each sentence, emphasize your point by expressing it in the subject and verb, the words that receive the most attention from readers. As a rule, choose an active verb and pair it with a subject that names the person or thing doing the action.

Within longer stretches of prose, you can draw attention to ideas deserving special emphasis by using a variety of techniques, usually involving some element of surprise.

14a Prefer active verbs.

Active verbs express meaning more emphatically and vigorously than their weaker counterparts — forms of the verb *be* or verbs in the passive voice. Forms of the verb *be* (*be, am, is, are, was, were, being, been*) lack vigor because they convey no action. Verbs in the passive voice lack strength because their subjects receive the action instead of doing it (see 28c and 58c).

Although the forms of *be* and passive verbs have legitimate uses, if an active verb can carry your meaning, use it.

BE VERB A surge of power *was* responsible for the destruction of the coolant pumps.

PASSIVE The coolant pumps *were destroyed* by a surge of power.

ACTIVE A surge of power *destroyed* the coolant pumps.

Even among active verbs, some are more active — and therefore more vigorous and colorful—than others. Carefully selected verbs can energize a piece of writing.

▶ The goalie crouched low, ~~reached~~ *swept* out his stick, and ~~sent~~ *hooked* the rebound away from the mouth of the net.

When to replace be *verbs*

Not every *be* verb needs replacing. The forms of *be* (*be, am, is, are, was, were, being, been*) work well when you want to link a subject to a noun that clearly renames it or to an adjective that describes it: *History is a bucket of ashes. Scoundrels are always sociable.* And when used as helping verbs before present participles (*is flying, are disappearing*) to express ongoing action, *be* verbs are fine: *Derrick was plowing the field when his wife went into labor.* (See 29a.)

If using a *be* verb makes a sentence needlessly wordy, however, consider replacing it. Often a phrase following the verb will contain a word (such as *destruction*) that suggests a more vigorous, active alternative (*destroyed*).

▶ Burying nuclear waste in Antarctica would ~~be in violation of~~ *violate* an international treaty.

Violate is less wordy and more vigorous than *be in violation of.*

▶ Escaping into the world of drugs, I ~~was rebellious about~~ *rebelled against* every

rule set down by my parents.

Rebelled against is more active than *was rebellious about.*

When to replace passive verbs

In the active voice, the subject of the sentence does the action; in the passive, the subject receives the action.

> **ACTIVE**   Hernando *caught* the fly ball.
>
> **PASSIVE**   The fly ball *was caught* by Hernando.

In passive sentences, the actor (in this case *Hernando*) frequently disappears from the sentence: The fly ball *was caught.*

In most cases, you will want to emphasize the actor, so you should use the active voice. To replace a passive verb with an active alternative, make the actor the subject of the sentence.

▶ ~~The transformer was struck by a bolt of lightning,~~ *A bolt of lightning struck the transformer,* plunging us into darkness.

The active verb (*struck*) makes the point more forcefully than the passive verb (*was struck*).

The passive voice is appropriate when you wish to emphasize the receiver of the action or to minimize the importance of the actor. For example, in the sentence about the fly ball, you would choose the active voice if you wanted to emphasize the actor, Hernando: *Hernando caught the fly ball.* But you would choose the passive voice if you wanted to emphasize the fly ball's being caught: *The fly ball was caught by Hernando.* (See 28c.)

ESL NOTE: Some speakers of English as a second language avoid the passive voice even when it is appropriate. For advice on appropriate uses of the passive, see 28c.

14b As a rule, choose a subject that names the person or thing doing the action.

In weak, unemphatic prose, both the actor and the action may be buried in sentence elements other than the subject and the verb. In the following sentence, for example, the actor and the action both appear in prepositional phrases, word groups that do not receive much attention from readers.

> **WEAK**   Exposure to Dr. Martinez's excellent teaching had the effect of inspiring me to major in education.
>
> **EMPHATIC**   Dr. Martinez's excellent teaching inspired me to major in education.

Consider the subjects and verbs of the two versions — *exposure had* versus *teaching inspired.* Clearly the latter expresses the writer's point more emphatically.

> ▶ *Cocaine used*
>
> ~~The use of cocaine~~ by pregnant women can ~~be a major~~ *Cause*
> ~~contributor to~~ severe brain damage in infants.

In the original version, the subject and verb — *use can be* — express the point blandly. *Cocaine can cause* alerts readers to the dangers of cocaine more emphatically than *use can be.*

EXERCISE 14–1

Revise any weak, unemphatic sentences by replacing *be* verbs or passive verbs with active alternatives and, if necessary, by naming in the subject the person or thing doing the action. Some sentences are emphatic; do not change them. Revisions of lettered sentences appear in the back of the book. Example:

The ranger doused the campfire before giving us
~~The campfire was doused by the ranger before we were given~~
∧
a ticket for unauthorized use of a campsite.

a. Her letter was in acknowledgment of the students' participation in the literacy program.
b. The entire operation is managed by Ahmed, the producer.
c. Finally the chute caught air and popped open with a jolt at about 2,000 feet.
d. There were fighting players on both sides of the rink.
e. At the crack of rocket and mortar blasts, I jumped from the top bunk and landed on my buddy below, who was crawling on the floor looking for his boots.

1. Just as the police were closing in, two shots were fired by the terrorists from the roof of the hotel.
2. Julia was successful in her first attempt to pass the bar exam.
3. The bomb bay doors rumbled open and freezing air whipped through the plane.
4. C.B.'s are used to find parts, equipment, food, lodging, and anything else that is needed by a trucker.
5. Fireworks were exploding all around us.

14c Experiment with techniques for gaining special emphasis.

By experimenting with certain techniques, usually involving some element of surprise, you can draw attention to ideas that deserve special emphasis. Use such techniques sparingly, however, or they will lose their punch. The writer who tries to emphasize everything ends up emphasizing nothing.

Using sentence endings for emphasis

You can highlight an idea simply by withholding it until the end of a sentence. The technique works something like a punch line. In the following example, the sentence's meaning is not revealed until its very last word.

> The only completely consistent people are dead.
> — Aldous Huxley

Two types of sentence that withhold information until the end deserve special mention: the inversion and the periodic sentence. The *inversion* reverses the normal subject-verb order, placing the subject at the end, where it receives unusual emphasis. (Also see 15c.)

> In golden pots are hidden the most deadly poisons.
> — Thomas Draxe

The *periodic* sentence opens with a pile-up of modifiers and withholds the subject and verb until the end. It draws attention to itself because it contrasts with the cumulative sentence, which is used more frequently. A *cumulative* sentence begins with the subject and verb and adds modifying elements at the end.

PERIODIC
Twenty-five years ago, at the age of thirteen, while hiking in the mountains near my hometown of Vancouver, Washington, I came face to face with the legendary Goat Woman of Livingston Mountain. — Tom Weitzel, student

CUMULATIVE
A metaphysician is one who goes into a dark cellar at midnight without a light, looking for a black cat that is not there.
— Baron Bowan of Colwood

Using parallel structure for emphasis

Parallel grammatical structure draws special attention to paired ideas or to items in a series. (See 9.) When parallel ideas are paired, the emphasis falls on words that underscore comparisons or contrasts, especially when they occur at the end of a phrase or clause.

> We must *stop talking* about the *American dream* and *start listening* to the *dreams of Americans.*   — Reubin Askew

In a parallel series, the emphasis falls at the end, so it is generally best to end with the most dramatic or climactic item in the series.

> Sister Charity enjoyed passing out writing punishments: translate the Ten Commandments into Latin, type a thousand-word essay on good manners, copy the New Testament with a quill pen.   — Marie Visosky, student

Using punctuation for emphasis

Obviously the exclamation point can add emphasis, but you should not overuse it. As a rule, the exclamation point is more appropriate in dialogue than in ordinary prose.

> I oozed a glob of white paint onto my palette, whipped some medium into it, loaded my brush, and announced to the class, "Move over, Michelangelo. Here I come!"
> — Carolyn Goff, student

A dash or a colon may be used to draw attention to word groups worthy of special attention. (See 35a, 35b, an 39a.)

> The middle of the road is where the white line is — and that's the worst place to drive.   — Robert Frost

I turned to see what the anemometer read: The needle had
pegged out at 106 knots.   —Jonathan Shilk, student

Occasionally, a pair of dashes may be used to highlight a
word or an idea.

[My friend] was a gay and impudent and satirical and delightful
young black man—a slave—who daily preached sermons
from the top of his master's woodpile, with me for sole
audience.   —Mark Twain

Using an occasional short sentence for emphasis

Too many short sentences in a row will fast become monotonous (see 8a), but an occasional short sentence, when played
off against longer sentences in the same passage, will draw
attention to an idea.

The great secret, known to internists and learned early in
marriage by internists' wives [or husbands], but still hidden
from the general public, is that most things get better by
themselves. Most things, in fact, are better by morning.
                                                    —Lewis Thomas

EXERCISE 14-2

Discuss the methods used to achieve emphasis in the following paragraphs.

Unseen in the jungle, but present, are tapirs, jaguars,
many species of snake and lizard, ocelots, armadillos, mar-
mosets, howler monkeys, toucans and macaws and a hundred
other birds, deer, bats, peccaries, capybaras, agoutis, and
sloths. Also present in this jungle, but variously distant, are
Texaco derricks and pipelines, and some of the wildest Indians
in the world, blowgun-using Indians, who killed missionaries
in 1956 and ate them.   —Annie Dillard

My Uncle Tom worked as a blacksmith in the B & O yards near Harpers Ferry. That was a good job too. Though he walked the four-mile round trip to and from the shop daily in sooty railroader's clothes, Uncle Tom was well off. His house contained a marvel I had never seen before: an indoor bathroom. This was enough to mark Uncle Tom a rich man, but in addition he had a car. And such a car. It was an Essex, with windows that rolled up and down with interior hand cranks, not like my father's Model T with the isinglass windows in side curtains that had to be buttoned onto the frame in bad weather. Uncle Tom's Essex even had cut-glass flower vases in sconces in the backseat. He was a man of substance. When he rolled up in his Essex for Ida Rebecca's command appearances on Sunday afternoons in Morrisonville, wearing a white shirt and black suit, smoking his pipe, his pretty red-haired wife Goldie on the seat beside him, I felt pride in kinship to so much grandeur.   — Russell Baker

15

Provide some variety.

When a rough draft is filled with too many same-sounding sentences, try injecting some variety — as long as you can do so without sacrificing clarity or ease of reading.

15a   Vary your sentence openings.

Most sentences in English begin with the subject, move to the verb, and continue along to the object, with modifiers tucked in along the way or put at the end. For the most part, such sentences are fine. Put too many of them in a row, however, and they become monotonous.

Adverbial modifiers, being easily movable, can often be inserted ahead of the subject. Such modifiers might be single words, phrases, or clauses.

▶ *Eventually a* ~~A~~ few drops of sap ~~eventually~~ began to trickle into the pail.

Like most adverbs, *eventually* does not need to appear close to the verb it modifies (*began*).

▶ *Just as the sun was coming up, a* ~~A~~ pair of black ducks flew over the blind. ~~just as the sun was coming up.~~

The adverb clause, which modifies the verb *flew*, is as clear at the beginning of the sentence as it is at the end.

Adjectives and participial phrases can frequently be moved to the beginning of a sentence without loss of clarity.

▶ *Dejected and withdrawn,* Edward, ~~dejected and withdrawn,~~ nearly gave up his search for a job.

▶ *A* ~~John and I,~~ anticipating a peaceful evening, *John and I* sat down at the campfire to brew a cup of coffee.

CAUTION: When beginning a sentence with an adjective or a participial phrase, make sure that the subject of the sentence names the person or thing described in the introductory phrase. If it doesn't, the phrase will dangle. (See 12e.)

15b Use a variety of sentence structures.

A writer should not rely too heavily on simple sentences and compound sentences, for the effect tends to be both monotonous and choppy. (See 8a and 8b.) Too many complex or compound-complex sentences, however, can be equally monotonous. If your style tends to one or the other extreme, try to achieve a better mix of sentence types.

The major sentence types are illustrated in the following sentences, all taken from Flannery O'Connor's "The King of the Birds," an essay describing the author's pet peafowl.

SIMPLE	Frequently the cock combines the lifting of his tail with the raising of his voice.
COMPOUND	Any chicken's dusting hole is out of place in a flower bed, but the peafowl's hole, being the size of a small crater, is more so.
COMPLEX	The peacock does most of his serious strutting in the spring and summer when he has a full tail to do it with.
COMPOUND-COMPLEX	The cock's plumage requires two years to attain its pattern, and for the rest of his life, this chicken will act as though he designed it himself.

For a fuller discussion of sentence types, see 60a.

15c Try inverting sentences occasionally.

A sentence is inverted if it does not follow the normal subject-verb-object pattern. (See 58.) Many inversions sound artificial and should be avoided except in the most formal contexts. But if an inversion sounds natural, it can provide a welcome touch of variety.

▶ *Opposite the produce section is a*
~~A~~ refrigerated case of mouth-watering cheeses ; ~~is opposite~~
~~the produce section;~~ a friendly attendant will cut off just the
amount you want.

The revision inverts the normal subject-verb order by moving the verb, *is,* ahead of its subject, *case.*

Set at the top two corners of the stage were huge

▶ ~~Huge~~ lavender hearts outlined in bright white lights ~~, were set~~
  ^
~~at the top two corners of the stage.~~

In the revision the subject, *hearts,* appears after the verb, *were set.* Notice that the two parts of the verb are also inverted—and separated from one another—without any awkwardness or loss of meaning.

Inverted sentences are used for emphasis as well as for variety. See 14c.

15d Consider adding an occasional question or quotation.

An occasional question can provide a welcome change of pace, especially at the beginning of a paragraph, where it engages the reader's interest.

> Virginia Woolf, in her book *A Room of One's Own,* wrote that in order for a woman to write fiction she must have two things, certainly: a room of her own (with key and lock) and enough money to support herself.
> *What then are we to make of Phillis Wheatley, a slave, who owned not even herself?* This sickly, frail black girl who required a servant of her own at times — her health was so precarious — and who, had she been white, would have been easily considered the intellectual superior of all the women and most of the men in the society of her day. [Italics added.]
> —Alice Walker

Quotations can also provide variety, for they add other people's voices to your own. These other voices might be bits of dialogue.

When we got back upstairs, Dr. Haney and Captain Shiller, the head nurse, were waiting for us by the elevator. As the nurse hurried off, pushing Todd, the doctor explained to us what would happen next.

"Mrs. Barrus," he began, "this last test is one we do only when absolutely necessary. It is very painful and hard on the patient but we have no other choice." Apologetically, he went on. "I cannot give him an anesthetic." He waited for the statement to sink in.   — Celeste L. Barrus, student

Or they might be quotations from written sources:

Even when she enters the hospital on the brink of death, the anorexic will refuse help from anyone and will continue to deny needing help, especially from a doctor. At this point, reports Dr. Steven Levenkron, the anorexic is most likely "a frightened, cold, lonely, starved, and physically tortured, exhausted person — not unlike an actual concentration camp inmate" (29). In this condition she is ultimately force-fed through a tube inserted in the chest.   — Jim Drew, student

Notice that the quotation from a written source is documented with a citation in parentheses. See 50.

EXERCISE 15–1

Edit the following paragraph to increase variety in sentence structure.

I have spent thirty years of my life on a tobacco farm, and I cannot understand why people smoke. The whole process of raising tobacco involves deadly chemicals. The ground is treated for mold and chemically fertilized before the tobacco seed is ever planted. The seed is planted and begins to grow, and then the bed is treated with weed killer. The plant is then transferred to the field. It is sprayed with poison to kill worms about two months later. Then the time for harvest approaches, and the plant is sprayed once more with a chemical to retard the growth of suckers. The tobacco is harvested and hung in a

barn to dry. These barns are havens for birds. The birds
defecate all over the leaves. After drying, these leaves are
divided by color, and no feces are removed. They are then sold
to the tobacco companies. I do not know what the tobacco
companies do after they receive the tobacco. I do not need to
know. They cannot remove what I know is in the leaf and on
the leaf. I don't want any of it to pass through my mouth.

EXERCISE 15–2

Discuss how the writers of the following paragraphs provide variety.

> I was then a listening child, careful to hear the very
> different sounds of Spanish and English. Wide-eyed with
> hearing, I'd listen to sounds more than to words. First, there
> were English (*gringo*) sounds. So many words were still
> unknown to me that when the butcher or the lady at the
> drugstore said something, exotic polysyllabic sounds would
> bloom in the midst of their sentences. Often the speech of
> people in public seemed to me very loud, booming with
> confidence. The man behind the counter would literally ask,
> "What can I do for you?" But by being so firm and clear, the
> sound of his voice said that he was a *gringo*; he belonged in
> public society.   — Richard Rodriguez

> Our own house was an appalling sight from the outside.
> The siding, originally white, sprouted leprous gray patches
> where the paint was peeling away. Bark hung down from the
> huge dead elm in the front yard like long, limp scabs. The tree
> and a doorless garage leaned ominously toward our house. To
> the north, weeds grew up around a lonely, abandoned shack.
> To the south, a run-down house covered with rotting, gray
> asbestos shingles crouched, a weathered outhouse several
> steps from the back door. Farther south along the frozen,
> muddy road huddled a tiny one-room dwelling isolated in a
> swampy hollow. Barely glimpsed through a sea of stiffly dried
> weeds, the roofs of two ramshackle chicken coops rounded out
> the view from our yard. Our forgotten lane lacked street lamps
> and house numbers and was denied even the dignity of a street
> sign at the corner.   — Julie Reardon, student

PART IV

Choosing Words

16

Tighten wordy sentences.

In a rough draft we are rarely economical: We repeat ourselves, we belabor the obvious, we cushion our thoughts in verbiage. As a general rule, advises writer Sidney Smith, "run a pen through every other word you have written; you have no idea what vigor it will give your style."

Long sentences are not necessarily wordy, nor are short sentences always concise. A sentence is wordy if it can be tightened without loss of meaning.

16a Eliminate redundancies.

Writers often repeat themselves unnecessarily. Afraid, perhaps, that they won't be heard the first time, they insist that a teacup is small *in size* or yellow *in color,* that married people should cooperate *together,* that a fact is not just a fact but a *true* fact. Such redundancies may seem at first to add emphasis. In reality they do just the opposite, for they divide the reader's attention.

▶ Mr. Barker still hasn't paid last month's rent. ~~yet.~~

▶ Black slaves were ~~called or~~ stereotyped as lazy even though they were the main labor force of the South.

Though modifiers ordinarily add meaning to the words they modify, occasionally they are redundant.

▶ Sylvia ~~very hurriedly~~ scribbled her name, address, and phone number on the back of a greasy napkin.

▶ Joel was determined ~~in his mind~~ to lose weight.

The words *scribbled* and *determined* already contain the notions suggested by the modifiers *very hurriedly* and *in his mind.*

16b Avoid unnecessary repetition of words.

Though words may be repeated deliberately, for effect, repetitions will seem awkward if they are clearly unnecessary. When a more concise version is possible, choose it.

▶ Our fifth patient, in room six, is ~~a~~ mentally ill ~~.patient.~~

▶ The best teachers help each student to ~~become a better~~ grow ~~student~~ both academically and emotionally.

16c Cut empty or inflated phrases.

An empty phrase can be cut with little or no loss of meaning. Common examples are introductory word groups that apologize or hedge: *in my opinion, I think that, it seems that, one must admit that,* and so on.

▶ ~~In my opinion, our~~ Our current policy in Central America is misguided on several counts.

▶ ~~It seems that~~ *Lonesome Dove* is one of Larry McMurtry's

most ambitious novels.

Readers understand without being told that they are hearing the writer's opinion or educated guess.

Inflated phrases can be reduced to a word or two without loss of meaning.

INFLATED	CONCISE
along the lines of	like
as a matter of fact	in fact
at all times	always
at the present time	now, currently
at this point in time	now, currently
because of the fact that	because
by means of	by
by virtue of the fact that	because
due to the fact that	because
for the purpose of	for
for the reason that	because
have the ability to	be able to
in light of the fact that	because
in the nature of	like
in order to	to
in spite of the fact that	although, though
in the event that	if
in the final analysis	finally
in the neighborhood of	about
until such time as	until

▶ We will file the appropriate papers ~~in the event that~~ *if* we are

unable to meet the deadline.

▶ ~~Due to the fact that~~ *Because* the guest of honor is ill, the party is being

postponed until next Saturday.

16d Simplify the structure.

If the structure of a sentence is needlessly indirect, try simplifying it. Look for opportunities to strengthen the verb.

▶ The financial analyst claimed that because of volatile market conditions she could not ~~make an~~ estimate ~~of~~ the company's future profits.

The verb *estimate* is more vigorous and more concise than *make an estimate of*.

The colorless verbs *is, are, was,* and *were* frequently generate excess words.

▶ The secretary ~~is responsible for monitoring and balancing~~ **monitors and balances** the budgets for travel, contract services, and personnel.

The revision is more direct and concise. Actions originally appearing in subordinate structures have become verbs replacing *is*.

The expletive constructions *there is* and *there are* (or *there was* and *there were*) can also generate excess words. The same is true of expletive constructions beginning with *it*. (See 58c.)

▶ ~~There is~~ **A**nother module ~~that~~ tells the story of Charles Darwin and introduces the theory of evolution.

▶ ~~It is important that~~ **H**ikers **must** remain inside the park boundaries.

Reviewing your writing for wordy sentences

Look especially for these common trouble spots:

REDUNDANCIES (16a)

▶ Passive euthanasia is the ~~act or~~ practice of allowing terminally ill patients to die.

▶ The colors of the reproductions were ~~precisely~~ exact.

UNNECESSARY REPETITION OF WORDS (16b)

▶ ~~The quilt that was~~ ^T^ he highlight of Grandmother's collection was a crazy quilt dating from 1889.

EMPTY OR INFLATED PHRASES (16c)

▶ Although ~~it seemed that~~ it was unlikely that the call was for me, I was so excited that I ran to the phone.

▶ The ring costs *about* ~~in the neighborhood of~~ sixty dollars.

NEEDLESSLY INDIRECT STRUCTURES (16d)

▶ The institute was established to ~~develop and provide~~ *train* ~~training for~~ highway agency employees.

Wordy sentences (continued)

▶ ~~There was a~~ deranged vagrant [A] pestering the persons in [was] line, spouting biblical quotations one minute and shouting obscenities the next.

▶ ~~It is imperative that~~ [A]ll police officers [must] follow strict procedures when apprehending a suspect.

▶ Last summer, a horse. [my parents gave me] ~~was given to me by my parents.~~

NEEDLESSLY COMPLEX STRUCTURES (16e)

▶ We took a side trip to Monticello, ~~which was~~ the home of Thomas Jefferson.

▶ Our landlord was an elderly bachelor, [who taught us] ~~and it was through his guidance that we were able~~ to appreciate country life.

▶ When I approached the window, the guard took the form. ~~He~~ asked me a few questions, and then ~~he~~ told me to see another guard, who would do a physical search.

Expletive constructions do have legitimate uses, however. For example, they are appropriate when a writer has a good reason for delaying the subject. (See 58c.)

Finally, verbs in the passive voice may be needlessly indirect. When the active voice expresses your meaning as well, use it. (See 14a and 28c.)

▶ All too often, athletes with marginal academic skills. ~~have~~ *our coaches have recruited*

~~been recruited by our coaches.~~

16e   Reduce clauses to phrases, phrases to single words.

Word groups functioning as modifiers can often be made more compact. Look for any opportunities to reduce clauses to phrases or phrases to single words.

▶ The Lanier, ~~was~~ one of the first word processors on the market, ~~It~~ was much more limited than those available now.

Part of an independent clause has become an appositive phrase. (See also 8a.)

▶ For her birthday we gave Jess a stylish vest. ~~made of silk~~ *silk*

A verbal phrase has become a single word.

EXERCISE 16–1

Edit the following sentences for wordiness. Revisions of lettered sentences appear in the back of the book. Example:

The Wilsons moved into the house ~~in spite of the fact that~~ *even though* the back door was only ten yards from the train tracks.

LOOKING AT YOURSELF AS A WRITER
Wordy sentences

Editing for wordiness is a natural part of the writing process, especially in the business world, where conciseness (without loss of meaning) is highly valued. In the academic world, you may be tempted to adopt a wordy style for the following reasons.

CAUSE   You are padding your essay to reach the word limit established in the assignment.

CURE   Find an approach to the assignment that interests you; then do prewriting activities such as listing or clustering before you begin drafting. (See pp. 18–19.)

CAUSE   You are mimicking the indirect, wordy style that is unfortunately common in academic textbooks and journal articles.

CURE   Try not to be impressed by intelligent people who write badly. In your reading, notice that the best writers waste no words; they make each word count.

CAUSE   You fear that a simple, direct style will not sound intelligent — that more words will suggest a greater depth of ideas.

CURE   Look at yourself as a reader. Don't you resent having to wade through wordy sentences? Do you view them as a sign of the writer's intelligence?

a. The drawing room in the west wing is the room that is said to be haunted.
b. Dr. Santini has seen problems like yours countless numbers of times.
c. In my opinion, Bloom's race for the governorship is a futile exercise.
d. If there are any new fares, then they must be reported by message to our transportation offices in Chicago, Peoria, and Springfield.
e. In the heart of Beijing lies the Forbidden City, which is an imperial palace built in very ancient times during the Ming dynasty.

1. Seeing the barrels, the driver immediately slammed on his brakes.
2. The thing data sets are used for is communicating with other computers.
3. The town of New Harmony, located in Indiana, was founded as a utopian community.
4. In the early eighties, some analysts viewed Soviet expansion as an effort to achieve nothing less than world dominance, if not outright control of the world.
5. You will be the departmental travel coordinator for all members of the department.
6. Martin Luther King, Jr., was a man who set a high standard for future leaders to meet.
7. Your task will be the deliverance of correspondence to all employees of the company.
8. A typical autocross course consists of at least two straightaways, and the rest of the course is made up of numerous slaloms and several sharp turns.
9. The program is called the Weight Control Program, and it has been remarkably successful in helping airmen and airwomen lose weight.
10. The price of driving while drunk or while intoxicated can be extremely high.

17

Choose appropriate language.

Language is appropriate when it suits your subject, engages your audience, and blends naturally with your own voice.

To some extent, your choice of language will be governed by the conventions of the genre in which you are writing. When in doubt about the conventions of a particular genre—lab reports, informal essays, business memos, and so on—take a look at models written by experts in the field.

17a Stay away from jargon.

Jargon is specialized language used among members of a trade, profession, or group. Use jargon only when readers will be familiar with it; even then, use it only when plain English will not do as well.

Sentences filled with jargon are likely to be long and lumpy. To revise such sentences, you must rewrite them, usually in fewer words.

> **JARGON** For years the indigenous body politic of South Africa attempted to negotiate legal enfranchisement without result.
>
> **REVISED** For years the indigenous people of South Africa negotiated in vain for the right to vote.

Though a political scientist might feel comfortable with the original version, jargon such as *indigenous body politic* and *legal enfranchisement* is needlessly complicated for ordinary readers.

Broadly defined, jargon includes puffed-up language designed more to impress readers than to inform them. The following are common examples from business, government, higher education, and the military, with plain English translations in parentheses.

ameliorate (improve)
commence (begin)
components (parts)
endeavor (try)
exit (leave)
facilitate (help)
factor (consideration, cause)
impact on (affect)

indicator (sign)
optimal (best, most favorable)
parameters (boundaries, limits)
peruse (read, look over)
prior to (before)
utilize (use)
viable (workable)

▶ ~~In order that I may increase my expertise in the area of~~

~~delivery of services to clients, I feel that participation in this~~

This ^ conference will ~~be beneficial.~~ *train me to serve clients better.* ^

At first the writer tinkered with this sentence—changing *in order that I may* to *to, the area of delivery of* to *delivering,* and so on. The sentence was improved, but it still sounded unnatural. A better solution, this writer discovered, was to rethink what he wanted to say and then rewrite the sentence.

17b Avoid pretentious language, most euphemisms, and "doublespeak."

Hoping to sound profound or poetic, some writers embroider their thoughts with large words and flowery phrases, language that in fact sounds pretentious. Pretentious language is so ornate and often so wordy that it obscures the thought that lies beneath.

> parents become old,
> When our ~~progenitors reach their silver-haired and golden~~
>   entomb   old-age homes
> ~~years~~, we frequently ~~ensepulcher~~ them in ~~homes for~~
>   ∧   ∧   dead.
> ~~senescent beings~~ as if they were already among the ~~deceased.~~
>   ∧

The writer of the original sentence had turned to a thesaurus (a dictionary of synonyms and antonyms) in an attempt to sound educated. When such a writer gains enough confidence to speak in his or her own voice, pretentious language disappears.

Related to pretentious language are euphemisms, nice-sounding words or phrases substituted for words thought to sound harsh or ugly. Like pretentious language, euphemisms are wordy and indirect. Unlike pretentious language, they are sometimes appropriate. It is our social custom, for example, to use euphemisms when speaking or writing about death (*Her sister passed on*), excretion (*I have to go to the bathroom*), sexual intercourse (*They did not sleep together until they were married*), and the like. We may also use euphemisms out of concern for someone's feelings. Telling parents, for example, that their daughter is "unmotivated" is more sensitive than saying she's lazy. Tact or politeness, then, can justify an occasional euphemism.

Most euphemisms, however, are needlessly evasive or even deceitful. Like pretentious language, they obscure the intended meaning.

EUPHEMISM	PLAIN ENGLISH
adult entertainment	pornography
preowned automobile	used car
economically deprived	poor
selected out	fired
negative savings	debts
strategic withdrawal	retreat or defeat

EUPHEMISM	PLAIN ENGLISH
revenue enhancers	taxes
chemical dependency	drug addiction
nuclear engagement	nuclear war
correctional facility	prison

The term *doublespeak*, coined by George Orwell in his novel *1984*, applies to any deliberately evasive or deceptive language, including euphemisms. Doublespeak is especially common in politics, where missiles are named "Peacekeepers," airplane crashes are termed "uncontrolled contact with the ground," and a military retreat is described as "tactical redeployment." Business also gives us its share of doublespeak. When the manufacturer of a pacemaker writes that its product "may result in adverse health consequences in pacemaker-dependent patients as a result of sudden 'no output' failure," it takes an alert reader to grasp the message: The pacemakers might suddenly stop functioning and cause a heart attack or even death.

EXERCISE 17–1

Edit the following sentences to eliminate jargon, pretentious or flowery language, euphemisms, and doublespeak. You may need to make substantial changes in some sentences. Revisions of lettered sentences appear in the back of the book. Example:

> After two weeks in the legal department, Sue has ~~worked into~~ *mastered*
> the routine, ~~of the office,~~ and her ~~functional and self-~~ *office* *performance has*
> ~~management skills have~~ exceeded all expectations.

a. It is a widespread but unproven hypothesis that the parameters of significant personal change for persons in midlife are extremely narrow.

b. All employees functioning in the capacity of work-study students will be required to give evidence of current enrollment.

LOOKING AT YOURSELF AS A WRITER
Jargon and pretentious language

In the academic and business worlds, you may be tempted to use jargon and pretentious language for several reasons.

CAUSE You're surrounded by jargon and pretentious language—at work or in your academic field—so you are picking it up, by osmosis.

CURE Develop an appreciation for good writing. Notice that the best writers can manage an elevated style without losing their human voices.

CAUSE You're afraid that if you present your ideas clearly, they will seem too simple.

CURE Give clear writing a try—and see if it sells. You can usually tell which professors or supervisors value a straightforward style and which are impressed by pompous language.

CAUSE Having discovered a thesaurus, you are using it for the wrong reason.

CURE Use a thesaurus or a dictionary to choose the best word, not necessarily the fanciest one. (See pp. 202–203.)

CAUSE You are experimenting with style, and your attempts at creativity and sophistication sometimes backfire.

CURE Continue to experiment, but be prepared—in the words of one writer—to "murder your darlings."

c. In 1985 I purchased a residential property that was in need of substantial upgrading.
d. When Sal was selected out from his high-paying factory job, he learned what it was like to be economically depressed.
e. Passengers should endeavor to finalize the customs declaration form prior to exiting the aircraft.

1. Mayor Summers will commence his term of office by ameliorating living conditions in economically deprived zones.
2. As I approached the edifice of confinement where my brother was incarcerated, several inmates loudly vocalized a number of lewd remarks.
3. The nurse announced that there had been a negative patient-care outcome due to a therapeutic misadventure on the part of the surgeon.
4. When we returned from our evening perambulation, we shrank back in horror as we surmised that our domestic dwelling was being swallowed up in hellish flames.
5. The bottom line is that the company is experiencing a negative cash flow.

17c Avoid obsolete, archaic, and invented words.

Obsolete words are words found in the writing of the past that have dropped out of use entirely. Archaic words are old words that are still used, but only in special contexts such as literature or advertising. Although dictionaries list obsolete words such as *recomfort* and *reechy* and archaic words such as *anon* and *betwixt*, these words are not appropriate for current use.

Invented words (also called *neologisms*) are words too recently created to be part of standard English. Many invented words fade out of use without becoming standard. *Build-down*, *throughput*, and *palimony* are neologisms that may not last. *Scuba, disco, sexist, software*, and *spinoff* are no longer neologisms; they have become standard English. Avoid using invented words in your writing unless they are given in the dictionary as standard or unless no other word expresses your meaning.

17d In most contexts, avoid slang, regional expressions, and nonstandard English.

Slang is an informal and sometimes private vocabulary that expresses the solidarity of a group such as teenagers, rock musicians, or football fans; it is subject to more rapid change than standard English. For example, the slang teenagers use to express approval changes every few years; *cool, groovy, neat, wicked,* and *awesome* have replaced one another within the last three decades. Sometimes slang becomes so widespread that it is accepted as standard vocabulary. *Jazz,* for example, started out as slang but is now generally accepted to describe a style of music.

Although slang has a certain vitality, it is a code that not everyone understands, and it is very informal. Therefore, it is inappropriate in most written work.

▶ If we don't begin studying for the final, a whole semester's
  will be wasted.
  work ~~is going down the tubes.~~
  ∧

▶ The government's "filth" guidelines for food will ~~gross you~~ *disgust you.*
  ∧
  ~~out.~~

Regional expressions are common to a group in a geographical area. *Let's talk with the bark off* (for *Let's speak frankly*) is an expression in the southern United States, for example. Regional expressions have the same limitations as slang and are therefore inappropriate in most writing.

▶ John was four blocks from the house before he remembered
  turn on
  to ~~cut~~ the headlights ● ~~on.~~
  ∧   ∧

▶ I'm not ~~for~~ sure, but I think the dance has been postponed.

As you probably know, many people speak two varieties of English — standard English, used in academic and business situations, and a nonstandard dialect, spoken with close acquaintances who share a regional or social heritage. In written English, a dialect may be used in dialogue, to reflect actual speech, but in most other contexts it is out of place. Like slang and regionalisms, nonstandard English is a language shared by a select group. Standard English, by contrast, is accessible to all.

If you speak a nonstandard dialect, try to identify the ways in which your dialect differs from standard English. Look especially for the following features of nonstandard English, which commonly cause problems in writing.

Misuse of verb forms such as *began* and *begun* (See 27a.)

Omission of *-s* endings on verbs (See 27c.)

Omission of *-ed* endings on verbs (See 27d.)

Omission of necessary verbs (See 27e.)

Double negatives (See 26d.)

17e   Choose an appropriate level of formality.

In deciding on a level of formality, consider both your subject and your audience. Does the subject demand a dignified treatment, or is a relaxed tone more suitable? Will readers be put off if you assume too close a relationship with them, or might you alienate them by seeming too distant?

Formal writing emphasizes the importance of its subject and the exactness of its information. Its tone is dignified, and it maintains a certain distance between writer and audience. A sophisticated vocabulary and complex sentence structures are compatible with a formal writing style, although simple words and short sentences do not necessarily destroy it. Contractions (*don't, he'll*) and colloquial words (*kids, buddy*) tend to be out of place.

For most college and professional writing, some degree of formality is appropriate. In a letter applying for a job, for example, it is a mistake to sound too breezy and informal.

TOO INFORMAL	I'd like to get that receptionist's job you've got in the paper.
MORE FORMAL	I would like to apply for the receptionist's position listed in the *Peoria Journal Star.*

Informal writing is appropriate for private letters, articles in popular magazines, and business correspondence between close associates. Like spoken conversation, it allows contractions and colloquial words. Vocabulary and sentence structure are rarely complex.

In choosing a level of formality, above all be consistent. When a writer's voice shifts from one level of formality to another, readers receive mixed messages.

▶ Once a pitcher for the Cincinnati Reds, Bob shared with me the secrets of his trade. His lesson ~~commenced~~ *began* with his famous curveball, ~~implemented~~ *thrown* by tucking the little finger behind the ball instead of holding it straight out. Next he ~~elucidated~~ *revealed* the mysteries of the sucker pitch, a slow ball coming behind a fast windup.

Words such as *commenced* and *elucidated* are inappropriate for the subject matter, and they clash with informal terms such as *sucker pitch* and *fast windup.*

EXERCISE 17–2

Edit the following paragraph to eliminate slang and maintain a consistent level of formality.

The graduation speaker really blew it. He should have discussed the options and challenges facing the graduating class. Instead, he shot his mouth off at us and trashed us for being lazy and pampered. He did make some good points, however. Our profs have certainly babied us by not holding fast to deadlines, by dismissing assignments that the class ragged them about, by ignoring our tardiness, and by handing out easy C's like hotcakes. Still, we resented this speech as the final word from the college establishment. It should have been the orientation speech when we started college.

17f Avoid sexist language.

Sexist language is language that stereotypes or demeans men or women, usually women. Some sexist language reflects genuine contempt for women: referring to a woman as a "broad," for example, or calling a lawyer a "lady lawyer," or saying in an advertisement, "If our new sports car were a lady, it would get its bottom pinched."

Other forms of sexist language, while they may not suggest conscious sexism, reflect stereotypical thinking: referring to nurses as women and doctors as men, using different conventions when naming or identifying women and men, or assuming that all of one's readers are men. (See the chart on page 200.)

Still other forms of sexist language result from outmoded traditions. The pronouns *he, him,* and *his,* for instance, were traditionally used to refer indefinitely to persons of either sex.

TRADITIONAL   A journalist is stimulated by *his* deadline.

Today, however, such usage is widely viewed as sexist because it excludes women and encourages sex-role stereotyping — the view that men are somehow more suited than women to be journalists, doctors, and so on.

One option, of course, is to substitute *his or her* for *his: A journalist is stimulated by his or her deadline.* This strategy is fine in small doses, but it generates needless words that become awkward when repeated throughout an essay. A better strategy, many writers have discovered, is simply to write in the plural.

REVISED   *Journalists* are stimulated by *their* deadlines.

Yet another strategy is to recast the sentence so that the problem does not arise:

REVISED   A journalist is stimulated by *a* deadline.

When sexist language occurs throughout an essay, it is sometimes possible to adjust the essay's point of view. If the essay might be appropriately rewritten from the *I*, the *we*, or the *you* point of view, the problem of sexist English will not arise. (See pages 47–51.)

Like the pronouns *he, him,* and *his,* the nouns *man* and *men* were once used indefinitely to refer to persons of either sex. Current usage demands gender-neutral terms instead.

INAPPROPRIATE	APPROPRIATE
chairman	chairperson, moderator, chair, head
clergyman	member of the clergy, minister, pastor
congressman	member of Congress, representative, legislator
fireman	firefighter
foreman	supervisor
mailman	mail carrier, postal worker, letter carrier
mankind	people, humans
manpower	personnel
policeman	police officer
salesman	salesperson, sales associate, salesclerk
to man	to operate, to staff
weatherman	weather forecaster, meteorologist
workman	worker, laborer

Avoiding sexist language

1. Avoid occupational stereotypes.

   ▶ After the nursing student graduates, ~~she~~ *he or she* must face a

   difficult state board examination.

2. When naming and identifying men and women, be consistent.

   ▶ Running for city council are Jake Stein, an attorney,

   and ~~Mrs.~~ Cynthia Jones, a professor of English~~, and~~

   ~~mother of three.~~

3. Do not write to an audience of men alone.

   ▶ If you are a senior government official, your ~~wife~~ *spouse* is

   required to report any gifts ~~she~~ *he or she* receives that are valued

   at more than $100.

4. Avoid using *he* to mean "he or she" or *him* to mean "him
   or her." (For a variety of revision strategies, see the chart
   on pages 260–61.)

   ▶ ~~Every applicant wants~~ *All applicants want* to know how much ~~he~~ *they* will make.

5. Avoid using *-man* words to refer to persons of either sex.

   ▶ A ~~fireman~~ *firefighter* must always be on call, even when ~~he is~~ off

   duty.

EXERCISE 17-3

Edit the following sentences to eliminate sexist language or sexist assumptions. Revisions of lettered sentences appear in the back of the book. Example:

> *Scholarship athletes*
> ~~A scholarship athlete~~ must be as concerned about ~~his~~ *their*
> academic performance as ~~he is~~ *they are* about ~~his~~ *their* athletic
>
> performance.

a. Mrs. Asha Purpura, who is a doctor's wife, is the defense attorney appointed by the court. Al Jones has been assigned to work with her on the case.

b. If a young graduate is careful about investments, he can accumulate a significant sum in a relatively short period.

c. An elementary school teacher should understand the concept of nurturing if she intends to be a success.

d. Because Dr. Brown and Dr. Dorothy Coombs were the senior professors in the department, they served as co-chairmen of the promotion committee.

e. If man does not stop polluting his environment, mankind will perish.

1. I have been trained to doubt an automobile mechanic, even if he has an excellent reputation.

2. After a new president is elected, he must wait several months before his inauguration.

3. In the recent gubernatorial race, Lena Weiss, a defense lawyer and mother of two, easily defeated Harvey Tower, an architect.

4. In my hometown, the lady mayor has led the fight for a fair share of federal funds for new schools.

5. As partners in a successful real estate firm, John Crockett and Sarah Cooke have been an effective sales team; he is particularly skillful at arranging attractive mortgage packages; she is a vivacious blonde who stays fit by doing aerobics daily.

18

Find the exact words.

Whatever you want to say, claimed French writer Gustave Flaubert, "there is but one word to express it, one verb to give it movement, one adjective to qualify it; you must seek until you find this noun, this verb, this adjective." Even if you are not reaching for such perfection in your writing, you will sometimes find yourself wishing for better words. The dictionary is the obvious first place to turn, a thesaurus the second.

A good desk dictionary— such as *The American Heritage Dictionary, The Random House College Dictionary,* or *Merriam-Webster's Collegiate* or *New World Dictionary of the American Language* — lists synonyms and antonyms for many words, with helpful comments on shades of meaning. Under *fertile,* for example, *Webster's New World Dictionary* carefully distinguishes the meanings of *fertile, fecund, fruitful,* and *prolific:*

> SYN. —*fertile* implies a producing, or power of producing, fruit or offspring, and may be used figuratively of the mind; *fecund* implies the abundant production of offspring or fruit, or, figuratively, of creations of the mind; *fruitful* specifically suggests the bearing of much fruit, but it is also used to imply fertility (of soil), favorable results, profitableness, etc.; *prolific,* a close synonym for *fecund,* more often carries derogatory connotations of overly rapid production or reproduction— ANT. *sterile, barren*

If the dictionary doesn't yield the word you need, try a book of synonyms and antonyms such as *Roget's International Thesaurus.* In the back of *Roget's* is an index to the groups of synonyms that make up the bulk of the book. Look up the adjective *still,* for example, and you will find references to lists containing the words *dead, motionless, silent,* and *tranquil.* If *tranquil* is close to the word you have in mind, turn to its section in the front of the book. There you will find a long list of synonyms, including such words as *quiet, quiescent, reposeful, calm, pacific, halcyon, placid,* and *unruffled.* Unless your vocabulary is better than average, the list will contain words you've never heard or with which you are only vaguely familiar. Whenever you are tempted to use one of these words, look it up in the dictionary first to avoid misusing it.

On discovering the thesaurus, many writers use it for the wrong reasons, so a word of caution is in order. Do not turn to a thesaurus in search of exotic, fancy words—such as *halcyon*—with which to embellish your essays. Look instead for words that exactly express your meaning. Most of the time these words will be familiar to both you and your readers. *Tranquil* was probably the word you were looking for all along.

18a Select words with appropriate connotations.

In addition to their strict dictionary meanings (or *denotations*), words have *connotations,* emotional colorings that affect how readers respond to them. The word *steel* denotes "made of or resembling commercial iron that contains carbon," but it also calls up a cluster of images associated with steel, such as the sensation of touching it. These associations give the word its connotations—cold, smooth, unbending.

If the connotation of a word does not seem appropriate for your purpose, your audience, or your subject matter, you should change the word. When a more appropriate synonym does not come quickly to mind, consult a dictionary or a thesaurus.

▶ The model was ~~skinny~~ *slender* and fashionable.

The connotation of the word *skinny* is too negative.

▶ As I covered the boats with marsh grass, the ~~perspiration~~ *sweat* I

had worked up evaporated in the wind, making the cold

morning air seem even colder.

The term *perspiration* is too dainty for the context, which suggests vigorous exercise.

EXERCISE 18–1

Use a dictionary or thesaurus to find at least four synonyms for each
of the following words. Be prepared to explain any slight differences
in meaning.

1. decay (verb)   3. hurry (verb)   5. secret (adjective)
2. difficult (adjective) 4. pleasure (noun)   6. talent (noun)

EXERCISE 18–2

For each of the words italicized in the following passages, consider
alternatives that the writer might have chosen instead. (A dictionary
and a thesaurus will lead you to other possibilities.) Then discuss why
the author probably selected the word he or she did.

1. The forest, *choked* by growth and *shadow*, was like a jungle; the
   air hung thick with heat, *muting* the sound of their progress.
   Breathing in a *pungent steam* of sweet grasses and tangy nee-
   dles, rotting wood and sunbaked fungi, she followed as best she
   could, *plunging* through the thicket to keep up with the young
   man ahead.   —Diana West
2. A change of just a few degrees in atmospheric temperature over
   the next century would be *catastrophic*. A *parade* of scientists
   appearing before a Senate committee in June *painted* a *graphic*
   picture of what that could mean: melting icecaps and rising sea
   levels that would *inundate* seaboard cities and drown thousands

in *fierce* storms; rainfall shifts that would make the deserts *bloom* and turn *breadbaskets* into *dustbowls*; and, of course, heat everywhere. — Matthew L. Wald

18b Prefer specific, concrete nouns.

Unlike general nouns, which refer to broad classes of things, specific nouns point to definite and particular items. *Film*, for example, names a general class, *science fiction film* names a narrower class, and *Jurassic Park* is more specific still. Other examples: *team, football team, Denver Broncos; music, symphony, Beethoven's Ninth; work, carpentry, cabinetmaking.*

Unlike abstract nouns, which refer to qualities and ideas (*justice, beauty, realism, dignity*), concrete nouns point to immediate, often sensory experience and to physical objects (*steeple, asphalt, lilac, stone, garlic*).

Specific, concrete nouns express meaning more vividly than general or abstract ones. Although general and abstract language is sometimes necessary to convey your meaning, ordinarily prefer specific, concrete alternatives.

▶ The senator spoke about the challenges of the future: problems ~~concerning the environment and world peace~~.
   ∧ *of famine, pollution, dwindling resources, and arms control.*

Nouns such as *thing, area, aspect, factor,* and *individual* are especially dull and imprecise.

▶ A career in transportation management offers many ~~things.~~
   ∧ *rewards.*

▶ Try pairing a trainee with an ~~individual with technical~~
   ∧ *experienced technician.*
   ~~experience.~~

18c Do not misuse words.

If a word is not in your active vocabulary, you may find your-self misusing it, sometimes with embarrassing consequences. Imagine the chagrin of the young woman who wrote that the "aroma of pumpkin pie and sage stuffing acted as an *aphrodisiac*" when she learned that aphrodisiacs are drugs or foods stimulating sexual desire. Such blunders are easily prevented: When in doubt, check the dictionary.

▶ The fans were ~~migrating~~ up the bleachers in search of seats.
  Climbing

▶ Mrs. Johnson tried to fight but to no ~~prevail.~~ *avail.*

▶ Drugs have so ~~diffused~~ our culture that they touch all *permeated*

segments of society.

EXERCISE 18–3

Edit the following sentences to correct misused words. Revisions of lettered sentences appear in the back of the book. Example:

The training required for a ballet dancer is ~~all-absorbent.~~ *all-absorbing.*

a. Many of us are not persistence enough to make a change for the better.

b. It is sometimes difficult to hear in church because the agnostics are so terrible.

c. Liu Kwan began his career as a lawyer, but now he is a real estate mongrel.

d. When Robert Frost died at age eighty-eight, he left a legacy of poems that will make him immortal for years to come.

e. This patient is kept in isolation to prevent her from obtaining our germs.

LOOKING AT YOURSELF AS A WRITER
Misused words

Most writers choose the wrong word now and then, but if you find yourself misusing a great many words, consider why. Here are some common causes and cures.

CAUSE You have a fondness for fancy words, such as *penultimate,* that are not in your active vocabulary.

CURE Write in a simpler style. Readers appreciate plain English more than you may think. (See 17a and 17b.) *Penultimate* probably isn't in their active vocabulary either.

CAUSE You tend to mix up easily confused words such as *accept* and *except.*

CURE Turn to the Glossary of Usage at the back of this book whenever you are in doubt about such words. Or consult a dictionary.

CAUSE Your vocabulary is not as strong as you'd like it to be.

CURE This cure will take time. The best way to improve your vocabulary is to read, and the best way to develop the habit of reading is to choose magazines and books that you enjoy. Seeing new words used properly, in context, will help you learn to use them in your own writing.

1. Waste, misuse of government money, security and health violations, and even pilfering have become major dilemmas at the FBI.
2. Trifle, a popular English dessert, contains a ménage of ingredients that do not always appeal to American tastes.
3. Grand Isle State Park is surrounded on three sides by water.
4. Frequently I cannot do my work because the music blaring from my son's room detracts me.
5. Tom Jones is an illegal child who grows up under the care of Squire Western.

18d Use standard idioms.

Idioms are speech forms that follow no easily specified rules. The English say "Maria went *to hospital*," an idiom strange to American ears, which are accustomed to hearing *the* in front of *hospital*. Native speakers of a language seldom have problems with idioms, but prepositions sometimes cause trouble, especially when they follow certain verbs and adjectives. When in doubt, consult a good desk dictionary.

UNIDIOMATIC	IDIOMATIC
according with	according to
abide with (a decision)	abide by (a decision)
agree to (an idea)	agree with (an idea)
angry at (a person)	angry with (a person)
capable to	capable of
comply to	comply with
desirous to	desirous of
different than	different from
intend on doing	intend to do
off of	off
plan on doing	plan to do
preferable than	preferable to
prior than	prior to
superior than	superior to

UNIDIOMATIC	IDIOMATIC
sure and	sure to
try and	try to
type of a	type of

> **ESL NOTE:** Because idioms follow no particular rules, you must learn them individually. You may find it helpful to keep a list of idioms that you frequently encounter in conversation and in reading.

EXERCISE 18–4

Edit the following sentences to eliminate errors in the use of idiomatic expressions. If a sentence is correct, write "correct" after it. Answers to lettered sentences appear in the back of the book. Example:

We agreed to abide ~~with~~ *by* the decision of the judge.

a. Queen Anne was so angry at Sarah Churchill that she refused to see her again.

b. Prior to the Russians' launching of *Sputnik, nik* was not an English suffix.

c. Try and come up with the rough outline, and Marika will fill in the details.

d. For the frightened refugees, the dangerous trek across the mountains was preferable than life in a war zone.

e. The parade moved off of the street and onto the beach.

1. Be sure and report on the danger of releasing genetically engineered bacteria into the atmosphere.

2. Why do you assume that embezzling bank assets is so different than robbing the bank?

3. Most of the class agreed to Sylvia's view that nuclear proliferation is potentially a very dangerous problem.

4. What type of a wedding are you planning?

5. Andrea intends on joining the Peace Corps after graduation.

18e Avoid worn-out expressions.

The frontiersman who first announced that he had "slept like a log" no doubt amused his companions with a fresh and unlikely comparison. Today, however, that comparison is a cliché, a saying that has lost its dazzle from overuse. No longer can it surprise.

To see just how dully predictable clichés are, put your hand over the right-hand column below and then finish the phrases on the left.

cool as a	cucumber
beat around	the bush
blind as a	bat
busy as a	bee, beaver
crystal	clear
dead as a	doornail
out of the frying pan	into the fire
light as a	feather
like a bull	in a china shop
playing with	fire
nutty as a	fruitcake
selling like	hotcakes
starting out at the bottom	of the ladder
water over the	dam
white as a	sheet, ghost
avoid clichés like the	plague

The cure for clichés is frequently simple: Just delete them. When this won't work, try adding some element of surprise. One student, for example, who had written that she had butterflies in her stomach, revised her cliché like this:

> If all of the action in my stomach is caused by butterflies, there must be a horde of them, with horseshoes on.

The image of butterflies wearing horseshoes is fresh and unlikely, not dully predictable like the original cliché.

18f Use figures of speech with care.

A figure of speech is an expression that uses words imaginatively (rather than literally) to invigorate an idea or make abstract ideas concrete. Most often, figures of speech compare two seemingly unlike things to reveal surprising similarities. For example, Richard Selzer compares an aging surgeon who has lost his touch to an old lion whose claws have become blunted. Readers enjoy such fresh comparisons, and you will find that creating them is one of the greatest pleasures in writing.

In a *simile,* the writer makes a comparison explicitly, usually by introducing it with *like* or *as.* One student, for instance, writes of his grandfather, "By the time cotton had to be picked, his neck was as red as the clay he plowed." In one of his short stories, William Faulkner describes the eyes of a plump old woman who had locked herself in her house for years as "like two small pieces of coal pressed into a lump of dough." J. D. Salinger's troubled adolescent Holden Caulfield in *The Catcher in the Rye* finds one of his fellow students "as sensitive as a goddam toilet seat," and actress Mae West tells us that men are "like streetcars. There's always another one around the corner."

In a *metaphor,* the *like* or *as* is omitted, and the comparison is implied. For example, Mark Twain's Huck Finn describes his drunken father's face as "fish-belly white." In the Old Testament's Song of Solomon, a young woman compares the man she loves to a fruit tree: "With great delight I sat in his shadow, and his fruit was sweet to my taste." And a student poet describes a fierce summer storm like this: "It growls and barks at me, / jumping at its leash, / as if it guards the gates of heaven."

Although figures of speech are useful devices, writers sometimes use them without thinking through the images they evoke. This can result in a *mixed metaphor,* the combination of two or more images that don't make sense together.

▶ Crossing Utah's salt flats in his new Corvette, my father flew *at jet speed.*
~~under a full head of steam.~~
⌃

Flew suggests an airplane, while *under a full head of steam* suggests a steamboat or a train. To clarify the image, the writer should stick with one comparison or the other.

▶ Our office had decided to put all controversial issues on a

back burner, ~~in a holding pattern.~~
⌃

Here the writer is mixing stoves and airplanes. Simply deleting one of the images corrects the problem.

EXERCISE 18–5

Edit the following sentences to replace worn-out expressions and clarify mixed figures of speech. Revisions of lettered sentences appear in the back of the book. Example:

the color drained from his face.
When he heard about the accident, ~~he turned white as a~~
⌃

~~sheet.~~

a. Juanita told Kyle that keeping skeletons in the closet would be playing with fire.
b. The president thought that the scientists were using science as a sledgehammer to grind their political axes.
c. Ours was a long courtship; we waited ten years before finally deciding to tie the knot.

d. We ironed out the sticky spots in our relationship.

e. Sasha told us that he wasn't willing to put his neck out on a limb.

1. I could read him like a book; he had egg all over his face.
2. Tears were strolling down the child's face.
3. High school is a seething caldron of raw human emotion.
4. There are too many cooks in the broth here at corporate head-quarters.
5. Once she had sunk her teeth into it, Helen burned through the assignment.

EXERCISE 18–6

Identify the figurative language in the following sentences. Be prepared to discuss why you think these passages are effective.

1. The kitchen was a great machine that set our lives running; it whirred down a little only on Saturdays and holy days.
   — Alfred Kazin
2. If growing up is painful for the Southern Black girl, being aware of her displacement is the rust on the razor that threatens the throat. — Maya Angelou
3. She sat looking about her with eyes as impersonal, almost as stony, as those with which the granite Rameses in a museum watches the froth and fret that ebbs and flows about his pedestal.
   — Willa Cather
4. As the sweeping scythe of plague turned bustling towns into sepulchers and emptied the countryside, it reshaped European history. — Nicole Duplaix
5. In a word, we [Afro-Americans] are bringing down the curtain on this role you have cast us in and we will no longer be a party to our own degradation. — John Oliver Killens

PART V

Editing for Grammar

19

___

Repair sentence fragments.

___

A sentence fragment is a word group that pretends to be a sentence. Some fragments are clauses that contain a subject and a verb but begin with a subordinating word. Others are phrases that lack a subject, a verb, or both.

Sentence fragments are easy to recognize when they appear out of context, like this one:

> On the old wooden stool in the corner of my grandmother's kitchen.

When they appear next to related sentences, however, they are harder to spot.

> On that morning I sat in my usual spot. On the old wooden stool in the corner of my grandmother's kitchen.

To be a sentence, a word group must consist of at least one full independent clause. An independent clause has a subject and a verb, and it either stands alone or could stand alone. To test a word group for sentence completeness, use the flow chart on page 225. For example, by using the flow chart, you can see exactly why *On the old wooden stool in the corner of my grandmother's kitchen* is a fragment: It lacks both a verb and a subject.

You can repair most fragments in one of two ways: Either pull the fragment into a nearby sentence, making sure to punctuate the new sentence correctly, or turn the fragment into a sentence. To repair the sample fragment, you would probably choose to combine it with the sentence that precedes it, like this:

On that morning I sat in my usual spot, on the old wooden stool in the corner of my grandmother's kitchen.

> **ESL NOTE:** Unlike some languages, English does not allow omission of subjects (except in imperative sentences); nor does it allow omission of verbs. See 31a and 29e.

19a Attach fragmented subordinate clauses or turn them into sentences.

A subordinate clause is patterned like a sentence, with both a subject and a verb, but it begins with a word that marks it as subordinate. The following words commonly introduce subordinate clauses:

after	even though	so that	when	whom
although	how	than	where	whose
as	if	that	whether	why
as if	in order that	though	which	
because	rather than	unless	while	
before	since	until	who	

Subordinate clauses function within sentences as adjectives, as adverbs, or as nouns. They cannot stand alone. (See 59b.)

Most fragmented clauses beg to be pulled into a sentence nearby.

▶ Jane will address the problem of limited on-campus parking,/
   if
   ~~I~~f she is elected special student adviser.

If introduces a subordinate clause that modifies the verb *will address.* For punctuation of subordinate clauses appearing at the end of a sentence, see 33f.

▶ Although we seldom get to see wildlife in the city/, ~~At~~ the zoo *at*

we can still find some of our favorites.

Although introduces a subordinate clause that modifies the verb
can find. For punctuation of subordinate clauses appearing at
the beginning of a sentence, see 32b.

If a fragmented clause cannot be attached to a nearby
sentence or if you feel that attaching it would be awkward, try
rewriting it. The simplest way to turn a subordinate clause
into a sentence is to delete the opening word or words that
mark it as subordinate.

▶ Violence has produced a great deal of apprehension among
teachers at Dean Junior High. ~~So that self-preservation~~, in
Self-preservation,

fact, has become their primary aim.

19b Attach fragmented phrases or turn them into sentences.

Like subordinate clauses, phrases function within sentences
as adjectives, as adverbs, or as nouns. They cannot stand
alone. Fragmented phrases are often prepositional or verbal
phrases; sometimes they are appositives, words or word
groups that rename nouns or pronouns. (See 59a, 59c, and
59d.)

Many fragmented phrases may simply be pulled into
nearby sentences.

▶ On Sundays James scrupulously read the newspaper's
employment listings/, ~~Scrutinizing~~ every position that held
scrutinizing

even the remotest possibility.

Scrutinizing every position that held even the remotest possibility is a verbal phrase modifying *James.* For punctuation of verbal phrases, see 32e.

▶ Wednesday morning Phil allowed himself half a grapefruit/ ,̸
†
/̸The only food he had eaten in two days.

The only food he had eaten in two days is an appositive renaming the noun *grapefruit.* For punctuation of appositives, see 32e.

If a fragmented phrase cannot be pulled into a nearby sentence effectively, turn the phrase into a sentence. You may need to add a subject, a verb, or both.

▶ In the study skills workshop, we learned the value of
discipline and hard work. ~~Also~~ how to organize our time, take
We also learned
meaningful notes, interpret assignments, pinpoint trouble
spots, and seek help.

The word group beginning *Also how to organize* is a fragmented verbal phrase. The revision turns the fragment into a sentence by adding a subject and a verb.

19c Attach other fragmented word groups or turn them into sentences.

Other word groups that are commonly fragmented include parts of compound predicates, lists, and examples introduced by *such as, for example,* or similar expressions.

Parts of compound predicates

A predicate consists of a verb and its objects, complements, and modifiers (see 58b). A compound predicate includes two or more predicates joined by a coordinating conjunction such as *and, but,* or *or.* Because the parts of a compound predicate share the same subject, they should appear in the same sentence.

▶ Aspiring bodybuilders must first ascertain their strengths

and weaknesses/ And then decide what they want to achieve.

Notice that no comma appears between the parts of a compound predicate. (See 33a.)

Lists

When a list is mistakenly fragmented, it can often be attached to a nearby sentence with a colon or a dash. (See 35a and 39a.)

▶ The side effects of lithium are many/: Nausea, stomach

cramps, thirst, muscle weakness, vomiting, diarrhea,

confusion, and tremors.

Examples introduced by such as, for example, *or similar expressions*

Expressions that introduce examples (or explanations) can lead to unintentional fragments. Although you may begin a sentence with some of the following words or phrases, make sure that what you have written is a sentence, not a fragment.

also	especially	in addition	namely	that is
and	for example	like	or	
but	for instance	mainly	such as	

Sometimes fragmented examples can be attached to the preceding sentence.

▶ The South has produced some of our greatest twentieth-
century writers/, ~~Such~~ as Flannery O'Connor, William
Faulkner, Alice Walker, Tennessee Williams, and Thomas
Wolfe.

At times, however, it may be necessary to turn the fragment into a sentence.

▶ If Eric doesn't get his way, he goes into a fit of rage. For
example, ~~lying~~ *he lies* on the floor screaming or ~~opening~~ *opens* the cabinet
doors and then ~~slamming~~ *slams* them shut.

The writer corrected this fragment by adding a subject — he —
and substituting verbs for the verbals *lying, opening,* and
slamming.

LOOKING AT YOURSELF AS A WRITER
Sentence fragments

An occasional sentence fragment, used deliberately, can be effective, but unintentional sentence fragments are serious
errors. If you tend to write unintentional fragments, try to
discover why.

CAUSE You worry that you will write a run-on sentence (a
comma splice or a fused sentence).

CURE You are right to be concerned about run-on
sentences, but you may be worrying too much
about them while drafting. When you reach the
editing stage of the writing process, try proofreading
for both fragments and run-ons by using the flow
charts on pages 225 and 237.

	Sentence fragments (continued)
CAUSE	Feeling that a sentence should be a certain length, you insert a period at some convenient point when it has reached that length.
CURE	Make punctuation decisions based on sentence structure, not length. The following comma rules tell you when to use a comma (or no punctuation) instead of a period: 32b, 32e, 33e, and 33f.
CAUSE	You are trying to emphasize the idea in the fragment by putting it in its own sentence.
CURE	Consider using other strategies for emphasis, such as the dash or the colon. See 19c.

19d Exception: Occasionally a fragment may be used deliberately, for effect.

Skilled writers occasionally use sentence fragments for emphasis. In the following passage, Richard Rodriguez uses a fragment (italicized) to draw attention to his mother.

> Following the dramatic Americanization of their children, even my parents grew more publicly confident. *Especially my mother.* She learned the names of all the people on our block.
> — *Hunger of Memory*

Fragments are occasionally used to save words. For example, a fragment may be a concise way to mark a transition (*And now the opposing arguments*) or to answer a question (*Are these new drug tests 100% reliable? Not in the opinion of most experts*).

When deciding whether to risk using a fragment, consider your writing situation. Are readers likely to object to fragments, even when used deliberately? Does your subject demand a formal approach? If the answer to either of these questions is yes, you will find it safer to write in complete sentences.

EXERCISE 19–1

Repair any fragment by attaching it to a nearby sentence or by rewriting it as a complete sentence. If a word group is correct, write "correct" after it. Revisions of lettered sentences appear in the back of the book. Example:

> One Greek island that should not be missed is Mykonos, a
> vacation spot for Europeans and a playpen for the rich.

a. As I stood in front of the microwave, I recalled my grandmother bending over her old black stove. And remembered what she taught me: that any food can have soul if you love the people you are cooking for.

b. It has been said that there are only three indigenous American art forms. Jazz, musical comedy, and soap opera.

c. I stepped on some frozen moss and started sliding down the face of a flat rock toward the falls. Suddenly I landed on another rock.

d. We need to stop believing myths about drinking. That strong black coffee will sober you up, for example, or that a cold shower will straighten you out.

e. As we walked up the path, we came upon the gun batteries. Large gray concrete structures covered with ivy and weeds.

1. Sitting at a sidewalk café near the Sorbonne, I could pass as a French student. As long as I kept my mouth shut.

2. Mother loved to play all our favorite games. Canasta, Monopoly, hide-and-seek, and even kick the can.

3. The horses were dressed up with hats and flowers. Some even wore sunglasses.

4. I had pushed these fears into one of those quiet places in my mind. Hoping they would stay there asleep.

Reviewing your writing for sentence fragments

First look for the most common trouble spots:

WORDS INTRODUCING SUBORDINATE CLAUSES (19a)

although	even though	that	where	who
as if	if	though	whether	whom
because	how	unless	which	whose
before	so that	when	while	why

▶ Pat could not come skiing with us/ ᵇBecause she had

broken her leg.

PHRASES (19b)

▶ Mary is suffering from agoraphobia/, ᵃ̶A̶ fear of the

outside world.

PARTS OF COMPOUND PREDICATES (19c)

▶ Pressing the gun to my shoulder, I laid my cheek to the

stock/ ᵃA̶nd sighted the target.

WORDS INTRODUCING LISTS OR EXAMPLES (19c)

for example	like	namely
for instance	mainly	such as

▶ You already know some gestures in sign language/,

such
S̶u̶c̶h̶ as a wave for "hello" and a shake of the head for

"no."

Sentence fragments (continued)

Next test possible fragments for sentence completeness:

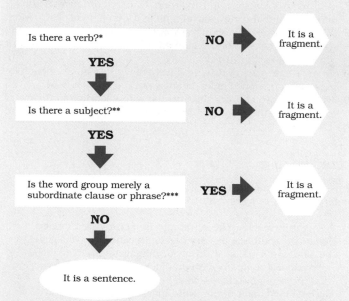

*Do not mistake verbals for verbs. (See 59c.)

**The subject of a sentence may be *you,* understood. (See 58a.)

***A sentence may open with a subordinate clause, but the sentence must also include an independent clause. (See 59b.)

If you find any fragments, try one of these methods of revision:

1. Attach the fragment to a nearby sentence.
2. Turn the fragment into a sentence.

5. To give my family a comfortable, secure home life. That is my most important goal.
6. If a woman from the desert tribe showed anger toward her husband, she was whipped in front of the whole village. And shunned by the rest of the women.
7. A tornado is a violent whirling wind. One that produces a funnel-shaped cloud and moves over land in a slim path of destruction.
8. With machetes, the explorers cut their way through the tall grasses to the edge of the canyon. Where they began to lay out their tapes for the survey.
9. In my three years of driving, I have never had an accident. Not one wreck, not one fender-bender, not even a little dent.
10. The pilots ejected from the burning plane, landing in the water not far from the ship. And immediately popped their flares and life vests.

EXERCISE 19–2

Repair each fragment in the following paragraphs by attaching it to a sentence nearby or by rewriting it as a complete sentence.

Until recently, Maria thought that studying a foreign language would not be very useful. Because she was going to be a business major, training for management. Even if she worked for a company with an office overseas, she was sure that international clients would communicate in English. The accepted language of the world marketplace. But Maria's adviser, Professor Will, told her that many U.S. firms are owned by foreign corporations. Or rely on the sales of subsidiaries in foreign markets. English is therefore not always the language of preference.

Professor Will advised Maria to learn a foreign language. Such as French, German, or Japanese. These are the most useful languages, he told her. In addition to preparing her to use the language, the classes would expose her to the history, culture, and politics of another country. Factors that often affect business decisions. After talking with Professor Will, Maria was convinced. To begin immediately to prepare for her business career by studying a foreign language.

20

Revise comma splices and fused sentences.

Comma splices and fused sentences, more commonly known as "run-on sentences," are independent clauses that have not been joined correctly. An independent clause is a word group that can stand alone as a sentence. (See 60.) When two independent clauses appear in one sentence, they must be joined in one of these ways:

— with a comma and a coordinating conjunction (*and, but, or, nor, for, so, yet*)

— with a semicolon (or occasionally a colon or a dash)

When a writer puts no mark of punctuation and no coordinating conjunction between independent clauses, the result is a fused sentence.

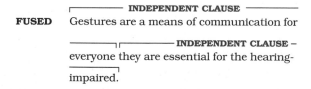

FUSED

Gestures are a means of communication for everyone they are essential for the hearing-impaired.

A far more common error is the comma splice — independent clauses joined by a comma without a coordinating conjunction. In some comma splices, the comma appears alone.

COMMA SPLICE   Gestures are a means of communication for everyone, they are essential for the hearing-impaired.

In other comma splices, the comma is accompanied by a joining word that is *not* a coordinating conjunction. There are only seven coordinating conjunctions in English: *and, but, or, nor, for, so, yet.* Notice that all of these words are short—only two or three letters long.

> **COMMA**   Gestures are an important means of communication
> **SPLICE**   for everyone, however, they are essential for the
>   hearing-impaired.

In the second example, *however* is a conjunctive adverb, not a coordinating conjunction. When a conjunctive adverb such as *however, therefore,* or *moreover* or a transitional phrase such as *in fact* or *for example* appears between independent clauses, it must be preceded by a semicolon. (See page 236 for a more complete list of these words and phrases.)

To correct a fused sentence or a comma splice, you have four choices:

1. Use a comma and a coordinating conjunction (*and, but, or, nor, for, so, yet*).

▶ Gestures are a means of communication for everyone, ~~they~~ *but* they

   are essential for the hearing-impaired.

2. Use a semicolon (or, if appropriate, a colon or a dash). A semicolon may be used alone; it can also be accompanied by a conjunctive adverb or transitional phrase.

▶ Gestures are a means of communication for everyone/*;* they

   are essential for the hearing-impaired.

▶ Gestures are a means of communication for everyone/ *; however,* they

   are essential for the hearing-impaired.

3. Make the clauses into separate sentences.

▶ Gestures are a means of communication for everyone. they

are essential for the hearing-impaired.

4. Restructure the sentence, perhaps by subordinating one of the clauses.

Although gestures
▶ ~~Gestures~~ are a means of communication for everyone, they

are essential for the hearing-impaired.

One of these revision techniques will often work better than the others for a particular sentence. The fourth technique, the one requiring the most extensive revision, is frequently the most effective.

20a Consider separating the clauses with a comma and a coordinating conjunction.

There are seven coordinating conjunctions in English: *and, but, or, nor, for, so,* and *yet.* When a coordinating conjunction joins independent clauses, it is usually preceded by a comma. (See 32a.)

and
▶ The paramedic asked where I was hurt, as soon as I told him,

he cut up the leg of my favorite pair of jeans.

▶ Many government officials privately admit that the polygraph
yet
is unreliable, ~~however,~~ they continue to use it as a security

measure.

However is a conjunctive adverb, not a coordinating conjunction, so it cannot be used with only a comma to join independent clauses. (See 20b.)

20b Consider separating the clauses with a semicolon (or, if appropriate, with a colon or a dash).

When the independent clauses are closely related and their relation is clear without a coordinating conjunction, a semicolon is an acceptable method of revision. (See 34a.)

▶ Tragedy depicts the individual confronted with the fact of

death/;comedy depicts the adaptability and ongoing survival

of human society.

A semicolon is required between independent clauses that have been linked with a conjunctive adverb (such as *however, therefore,* or *moreover*) or with a transitional phrase (such as *in fact* or *for example*). For a longer list, see the chart on page 236. (See also 34b.)

▶ The timber wolf looks much like a large German shepherd/;

however, the wolf has longer legs, larger feet, a wider head,

and a long, bushy tail.

▶ Everyone in my outfit had a specific job/;as a matter of fact,

most of the officers had three or four duties.

If the first independent clause introduces the second or if the second clause summarizes or explains the first, a colon or a dash may be an appropriate method of revision. (See 35b and 39a.) In formal writing, the colon is usually preferred to the dash.

▶ The experience taught Juanita a lesson/: ~~she~~ *She* could not

always rely on her parents to bail her out of trouble.

20c Consider making the clauses into separate sentences.

▶ Why shouldn't a divorced wife receive half of her husband's

pension and other retirement benefits/? ~~she~~ *She* was her

husband's partner for many years.

Since one independent clause is a question and the other is a statement, they should be separate sentences.

▶ I gave the necessary papers to the police officer. *T*hen he said

I would have to accompany him to the police station, where a

counselor would talk with me and call my parents.

Because the second independent clause is quite long, a sensible revision is to use separate sentences.

20d Consider restructuring the sentence, perhaps by subordinating one of the clauses.

If one of the independent clauses is less important than the other, turn it into a subordinate clause or phrase. (For more about subordination, see 8, especially the chart on page 119.)

▶ Lindsey is a top competitor ~~she~~ ^{who} has been riding since the age

of seven.

▶ ^{When the} ~~The~~ new health plan was explained to the employees in my

division, everyone agreed to give it a try.

▶ Saturday afternoon Julie came running into the house/ ~~she~~

~~wanted~~ to get permission to go to the park.

Minor ideas in these sentences are now expressed in subordinate
clauses or phrases.

LOOKING AT YOURSELF AS A WRITER
Comma splices and fused sentences

More commonly known as "run-on-sentences," comma splices
and fused sentences are considered serious errors because
they suggest that the writer doesn't understand basic sentence
structure. Unfortunately, comma splices are fairly common,
even among writers who are otherwise reasonably proficient. If
you frequently write comma splices or fused sentences, consider the following possible causes and cures.

CAUSE Because you want your writing to flow smoothly
from one idea to the next, you tend to string ideas
together with commas. Comma splices sound better
to you than a series of short, choppy sentences or a
chain of ideas strung together with *and*'s.

CURE You are right to want your writing to flow, but you'll
need to turn to other strategies for making this
happen. One of the best strategies for achieving
sentence flow is subordination. See 20d and 8a
and 8b.

Comma splices and fused sentences (continued)

CAUSE Feeling that a sentence should be a certain length, you tend to keep it going until it has reached that length.

CURE Make punctuation decisions based on sentence structure, not length. The following punctuation rules show you ways of joining independent clauses correctly: 32a, 34a, 34b, 35a, 35b, 38a.

CAUSE You enjoy using formal-sounding transition words like *therefore, however,* and *moreover,* and you confuse these words with coordinating conjunctions meaning the same thing (*so, but,* and).

CURE In most contexts, prefer the simpler coordinating conjunctions (*and, but, or, nor, for, so, yet*), which do not create comma splices or fused sentences.

CAUSE You are confused by the term "comma splice," which focuses your attention on the comma and prevents you from seeing several possibilities for revision.

CURE The term "comma splice" is perhaps unfortunate, since the problem it names is not a simple comma error. If the term "run-on sentence" makes more sense to you, use it instead. Whatever you call the error, just be aware that there are several ways to fix it — and that some revision strategies will work better than others for achieving the effect you were aiming for when you wrote the sentence.

EXERCISE 20–1

Revise any comma splices or fused sentences using the method of revision suggested in brackets. Revisions of lettered sentences appear in the back of the book. Example:

Because
^Orville was obsessed with his weight, he rarely ate anything

sweet and delicious. [*Restructure the sentence.*]

a. The city had one public swimming pool, it stayed packed with children all summer long. [*Restructure the sentence.*]
b. The building is being renovated, therefore at times we have no heat, water, or electricity. [*Use a comma and a coordinating conjunction.*]
c. Why should we pay taxes to support public transportation, we prefer to save energy dollars by carpooling. [*Make two sentences.*]
d. Suddenly there was a loud silence, the shelling had stopped. [*Use a semicolon.*]
e. In Garvey's time the caste system in the West Indies was simple, the lighter the skin tone, the higher the status. [*Use a colon.*]

1. For the first time in her adult life, Lucia had time to waste, she could spend a whole day curled up with a good book. [*Use a semicolon.*]
2. Be sure to take your credit card, Disney has a way of making you want to spend money. [*Restructure the sentence.*]
3. The next time an event is canceled because of bad weather, don't blame the meteorologist, blame nature. [*Make two sentences.*]
4. While we were walking down Grover Avenue, Gary told us about his Aunt Elsinia, she was an extraordinary woman. [*Restructure the sentence.*]
5. The president of Algeria was standing next to the podium he was waiting to be introduced. [*Restructure the sentence.*]
6. On most days I had only enough money for bus fare, lunch was a luxury I could not afford. [*Use a semicolon.*]
7. There was one major reason for John's wealth, his grandfather had been a multimillionaire. [*Use a colon.*]
8. The homeless shelter was filled with alcoholics, drug addicts, and crazy people, what kind of environment was this for my four-year-old daughter. [*Make two sentences.*]
9. Of the many geysers in Yellowstone National Park, the most famous is Old Faithful, it sometimes reaches 150 feet in height. [*Restructure the sentence.*]

10. Wind power for the home is a supplementary source of energy, it can be combined with electricity, gas, or solar energy. [*Restructure the sentence.*]

EXERCISE 20–2

Revise any comma splices or fused sentences using a technique that you find effective. If a sentence is correct, write "correct" after it. Revisions of lettered sentences appear in the back of the book. Example:

> I ran the three blocks as fast as I could, ~~however~~ *but* I still
>
> missed the bus.

a. The trail up Mount Finegold was declared impassable, therefore, we decided to return to our hotel a day early.

b. The duck hunter set out his decoys in the shallow bay and then settled in to wait for the first real bird to alight.

c. The instructor never talked to the class, she just assigned busywork and sat at her desk reading the newspaper.

d. Researchers were studying the fertility of Texas land tortoises they X-rayed all the female tortoises to see how many eggs they had.

e. The suburbs seemed cold, they lacked the warmth and excitement of our Italian neighborhood.

1. Are you able to endure boredom, isolation, and potential violence, then the army may well be the adventure for you.

2. Jet funny cars are powered by jet engines, these engines are the same type that are used on fighter aircraft and helicopters.

3. If one of the dogs should happen to fall through the ice, it would be cut loose from the team and left to its fate, the sled drivers could not endanger the rest of the team for just one dog.

4. The volunteers worked hard to clean up and restore calm after the tornado, as a matter of fact, many of them did not sleep for the first three days of the emergency.

5. Nuclear power plants produce energy by fission, a process that generates radioactive waste.

Reviewing your writing for comma splices and fused sentences

First look for the most common trouble spots:

CONJUNCTIVE ADVERB OR TRANSITIONAL PHRASE

also	in addition	now
as a result	in fact	of course
besides	in other words	on the other hand
consequently	in the first place	otherwise
finally	meanwhile	still
for example	moreover	then
for instance	nevertheless	therefore
furthermore	next	thus
however		

▶ We usually think of children as innocent and guileless /;
 however, they are often cruel and unjust.

EXAMPLE OR EXPLANATION IN SECOND CLAUSE

▶ Martin looked out the window in astonishment: He had
 never seen snow before.

CLAUSES EXPRESSING CONTRAST

▶ Most of his contemporaries had made plans for their
 retirement , but Tom had not.

PRONOUN AS SUBJECT OF SECOND CLAUSE

▶ Claudia , who was full of energy and enthusiasm, ~~she~~ tackled
 the job at once.

Comma splices and fused sentences *(continued)*

Next test your sentences for correctness:

Does the sentence contain two independent clauses (word groups that can be punctuated as sentences)?

NO No problem

YES

Are the clauses joined with a comma and a coordinating conjunction (*and, but, or, nor, for, so,* or *yet*)?

YES No problem

NO

Are the clauses joined with a semicolon?

YES No problem

NO

Revise.
It is a comma splice or
a fused sentence.

If you find an error, choose an effective method of revision. See 20a–d for specific revision strategies.

6. After days of struggling with her dilemma, Rosa came to a decision, she would sacrifice herself for her people and her cause.
7. The Carrier Air Wing Eight, called CAG-8, is made up of ten squadrons, each has its own mission and role.
8. We didn't trust her, she had lied before.
9. I pushed open the first door with my back, turning to open the second door, I encountered a young woman in a wheelchair holding it open for me.
10. If you want to lose weight and keep it off, consider this advice, don't try to take it off faster than you put it on.

EXERCISE 20–3

In the following rough draft, repair any sentence fragments and revise any comma splices or fused sentences. (See 19 and 20, especially the charts on pages 224 and 236.)

Teri, Karen, and I took introductory foreign language courses last year. Each of us was interested in learning a different language, however, we were all trying to accomplish the same goal. To begin mastering a new language. When we compared our classes and the results, we found that each course used a quite different approach to language learning.

In my Spanish course, Professor Cruz introduced lists of new vocabulary words every week, she devoted half of each class to grammar rules. I spent most of my time memorizing lists and rules. In addition to vocabulary and grammar study, I read passages of Spanish literature. Translating them into English. And wrote responses to the reading in Spanish. The only time I spoke Spanish, however, was when I translated a passage or answered questions in class. Although Professor Cruz spoke Spanish for the entire class period.

Instead of memorizing vocabulary lists and grammar rules and translating reading selections, Teri's Portuguese class rehearsed simple dialogues useful for tourists. Conducting every class in Portuguese, Teri's professor asked students to recite the dialogues, she corrected the students' pronunciation and grammar as they spoke. Teri's homework was to go to the language lab, she listened to various dialogues and practiced ordering meals, asking for directions to a train station, and so on. Teri learned to pronounce the language well, she mastered the simple dialogues. But she did not get much practice in reading.

Karen took a course in Russian, her experience was different from Teri's and from mine. Her professor asked the students to read articles from the Soviet press. And to listen to recent news programs from the Soviet Union. In class, students discussed the articles and programs. Teri's professor encouraged the students to use Russian as much as possible in their discussions, she also allowed them to use English. Other class activities included writing letters in response to articles in Soviet publications and role playing to duplicate real-life situations. Such as a discussion with a neighbor about the lack of meat in the shops. Karen learned to understand spoken Russian and to speak the language, in addition, she regularly practiced reading and writing. Although her Russian course was difficult, Karen thinks it will help her when she visits the Soviet Union this summer.

Of the three of us, Karen is the most positive about her course. She is certain that she will further develop her language skills when visiting the Soviet Union, moreover, she is confident that she can communicate without struggling too much with a dictionary. Teri and I feel less positive about our courses. Because we both have forgotten the vocabulary and grammar rules. If I were asked to read a passage in Spanish now, I couldn't, Teri says she would not understand Portuguese or be able to respond to a single dialogue if she had to.

21

Make subjects and verbs agree.

In the present tense, verbs agree with their subjects in number (singular or plural) and in person (first, second, or third). The present-tense ending -*s* is used on a verb if its subject is third-person singular; otherwise the verb takes no ending.

Consider, for example, the present-tense forms of the verb *give:*

	SINGULAR	PLURAL
FIRST PERSON	I give	we give
SECOND PERSON	you give	you give
THIRD PERSON	he/she/it gives	they give
	Alison gives	parents give

The verb *be* varies from this pattern; unlike any other verb, it has special forms in *both* the present and the past tense.

PRESENT-TENSE FORMS OF *BE*		PAST-TENSE FORMS OF *BE*	
I am	we are	I was	we were
you are	you are	you were	you were
he/she/it is	they are	he/she/it was	they were

Speakers of standard English know by ear that *he talks, she has,* and *it doesn't* (not *he talk, she have,* and *it don't*) are the standard forms. For such speakers, problems with subject-verb agreement arise only in certain tricky situations, which are detailed in this section.

If you don't trust your ear, consult 27c, which contrasts the present-tense verb systems of standard and nonstandard English. Also see 58a and 58b on subjects and verbs.

21a Make the verb agree with its subject, not with a word that comes between.

Word groups often come between the subject and the verb. Such word groups, usually modifying the subject, may contain a noun that at first appears to be the subject. By mentally stripping away such modifiers, you can isolate the noun that is in fact the subject.

The *tulips* in the pot on the balcony *need* watering.

▶ High levels of air pollution causes / damage to the respiratory

tract.

The subject is *levels*, not *pollution*. Strip away the phrase *of air pollution* to hear the correct verb: *levels cause.*

Costs
▶ A good set of golf clubs ~~cost~~ about eight hundred dollars.
                          ^

The subject is *set*, not *clubs*. Strip away the phrase *of golf clubs* to hear the correct verb: *set costs.*

NOTE: Phrases beginning with the prepositions *as well as, in addition to, accompanied by, together with,* and *along with* do not make a singular subject plural.

                                              was
▶ The governor, as well as his press secretary, ~~were~~ shot.
                                               ^

To emphasize that two people were shot, the writer could use *and* instead: *The governor and his press secretary were shot.*

21b Treat most compound subjects connected by *and* as plural.

A subject with two or more parts is said to be compound. If the parts are connected by *and*, the subject is nearly always plural.

⌐   ⌐
Leon and Jan often *jog* together.

                                         are
▶ Remember that your safety and welfare ~~is~~ in your own hands.
                                        ^

The compound subject *safety and welfare* is plural, requiring the verb *are.*

▶ Jill's natural ability and her desire to help others ~~has~~ *have* led to a
career in the ministry.

Ability and desire is a plural subject, so its verb should be *have*.

EXCEPTIONS: When the parts of the subject form a single unit
or when they refer to the same person or thing, treat the subject as singular.

Strawberries and cream was a last-minute addition to the menu.

Sue's friend and adviser was surprised by her decision.

When a compound subject is preceded by *each* or *every*, treat
it as singular.

Each tree, shrub, and vine needs to be sprayed.

Every car, truck, and van is required to pass inspection.

This exception does not apply when a compound subject is
followed by *each: Alan and Marcia each have different ideas.*

21c With compound subjects connected by *or* or *nor*
(or by *either . . . or* or *neither . . . nor*), make the verb agree
with the part of the subject nearer to the verb.

A driver's *license* or credit *card is* required.

A driver's *license* or two credit *cards are* required.

▶ If a relative or neighbor ~~are~~ *is* abusing a child, notify the police
immediately.

▶ Neither the instructor nor her students ~~was~~ *were* able to find the

classroom.

The verb must be matched with the part of the subject closer to it: *neighbor is* in the first sentence, *students were* in the second.

NOTE: If one part of the subject is singular and the other is plural, put the plural one last to avoid awkwardness.

21d Treat most indefinite pronouns as singular.

Indefinite pronouns are pronouns that do not refer to specific persons or things. The following commonly used indefinite pronouns are singular:

any	each	everybody	none	someone
anyone	either	everything	no one	something
anybody	everyone	neither		

Many of these words appear to have plural meanings, and they are often treated as such in casual speech. In formal written English, however, they are nearly always treated as singular.

Everyone on the team *supports* the coach.

▶ Each of the furrows ~~have~~ *has* been seeded.

▶ Everybody who signed up for the ski trip ~~were~~ *was* taking lessons.

The subjects of these sentences are *each* and *everybody.* These indefinite pronouns are third-person singular, so the verbs must be *has* and *was.*

The indefinite pronouns *none* and *neither* are considered singular when used alone.

None is immune from this disease.

Neither is able to attend.

When these pronouns are followed by prepositional phrases with a plural meaning, however, usage varies. Some experts insist on treating the pronouns as singular, but many writers disagree. It is safer to treat them as singular.

None of these trades *requires* a college education.

Neither of those pejoratives *fits* Professor Brady.

A few indefinite pronouns (*all, any, some*) are singular or plural depending on the noun or pronoun they refer to.

Some of the *lemonade has* disappeared.

Some of the *rocks were* slippery.

21e Treat collective nouns as singular unless the meaning is clearly plural.

Collective nouns such as *jury, committee, audience, crowd, class, troop, family,* and *couple* name a class or a group. In American English, collective nouns are nearly always treated as singular: They emphasize the group as a unit. Occasionally, when there is some reason to draw attention to the individual members of the group, a collective noun may be treated as plural. (Also see 22b.)

SINGULAR   The *class respects* the teacher.

PLURAL   The *class are* debating among themselves.

To underscore the notion of individuality in the second sentence, many writers would add a clearly plural noun such as *members:*

PLURAL   The class *members are* debating among themselves.

meets
▶ The scout troop ~~meet~~ in our basement on Tuesdays.

The troop as a whole meets in the basement; there is no reason to draw attention to its individual members.

were
▶ A young couple ~~was~~ arguing about politics while holding hands.

The meaning is clearly plural. Only individuals can argue and hold hands.

NOTE: The phrase *the number* is treated as singular, *a number* as plural.

SINGULAR   *The number* of school-age children *is* declining.

PLURAL   *A number* of children *are* attending the wedding.

NOTE: When units of measurement are used collectively, treat them as singular; when they refer to individual persons or things, treat them as plural.

SINGULAR   *Three-fourths* of the pie *has* been eaten.

PLURAL   *One-fourth* of the drivers *were* drunk.

21f **Make the verb agree with its subject even when the subject follows the verb.**

Verbs ordinarily follow subjects. When this normal order is reversed, it is easy to become confused. Sentences beginning with *there is* or *there are* (or *there was* or *there were*) are inverted; the subject follows the verb.

There *are* surprisingly few *children* in our neighborhood.

▶ There ~~was~~ a social worker and a crew of twenty volunteers at
   were

the scene of the accident.

The subject *worker and crew* is plural, so the verb must be *were*.

Occasionally you may decide to invert a sentence for variety or effect. When you do so, check to make sure that your subject and verb agree.

▶ At the back of the room ~~is~~ a small aquarium and an
   are

enormous terrarium.

The subject *aquarium and terrarium* is plural, so the verb must be *are*.

21g **Make the verb agree with its subject, not with a subject complement.**

One basic sentence pattern in English consists of a subject, a linking verb, and a subject complement: *Jack is a securities lawyer.* Because the subject complement names or describes the subject (*Jack*), it is sometimes mistaken for the subject. (See 58b on subject complements.)

These *problems* are a way to test your skill.

▶ A tent and a sleeping bag ~~is~~ *are* the required equipment for all

campers.

Tent and bag is the subject, not *equipment*.

▶ A major force in today's economy ~~are~~ *is* women — as earners,

consumers, and investors.

Force is the subject, not *women*. If the corrected version seems awkward, make *women* the subject: *Women are a major force in today's economy — as earners, consumers, and investors.*

21h *Who, which,* and *that* take verbs that agree with their antecedents.

Like most pronouns, the relative pronouns *who, which,* and *that* have antecedents, nouns or pronouns to which they refer. Relative pronouns used as subjects of subordinate clauses take verbs that agree with their antecedents.

Take a *suit that travels* well.

Problems can arise with the constructions *one of the* and *only one of the.* As a rule, treat *one of the* constructions as plural, *only one of the* constructions as singular.

▶ Our ability to use language is one of the things that sets us

apart from animals.

The antecedent of *that* is *things,* not *one.* Several things set us apart from animals.

▶ Dr. Barker knew that Frank was the only one of his sons who

   was

   ~~were~~ responsible enough to handle the estate.

The antecedent of *who* is *one*, not *sons*. Only one son was responsible enough.

LOOKING AT YOURSELF AS A WRITER
Subject-verb agreement

Subject-verb agreement causes trouble for most of us, largely because of the many tricky contexts that tempt us to choose the wrong verb. But if you find subject-verb agreement unusually troublesome, consider possible sources of your difficulties.

CAUSE   You are confused about the rules on when to use the -*s* form of a verb. For example, you may think that a "plural" verb takes an -*s* ending, just like most plural nouns. Or you may think that *all* singular subjects demand a verb with an -*s* ending, not just third-person singular subjects.

CURE   Trust the chart on page 253. Don't let yourself get confused by half-learned rules.

CAUSE   You can't find the simple subject of the sentence (or clause).

CURE   You are at a serious disadvantage as a writer if you cannot find the subject of a sentence. Turn to 58a for help. If you need more practice, check with your instructor or a writing center tutor.

CAUSE   You aren't sure whether the subject is singular or plural.

CURE   Look up the appropriate rule in 21. There is no need to memorize all of these rules; just know where to find them.

See also "Looking at Yourself as a Writer: Problems with -*s* endings on verbs" (p. 299).

21i Words such as *athletics, economics, mathematics, physics, statistics, measles, mumps,* and *news* are usually singular, despite their plural form.

▶ Statistics ~~are~~ *is* among the most difficult courses in our program.

EXCEPTION: When they describe separate items rather than a collective body of knowledge, words such as *athletics, mathematics, physics,* and *statistics* are plural: *The statistics on school retention rates are impressive.*

21j Titles of works and words mentioned as words are singular.

▶ *Lost Cities* ~~describe~~ *describes* the discoveries of many ancient civilizations.

▶ *Controlled substances* ~~are~~ *is* a euphemism for illegal drugs.

EXERCISE 21–1

Underline the subject (or compound subject) and then select the verb that agrees with it. (If you have difficulty identifying the subject, consult 58a.) Answers to lettered sentences appear in the back of the book. Example:

Someone in the audience (has/have) volunteered to

participate in the experiment.

a. Your friendship over the years and your support on a wide variety of national issues (has/have) meant a great deal to us.

b. Two-week-old onion rings in the ashtray (is/are) not a pretty sight.

c. Each of the twenty-five actors (was/were) given a five-minute try-out, and only three of us were called back for a more intensive audition.

d. The main source of income for Trinidad (is/are) oil and pitch.

e. When Governor John White returned to Roanoke, he found that there (was/were) no signs of life or traces of the settlers he had left behind.

1. Neither the professor nor his assistants (was/were) able to solve the mystery of the eerie glow in the laboratory.

2. Quilts made by the Amish (commands/command) high prices.

3. Located at the south end of the complex (was/were) an Olympic-size pool, two basketball courts, and four tennis courts.

4. The most significant lifesaving device in automobiles (is/are) seat belts.

5. The old iron gate and the brick wall (makes/make) our court-house appear older than its fifty years.

6. The dangers of smoking (is/are) well documented.

7. There (was/were) a Peanuts cartoon and a few Mother Goose rhymes pinned to the bulletin board.

8. When food supplies (was/were) scarce, the slaves had to make do with the less desirable parts of the animals.

9. The slaughter of pandas for their much-sought-after pelts (has/have) caused the panda population to decline dramatically.

10. Hidden under the floorboards (was/were) a bag of coins and a rusty sword.

EXERCISE 21–2

Edit the following sentences for problems with subject-verb agreement. If a sentence is correct, write "correct" after it. Answers to lettered sentences appear in the back of the book. Example:

> Jack's first days in the infantry ~~was~~ *were* grueling.

a. High concentrations of carbon monoxide results in headaches, dizziness, unconsciousness, and even death.

b. Not until my interview with Dr. Hwang were other possibilities opened to me.
c. After hearing the evidence and the closing arguments, the jury was sequestered.
d. Crystal chandeliers, polished floors, and a new oil painting has transformed Sandra's apartment.
e. Either Gertrude or Alice take the dog out for its nightly walk.

1. Small pieces of fermented bread was placed around the edge of the platter.
2. Of particular concern are penicillin and tetracycline, antibiotics used to make animals more resistant to disease.
3. The presence of certain bacteria in our bodies is one of the factors that determine our overall health.
4. Nearly everyone on the panel favor the arms control agreement.
5. Every year a number of kokanee salmon, not native to the region, is introduced into Flathead Lake.
6. Measles is a contagious childhood disease.
7. Neither Paul nor Arthur is usually here on Sundays.
8. At MGM Studios at Disney World, the wonders of moviemaking comes alive.
9. SEACON is the only one of our war games that emphasize scientific and technical issues.
10. The key program of Alcoholics Anonymous are the twelve steps to recovery.

EXERCISE 21-3

In the following paragraphs, circle the verb in parentheses that agrees with its subject.

Natalie, together with many other students in her educational philosophy class, (supports/support) a program to standardize cultural literacy in the high school curriculum. Natalie and those who agree with her (argues/argue) that students should have a broad background of shared knowledge. This shared knowledge (helps/help) bind a culture together and (encourages/encourage) pride in our country's heritage. In deciding which knowledge to include in a

Reviewing your writing for problems with subject-verb agreement

First look for the most common trouble spots:

WORDS BETWEEN THE SUBJECT AND VERB (21a)

A *line* of cars behind the snowplows *stretches* a mile.

COMPOUND SUBJECTS WITH *AND* — USUALLY PLURAL (21b)

Nan's *skills and experience qualify* her for the job.

COMPOUND SUBJECTS WITH *OR* OR *NOR* (21c)

Dr. Brown or *Dr. Mullings* usually *works* the late shift.

Neither Ms. Cox nor her *students want* to attend.

SINGULAR INDEFINITE PRONOUNS (21d)

any	each	everybody	none	someone
anyone	either	everything	no one	something
anybody	everyone	neither		

None of the suspects *has* confessed.

COLLECTIVE NOUNS — USUALLY SINGULAR (21e)

| audience | club | couple | family | troop |
| class | committee | crowd | jury | |

The philosophy *club* usually *meets* in the seminar room.

SUBJECT AFTER THE VERB (21f)

There *are* several street *people* living under Key Bridge.

Subject-verb agreement (continued)

Then test for the correct verb form.

Once you have found the subject and decided whether it is singular or plural, your ear will probably tell you which form of the verb to choose. If you don't trust your ear, consult the models here. (See also 27c.)

PRESENT-TENSE FORMS OF *LOVE* (A TYPICAL VERB)

	SINGULAR		PLURAL	
FIRST PERSON	I	love	we	love
SECOND PERSON	you	love	you	love
THIRD PERSON	he/she/it	loves	they	love

PRESENT-TENSE FORMS OF *HAVE*

	SINGULAR		PLURAL	
FIRST PERSON	I	have	we	have
SECOND PERSON	you	have	you	have
THIRD PERSON	he/she/it	has	they	have

PRESENT-TENSE FORMS OF *DO*

	SINGULAR		PLURAL	
FIRST PERSON	I	do/don't	we	do/don't
SECOND PERSON	you	do/don't	you	do/don't
THIRD PERSON	he/she/it	does/doesn't	they	do/don't

PRESENT- AND PAST-TENSE FORMS OF *BE*

	SINGULAR		PLURAL	
FIRST PERSON	I	am/was	we	are/were
SECOND PERSON	you	are/were	you	are/were
THIRD PERSON	he/she/it	is/was	they	are/were

standardized curriculum, advocates of cultural literacy (looks/ look) primarily to the past: If a book (has/have) stood the test of time, they say, it is a part of our culture worth preserving.

Kimberly and several other students in the class (opposes/oppose) the idea of a standardized high school curriculum. They argue that the content of such a curriculum is not easily determined in a multicultural society, especially in subjects such as sociology, history, and literature that (examines/examine) values and beliefs. Kimberly and other opponents of cultural literacy (believes/believe) that knowledge survives over time because a dominant culture preserves it. Kimberly (doesn't/don't) question the value of that knowledge, but she recognizes that the dominant culture over the years (neglects/neglect) to preserve and transmit knowledge that is important to less powerful cultures. The important factor in this debate (is/are) the students: Each of them (deserves/ deserve) attention and respect. Kimberly worries that plans to standardize cultural literacy (ignores/ignore) the cultures of too many students. She represents those in her class who (feels/feel) that a true cultural literacy program has to include knowledge from many cultures and that standardizing a multi-cultural curriculum may not be practical on any large scale.

22

Make pronouns and antecedents agree.

A pronoun is a word that substitutes for a noun. (See 57b.) Many pronouns have antecedents, nouns or pronouns to which they refer. A pronoun and its antecedent agree when they are both singular or both plural.

SINGULAR   *Dr. Sarah Simms* finished *her* rounds.

PLURAL   The *doctors* finished *their* rounds.

> **ESL NOTE:** The pronouns *he, his, she, her, it,* and *its* must
> agree in gender (masculine, feminine, or neuter) with their
> antecedents, not with the words they modify.
>
> *Jane* visited *her* [not *his*] brother in Denver.

22a   Do not use plural pronouns to refer to singular antecedents.

Writers are frequently tempted to use plural pronouns to refer
to two kinds of singular antecedents: indefinite pronouns and
generic nouns.

Indefinite pronouns

Indefinite pronouns refer to nonspecific persons or things.
Even though some of the following indefinite pronouns may
seem to have plural meanings, treat them as singular in formal English.

any	each	everything	no one
anybody	either	neither	somebody
anyone	everybody	nobody	someone
anything	everyone	none	something

In class *everyone* performs at *his or her* [not *their*] fitness level.

When a plural pronoun refers mistakenly to a singular
indefinite pronoun, you can usually choose one of three options for revision.

1. Replace the plural pronoun with *he or she* (or *his or her*).
2. Make the antecedent plural.

3. Rewrite the sentence so that no problem of agreement exists.

▶ When someone has been drinking, ~~they are~~ *he or she is* likely to speed.

▶ When ~~someone has~~ *drivers have* been drinking, they are likely to speed.

▶ ~~When someone~~ *A driver who* has been drinking/ ~~they are~~ *is* likely to speed.

Because the *he or she* construction is wordy, often the second or third revision strategy is more effective. Be aware that the traditional use of *he* (or *his*) to refer to persons of either sex is now widely considered sexist. (See 17f.)

Generic nouns

A generic noun represents a typical member of a group, such as a typical student, or any member of a group, such as any lawyer. Although generic nouns may seem to have plural meanings, they are singular.

Every *runner* must train rigorously if *he or she wants* [not *they want*] to excel.

When a plural pronoun refers mistakenly to a generic noun, you will usually have the same three revision options as just mentioned for indefinite pronouns.

▶ A medical student must study hard if ~~they want~~ *he or she wants* to succeed.

▶ ~~A medical student~~ *Medical students* must study hard if they want to succeed.

▶ A medical student must study hard ~~if they want~~ to succeed.

22b Treat collective nouns as singular unless the meaning is clearly plural.

Collective nouns such as *jury, committee, audience, crowd, class, troop, family, team,* and *couple* name a class or a group. Ordinarily the group functions as a unit, so the noun should be treated as singular; if the members of the group function as individuals, however, the noun should be treated as plural. (See also 21e.)

AS A UNIT The *committee* granted *its* permission to build.

AS INDIVIDUALS The *committee* put *their* signatures on the document.

▶ The jury has reached ~~their~~ *its* decision.

There is no reason to draw attention to the individual members of the jury, so *jury* should be treated as singular. Notice also that the writer treated the noun as singular when choosing the verb *has,* so for consistency the pronoun must be *its.*

▶ The audience shouted "Bravo" and stamped ~~its~~ *their* feet.

It is difficult to see how the audience as a unit can stamp *its* feet. The meaning here is clearly plural, requiring *their.*

22c Treat most compound antecedents connected by *and* as plural.

Joanne and John moved to the mountains, where *they* built a log cabin.

22d With compound antecedents connected by *or* or *nor* (or by *either . . . or* or *neither . . . nor*), make the pronoun agree with the nearer antecedent.

> Either *Bruce* or *James* should receive first prize for *his* sculpture.

> Neither the *mouse* nor the *rats* could find *their* way through the maze.

NOTE: If one of the antecedents is singular and the other plural, as in the second example, put the plural one last to avoid awkwardness.

EXCEPTION: If one antecedent is male and the other female, do not follow the traditional rule. The sentence *Either Bruce or Ann should receive the blue ribbon for her sculpture* makes no sense. The best solution is to recast the sentence: *The blue ribbon for best sculpture should go to Bruce or Ann.*

EXERCISE 22–1

Edit the following sentences to eliminate problems with pronoun-antecedent agreement. Most of the sentences can be revised in more than one way, so experiment before choosing a solution. If a sentence is correct, write "correct" after it. Revisions of lettered sentences appear in the back of the book. Example:

> *Recruiters*
> ~~The recruiter~~ may tell the truth, but there is much that they
>   ∧
> choose not to tell.

a. I can be standing in front of a Xerox machine, with parts scattered around my feet, and someone will ask me to let them make a copy.

LOOKING AT YOURSELF AS A WRITER
Pronoun-antecedent agreement

Like all writers, at times you will find yourself wrestling with the problem of pronoun-antecedent agreement. Here is why the problem is so pervasive.

CAUSE You hear faulty pronoun agreement in speech all the time, and you probably don't see much wrong with it, since it rarely interferes with clarity.

CURE Be aware that standards in writing tend to be stricter than those in speech.

CAUSE You don't want to use sexist English, and you find *he or she* awkward — so you resort to using plural pronouns such as *their* with singular antecedents such as *swimmer*.

CURE Choose plural antecedents or find a clever way around the problem. The chart on page 261 shows several possibilities.

b. The sophomore class elects its president tomorrow.
c. The instructor has asked everyone to bring their own tools to carpentry class.
d. An eighteenth-century architect was also a classical scholar; they were often at the forefront of archeological research.
e. On the first day of class, Mr. Bhatti asked each individual why they wanted to stop smoking.

1. If a driver refuses to take a blood or breath test, he or she will have their licenses suspended for six months.
2. Why should we care about the timber wolf? One answer is that they have proven beneficial to humans by killing off weakened prey.

Reviewing your writing for problems with pronoun-antecedent agreement

First look for the most common trouble spots:

INDEFINITE PRONOUNS (SINGULAR) (22a)

any	each	everyone	none	someone
anybody	either	everything	no one	something
anyone	everybody	neither		

No one will see a salary increase until *he or she has* [not *they have*] been employed for two years.

GENERIC NOUNS (SINGULAR) (22a)

A generic noun names a typical person or thing (such as a typical teacher) or any person or thing (such as any employee of a company).

An adult panda must consume ninety pounds of bamboo if *it is* [not *they are*] to remain healthy.

COLLECTIVE NOUNS (SINGULAR UNLESS THE MEANING IS CLEARLY PLURAL) (22b)

audience	committee	couple	majority	team
class	crowd	family	minority	troop

The *committee* selected *its* [not *their*] new chairperson last night.

Choose an effective revision strategy that avoids sexist language.

Because many readers object to sexist language, avoid the use of *he, him,* and *his* as shorthand for *he or she, him or her,* and

Pronoun-antecedent agreement *(continued)*

his or hers. Also try to be sparing in your use of *he or she* and *his or her,* since these expressions can become awkward, especially when repeated several times in a short passage. Where possible, seek out more graceful alternatives.

1. Use an occasional *he or she* (or *his or her*).

▶ In our office, everyone works at ~~their~~ own pace. *(his or her)*

2. Make the antecedent plural.

▶ ~~An employee~~ on extended leave may continue their life *(Employees)*

insurance.

3. Recast the sentence.

▶ The amount of annual leave a federal worker may

accrue depends on their length of service.

▶ ~~If a~~ child ~~is~~ born to parents who are both *(A)*

schizophrenic, ~~they have~~ a high chance of being *(has)*

schizophrenic.

▶ A year later someone finally admitted ~~that they were~~ *(to being)*

involved in the kidnapping.

▶ I was taught that no one could escape the fires of *(who wanted to reach heaven)*

purgatory. ~~if they wanted to reach heaven.~~

3. No one should be forced to sacrifice their prized possession — life — for someone else.

4. Seven qualified Hispanic agents applied, each hoping for a career move that would let them use their language and cultural training on more than just translations and drug deals; the job went to a non-Hispanic who was taking a crash course in Spanish.

5. If anyone notices any suspicious activity, they should report it to the police.

6. The crowd grew until they filled not only the plaza but also the surrounding streets.

7. David lent his motorcycle to someone who allowed their friend to use it.

8. By the final curtain, ninety percent of the audience had voted with their feet.

9. A good teacher is patient with his or her students, and they should maintain an even temper.

10. A graduate student needs to be willing to take on a sizable debt unless they have wealthy families.

23

Make pronoun references clear.

Pronouns substitute for nouns; they are a kind of shorthand. In a sentence like *After Andrew intercepted the ball, he kicked it as hard as he could,* the pronouns *he* and *it* substitute for the nouns *Andrew* and *ball.* The word a pronoun refers to is called its *antecedent.*

23a Avoid ambiguous or remote pronoun reference.

Ambiguous pronoun reference occurs when the pronoun could refer to two possible antecedents.

▶ *The pitcher broke when Gloria set it*
~~When Gloria set the pitcher~~ on the glass-topped table *, . it*
~~broke.~~

▶ Tom told James *"You have* ~~that he had~~ won the lottery *."*

What broke — the table or the pitcher? Who won the lottery — Tom or James? The revisions eliminate the ambiguity.

Remote pronoun reference occurs when a pronoun is too far away from its antecedent for easy reading.

▶ After the court ordered my ex-husband to pay child support,

he refused. Approximately eight months later, we were back

in court. This time the court ordered him to make payments

directly to the Support and Collections Unit, which would in

turn pay me. For the first six months I received regular

payments, but then they stopped. Again ~~he~~ *my ex-husband* was summoned to

appear in court; he did not respond.

The pronoun *he* was too distant from its antecedent, *ex-husband,* which appeared several sentences earlier.

23b Generally, avoid broad reference of *this, that, which,* and *it.*

For clarity, the pronouns *this, that, which,* and *it* should ordinarily refer to specific antecedents rather than to whole ideas or sentences. When a pronoun's reference is needlessly broad, either replace the pronoun with a noun or supply an antecedent to which the pronoun clearly refers.

▶ More and more often, especially in large cities, we are finding
                                                                               our fate
  ourselves victims of serious crimes. We learn to accept ~~this~~

  with minor gripes and groans.

For clarity the writer substituted a noun (*fate*) for the pronoun
this, which referred broadly to the idea expressed in the preceding sentence.

▶ Romeo and Juliet were both too young to have acquired much
    a fact
  wisdom, which accounts for their rash actions.

The writer added an antecedent (*fact*) that the pronoun *which*
clearly refers to.

EXCEPTION: Many writers view broad reference as acceptable
when the pronoun refers clearly to the sense of an entire
clause.

If you pick up a starving dog and make him prosperous, he will
not bite you. This is the principal difference between a dog and
a man.   — Mark Twain

23c   Do not use a pronoun to refer to an implied antecedent.

A pronoun must refer to a specific antecedent, not to a word
that is implied but not present in the sentence.

                                             the braids
▶ After braiding Ann's hair, Sue decorated ~~them~~ with ribbons.

The pronoun *them* referred to Ann's braids (implied by the term
braiding), but the word *braids* did not appear in the sentence.

Modifiers, such as possessives, cannot serve as antecedents. A modifier may strongly imply the noun that the pronoun might logically refer to, but it is not itself that noun.

▶ In ~~Euripides'~~ *Medea,* ~~he~~ *Euripides* describes the plight of a woman

     rejected by her husband.

The pronoun *he* cannot refer logically to the possessive modifier *Euripides'*. The revision substitutes the noun *Euripides* for the pronoun *he*, thereby eliminating the problem.

23d   Avoid the indefinite use of *they, it,* and *you.*

Do not use the pronoun *they* to refer indefinitely to persons who have not been specifically mentioned. *They* should always refer to a specific antecedent.

▶ Sometimes a list of ways to save energy is included with the
     gas bill. For example, ~~they suggest~~ *the gas company suggests* setting a moderate

     temperature for the hot water heater.

The word *it* should not be used indefinitely in constructions such as "It is said on television . . ." or "In the article it says that. . . ."

▶ ~~In the~~ *The* report ~~it~~ points out that lifting the ban on Compound

     1080 would prove detrimental, possibly even fatal, to the bald

     eagle.

The pronoun *you* is appropriate when the writer is addressing the reader directly: *Once you have kneaded the dough, let it rise in a warm place for at least twenty-five minutes.* (See page 49.) Except in very informal contexts, however, the indefinite *you* (meaning "anyone in general") is inappropriate.

▶ In Ethiopia ~~you don't~~ *one doesn't* need much property to be considered

well-off.

If the pronoun *one* seems too stilted, the writer might recast the sentence: *In Ethiopia, a person doesn't need much property to be considered well-off.*

23e   To refer to persons, use *who, whom,* or *whose,* not *that* or *which.*

In most contexts, use *who, whom,* or *whose* to refer to persons, *that* or *which* to refer to animals or things. Although *that* is occasionally used to refer to persons, it is more polite to use a form of *who. Which* is reserved only for animals or things, so it is impolite to use it to refer to persons.

▶ When he heard about my seven children, four of ~~which~~ *whom* lived

at home, Gill smiled and said, "I love children."

▶ Fans wondered how an out-of-shape old man ~~that~~ *who* walked with

a limp could play football.

NOTE: Occasionally *whose* may be used to refer to animals and things to avoid the awkward *of which* construction.

▶ It is a tree ~~the~~ name ~~of which~~ *whose* I have forgotten.

EXERCISE 23-1

Edit the following sentences to correct errors in pronoun reference. In some cases you will need to decide on an antecedent that the pronoun might logically refer to. Revisions of lettered sentences appear in the back of the book. Example:

> Following the breakup of AT&T, many other companies began
> *The competition*
> to offer long-distance phone service. ~~This~~ has led to lower
>   ∧
>
> long-distance rates.

a. The detective removed the bloodstained shawl from the body and then photographed it.

b. In Professor Jamal's class, you are lucky to earn a C.

c. Please be patient with the elderly residents that have difficulty moving through the cafeteria line.

d. The Comanche braves' lifestyle was particularly violent; they gained respect for their skill as warriors.

e. All students can secure parking permits from the campus police office; they are open from 8 A.M. until 8 P.M.

1. He recognized her as the woman which had won an Olympic gold medal for swimming.

2. Many people believe that the polygraph test is highly reliable if you employ a licensed examiner.

3. We expected the concert to last for at least two hours. Since the average ticket sells for twenty dollars, this was not being unrealistic.

4. Because of Paul Robeson's outspoken attitude toward fascism, he was labeled a Communist.

5. In the encyclopedia it states that male moths can smell female moths from several miles away.

6. When Aunt Harriet put the cake on the table, it collapsed.

7. Employees are beginning to take advantage of the company's athletic facilities. They offer squash and tennis courts, a small track, and several trampolines.

8. Be sure to visit Istanbul's bazaar, where they sell everything from Persian rugs to electronic calculators.
9. If you have a sweet tooth, you can visit the confectioner's shop, where it is still made as it was a hundred years ago.
10. Time and time again, I fell for materialistic guys that gave me nothing but pain.

24

Use personal pronouns and nouns in the proper case.

The personal pronouns in the following chart change what is known as case form according to their grammatical function in a sentence. Pronouns functioning as subjects (or subject complements) appear in the *subjective* case; those functioning as objects appear in the *objective* case; and those showing ownership appear in the *possessive* case.

	SUBJECTIVE CASE	OBJECTIVE CASE	POSSESSIVE CASE
SINGULAR	I	me	my
	you	you	your
	he/she/it	him/her/it	his/her/its
PLURAL	we	us	our
	you	you	your
	they	them	their

Pronouns in the subjective and objective cases are frequently confused. Most of the rules in this section specify when to use one or the other of these cases (*I* or *me*, *he* or *him*, and so on). Rule 24g details a special use of pronouns and nouns in the possessive case.

24a Use the subjective case (*I, you, he, she, it, we, they*) for subjects and subject complements.

When personal pronouns are used as subjects, ordinarily your ear will tell you the correct pronoun. Problems sometimes arise, however, with compound word groups containing a pronoun, so it is not always safe to trust your ear.

▶ Joel ran away from home because his stepfather and ~~him~~ *he* had

quarreled.

> *His stepfather and he* is the subject of the verb *had quarreled*. If we strip away the words *his stepfather and,* the correct pronoun becomes clear: *he had quarreled* (not *him had quarreled*).

When a pronoun is used as a subject complement (a word following a linking verb), your ear may mislead you, since the incorrect form is frequently heard in casual speech. (See subject complement, 58b.)

▶ Sandra confessed that the artist was ~~her.~~ *she.*

> The pronoun *she* functions as a subject complement with the linking verb *was.* In formal, written English, subject complements must be in the subjective case. If your ear rejects *artist was she* as too stilted, try rewriting the sentence: *Sandra confessed that she was the artist.*

24b Use the objective case (*me, you, him, her, it, us, them*) for all objects.

When a personal pronoun is used as a direct object, an indirect object, or the object of a preposition, ordinarily your ear will lead you to the correct pronoun. When an object is compound, however, you may occasionally become confused.

▶ Janice was indignant when she realized that the salesclerk

was insulting her mother and ~~she~~ *her.*

Her mother and her is the direct object of the verb *was insulting.*
Strip away the words *her mother and* to hear the correct pronoun:
was insulting her (not *was insulting she*).

▶ Geoffrey went with my family and ~~I~~ *me* to King's Dominion.

Me is the object of the preposition *with.* We would not say
Geoffrey went with I.

When in doubt about the correct pronoun, some writers
try to avoid making the choice by using a reflexive pronoun
such as *myself.* Such evasions are nonstandard, even though
they are used by some educated persons.

▶ The Egyptian cab driver gave my husband and ~~myself~~ *me* some

good tips on traveling in North Africa.

My husband and me is the indirect object of the verb *gave.* For
correct uses of *myself,* see the Glossary of Usage.

24c Put an appositive and the word to which it refers in the same case.

Appositives are noun phrases that rename nouns or pronouns. A pronoun used as an appositive has the same function (usually subject or object) as the word(s) the appositive renames.

▶ At the drama festival, two actors, Christina and ~~me,~~ *I,* were

selected to do the last scene of *King Lear.*

The appositive *Christina and I* renames the subject, *actors.*

▶ The college interviewed only two applicants for the job,

Professor Stevens and ~~I.~~ *me.*

The appositive *Professor Stevens and me* renames the direct object *applicants.*

24d In elliptical constructions following *than* or *as,* choose the pronoun that expresses your meaning.

In an elliptical construction, words are omitted yet understood. When an elliptical construction follows a comparison beginning with *than* or *as,* your choice of a pronoun will depend on your intended meaning. Consider, for example, the difference in meaning between these sentences:

My husband likes football better than I.

My husband likes football better than me.

Finish each sentence mentally and its meaning becomes clear: *My husband likes football better than I* [do]. *My husband likes football better than* [he likes] *me.*

▶ Even though he is sometimes ridiculed by the other boys,

Norman is much better off than ~~them.~~ *they.*

They is the subject of the verb *are,* which is understood: *Norman is much better off than they* [are]. If the correct English seems too formal, you can always add the verb.

▶ We respected no other candidate as much as ~~she.~~ *her.*

> This sentence means that we respected no other candidate as much as *we respected her. Her* is the direct object of an understood verb.

24e   When deciding whether *we* or *us* should precede a noun, choose the pronoun that would be appropriate if the noun were omitted.

▶ *We* ~~Us~~ tenants would rather fight than move.

▶ Management is short-changing ~~we~~ *us* tenants.

> No one would say *Us would rather fight than move* or *Management is short-changing we.*

24f   Use the objective case for subjects and objects of infinitives.

An infinitive is the word *to* followed by the base form of a verb. (See 59c.) Subjects of infinitives are an exception to the rule that subjects must be in the subjective case. Whenever an infinitive has a subject, it must be in the objective case. Objects of infinitives also are in the objective case.

▶ The crowd expected Chris and *me* ~~I~~ to defeat Tracy and ~~he~~ *him* in the doubles championship.

> *Chris and me* is the subject of the infinitive *to defeat; Tracy and him* is the direct object of the infinitive.

24g Use the possessive case to modify a gerund.

A pronoun that modifies a gerund or a gerund phrase should appear in the possessive case (*my, our, your, his/her/its, their*). A gerund is a verb form ending in *-ing* that functions as a noun. Gerunds frequently appear in phrases, in which case the whole gerund phrase functions as a noun. (See 59c.)

▶ My father always tolerated ~~us~~ *our* talking after the lights were out.

The possessive pronoun *our* modifies the gerund *talking*.

Nouns as well as pronouns may modify gerunds. To form the possessive case of a noun, use an apostrophe and an *-s* (*a victim's rights*) or just an apostrophe (*victims' rights*). (See 36a.)

▶ We had to pay a fifty-dollar fine for ~~Brenda~~ *Brenda's* driving without a

permit.

The possessive noun *Brenda's* modifies the gerund phrase *driving without a permit.*

Gerund phrases should not be confused with participial phrases, which function as adjectives, not as nouns: *We saw Brenda driving a yellow convertible.* Here *driving a yellow convertible* is a participial phrase modifying the noun *Brenda.* (See 59c.)

Sometimes the choice between the objective or the possessive case conveys a subtle difference in meaning:

We watched *them* dancing.

We watched *their* dancing.

Reviewing your writing for problems with pronoun case

Look for the most common trouble spots; where possible, apply a test for the correct pronoun.

COMPOUND WORD GROUPS (24a, 24b)

Test: Mentally strip away the rest of the compound word group.

> While diving for pearls, [Ikiko and] *she* found a treasure chest full of gold bars.

> The most traumatic experience for [her father and] *me* occurred long after her operation.

PRONOUN AFTER *IS, ARE, WAS,* OR *WERE* (24a)

In formal English, remember to use the subjective-case pronouns *I, he, she, we,* and *they* after the linking verbs *is, are, was,* and *were.*

> The panel was shocked to learn that the undercover agent was *she.*

APPOSITIVES (24c)

Test: Mentally strip away the word group that the appositive renames.

> [The chief strategists], Dr. Bell and *I,* could not agree on a plan.

> The company could afford to send only [one of two researchers], Dr. Davis or *me,* to Paris.

Pronoun case (continued)

PRONOUN AFTER *THAN* OR *AS* (24d)

Test: Mentally complete the sentence.

> The supervisor claimed that she was much more experienced than *I* [was].

> Gloria admitted that she liked Greg's twin better than [she liked] *him.*

WE OR *US* BEFORE A NOUN (24e)

Test: Mentally delete the noun.

> *We* [women] really have come a long way.

> Sadly, discrimination against *us* [women] occurs in most cultures.

PRONOUN BEFORE OR AFTER AN INFINITIVE (24f)

Remember that both subjects and objects of infinitives take the objective case.

> Ms. Wilson asked John and *me* to drive the senator and *her* to the airport.

PRONOUN OR NOUN BEFORE A GERUND (24g)

Remember to use the possessive case when a pronoun modifies a gerund.

> There is only a small chance of *his* bleeding excessively because of this procedure.

In the first sentence the emphasis is on the people; *dancing* is a participle modifying the pronoun *them*. In the second sentence the emphasis is on the dancing; *dancing* is a gerund, and *their* is a possessive pronoun modifying the gerund.

NOTE: Do not use the possessive if it creates an awkward effect. Try to reword the sentence instead.

AWKWARD   The president agreed to the applications' being reviewed by a faculty committee.

REVISED   The president agreed that the applications could be reviewed by a faculty committee.

REVISED   The president agreed that a faculty committee could review the applications.

EXERCISE 24–1

Edit the following sentences to eliminate errors in case. If a sentence is correct, write "correct" after it. Answers to lettered sentences appear in the back of the book. Example:

Grandfather cuts down trees for neighbors much younger
than ~~him.~~ *he.*

a. My Ethiopian neighbor was puzzled by the dedication of we joggers.
b. The jury was astonished when the witness suddenly confessed that the murderer was none other than he.
c. Sue's husband is ten years older than her.
d. Everyone laughed whenever Sandra described how her brother and her had seen the Loch Ness monster and fed it sandwiches.
e. There is only a slim chance of his getting an infection from the procedure.

1. Doctors should take more seriously what us patients say about our treatment.
2. Grandfather said he would give anything to live nearer to Paulette and me.

3. The patient began suffering from the delusion that him and his family were constantly being followed and observed.
4. A professional counselor advised the division chief that Marco, Fidelia, and myself should be allowed to apply for the opening.
5. Because of last night's fire, we are fed up with him drinking and smoking.
6. The student ethics board gave Marlo and I the opportunity to defend ourselves against the instructor's false charges.
7. The swirling cyclone caused he and his horse to race for shelter.
8. The winners of the art competition, Justine and I, will spend a month studying painting in Florence.
9. During the testimony the witness pointed directly at the defendant and announced that the thief was him.
10. Despite our different backgrounds, a close friendship developed between Esperanza and I.

25

Use *who* and *whom* in the proper case.

The choice between *who* and *whom* (or *whoever* and *whomever*) occurs primarily in subordinate clauses and in questions. *Who* and *whoever*, subjective-case pronouns, are used for subjects and subject complements. *Whom* and *whomever*, objective-case pronouns, are used for objects. (For more about pronoun case, see 24.)

25a In subordinate clauses, use *who* and *whoever* for subjects or subject complements, *whom* and *whomever* for all objects.

When *who* and *whom* (or *whoever* and *whomever*) introduce subordinate clauses, their case is determined by their function *within the clause they introduce.* To choose the correct pronoun, you must isolate the subordinate clause and then decide how the pronoun functions within it. (See subordinate clauses, 59b.)

In the following two examples, the pronouns *who* and *whoever* function as the subjects of the clauses they introduce.

▶ The prize goes to the runner ~~whom~~ *who* collects the most points.

The subordinate clause is *who collects the most points.* The verb of the clause is *collects,* and its subject is *who.*

▶ He tells that story to ~~whomever~~ *whoever* will listen.

The writer selected the pronoun *whomever,* thinking that it was the object of the preposition *to.* However, the object of the preposition is the entire subordinate clause *whoever will listen.* The verb of the clause is *will listen,* and its subject is *whoever.*

Who occasionally functions as a subject complement in a subordinate clause. Subject complements occur with linking verbs (usually *be, am, is, are, was, were, being,* and *been*). (See 58b.)

▶ The receptionist knows ~~whom~~ *who* you are.

The subordinate clause is *who you are.* Its subject is *you,* and its subject complement is *who.*

When functioning as an object in a subordinate clause, *whom* (or *whomever*) appears out of order, before both the subject and the verb. To choose the correct pronoun, you must mentally restructure the clause.

▶ You will work with our senior industrial engineers, ~~who~~ *whom* you will meet later.

The subordinate clause is *whom you will meet later.* The subject of the clause is *you,* the verb is *will meet,* and *whom* is the direct object of the verb. This becomes clear if you mentally restructure the clause: *you will meet whom.*

When functioning as the object of a preposition in a subordinate clause, *whom* is often separated from its preposition.

▶ The tutor ~~who~~ **whom** I was assigned to was very supportive.

Whom is the object of the preposition *to.* In this sentence, the writer might choose to drop *whom: The tutor I was assigned to was very supportive.*

NOTE: Inserted expressions such as *they know, I think,* and *she says* should be ignored in determining the case of a relative pronoun.

▶ All of the show-offs, bullies, and tough guys in school want to take on a big guy ~~whom~~ **who** they know will not hurt them.

Who is the subject of *will hurt,* not the object of *know.*

25b In questions, use *who* and *whoever* for subjects, *whom* and *whomever* for all objects.

When *who* and *whom* (or *whoever* and *whomever*) are used to open questions, their case is determined by their function within the question. In the following example, *who* functions as the subject of the question.

▶ ~~Whom~~ **Who** is responsible for this dastardly deed?

When *whom* functions as the object of a verb or the object of a preposition in a question, it appears out of normal order.

To choose the correct pronoun, you must mentally restructure the question.

▶ ~~Who~~ did the committee select?
   Whom

Whom is the direct object of the verb *did select*. To choose the correct pronoun, restructure the question: *The committee did select whom?*

▶ ~~Who~~ did you enter into the contract with?
   Whom

Whom is the object of the preposition *with*, as is clear if you restructure the question: *You did enter into the contract with whom?*

USAGE NOTE: In spoken English, *who* is frequently used to open a question even when it functions as an object: *Who did Joe replace?* Although some readers will accept such constructions in informal written English, it is safer to use the correct form *whom: Whom did Joe replace?*

EXERCISE 25–1

Edit the following sentences to eliminate errors in the use of *who* and *whom* (or *whoever* and *whomever*). If a sentence is correct, write "correct" after it. Answers to lettered sentences appear in the back of the book. Example:

What is the name of the person ~~who~~ you are sponsoring for
   whom

membership in the club?

a. In his first production of *Hamlet,* who did Laurence Olivier replace?
b. Who was Martin Luther King's mentor?
c. Datacall allows you to talk to whoever needs you no matter where you are in the building.

Reviewing your writing for problems with who *and* whom

Look for common trouble spots; where possible, apply a test for correct usage.

IN A SUBORDINATE CLAUSE

Isolate the subordinate clause. Then read its subject, verb, and any objects, restructuring the clause if necessary. Some writers find it helpful to substitute *he* for *who* and *him* for *whom.*

> Samuels hoped to become the business partner of (whoever/whomever) found the treasure.

> Test: . . . *whoever* found the treasure. [. . . *he* found the treasure.]

> Ada always seemed to be bestowing a favor on (whoever/ whomever) she worked for.

> Test: . . . she worked for *whomever.* [. . . she worked for *him.*]

IN A QUESTION

Read the subject, verb, and any objects, rearranging the sentence structure if necessary.

> (Who/Whom) conferred with Roosevelt and Stalin at Yalta in 1945?

> Test: *Who* conferred . . . ?

> (Who/Whom) did the committee nominate?

> Test: The committee did nominate *whom?*

d. Some group leaders cannot handle the pressure; they give whomever makes the most noise most of their attention.
e. One of the women who Martinez hired became the most successful lawyer in the agency.

1. When medicine is scarce and expensive, physicians must give it to whomever has the best chance to survive.
2. Who was accused of receiving Mafia funds?
3. They will become business partners with whomever is willing to contribute to the company's coffers.
4. The only interstate travelers who get pulled over for speeding are the ones whom cannot afford a radar detector.
5. The elderly woman who I was asked to take care of was a clever, delightful companion.

26

Choose adjectives and adverbs with care.

Adjectives ordinarily modify nouns or pronouns; occasionally they function as subject complements following linking verbs. Adverbs modify verbs, adjectives, or other adverbs. (See 57d and 57e.)

Many adverbs are formed by adding -ly to adjectives (*formal, formally; smooth, smoothly*). But don't assume that all words ending in -ly are adverbs or that all adverbs end in -ly. Some adjectives end in -ly (*lovely, friendly*) and some adverbs don't (*always, here, there*). When in doubt, consult a dictionary.

ESL NOTE: In English, adjectives are not pluralized to agree with the words they modify: *The red* [not *reds*] *roses were a wonderful surprise.*

26a Use adverbs, not adjectives, to modify verbs, adjectives, and adverbs.

When adverbs modify verbs (or verbals), they nearly always answer the question When? Where? How? Why? Under what conditions? How often? or To what degree? When adverbs modify adjectives or other adverbs, they usually qualify or intensify the meaning of the word they modify. (See 57e.)

The incorrect use of adjectives in place of adverbs to modify verbs occurs primarily in casual or nonstandard speech.

▶ The arrangement worked out ~~perfect~~ *perfectly* for everyone.

▶ We discovered that the patients hadn't been bathed ~~regular.~~ *regularly.*

Perfect and *regular* are adjectives, so they should not be used to modify the verbs *worked* and *had been bathed.*

The incorrect use of the adjective *good* in place of the adverb *well* is especially common in casual and nonstandard speech.

▶ We were surprised to hear that Louise had done so ~~good~~ *well* on the CPA exam.

The adverb *well* (not the adjective *good*) should be used to modify the verb *had done.*

NOTE: The word *well* is an adjective when it means "healthy," "satisfactory," or "fortunate": *I am very well, thank you. All is well. It is just as well.*

Adjectives are sometimes used incorrectly to modify adjectives or adverbs.

▶ For a man eighty years old, Joe plays golf ~~real~~ *really* well.

▶ We were ~~awful~~ *awfully* sorry to hear about your uncle's death.

Only adverbs can be used to modify adjectives or other adverbs. *Really* intensifies the meaning of the adverb *well*, and *awfully* intensifies the meaning of the adjective *sorry*. The writers could substitute other intensifiers: *very well, terribly sorry.*

> **ESL NOTE:** Placement of adjectives and adverbs can be a tricky matter for second language speakers. See 31c.

26b Use adjectives, not adverbs, as complements.

Adjectives ordinarily precede nouns, but they can also function as subject complements or as object complements.

Subject complements

A subject complement follows a linking verb and completes the meaning of the subject. (See 58b.) When an adjective functions as a subject complement, it describes the subject.

> Justice is *blind.*

Problems can arise with verbs such as *smell, taste, look,* and *feel,* which sometimes, but not always, function as linking verbs. If the word following one of these verbs describes the subject, use an adjective; if it modifies the verb, use an adverb.

ADJECTIVE   The detective looked *cautious.*

ADVERB   The detective looked *cautiously* for fingerprints.

The adjective *cautious* describes the detective; the adverb *cautiously* modifies the verb *looked.*

Linking verbs suggest states of being, not actions. Notice, for example, the different meanings of *looked* in the preceding examples. To look cautious suggests the state of being cautious; to look cautiously is to perform an action in a cautious way.

▶ The lilacs in our backyard smell especially ~~sweetly~~ *sweet* this year.

▶ Lori looked ~~well~~ *good* in her new raincoat.

> The verbs *smell* and *looked* suggest states of being, not actions. Therefore, they should be followed by adjectives, not adverbs. (Contrast with action verbs: *We smelled the flowers. Lori looked for her raincoat.*)

Object complements

An object complement follows a direct object and completes its meaning. (See 58b.) When an adjective functions as an object complement, it describes the direct object.

> Sorrow makes us *wise.*

Object complements occur with verbs such as *call, consider, create, find, keep,* and *make.* When a modifier follows the direct object of one of these verbs, check to see whether it functions as an adjective describing the direct object or as an adverb modifying the verb.

ADJECTIVE	The referee called the plays *perfect.*
ADVERB	The referee called the plays *perfectly.*

The first sentence means that the referee considered the plays to be perfect; the second means that the referee did an excellent job of calling the plays.

► God created all men and women ~~equally.~~ *equal.*

The adjective *equal* is an object complement describing the direct object *men and women.*

26c Use comparatives and superlatives with care.

Most adjectives and adverbs have three forms: the positive, the comparative, and the superlative.

POSITIVE	COMPARATIVE	SUPERLATIVE
soft	softer	softest
fast	faster	fastest
careful	more careful	most careful
bad	worse	worst
good	better	best

Comparative versus superlative

Use the comparative to compare two things, the superlative to compare three or more.

► Which of these two brands of toothpaste is ~~best?~~ *better?*

► Though Shaw and Jackson are impressive, Hobbs is the ~~more~~ *most*

qualified of the three candidates running for mayor.

Form of comparatives and superlatives

To form comparatives and superlatives of most one- and two-syllable adjectives, use the endings *-er* and *-est: smooth, smoother, smoothest; easy, easier, easiest.* With longer adjectives, use *more* and *most* (or *less* and *least* for downward comparisons): *exciting, more exciting, most exciting; helpful, less helpful, least helpful.*

Some one-syllable adverbs take the endings -*er* and -*est* (*fast, faster, fastest*), but longer adverbs and all of those ending in -*ly* form the comparative and superlative with *more* and *most* (or *less* and *least*).

The comparative and superlative forms of the following adjectives and adverbs are irregular: *good, better, best; bad, worse, worst; badly, worse, worst.*

▶ The Kirov was the ~~talentedest~~ *most talented* ballet company we had ever

seen.

▶ Lloyd's luck couldn't have been ~~worser~~ *worse* than David's.

Double comparatives or superlatives

Do not use double comparatives or superlatives. When you have added -*er* or -*est* to an adjective or adverb, do not also use *more* or *most* (or *less* or *least*).

▶ Of all her family, Julia is the ~~most~~ happiest about the move.

▶ That is the most ~~inanest~~ *inane* joke I have ever heard.

Absolute concepts

Avoid expressions such as *more straight, less perfect, very round,* and *most unique.* Either something is *unique* or it isn't. It is illogical to suggest that absolute concepts come in degrees.

▶ That is the most ~~unique~~ *unusual* wedding gown I have ever seen.

▶ The painting would have been even more ~~priceless~~ *valuable* had it been

signed.

26d Avoid double negatives.

Standard English allows two negatives only if a positive meaning is intended: *The orchestra was not unhappy with its performance.* Double negatives used to emphasize negation are nonstandard.

Negative modifiers such as *never, no,* and *not* should not be paired with other negative modifiers or with negative words such as *neither, none, no one, nobody,* and *nothing.*

▶ Management is not doing ~~nothing~~ anything to see that the trash is

picked up.

▶ George won't ~~never~~ ever forget that day.

▶ I enjoy living alone because I don't have to answer to ~~nobody~~ anybody.

The double negatives *not . . . nothing, won't never,* and *don't . . . nobody* are nonstandard.

The modifiers *hardly, barely,* and *scarcely* are considered negatives in standard English, so they should not be used with negatives such as *not, no one,* or *never.*

▶ Maxine is so weak she ~~can't~~ can hardly climb stairs.

EXERCISE 26–1

Edit the following sentences to eliminate errors in the use of adjectives and adverbs. If a sentence is correct, write "correct" after it. Answers to lettered sentences appear in the back of the book. Example:

> When I watched Carl run the 440 on Saturday, I was amazed
> at how ~~good~~ well he paced himself.

a. When Tina began breathing normal, we could relax.
b. All of us on the team felt badly about our performance.
c. Tim's friends cheered and clapped very loud when he made it to the bottom of the beginners' slope.
d. The vaulting box, commonly known as the horse, is the easiest of the four pieces of equipment to master.
e. Last Christmas was the most perfect day of my life.

1. When answering the phone, you should speak clearly and courteous.
2. Doug wanted to know which of the two airlines offered the cheapest fares.
3. We wanted a hunting dog. We didn't care if he smelled badly, but we really did not want him to smell bad.
4. In the early 1970s, chances for survival of the bald eagle looked real slim.
5. After checking to see how bad I had been hurt, my sister dialed 911.
6. The manager must see that the office runs smooth and efficient.
7. Professor Brown's public praise of my performance on the exam made me feel a little strangely.
8. Of all my relatives, Uncle Roberto is the most cleverest.
9. The hall closet is so filled with ski equipment that the door won't hardly close.
10. Marcia performed very well at her Drama Club audition.

27

Choose standard English verb forms.

In nonstandard English, spoken by those who share a regional or cultural heritage, verb forms sometimes differ from those of standard English. In writing, use standard English verb forms unless you are quoting nonstandard speech or using nonstandard forms for literary effect. (See 17d.)

Except for the verb *be,* all verbs in English have five forms.

The following chart lists the five forms and provides a sample sentence in which each might appear.

BASE FORM	Usually I (*walk, ride*).
PAST TENSE	Yesterday I (*walked, rode*).
PAST PARTICIPLE	I have (*walked, ridden*) many times before.
PRESENT PARTICIPLE	I am (*walking, riding*) right now.
-S FORM	He/she/it (*walks, rides*) regularly.

Both the past-tense and past-participle forms of regular verbs end in *-ed* (*walked, walked*). Irregular verbs form the past tense and past participle in other ways (*rode, ridden*).

The verb *be* has eight forms instead of the usual five: *be, am, is, are, was, were, being, been.*

27a Use the correct forms of irregular verbs.

For all regular verbs, the past-tense and past-participle forms are the same (ending in *-ed* or *-d*), so there is no danger of confusion. This is not true, however, for irregular verbs, such as the following.

BASE FORM	PAST TENSE	PAST PARTICIPLE
go	went	gone
fight	fought	fought
fly	flew	flown

The past-tense form, which never has a helping verb, expresses action that occurred entirely in the past. The past participle is used with a helping verb—either with *has, have,* or *had* to form one of the perfect tenses or with *be, am, is, are, was, were, being,* or *been* to form the passive voice.

PAST TENSE	Last July, we *went* to Paris.
PAST PARTICIPLE	We have *gone* to Paris twice.

When you aren't sure which verb form to choose (*went* or *gone, began* or *begun,* and so on), consult the list of common irregular verbs that starts below. Choose the past-tense form if the verb in your sentence doesn't have a helping verb; choose the past-participle form if it does.

In nonstandard English speech, the past-tense and past-participle forms may differ from those of standard English, as in the following sentences.

▶ Yesterday we ~~seen~~ an unidentified flying object.
        saw ∧

▶ The reality of the situation finally ~~sunk~~ in.
        sank ∧

The past-tense forms *saw* and *sank* are required because there are no helping verbs.

▶ The truck was apparently ~~stole~~ while the driver ate lunch.
        stolen ∧

▶ The teacher asked Dwain if he had ~~did~~ his homework.
        done ∧

Because of the helping verbs, the past-participle forms are required: *was stolen, had done.*

When in doubt about the standard English forms of irregular verbs, consult the following list or look up the base form of the verb in the dictionary, which also lists any irregular forms. (If no additional forms are listed in the dictionary, the verb is regular, not irregular.)

Common irregular verbs

BASE FORM	PAST TENSE	PAST PARTICIPLE
arise	arose	arisen
awake	awoke, awaked	awaked, awoke
be	was, were	been
beat	beat	beaten, beat
become	became	become
begin	began	begun

BASE FORM	PAST TENSE	PAST PARTICIPLE
bend	bent	bent
bite	bit	bitten, bit
blow	blew	blown
break	broke	broken
bring	brought	brought
build	built	built
burst	burst	burst
buy	bought	bought
catch	caught	caught
choose	chose	chosen
cling	clung	clung
come	came	come
cost	cost	cost
deal	dealt	dealt
dig	dug	dug
dive	dived, dove	dived
do	did	done
drag	dragged	dragged
draw	drew	drawn
dream	dreamed, dreamt	dreamed, dreamt
drink	drank	drunk
drive	drove	driven
eat	ate	eaten
fall	fell	fallen
fight	fought	fought
find	found	found
fly	flew	flown
forget	forgot	forgotten, forgot
freeze	froze	frozen
get	got	gotten, got
give	gave	given
go	went	gone
grow	grew	grown
hang (suspend)	hung	hung
hang (execute)	hanged	hanged
have	had	had
hear	heard	heard
hide	hid	hidden

BASE FORM	PAST TENSE	PAST PARTICIPLE
hurt	hurt	hurt
keep	kept	kept
know	knew	known
lay (put)	laid	laid
lead	led	led
lend	lent	lent
let (allow)	let	let
lie (recline)	lay	lain
lose	lost	lost
make	made	made
prove	proved	proved, proven
read	read	read
ride	rode	ridden
ring	rang	rung
rise (get up)	rose	risen
run	ran	run
say	said	said
see	saw	seen
send	sent	sent
set (place)	set	set
shake	shook	shaken
shoot	shot	shot
shrink	shrank	shrunk
sing	sang	sung
sink	sank	sunk
sit (be seated)	sat	sat
slay	slew	slain
sleep	slept	slept
speak	spoke	spoken
spin	spun	spun
spring	sprang	sprung
stand	stood	stood
steal	stole	stolen
sting	stung	stung
strike	struck	struck, stricken
swear	swore	sworn
swim	swam	swum
swing	swung	swung

BASE FORM	PAST TENSE	PAST PARTICIPLE
take	took	taken
teach	taught	taught
throw	threw	thrown
wake	woke, waked	waked, woken
wear	wore	worn
wring	wrung	wrung
write	wrote	written

27b Distinguish among the forms of *lie* and *lay*.

Writers and speakers frequently confuse the various forms of *lie* (meaning "to recline or rest on a surface") and *lay* (meaning "to put or place something"). *Lie* is an intransitive verb; it does not take a direct object: *The tax forms lie on the table.* The verb *lay* is transitive; it takes a direct object: *Please lay the tax forms on the coffee table.* (See 58b.)

In addition to confusing the meaning of *lie* and *lay*, writers and speakers are often unfamiliar with the standard English forms of these verbs.

BASE FORM	PAST TENSE	PAST PARTICIPLE	PRESENT PARTICIPLE
lie	lay	lain	lying
lay	laid	laid	laying

▶ Sue was so exhausted that she ~~laid~~ *lay* down for a nap.

The past-tense form of *lie* (to recline) is *lay.*

▶ The patient had ~~laid~~ *lain* in an uncomfortable position all night.

The past-participle form of *lie* (to recline) is *lain.*

▶ Mary ~~lay~~ *laid* the baby on my lap.

The past-tense form of *lay* (to place) is *laid.*

lying
▶ My mother's letters were ~~laying~~ in the corner of the chest.

The present participle of *lie* (to rest on a surface) is *lying*.

EXERCISE 27–1

Edit the following sentences for problems with irregular verbs. If a sentence is correct, write "correct" after it. Answers to lettered sentences appear in the back of the book. Example:

Saw
Was it you I ~~seen~~ last night at the concert?

a. Noticing that my roommate was shivering and looking pale, I rung for the nurse.
b. When I get the urge to exercise, I lay down until it passes.
c. Grandmother had drove our new jeep to the sunrise church service on Savage Mountain, so we were left with the station wagon.
d. I just heard on the news that Claudia Brandolini has broke the world record for the high jump.
e. For thousands of years, people have lain under the stars and gazed into the night sky.

1. How many times have you swore to yourself, "I'll diet tomorrow, after one more piece of cheesecake"?
2. Laying there in a bed of wet leaves with mist falling lightly on my face, I could hear Linda call my name, but I never answered, not even to say I was alive.
3. The burglar must have gone immediately upstairs, grabbed what looked good, and took off.
4. In just a week the ground had froze, and the first winter storm had left over a foot of snow.
5. All parents were asked to send a mat for their children to lay on.
6. Lincoln took good care of his legal clients; the contracts he drew for the Illinois Central Railroad could never be broke.
7. Have you ever dreamed that you were falling from a cliff or flying through the air?
8. I locked my brakes, leaned the motorcycle to the left, and laid it down to keep from slamming into the fence.

9. In her junior year, Cindy run the 440-yard dash in 51.1 seconds.
10. Larry claimed that he had drank a bad soda, but Esther suspected the truth.

27c Use -*s* (or -*es*) endings on present-tense verbs that have third-person singular subjects.

All singular nouns (*child, tree*) and the pronouns *he, she,* and *it* are third-person singular; indefinite pronouns such as *everyone* and *neither* are also third-person singular. When the subject of a sentence is third-person singular, its verb takes an -*s* or -*es* ending in the present tense. (See also 21.)

	SINGULAR		PLURAL	
FIRST PERSON	I	know	we	know
SECOND PERSON	you	know	you	know
THIRD PERSON	he/she/it	knows	they	know
	child	knows	parents	know
	everyone	knows		

In nonstandard speech, the -*s* ending required by standard English is sometimes omitted.

▶ Ellen taught him what he ~~know~~ *knows* about the paperwork.

▶ Sulfur dioxide ~~turn~~ *turns* leaves yellow, ~~dissolve~~ *dissolves* marble, and ~~eat~~ *eats* away iron and steel.

The subjects *he* and *sulfur dioxide* are third-person singular, so the verbs must end in -*s*.

CAUTION: Do not add the -*s* ending to the verb if the subject is not third-person singular.

The writers of the following sentences, knowing they sometimes dropped -*s* endings from verbs, overcorrected by adding the endings where they don't belong.

▶ I prepare~~s~~ program specifications and logic diagrams.

The writer mistakenly concluded that the -s ending belongs on present-tense verbs used with *all* singular subjects, not just *third-person* singular subjects. The pronoun *I* is first-person singular, so its verb does not require the -s.

▶ The dirt floors require~~s~~ continual sweeping.

The writer mistakenly thought that the -s ending on the verb indicated plurality. The -s goes on present-tense verbs used with third-person *singular* subjects.

Has *versus* have

In the present tense, use *has* with third-person singular subjects; all other subjects require *have.*

	SINGULAR		PLURAL	
FIRST PERSON	I	have	we	have
SECOND PERSON	you	have	you	have
THIRD PERSON	he/she/it	has	they	have

In some dialects, *have* is used with all subjects. But standard English requires *has* for third-person singular subjects.

▶ This respected musician almost always ~~have~~ *has* a message to convey in his work.

▶ As for the retirement income program, it ~~have~~ *has* finally been established.

The subjects *musician* and *it* are third-person singular, so the verb should be *has* in each case.

CAUTION: Do not use *has* if the subject is not third-person singular. The writers of the following sentences were aware that they often wrote *have* when standard English requires *has*. Here they are using what appears to them to be the "more correct" form, but in an inappropriate context.

▶ My business law classes ~~has~~ *have* helped me to understand more

about contracts.

▶ I ~~has~~ *have* much to be thankful for.

The subjects of these sentences — *classes* and *I* — are third-person plural and first-person singular, so standard English requires *have. Has* is used with third-person singular subjects only.

Does *versus* do and doesn't *versus* don't

In the present tense, use *does* and *doesn't* with third-person singular subjects; all other subjects require *do* and *don't*.

	SINGULAR		PLURAL	
FIRST PERSON	I	do/don't	we	do/don't
SECOND PERSON	you	do/don't	you	do/don't
THIRD PERSON	he/she/it	does/doesn't	they	do/don't

The use of *don't* instead of the standard English *doesn't* is a feature of many dialects in the United States. Use of *do* for *does* is rarer.

▶ Grandfather really ~~don't~~ *doesn't* have a place to call home.

▶ ~~Do~~ *Does* she know the correct procedure for setting up the

experiment?

Grandfather and *she* are third-person singular, so the verbs should be *doesn't* and *does*.

Am, is, *and* are; was *and* were

The verb *be* has three forms in the present tense (*am, is, are*) and two in the past tense (*was, were*). Use *am* and *was* with first-person singular subjects; use *is* and *was* with third-person singular subjects. With all other subjects, use *are* and *were*.

	SINGULAR		PLURAL	
FIRST PERSON	I	am/was	we	are/were
SECOND PERSON	you	are/were	you	are/were
THIRD PERSON	he/she/it	is/was	they	are/were

▶ Judy wanted to borrow Tim's notes, but she ~~were~~ too shy to
  was
  ^
ask for them.

The subject *she* is third-person singular, so the verb should be *was*.

LOOKING AT YOURSELF AS A WRITER
Problems with -s endings on verbs

If *-s* verb forms are a serious problem for you, ask yourself why. Here are the most common causes and cures.

CAUSE   Your informal spoken English may differ from standard English in its use of *-s* forms.

CURE   Listen carefully to your own casual speech (or the casual speech of family and friends) and compare it with the chart on page 253. Make a list of any differences that you need to be alert to.

CAUSE   You may be confused about the rules on when to use the *-s* form of a verb. For example, you may mistakenly think that a "plural" verb takes an *-s* ending, just like most plural nouns.

> ### Problems with -s endings on verbs (continued)
>
> **CURE** When proofreading, consult the chart on page 253, which shows when to use *-s* verb forms. Don't let yourself get confused by half-learned rules.
>
> **CAUSE** When you proofread your final draft, you read for meaning, so you don't notice small surface features such as missing word endings.
>
> **CURE** Proofread your draft out loud — slowly — articulating the words just as they are written on the page. If you still have trouble, ask your instructor or a writing center tutor for help.
>
> **CAUSE** When it is difficult to pronounce an *-s* ending, you may have trouble hearing that the *-s* is needed — even when you proofread out loud. For example, many speakers do not articulate the *-s* in verbs like *costs* and *asks* and nouns like *tests* and *desks*.
>
> **CURE** Be alert for words that give you difficulty. Probably they end in what grammarians call "consonant clusters." Here are some commonly used verbs and nouns that end in consonant clusters: *acts*, *asks*, *clasps*, *costs*, *crafts*, *desks*, *expects*, *grasps*, *lists*, *masks*, *risks*, *tests*, and *wasps*.

27d Do not omit *-ed* endings on verbs.

Speakers who do not fully pronounce *-ed* endings sometimes omit them unintentionally in writing. Failure to pronounce *-ed* endings is common in many dialects and in informal speech even in standard English. In the following frequently used words and phrases, for example, the *-ed* ending is not always fully pronounced.

advised	developed	prejudiced	stereotyped
asked	fixed	pronounced	used to
concerned	frightened	supposed to	

When a verb is regular, both the past tense and the past participle are formed by adding -ed to the base form of the verb. (See 27a.)

Past tense

Use an -ed or -d ending to express the past tense of regular verbs. The past tense is used when the action occurred entirely in the past.

▶ Over the weekend, Ed ~~fix~~ *fixed* his brother's skateboard and tuned up his mother's 1955 Thunderbird.

▶ Last summer my counselor ~~advise~~ *advised* me to ask my chemistry instructor for help.

Past participles

Past participles are used in three ways: (1) following *have, has,* or *had* to form one of the perfect tenses; (2) following *be, am, is, are, was, were, being,* or *been* to form the passive voice; and (3) as adjectives modifying nouns or pronouns. The perfect tenses are listed on page 307, and the passive voice is discussed in 28c. For a discussion of participles functioning as adjectives, see 59c.

▶ Robin has ~~ask~~ *asked* me to go to California with her.

Has asked is present perfect tense (*have* or *has* followed by a past participle).

▶ Though it is not a new phenomenon, wife battery is ~~publicize~~   *publicized*

more frequently than before.

Is publicized is a verb in the passive voice (a form of *be* followed
by a past participle).

LOOKING AT YOURSELF AS A WRITER
Problems with -ed endings on verbs

If you have difficulty spotting missing *-ed* endings, consider
possible sources of the problem.

CAUSE   Like most people, you don't always pronounce *-ed*
endings, so you tend not to hear them as you
proofread.

CURE   Try proofreading out loud in a formal-sounding
voice. When speaking formally, most people
enunciate word endings more clearly.

CAUSE   When you proofread a final draft, you read for
meaning, so you don't notice small surface features
such as missing word endings.

CURE   Again, reading out loud usually works. Read slowly,
articulating the words just as they are written on
the page. If you still have trouble, ask your
instructor or a writing center tutor for help.
Proofreading is a skill that can be learned.

CAUSE   You don't proofread your final draft carefully
enough or you try to proofread for too many
problems at once.

CURE   Take time to proofread. Until you become a skilled
proofreader, you may need to go over your work
several times.

▶ All aerobics classes end in a cool-down period to stretch

   tightened

  ~~tighten~~ muscles.
  ∧

  The past participle *tightened* functions as an adjective modifying
  the noun *muscles*.

27e Do not omit needed verbs.

Although standard English allows some linking verbs and
helping verbs to be contracted, at least in informal contexts,
it does not allow them to be omitted.

    Linking verbs, used to link subjects to subject comple-
ments, are frequently a form of *be: be, am, is, are, was, were,
being, been*. (See 58b.) Some of these forms may be contracted
(*I'm, she's, we're, you're, they're*), but they should not be
omitted altogether.

    are
▶ When we out there in the evening, we often hear the
      ∧

  helicopters circling above.

   is
▶ Alvin a man who can defend himself.
    ∧

    Helping verbs, used with main verbs, include forms of *be,
do,* and *have* or the words *can, will, shall, could, would,
should, may, might,* and *must*. (See 57c.) Some helping verbs
may be contracted (*he's leaving, we'll celebrate, they've been
told*), but they should not be omitted altogether.

   have
▶ We been in Chicago since last Thursday.
   ∧

would
▶ Do you know someone who ~~be~~ good for the job?
                              ∧

> **ESL NOTE:** Speakers of English as a second language
> sometimes have problems with omitted verbs and correct use
> of helping verbs. See 29e and 29a.

EXERCISE 27–2

Edit the following sentences for problems with *-s* and *-ed* verb forms
and for omitted verbs. If a sentence is correct, write "correct" after it.
Answers to lettered sentences appear in the back of the book.
Example:

has
The psychologist ~~have~~ so many problems in her own life that
doesn't   ∧
she ~~don't~~ know how to advise anyone else.
    ∧

a. I love to watch Anthony as he leaps off the balance beam and
   lands lightly on his feet.
b. The museum visitors were not suppose to touch the exhibits.
c. Our church has all the latest technology, even a close-circuit
   television.
d. We often don't know whether he angry or just joking.
e. Staggered working hours have reduce traffic jams and save motorists many gallons of gas.

1. The bald eagle feed mostly on carrion, such as the carcasses of
   deer or the bodies of dead salmon.
2. Have there ever been a time in your life when you were too depressed to get out of bed?
3. We were ask to sign a contract committing ourselves to not
   smoking for forty-eight hours.
4. Today a modern school building covers most of the old grounds.
5. Christos didn't know about Marlo's death because he never lis-
   tens. He always talking.
6. The training for security checkpoint screeners, which takes
   place in an empty airplane hangar, consist of watching out-of-
   date videos.

7. Our four children plays one or two instruments each.
8. The ball was pass from one player to the other so fast that even the TV crew miss some of the exchanges.
9. Do he have enough energy to hold down two jobs while going to night school?
10. How would you feel if a love one had been a victim of a crime like this?

28

Use verbs in the appropriate tense, mood, and voice.

28a Choose the appropriate verb tense.

Tenses indicate the time of an action in relation to the time of the speaking or writing about that action.

The most common problem with tenses — shifting confusingly from one tense to another—is discussed in 13. Other problems with tenses are detailed in this section, after the following survey of tenses.

Survey of tenses

English has three simple tenses (past, present, and future) and three perfect tenses (present perfect, past perfect, and future perfect). In addition, there is a progressive form of each of these six tenses.

SIMPLE TENSES The simple present tense is used primarily to describe habitual actions (*Jane walks to work*) or to refer to actions occurring at the time of speaking (*I see a cardinal in our maple tree*). It is also used to state facts or general truths and to describe fictional events in a literary work (see page 308). The present tense may even be used to express future actions that are to occur at some specified time (*The semester begins tomorrow*).

The simple past tense is used for actions completed entirely in the past (*Yesterday Jane walked to work*).

The simple future tense is used for actions that will occur in the future (*Tomorrow Jane will walk to work*) or for actions that are predictable, given certain causes (*Meat will spoil if not properly refrigerated*).

In the following chart, the simple tenses are given for the regular verb *walk,* the irregular verb *ride,* and the highly irregular verb *be.*

SIMPLE PRESENT

SINGULAR		PLURAL	
I	walk, ride, am	we	walk, ride, are
you	walk, ride, are	you	walk, ride, are
he/she/it	walks, rides, is	they	walk, ride, are

SIMPLE PAST

SINGULAR		PLURAL	
I	walked, rode, was	we	walked, rode, were
you	walked, rode, were	you	walked, rode, were
he/she/it	walked, rode, was	they	walked, rode, were

SIMPLE FUTURE

I, you, he/she/it, we, they   will walk, ride, be

PERFECT TENSES   More complex time relations are indicated by the perfect tenses (which consist of a form of *have* plus the past participle). The present perfect tense is used for an action that began in the past and is still going on in the present (*Jane has walked to work for years*) or an action that began in the past and is finished by the time of speaking or writing (*Jane has stopped walking to work*).

The past perfect tense is used for an action already completed by the time of another past action (*Jane hailed a cab after she had walked several blocks in the rain*) or for an action already completed at some specific past time (*By 8:30, Jane had walked two miles*). (See also page 309.)

The future perfect tense is used for an action that will be completed before or by a certain future time (*Jane will have left Troy by the time Jo arrives*).

PRESENT PERFECT

I, you, we, they	have walked, ridden, been
he/she/it	has walked, ridden, been

PAST PERFECT

I, you, he/she/it, we, they	had walked, ridden, been

FUTURE PERFECT

I, you, he/she/it, we, they	will have walked, ridden, been

PROGRESSIVE FORMS The simple and perfect tenses already discussed have progressive forms that describe actions in progress. The present progressive form is used for actions currently in progress (*Jane is writing a letter*) or for future actions that are to occur at some specified time (*Jane is leaving for Chicago on Monday*).

The past progressive is used for past actions in progress (*Jane was writing a letter last night*).

The future progressive is used for future actions in progress (*Jane will be traveling next week*).

PRESENT PROGRESSIVE

I	am walking, riding, being
he/she/it	is walking, riding, being
you, we, they	are walking, riding, being

PAST PROGRESSIVE

I, he/she/it	was walking, riding, being
you, we, they	were walking, riding, being

FUTURE PROGRESSIVE

I, you, he/she/it, we, they	will be walking, riding, being

Like the simple tenses, the perfect tenses have progressive forms. The perfect progressive forms express the length of time an action is, was, or will be in progress. *Jane has been walking to work for five years* (present perfect progressive). *Jane had been walking to work before she was mugged* (past perfect progressive). *Jane will have been walking to work for five years by the end of this month* (future perfect progressive).

PRESENT PERFECT PROGRESSIVE

I, you, we, they   have been walking, riding, being
he/she/it   has been walking, riding, being

PAST PERFECT PROGRESSIVE

I, you, he/she/it, we, they had been walking, riding, being

FUTURE PERFECT PROGRESSIVE

I, you, he/she/it, we, they will have been walking, riding, being

---

ESL NOTE: The progressive forms are not normally used with mental activity verbs such as *believe*. See 29a.

Special uses of the present tense

Use the present tense when writing about literature or when expressing general truths.

When writing about a work of literature, you may be tempted to use the past tense. The convention, however, is to describe fictional events in the present tense. (See also 13b.)

▶ In Masuji Ibuse's *Black Rain*, a child ~~reached~~ *reaches* for a pome-

granate in his mother's garden, and a moment later he
~~was~~ *is* dead, killed by the blast of the atomic bomb.

Scientific principles or general truths should appear in the present tense, unless such principles have been disproved.

▶ Galileo taught that the earth ~~revolved~~ around the sun.
               revolves ⌃

Since Galileo's teaching has not been discredited, the verb should be in the present tense. The following sentence, however, is acceptable: *Ptolemy taught that the sun revolved around the earth.*

The past perfect tense

The past perfect tense consists of a past participle preceded by *had* (*had worked, had gone*). (See page 307.) This tense is used for an action already completed by the time of another past action or for an action already completed at some specific past time.

Everyone *had spoken* by the time I arrived.

Everyone *had spoken* by 10:00 A.M.

Writers sometimes use the simple past tense when they should use the past perfect.

▶ We built our cabin high on a pine knoll, forty feet above an
                                had been
abandoned quarry that ~~was~~ flooded in 1920 to create a lake.
                               ⌃

The building of the cabin and the flooding of the quarry both occurred in the past, but the flooding was completed before the time of building.

▶ By the time we arrived at the party, the guest of honor left.
                                                  had ⌃

The past perfect tense is needed because the action of leaving was completed at a specific past time (by the time we arrived).

Some writers tend to overuse the past perfect tense. Do not use the past perfect if two past actions occurred at the same time.

▶ When we arrived in Paris, Pauline ~~had~~ met us at the train

station.

Sequence of tenses with infinitives and participles

An infinitive is the base form of a verb preceded by *to*. (See 59c.) Use the present infinitive to show action at the same time as or later than the action of the verb in the sentence.

▶ The club had hoped to ~~have raised~~ *raise* a thousand dollars by

April 1.

> The action expressed in the infinitive (*to raise*) occurred later than the action of the sentence's verb (*had hoped*).

Use the perfect form of an infinitive (*to have* followed by the past participle) for an action occurring earlier than that of the verb in the sentence.

▶ Dan would like to ~~join~~ *have joined* the navy, but he did not pass the physical.

> The liking occurs in the present; the joining would have occurred in the past.

Like the tense of an infinitive, the tense of a participle is also governed by the tense of the sentence's verb. Use the present participle (ending in *-ing*) for an action occurring at the same time as that of the sentence's verb.

> Hiking the Appalachian Trail in early spring, we spotted many wildflowers.

Use the past participle (such as *given* or *helped*) or the present perfect participle (*having* plus the past participle) for an action occurring before that of the verb.

Discovered off the coast of Florida, the *Atocha* yielded many treasures.

Having worked her way through college, Melanie graduated debt-free.

28b Use the subjunctive mood in the few contexts that require it.

There are three moods in English: the *indicative,* used for facts, opinions, and questions; the *imperative,* used for orders or advice; and the *subjunctive,* used in certain contexts to express wishes, requests, or conditions contrary to fact. Of these moods, only the subjunctive causes problems for writers.

Forms of the subjunctive

In the subjunctive mood, present-tense verbs do not change form to indicate the number and person of the subject (see 21). Instead, the subjunctive uses the base form of the verb (*be, drive, employ*) with all subjects.

> It is important that you *be* [not *are*] prepared for the interview.
>
> We asked that she *drive* [not *drives*] more slowly.

Also, in the subjunctive mood, there is only one past-tense form of *be: were* (never *was*).

> If I *were* [not *was*] you, I'd proceed more cautiously.

Uses of the subjunctive

The subjunctive mood appears only in a few contexts: in contrary-to-fact clauses beginning with *if* or expressing a wish; in *that* clauses following verbs such as *ask, insist, recommend, request,* and *suggest;* and in certain set expressions.

IN CONTRARY-TO-FACT CLAUSES BEGINNING WITH *IF* When a subordinate clause beginning with *if* expresses a condition contrary to fact, use the subjunctive mood.

>   *were*
> ► If I ~~was~~ a member of Congress, I would vote for that bill.

>   *were*
> ► We could be less cautious if Jake ~~was~~ more trustworthy.

The verbs in these sentences express conditions that do not exist: The writer is not a member of Congress, and Jake is not trustworthy.

Do not use the subjunctive mood in *if* clauses expressing conditions that exist or may exist.

If Dana *wins* the contest, she will leave for Barcelona in June.

IN CONTRARY-TO-FACT CLAUSES EXPRESSING A WISH In formal English the subjunctive is used in clauses expressing a wish or desire; in informal speech, however, the indicative is more common.

FORMAL   I wish that Dr. Kurtinitis *were* my professor.

INFORMAL   I wish that Dr. Kurtinitis *was* my professor.

IN *THAT* CLAUSES FOLLOWING VERBS SUCH AS *ASK, INSIST, RECOMMEND, REQUEST,* AND *SUGGEST* Because requests have not yet become reality, they are expressed in the subjunctive mood.

>   *be*
> ► Professor Moore insists that her students ~~are~~ on time.

>   *file*
> ► We recommend that Lambert ~~files~~ form 1050 soon.

IN CERTAIN SET EXPRESSIONS The subjunctive mood, once more widely used in English, remains in certain set expressions: *Be* that as it may, as it *were, come* rain or shine, far *be* it from me, and so on.

EXERCISE 28–1

Edit the following sentences to eliminate errors in verb tense or mood. If a sentence is correct, write "correct" after it. Answers to lettered sentences appear in the back of the book. Example:

> *had been*
> After the path ~~was~~ plowed, we were able to walk through the
>   ∧
> park.

a. The palace of Knossos in Crete is believed to have been destroyed by fire around 1375 B.C.E.

b. Watson and Crick discovered the mechanism that controlled inheritance in all life: the workings of the DNA molecule.

c. In 1941 Hitler decided to kill the Jews. But Himmler and his SS were three years ahead of him; they had mass murder in mind since 1938.

d. Toni could be an excellent student if she wasn't so distracted by problems at home.

e. Ken recommended that Juan remain on the beginners' slope for at least a week.

1. Our neighbor stood at the door looking so pale and ashen that we thought he just saw a ghost.

2. They had planned to have adopted a girl, but they got twin boys.

3. My sister Deanna was outside playing with the new puppies that were born only a few weeks earlier.

4. As soon as my aunt applied for the position of pastor, the post was filled by an inexperienced seminary graduate who had been so hastily snatched that his mortarboard was still in midair.

5. Sheila knew that Bruce would have preferred to have double-dated, but she really wanted to be alone with him.

6. Don Quixote, in Cervantes' novel, was an idealist ill suited for life in the real world.

7. The hurricane tore up the palm trees, lifted them over the hotel roof, and had dropped them into the swimming pool.

8. I would like to have been on the *Mayflower* but not to have lived through that first winter.
9. When the doctor said "It's a girl," I was stunned. For nine months I dreamed about playing baseball with my son.
10. If men and women were angels, no government would be necessary.

28c Prefer the active voice.

Transitive verbs (verbs that take a direct object) appear in either the active or the passive voice. (See 58c.) In the active voice, the subject of the sentence does the action; in the passive, the subject receives the action. Although both voices are grammatically correct, the active voice is usually more effective because it is simpler, more direct, and less wordy.

ACTIVE The committee *reached* a decision.

PASSIVE A decision *was reached* by the committee.

To transform a sentence from the passive to the active voice, make the actor the subject of the sentence.

▶ For the opening flag ceremony, ~~a dance was choreographed by~~
Choreographed a dance
Mr. Martins to the song "Two Hundred Years and Still a Baby."

The revision emphasizes Mr. Martins by making him the subject.

We did not take down the
▶ ~~The~~ Christmas decorations ~~were not taken down~~ until
Valentine's Day.

Very often the actor does not even appear in a passive-voice sentence. To turn such a sentence into the active voice, the writer must decide on an appropriate subject, depending on the context.

The passive voice is appropriate if you wish to emphasize the receiver of the action or to minimize the importance of the doer.

APPROPRIATE PASSIVE   Many native Hawaiians *are forced* to leave their beautiful beaches to make room for hotels and condominiums.

APPROPRIATE PASSIVE   As the time for harvest approaches, the tobacco plants *are sprayed* with a chemical to retard the growth of suckers.

The writer of the first sentence wished to emphasize the receivers of the action, Hawaiians. The writer of the second sentence wished to focus on the tobacco plants, not on the people spraying them.

> **ESL NOTE:** Some speakers of English as a second language tend to avoid the passive voice even when it is appropriate. For advice on transforming an active-voice sentence to the passive, see 58c.

EXERCISE 28–2

Change the following sentences from the passive to the active voice. You may need to invent an actor to be the subject in the active voice. Revisions of lettered sentences appear in the back of the book. Example:

> *We*
> ~~It was~~ learned from the test that our son was reading on the
> second-grade level.

a. Each bedroom in the monastery was painted by Fra Angelico.
b. Carbon dating is used by scientists to determine the approximate age of an object.
c. As the patient undressed, scars were seen on his back, stomach, and thighs. We suspected child abuse.

d. It was noted right away that the taxi driver had been exposed to Americans because he knew all the latest slang.
e. The holes were patched and sanded, the walls were primed, and the ceiling was painted.

1. All of my friends were invited to the party by my mother.
2. No loyalty at all was shown by the dog to his owner, who had mistreated him.
3. It can be concluded that a college education provides a significant economic advantage.
4. The land was ruthlessly stripped of timber before the settlers realized the consequences of their actions.
5. Home equity loans were explained to me by the assistant manager.

Editing for ESL Problems

Part VI is intended for speakers of English as a second language (ESL). It surveys rules that native speakers have mastered simply because they grew up speaking the language.

29

Be alert to special problems with verbs.

Both native and nonnative speakers of English encounter the following problems with verbs, which are treated elsewhere in this handbook:

> problems with subject-verb agreement (21),
>
> misuse of verb forms (27),
>
> problems with tense, mood, and voice (28).

This section focuses on features of the English verb system that cause special problems for second language speakers.

29a   Match helping verbs and main verbs appropriately.

Only certain combinations of helping verbs and main verbs are allowed in English. The correct combinations are discussed in this section, after the following review of helping verbs and main verbs.

Review of helping verbs and main verbs

Helping verbs always appear before main verbs. (See 57c.)

> HV MV   HV   MV
> We *will leave* for the picnic at noon. *Do* you *want* a ride?

Some helping verbs — *have, do,* and *be* — change form to indicate tense; others, known as modals, do not.

FORMS OF *HAVE, DO,* AND *BE*
have, has, had
do, does, did
be, am, is, are, was, were, being, been

MODALS
can, could, may, might, must, shall, should, will, would (*also* ought to)

Every main verb has five forms (except *be,* which has eight forms). The following list shows these forms for the regular verb *help* and the irregular verb *give.* (See 27a for a list of common irregular verbs.)

BASE FORM	help, give
PAST TENSE	helped, gave
PAST PARTICIPLE	helped, given
PRESENT PARTICIPLE	helping, giving
-S FORM	helps, gives

Modal + base form

After the modals *can, could, may, might, must, shall, should, will,* and *would,* use the base form of the verb.

▶ My cousin will send~~s~~ us photographs from her wedding.

▶ We could ~~spoke~~ speak Spanish when we were young.

CAUTION: Do not use *to* in front of a main verb that follows a modal. (*Ought to* is an exception.)

▶ Gina can ~~to~~ drive us home if we miss the bus.

Do, does, *or* **did** + *base form*

After helping verbs that are a form of *do*, use the base form of the verb.

The helping verbs *do, does,* and *did* are used in three ways: (1) to express a negative meaning with the adverbs *not* or *never*, (2) to ask a question, and (3) to emphasize a main verb used in a positive sense.

▶ Mariko does not wants̶ any more dessert.

▶ Did Janice b̶o̶u̶g̶h̶t̶ *buy* the gift for Katherine?

▶ We do h̶o̶p̶i̶n̶g̶ *hope* that you will come to the party.

Have, has, *or* **had** + *past participle* (*perfect tenses*)

After the helping verb *have, has,* or *had*, use the past participle to form one of the perfect tenses. (See 28a.) Past participles usually end in *-ed, -d, -en, -n,* or *-t.* (See 27a.)

▶ On cold nights many churches in the city have o̶f̶f̶e̶r̶ *offered* shelter to the homeless.

▶ An-Mei has not s̶p̶e̶a̶k̶i̶n̶g̶ *spoken* Chinese since she was a child.

The helping verbs *have, has,* and *had* are sometimes preceded by a modal helping verb such as *will: By nightfall, we will have driven five hundred miles.* (See also perfect tenses, 28a.)

Form of **be** + *present participle* (*progressive forms*)

After the helping verb *be, am, is, are, was, were,* or *been,* use the present participle to express a continuing action. (See 28a, progressive forms.)

▶ Carlos is ~~build~~ **building** his house on a cliff overlooking the Pacific Ocean.

▶ Uncle Roy was ~~driven~~ **driving** a brand new red Corvette.

The helping verb *be* must be preceded by a modal (*can, could, may, might, must, shall, should, will,* or *would*): *Edith will be going to Germany soon.* The helping verb *been* must be preceded by *have, has,* or *had: Andy has been studying English for five years.* (See also progressive forms, 28a.)

CAUTION: Certain verbs are not normally used in the progressive sense in English. In general, these verbs express a state of being or mental activity, not a dynamic action. Common examples are *appear, believe, belong, contain, have, hear, know, like, need, see, seem, taste, think, understand,* and *want.*

▶ I ~~am wanting~~ **want** to see August Wilson's *Fences* at Arena Stage.

Some of these verbs, however, have special uses in which progressive forms are normal. (*We are thinking about going to the Bahamas.*) You will need to make a note of exceptions as you encounter them.

Form of be + *past participle (passive voice)*

When a sentence is written in the passive voice, the subject receives the action instead of doing it (*Melissa was given a special award*). (See 28c.)

To form the passive voice, use *be, am, is, are, was, were, being,* or *been* followed by a past participle (usually ending in *-ed, -d, -en, -n,* or *-t*).

▶ *Bleak House* was ~~write~~ **written** by Charles Dickens.

honored
▶ The scientists were ~~honor~~ for their work with dolphins.
        ∧

When the helping verb is *be, being,* or *been,* it must be preceded by another helping verb. *Be* must be preceded by a modal such as *will: Senator Dixon will be defeated. Being* must be preceded by *am, is, are, was,* or *were: The child was being teased. Been* must be preceded by *have, has,* or *had: I have been invited to a party.*

CAUTION: Although they may seem to have passive meanings, verbs such as *occur, happen, sleep, die,* and *fall* may not be used to form the passive voice because they are intransitive. Only transitive verbs, those that take direct objects, may be used to form the passive voice. (See transitive and intransitive verbs, 58b.)

▶ The earthquake ~~was~~ occurred last Wednesday.

EXERCISE 29-1

Revise any sentences in which helping and main verbs do not match. You may need to look at the list of irregular verbs in 27a to determine the correct form of some irregular verbs. Answers to lettered sentences appear in the back of the book. Example:

Maureen should finds/ an apartment closer to campus.

a. We will making this a better country.
b. There is nothing in the world that TV has not touch on.
c. Did you understood my question?
d. A hard wind was blown while we were climbing the mountain.
e. The child's innocent world has been taking away from him.

1. Children are expose at an early age to certain aspects of adult life.

2. We've spend too much money this month, especially on things we don't really need.
3. Have you find your wallet yet?
4. I have ate Thai food only once before.
5. It would have help to know the cost before the work began.

29b In conditional sentences, choose verbs with care.

Conditional sentences state that one set of circumstances depends on whether another set of circumstances exists. Choosing verbs in such sentences can be tricky, partly because two clauses are involved: usually an *if* or a *when* or an *unless* clause and an independent clause.

Three kinds of conditional sentences are discussed in this section: factual, predictive, and speculative.

Factual

Factual conditional sentences express factual relationships. These relationships might be scientific truths, in which case the present tense is used in both clauses.

If water *cools* to 32°, it *freezes.*

Or they might be present or past relationships that are habitually true, in which case the same tense is used in both clauses.

When Sue *bicycles* along the canal, her dog *runs* ahead of her.

Whenever the coach *asked* for help, I *volunteered.*

Predictive

Predictive conditional sentences are used to predict the future or to express future plans or possibilities. In such a sentence, an *if* or *unless* clause contains a present-tense verb; the verb in the independent clause usually consists of the modal *will, can, may, should,* or *might* followed by the base form of the verb.

> If you *practice* regularly, your tennis game *will improve.*

> We *will lose* our remaining wetlands unless we *act* now.

Speculative

Speculative conditional sentences are used for three purposes: (1) to speculate about unlikely possibilities in the present or future, (2) to speculate about events that did not happen in the past, and (3) to speculate about conditions that are contrary to fact. Each of these purposes requires its own combination of verbs.

UNLIKELY POSSIBILITIES Somewhat confusingly, English uses the past tense in an *if* clause to speculate about a possible but unlikely condition in the present or future. The verb in the independent clause consists of *would, could,* or *might* plus the base form of the verb.

> If I *had* the time, I *would travel* to Senegal.

> If Stan *studied* harder, he *could master* calculus.

In the *if* clause, the past-tense form *were* is used with subjects that would normally take *was: Even if I were* [not *was*] *invited, I wouldn't go to the picnic.* (See also 28b.)

EVENTS THAT DID NOT HAPPEN English uses the past perfect tense in an *if* clause to speculate about an event that did not happen in the past or to speculate about a state of being that was unreal in the past. (See past perfect tense, 28a.) The verb in the independent clause consists of *would have, could have,* or *might have* plus the past participle.

> If I *had saved* enough money, I *would have traveled* to Senegal last year.

> If Aunt Grace *had been* alive for your graduation, she *would have been* very proud.

CONDITIONS CONTRARY TO FACT   To speculate about conditions that are currently unreal or contrary to fact, English usually uses the past-tense verb *were* (never *was*) in an *if* clause. (See 28b.) The verb in the independent clause consists of *would, could,* or *might* plus the base form of the verb.

> If Grandmother *were* alive today, she *would be* very proud of you.

> I *would make* children's issues a priority if I *were* president.

EXERCISE 29–2

Edit the following conditional sentences for problems with verbs. In some cases, more than one revision is possible. Suggested revisions of lettered sentences appear in the back of the book. Example:

> *had*
> If I ~~have~~ the money, I would meet my friends in Barcelona
>   ^
> next summer.

a. He would have won the election if he went to the inner city to campaign.
b. If Martin Luther King, Jr., was alive today, he would be appalled by the violence in our inner cities.
c. Whenever my uncle comes to visit, he brought me an expensive present.
d. We will lose our largest client unless we would update our computer system.
e. If Verena wins a fellowship, she would go to graduate school.

1. If it would not be raining, we could go fishing.
2. If Lee had followed the doctor's orders, he had recovered from his operation by now.
3. You would have met my cousin if you came to the party last night.
4. Whenever I washed my car, it rains.
5. Our daughter would have drowned if Officer Blake didn't risk his life to save her.

29c Become familiar with verbs that may be followed by gerunds or infinitives.

A gerund is a verb form that ends in *-ing* and is used as a noun: *sleeping, dreaming.* (See 59c.) An infinitive is the base form of the verb preceded by the word *to: to sleep, to dream.* The word *to* is not a preposition in this use but an infinitive marker. (See 59c.)

A few verbs may be followed by either a gerund or an infinitive; others may be followed by a gerund but not by an infinitive; still others may be followed by an infinitive (either directly or with a noun or pronoun intervening) but not by a gerund.

Verb + gerund or infinitive

These commonly used verbs may be followed by a gerund or an infinitive, with little or no difference in meaning:

begin	continue	like	start
can't stand	hate	love	

I love *skiing.*   I love *to ski.*

With a few verbs, however, the choice of a gerund or infinitive changes the meaning dramatically:

forget	remember	stop	try

She stopped *speaking* to Lucia. [She no longer spoke to Lucia.]

She stopped *to speak* to Lucia. [She paused so that she could speak to Lucia.]

Verb + gerund

These verbs may be followed by a gerund but not by an infinitive:

admit	discuss	imagine	put off	risk
appreciate	enjoy	miss	quit	suggest
avoid	escape	postpone	recall	tolerate
deny	finish	practice	resist	

Have you finished *decorating* [not *to decorate*] the tree?

Bill enjoys *playing* [not *to play*] the piano.

Verb + infinitive

These verbs may be followed by an infinitive but not by a gerund:

agree	decide	manage	pretend	wait
ask	expect	mean	promise	want
beg	have	offer	refuse	wish
claim	hope	plan		

We plan *to visit* [not *visiting*] the Yucatán next week.

Jill has offered *to water* [not *watering*] the plants while we are away.

Verb + noun (or pronoun) + infinitive

With certain verbs in the active voice, a noun or pronoun must come between the verb and the infinitive that follows it. The noun or pronoun usually names a person who is affected by the action.

advise	command	have	persuade	tell
allow	convince	instruct	remind	urge
cause	encourage	order	require	warn

The dean encourages *you to apply* for the scholarship.

The class asked *Luis to tell* the story of his escape.

A few verbs may be followed either by an infinitive directly or by an infinitive preceded by a noun or pronoun.

ask	expect	need	want	would like

We asked *to speak* to the congregation.

We asked *Rabbi Abrams to speak* to our congregation.

Verb + noun or pronoun + unmarked infinitive

An unmarked infinitive is an infinitive without *to*. A few verbs may be followed by a noun or pronoun and an unmarked (but not a marked) infinitive.

have ("cause")   let ("allow")   make ("force")

Absence makes *the heart grow* [not *to grow*] fonder.

Please let *me pay* [not *to pay*] for the tickets.

EXERCISE 29-3

Form sentences by adding gerund or infinitive constructions to the following sentence openings. In some cases, more than one kind of construction may be possible. Possible sentences for lettered items appear in the back of the book. Example:

Please remind your sister to call me.

a. I enjoy
b. Will you help Samantha

c. The team hopes
d. Ricardo and his brothers miss
e. The babysitter let

1. Pollen makes
2. The club president asked
3. Next summer we plan
4. Waverly intends
5. Please stop

29d Become familiar with commonly used two-word verbs.

Many verbs in English consist of a verb followed by a preposition or adverb known as a *particle*. (See 57c.) A two-word verb (also known as a *phrasal verb*) often expresses an idiomatic meaning that cannot be understood literally. Consider the verbs in the following sentences, for example.

> We *ran across* Professor Magnotto on the way to the bookstore.
>
> Calvin *dropped in* on his adviser this morning.
>
> Regina told me to *look* her *up* when I got to Seattle.

As you probably know, *ran across* means "encountered," *dropped in* means "paid an unexpected visit," and "*look up*" means "get in touch with." When you were first learning English, however, these two-word verbs must have suggested strange meanings.

Some two-word verbs are intransitive; they do not take direct objects. (See 58b.)

> This morning I *got up* at dawn.

Transitive two-word verbs (those that take direct objects) have particles that are either separable or inseparable. Separable particles may be separated from the verb by the direct object.

Lucy *called* the wedding *off.*

When the direct object is a noun, a separable particle may also follow the verb immediately:

At the last minute, Lucy *called off* the wedding.

When the direct object is a pronoun, however, the particle must be separated from the verb.

Why was there no wedding? Lucy *called* it *off* [not *called off* it].

Inseparable particles must follow the verb immediately. A direct object cannot come between the verb and the particle.

The police will *look into* the matter [not *look* the matter *into*].

The following list includes common two-word verbs. If a particle can be separated from the verb by a direct object, a pronoun is shown between the verb and the particle: *ask (someone) out.* When in doubt about the meaning of a two-word verb, consult the dictionary.

COMMON TWO-WORD VERBS

ask (someone) out
break down
burn (something) down
burn down
burn (something) up
burn up
bring (something or
   someone) up
call (something) off
call (someone) up
clean (something) up
clean up
come across
cut (something) up
do (something) over
drop in (on someone)
drop (someone or
   something) off
drop out (of something)
fill (something) out
fill (something) up
get along (with someone)

COMMON TWO-WORD VERBS

get away (with something)
get up
give (something) away
give (something) back
give in
give up
go out (with someone)
go over (something)
grow up
hand (something) in
hand (something) out
hang (something) up
help out
help (someone) out
keep on (doing something)
keep up (with someone or
     something)
leave (something) out
look into (something)
look (something) over
look (something) up
make (something) up
pick (something) out
pick (someone) up
pick (something) up
play around
point (something) out
put (something) away
put (something) back
put (something) off
put (something) on
put (something) out
put (something) together

put up (with someone or
     something)
quiet down
run across (someone or
     something)
run into (someone or
     something)
run out (of something)
see (someone) off
shut (something) off
speak to (someone)
speak up
stay away (from someone or
     something)
stay up
take care of (someone or
     something)
take off
take (something) off
take (someone) out
take (something) over
think (something) over
throw (something) away
throw (something) out
try (something) on
try (something) out
turn (something) down
turn (something) on
turn up
wake up
wake (someone) up
wear out
wrap (something) up

EXERCISE 29–4

From the list of two-word verbs, choose ten verbs, preferably ones
whose meaning you are not sure of. First look the verbs up in the
dictionary; then use each verb in a sentence of your own.

29e Do not omit needed verbs.

Some languages allow the omission of the verb when the meaning is clear without it; English does not.

▶ Jim $\overset{is}{\wedge}$ exceptionally intelligent.

▶ Many streets in San Francisco $\overset{are}{\wedge}$ very steep.

▶ Nancy $\overset{is}{\wedge}$ in the backyard.

30

Use the articles *a*, *an*, and *the* appropriately.

Except for occasional difficulty in choosing between *a* and *an*, native speakers of English encounter few problems with articles. To speakers whose native language is not English, however, articles can prove troublesome, for the rules governing their use are surprisingly complex. This section summarizes those rules.

The definite article *the* and the indefinite articles *a* and *an* signal that a noun is about to appear. The noun may follow the article immediately or modifiers may intervene (see 57a and 57d).

> *the candidate, the* exceptionally well qualified *candidate*
>
> *a sunset, a* spectacular *sunset*
>
> *an apple, an* appetizing *apple*

Articles are not the only words used to mark nouns. Other noun markers (sometimes called *determiners*) include possessive nouns (*Helen's*), numbers, and the following pronouns: *my, your, his, her, its, our, their, whose, this, that, these, those, all, any, each, either, every, few, many, more, most, much, neither, several, some.*

Usually an article is not used with another noun marker. Common exceptions include expressions such as *a few, the most,* and *all the.*

30a Use *a* (or *an*) with singular count nouns whose specific identity is not known to the reader.

Count nouns refer to persons, places, or things that can be counted: *one girl, two girls; one city, three cities; one apple, four apples.* Noncount nouns refer to entities or abstractions that cannot be counted: *water, steel, air, furniture, patience, knowledge.* It is important to remember that noncount nouns vary from language to language. To see what nouns English categorizes as noncount nouns, refer to the list on page 334.

If a singular count noun names something not known to the reader — perhaps because it is being mentioned for the first time, perhaps because its specific identity is unknown even to the writer — the noun should be preceded by *a* or *an* unless it has been preceded by another noun marker. *A* (or *an*) usually means "one among many" but can also mean "any one."

▶ Mary Beth arrived in ^*a*^ limousine.

▶ We are looking for ^*an*^ apartment close to the lake.

NOTE: *A* is used before a consonant sound: *a banana, a tree, a picture, a hand, a happy child. An* is used before a vowel sound: *an eggplant, an occasion, an uncle, an hour, an honorable person.* Notice that words beginning with *h* can have either a consonant sound (*hand, happy*) or a vowel sound (*hour, honorable*). (See also the Glossary of Usage.)

30b   Do not use *a* (or *an*) with noncount nouns.

A (or *an*) is not used to mark noncount nouns, such as *sugar*, *gold*, *honesty*, or *jewelry*.

▶ Claudia asked her mother for ~~an~~ advice.

If you want to express an amount for a noncount noun, you can use *some*, *any*, or *more*: *some paper, any information, more pasta*. Or you can add a count noun in front of the non-count noun: *a quart of milk, a piece of furniture, a bar of soap*.

▶ Mother asked us to pick up a *pound of* sugar at the corner store.

NOTE: A few noncount nouns may also be used as count nouns: *Bill loves chocolate; Bill offered me a chocolate.*

COMMONLY USED NONCOUNT NOUNS
Food and drink: bacon, beef, bread, broccoli, butter, cabbage, candy, cauliflower, celery, cereal, cheese, chicken, chocolate, coffee, corn, cream, fish, flour, fruit, ice cream, lettuce, meat, milk, oil, pasta, rice, salt, spinach, sugar, tea, water, wine, yogurt

Nonfood substances: air, cement, coal, dirt, gasoline, gold, paper, petroleum, plastic, rain, silver, snow, soap, steel, wood, wool

Abstract nouns: advice, anger, beauty, confidence, courage, employment, fun, happiness, health, honesty, information, intelligence, knowledge, love, poverty, satisfaction, truth, wealth

Other: biology (and other areas of study), clothing, equipment, furniture, homework, jewelry, luggage, lumber, machinery, mail, money, news, poetry, pollution, research, scenery, traffic, transportation, violence, weather, work

30c Use *the* with most nouns whose specific identity is known to the reader.

The definite article *the* is used with most nouns whose identity is known to the reader. (For exceptions, see 30d.) Usually the identity will be clear to the reader for one of the following reasons:

1. The noun has been previously mentioned.
2. A phrase or a clause following the noun restricts its identity.
3. A superlative such as *best* or *most intelligent* makes the noun's identity specific.
4. The noun describes a unique person, place, or thing.
5. The context or situation makes the noun's identity clear.

▶ A truck loaded with dynamite cut in front of our van. When
  the
  truck skidded a few seconds later, we almost plowed into it.
  ^

    The noun *truck* is preceded by *A* when it is first mentioned. When the noun is mentioned again, it is preceded by *the* since readers now know the specific truck being discussed.

                  the
▶ Bob warned me that gun on the top shelf of the cupboard was
                   ^

  loaded.

    The phrase *on the top shelf of the cupboard* identifies the specific gun.

                  the
▶ Our petite daughter dated tallest boy in her class.
                  ^

    The superlative *tallest* restricts the identity of the noun *boy*.

                        the
▶ During an eclipse, one should not look directly at sun.
                          ^

    There is only one sun in our solar system, so its identity is clear.

the

▶ Please don't slam door when you leave.

Both the speaker and the listener know which door is meant.

30d Do not use *the* with plural or noncount nouns meaning "all" or "in general"; do not use *the* with most proper nouns.

When a plural or a noncount noun means "all" or "in general," it is not marked with *the*.

F

▶ ~~The~~ fountains are an expensive element of landscape design.

▶ In some parts of the world, ~~the~~ rice is preferred to all other

grains.

Although there are many exceptions, *the* is not used with most singular proper nouns. Do not use *the* with names of persons (Jessica Webner), names of streets, squares, parks, cities, and states (Prospect Street, Union Square, Denali National Park, Miami, Idaho), names of continents and most countries (South America, Italy), and names of bays and single lakes, mountains, and islands (Tampa Bay, Lake Geneva, Mount Everest, Crete).

Exceptions to this rule include names of large regions, deserts, and peninsulas (the East Coast, the Sahara, the Iberian Peninsula) and names of oceans, seas, gulfs, canals, and rivers (the Pacific, the Dead Sea, the Persian Gulf, the Panama Canal, the Amazon).

NOTE: *The* is used to mark plural proper nouns: the United Nations, the Finger Lakes, the Andes, the Bahamas, and so on.

EXERCISE 30–1

Articles have been omitted from the following story, adapted from *Zen Flesh, Zen Bones*, compiled by Paul Reps. Insert the articles *a, an,* and *the* where English requires them and be prepared to explain the reasons for your choices.

Moon Cannot Be Stolen

Ryokan, who was Zen master, lived simple life in little hut at foot of mountain. One evening thief visited hut only to discover there was nothing in it to steal.

Ryokan returned and caught him. "You may have come long way to visit me," he told prowler, "and you should not return empty-handed. Please take my clothes as gift." Thief was bewildered. He took Ryokan's clothes and slunk away. Ryokan sat naked, watching moon. "Poor fellow," he mused, "I wish I could give him this beautiful moon."

31

Be aware of other potential trouble spots.

31a Do not omit subjects or the expletives *there* or *it*.

English requires a subject for all sentences except imperatives, in which the subject *you* is understood (*Give to the poor*). (See 58a.) If your native language allows the omission of an explicit subject in other sentences or clauses, be especially alert to this requirement in English.

▶ ~~Have~~ I have a large collection of baseball cards.

▶ Your aunt is very energetic; she seems young for her age.

When the subject has been moved from its normal position before the verb, English sometimes requires an expletive (*there* or *it*) at the beginning of the sentence or clause. (See 58c.) *There* is used at the beginning of a sentence or clause that draws the reader's (or listener's) attention to the location or existence of something.

There is
▶ ~~Is~~ an apple in the refrigerator.
     ^

                    there
▶ As you know, are many religious sects in India.
              ^

Notice that the verb agrees with the subject that follows it: *apple is, sects are.* (See 21f.)

In one of its uses, the word *it* functions as an expletive, to call attention to a subject following the verb.

It is
▶ ~~Is~~ healthy to eat fruit and grains.
    ^

It is
▶ ~~Is~~ clear that we must change our approach.
   ^

The subjects of these sentences are *to eat fruit and grains* (an infinitive phrase) and *that we must change our approach* (a noun clause). (See 59c and 59b.)

As you probably know, the word *it* is also used as the subject of sentences describing the weather or temperature, stating the time, indicating distance, or suggesting an environmental fact.

It is raining in the valley, and it is snowing in the mountains.

In July, it is very hot in Arizona.

It is 9:15 A.M.

It is three hundred miles to Chicago.

It gets noisy in our dorm on weekends.

31b Do not repeat the subject of a sentence.

English does not allow a subject to be repeated in its own clause.

▶ The doctor ~~she~~ advised me to cut down on salt.

The pronoun *she* repeats the subject *The doctor.*

The subject of a sentence should not be repeated even if a word group intervenes between the subject and the verb.

▶ The car that had been stolen ~~it~~ was found.

The pronoun *it* repeats the subject *car.*

31c Do not repeat an object or adverb in an adjective clause.

In some languages an object or an adverb is repeated later in the adjective clause in which it appears; in English such repetitions are not allowed. Adjective clauses begin with relative pronouns (*who, whom, whose, which, that*) or relative adverbs (*when, where*), and these words always serve a grammatical function within the clauses they introduce. (See 59b.) Another word in the clause cannot also serve that same grammatical function.

When a relative pronoun functions as the object of a verb or the object of a preposition, do not add another word with the same function later in the clause.

▶ The puppy ran after the car that we were riding in, ~~it.~~
                                                      ^

The relative pronoun *that* is the object of the preposition *in,* so the object *it* is not allowed.

Even when the relative pronoun has been omitted, do not add another word with its same function.

▶ The puppy ran after the car we were riding in, ~~it.~~
                                                    ∧

The relative pronoun *that* is understood even though it is not present in the sentence.

Like a relative pronoun, a relative adverb should not be echoed later in its clause.

▶ The place where I work ~~there~~ is one hour from my apartment

in the city.

The adverb *there* should not echo the relative adverb *where*.

EXERCISE 31–1

In the following sentences, add needed subjects or expletives and delete any repeated subjects, objects, or adverbs. Answers to lettered sentences appear in the back of the book. Example:

Nancy is the woman whom I talked to ~~her~~ last week.

a. The roses they brought home they cost three dollars each.
b. Are two grocery stores on Elm Street.
c. The prime minister she is the most popular leader in my country.
d. Pavel hasn't heard from the cousin that he wrote to her last month.
e. The king, who had served since the age of sixteen, he was an old man when he died.

1. Henri and Nicole they are good friends.
2. Is important to study the grammar of English.
3. The neighbor we trusted he was a thief.
4. I don't use the subway because am afraid.
5. Archeologists have excavated the city where the old Persian kings are buried there.

31d Place adjectives and adverbs with care.

Adjectives modify nouns or pronouns; adverbs modify verbs, adjectives, or other adverbs (see 57d and 57e). Both native and nonnative speakers encounter problems in the use of adjectives and adverbs (see 26). For nonnative speakers, the placement of adjectives and adverbs can also be troublesome.

Placement of adjectives

No doubt you have already learned that in English adjectives usually precede the nouns they modify and that they may also appear following linking verbs. (See 26b and 58b.)

Janine wore a *new* necklace. Janine's necklace was *new*.

When adjectives pile up in front of a noun, however, you may sometimes have difficulty arranging them. English is quite particular about the order of cumulative adjectives, those not separated by commas. (See 32d.)

> Janine was wearing a *beautiful antique silver* necklace [not *silver antique beautiful* necklace].

The chart on page 342 shows the order in which cumulative adjectives ordinarily appear in front of the noun they modify. This list is just a general guide; don't be surprised when you encounter exceptions.

NOTE: Long strings of cumulative adjectives tend to be awkward. As a rule, use no more than two or three of them between the article (or other noun marker) and the noun modified. Here are several examples:

a beautiful old pine table
two enormous French urns
an exotic purple jungle flower

Susan's large round painting
some small blue medicine bottles

Usual order of cumulative adjectives

ARTICLE OR OTHER NOUN MARKER

a, an, the, her, Joe's, two, many, some

EVALUATIVE WORD

attractive, dedicated, delicious, ugly, disgusting

SIZE

large, enormous, small, little

LENGTH OR SHAPE

long, short, round, square

AGE

new, old, young, antique

COLOR

yellow, blue, crimson

NATIONALITY

French, Scandinavian, Vietnamese

RELIGION

Catholic, Protestant, Jewish, Muslim

MATERIAL

silver, walnut, wool, marble

NOUN/ADJECTIVE

tree (as in *tree house*), kitchen (as in *kitchen table*)

THE NOUN MODIFIED

house, sweater, bicycle, bread, woman, priest

Placement of adverbs

Adverbs modifying verbs appear in various positions: at the beginning or end of the sentence, before or after the verb, or between a helping verb and its main verb.

> *Slowly,* we drove along the rain-slick road.
>
> Mia handled the teapot very *carefully.*
>
> Martin *always* wins our tennis matches.
>
> Christina is *rarely* late for our lunch dates.
>
> My daughter has *often* spoken of you.

An adverb may not, however, be placed between a verb and its direct object.

▶ Mother wrapped ~~carefully~~ the gift. *Carefully.*

> The adverb *carefully* may be placed at the beginning or at the end of this sentence or before the verb. It cannot appear after the verb because the verb is followed by the direct object *the gift.*

EXERCISE 31–2

Using the chart on page 342, arrange the following modifiers and nouns in their proper order. Answers to lettered items appear in the back of the book. Example:

two new French racing bicycles
new, French, two, bicycles, racing

a. woman, young, an, Vietnamese, attractive
b. dedicated, a, priest, Catholic
c. old, her, sweater, blue, wool
d. delicious, Joe's, Scandinavian, bread
e. many, cages, bird, antique, beautiful

1. round, two, marble, tables, large
2. several, yellow, tulips, tiny
3. a, sports, classic, car
4. courtyard, a, square, small, brick
5. charming, restaurants, Italian, several

31e Distinguish between present participles and past participles used as adjectives.

Both present and past participles may be used as adjectives. The present participle always ends in *-ing*. Past participles usually end in *-ed*, *-d*, *-en*, *-n*, or *-t*. (See 27a.)

> **PRESENT PARTICIPLES**   confusing, speaking
>
> **PAST PARTICIPLES**   confused, spoken

Participles used as adjectives can precede the nouns they modify; they can also follow linking verbs, in which case they will describe the subject of the sentence. (See 58b.)

It was a *depressing* movie. Jim was a *depressed* young man.

The essay was *confusing*. The student was *confused*.

A present participle should describe a person or thing causing or stimulating an experience; a past participle should describe a person or thing undergoing an experience.

> The lecturer was *boring* [not *bored*].
>
> The audience was *bored* [not *boring*].

In the first example, the lecturer is causing boredom, not experiencing it. In the second example, the audience is experiencing boredom, not causing it.

The participles that cause the most trouble for nonnative speakers are those describing mental states:

annoying / annoyed	exhausting / exhausted
boring / bored	fascinating / fascinated
confusing / confused	frightening / frightened
depressing / depressed	satisfying / satisfied
exciting / excited	surprising / surprised

When you come across these words in your drafts, check to see that you have used them correctly.

EXERCISE 31–3

Edit the following sentences for proper use of present and past participles. If a sentence is correct, write "correct" after it. Answers to lettered sentences appear in the back of the book. Example:

> *excited*
> Danielle and Monica were very ~~exciting~~ to be going to a
> Broadway show for the first time.

a. Having to listen to everyone's complaints was irritated.
b. The noise in the hall was distracted to me.
c. He was not pleased with his grades last semester.
d. The violence in recent movies is often disgusted.
e. I have never seen anyone as surprised as Mona when she walked through the door and we turned on the lights.

1. Megan worked on her art project for eight hours but still she was not satisfying.
2. That blackout was the most frightened experience I've ever had.
3. I couldn't concentrate on my homework because I was distracted.
4. Three weeks after his promotion, he decided that being the boss was bored.
5. The exhibit on the La Brea tar pits was fascinated.

31f Become familiar with common prepositions that show time and place.

The most frequently used prepositions in English are *at, by, for, from, in, of, on, to,* and *with.* Each of these prepositions has a variety of uses that must be learned gradually, in context.

Prepositions that indicate time and place can be difficult to master because the differences among them are subtle and idiomatic. The chart in this section limits itself to three troublesome prepositions that show time and place: *at, on,* and *in.*

Not every possible use is listed in the chart, so don't be surprised when you encounter exceptions and idiomatic uses that you must learn one at a time. For example, in English we ride *in* a car but *on* a bus, train, or subway. And when we fly *on* (not *in*) a plane, we are not sitting on top of the plane.

EXERCISE 31–4

In the following sentences, replace any prepositions that are not used correctly. If a sentence is correct, write "correct" after it. Answers to lettered sentences appear in the back of the book. Example:

> *at*
> The play begins ~~on~~ 7:00 P.M.
> ^

a. We spent seven days on June in the beach, and it rained every day.
b. In the 1980s, the gap between the rich and the poor in the United States became wider.
c. Usually she met with her patients on the afternoon, but in that day she stayed at home to take care of her son.
d. The clock is hanging on the wall on the dining room.
e. In Germany it is difficult for foreigners to become citizens even if they've lived at the country for a long time.

At, on, *and* in *to show time and place*

Showing time

AT

>*at* a specific time: *at* 7:00, *at* dawn, *at* dinner

ON

>*on* a specific day or date: *on* Tuesday, *on* June 4

IN

>*in* a part of a 24-hour period: *in* the afternoon, *in* the daytime [but *at* night]

>*in* a year or month: *in* 1999, *in* July

>*in* a period of time: finished *in* three hours

Showing place

AT

>*at* a meeting place or location: *at* home, *at* the club

>*at* the edge of something: sitting *at* the desk

>*at* the corner of something: turning *at* the intersection

>*at* a target: throwing the snowball *at* Lucy

ON

>*on* a surface: placed *on* the table, hanging *on* the wall

>*on* a street: the house *on* Spring Street

IN

>*in* an enclosed space: *in* the garage, *in* the envelope

>*in* a geographic location: *in* San Diego, *in* Texas

1. He sat on his bed in his room at the hotel.
2. Only the adults in the family were allowed to sit on the dining room table; the children ate in another room.
3. If the train is on time it will arrive on six o'clock at the morning.
4. She licked the stamp, stuck it in the envelope, put the envelope on her pocket, and walked to the nearest mailbox.
5. The mailbox was in the intersection of Laidlaw Avenue and Williams Street.

PART VII

Editing for Punctuation

32

The comma

The comma was invented to help readers. Without it, sentence parts can collide into one another unexpectedly, causing misreadings.

> **CONFUSING**   If you cook Elmer will do the dishes.

> **CONFUSING**   While we were eating a rattlesnake approached our campsite.

Add commas in the logical places (after *cook* and *eating*), and suddenly all is clear. No longer is Elmer being cooked, the rattlesnake being eaten.

Various rules have evolved to prevent such misreadings and to speed readers along through complex grammatical structures. Those rules are detailed in this section.

32a Use a comma before a coordinating conjunction joining independent clauses.

When a coordinating conjunction connects two or more independent clauses — word groups that could stand alone as separate sentences — a comma must precede it. There are seven coordinating conjunctions in English: *and, but, or, nor, for, so,* and *yet.*

A comma tells readers that one independent clause has come to a close and that another is about to begin.

▶ Nearly everyone has heard of love at first sight ‸ but I fell in

love at first dance.

EXCEPTION: If the two independent clauses are short and there is no danger of misreading, the comma may be omitted.

The plane took off and we were on our way.

CAUTION: As a rule, do *not* use a comma to separate coordinate word groups that are not independent clauses. See 33a.

▶ A good money manager controls expenses/ and invests surplus dollars to meet future needs.

The word group following *and* is not an independent clause; it is the second half of a compound predicate.

32b Use a comma after an introductory clause or phrase.

The most common introductory word groups are clauses and phrases functioning as adverbs. Such word groups usually tell when, where, how, why, or under what conditions the main action of the sentence occurred. See 59a, 59b, and 59c.

A comma tells readers that the introductory clause or phrase has come to a close and that the main part of the sentence is about to begin.

▶ When Irwin was ready to eat₊his cat jumped onto the table.

Without the comma, readers may have Irwin eating his cat. The comma signals that *his cat* is the subject of a new clause, not part of the introductory one.

▶ Near a small stream at the bottom of the canyon₊we discovered an abandoned shelter.

The comma tells readers that the introductory prepositional phrase has come to a close.

EXCEPTION: The comma may be omitted after a short adverb clause or phrase if there is no danger of misreading.

> In no time we were at 2,800 feet.

Sentences also frequently begin with phrases describing the noun or pronoun immediately following them. The comma tells readers that they are about to learn the identity of the person or thing described; therefore, the comma is usually required even when the phrase is short. See 59c.

▶ Knowing that he couldn't outrun a car, Sy took to the fields.

▶ Excited about the move, Alice and Don began packing their books.

The commas tell readers that they are about to hear the nouns described: *Sy* in the first sentence, *Alice and Don* in the second.

NOTE: Other introductory word groups include transitional expressions and absolute phrases. See 32f.

EXERCISE 32–1

Add or delete commas where necessary in the following sentences. If a sentence is correct, write "correct" after it. Answers to lettered sentences appear in the back of the book. Example:

> Because it rained all Labor Day, our picnic was rather soggy.

a. As he was writing up the report, Officer Sweet heard a strange noise coming from the trash dumpster.

b. The man at the next table complained loudly and the waiter stomped off in disgust.

c. Instead of eating half a cake or two dozen cookies I now grab a banana or an orange.

d. Nursing is physically, and mentally demanding, yet the pay is low.

e. Uncle Sven's dulcimers disappeared as soon as he put them up for sale but he always kept one for himself.

1. When the runaway race car hit the gas tank exploded.
2. He pushed the car beyond the toll gate and poured a bucket of water on the smoking hood.
3. Lighting the area like a second moon the helicopter circled the scene.
4. While one of the robbers tied Laureen to a chair, and gagged her with an apron, the other emptied the contents of the safe into a knapsack.
5. Many musicians of Bach's time played several instruments, but few mastered them as early or played with as much expression as Bach.

32c Use a comma between all items in a series.

When three or more items are presented in a series, those items should be separated from one another with commas. Items in a series may be single words, phrases, or clauses.

> At Dominique's one can order fillet of rattlesnake, bison burgers, or pickled eel.

Although some writers view the comma between the last two items as optional, most experts advise using the comma because its omission can result in ambiguity or misreading.

▶ Uncle David willed me all of his property, houses, and

warehouses.

> Did Uncle David will his property *and* houses *and* warehouses — or simply his property, consisting of houses and warehouses? If the former meaning is intended, a comma is necessary to prevent ambiguity.

▶ The activities include a search for lost treasure, dubious financial dealings, much discussion of ancient heresies, and midnight orgies.

Without the comma, the people seem to be discussing orgies, not participating in them. The comma makes it clear that *midnight orgies* is a separate item in the series.

32d Use a comma between coordinate adjectives not joined by *and*. Do not use a comma between cumulative adjectives.

When two or more adjectives each modify a noun separately, they are coordinate.

> With the help of a therapist, Mother has become a *strong, confident, independent* woman.

Adjectives are coordinate if they can be joined with *and* (strong *and* confident *and* independent) or if they can be scrambled (an *independent, strong, confident* woman).

Adjectives that do not modify the noun separately are cumulative.

> *Three large gray* shapes moved slowly toward us.

Beginning with the adjective closest to the noun *shapes*, these modifiers lean on one another, piggyback style, with each modifying a larger word group. *Gray* modifies *shapes*, *large* modifies *gray shapes*, and *three* modifies *large gray shapes*. We cannot insert the word *and* between cumulative adjectives (three *and* large *and* gray shapes). Nor can we scramble them (*gray three large* shapes).

COORDINATE ADJECTIVES

▶ Roberto is a warm ˏgentle ˏaffectionate father.

The adjectives *warm, gentle,* and *affectionate* modify *father* separately. They can be connected with *and* (warm *and* gentle *and* affectionate), and they can be scrambled (an *affectionate, warm, gentle* father).

CUMULATIVE ADJECTIVES

▶ Ira ordered a rich⁄ chocolate⁄ layer cake.

Ira didn't order a cake that was rich and chocolate and layer: He ordered a *layer cake* that was *chocolate,* a *chocolate layer cake* that was *rich.* These cumulative adjectives cannot be scrambled: a *layer chocolate rich cake.*

EXERCISE 32–2

Add or delete commas where necessary in the following sentences. If a sentence is correct, write "correct" after it. Answers to lettered sentences appear in the back of the book. Example:

We gathered our essentials, took off for the great outdoors ˏ

and ignored the fact that it was Friday the 13th.

a. She wore a black silk cape, a rhinestone collar, satin gloves and high-tops.
b. There is no need to prune, weed, fertilize or repot your air fern.
c. City Café is noted for its spicy vegetarian dishes and its friendly efficient service.
d. Juan walked through the room with casual elegant grace.
e. My cat's pupils had constricted to small black shining dots.

1. My brother and I found a dead garter snake, picked it up and placed it on Miss Eunice's doorstep.
2. For breakfast the children ordered cornflakes, English muffins with peanut butter and cherry Cokes.

3. Patients with severe irreversible brain damage should not be put on life support machines.
4. Cyril was clad in a luminous orange rain suit and a brilliant white helmet.
5. Anne Frank and thousands like her were forced to hide in attics, cellars and secret rooms in an effort to save their lives.

32e Use commas to set off nonrestrictive elements. Do not use commas to set off restrictive elements.

Word groups describing nouns or pronouns (adjective clauses, adjective phrases, and appositives) are restrictive or nonrestrictive. A *restrictive* element defines or limits the meaning of the word it modifies and is therefore essential to the meaning of the sentence. Because it contains essential information, a restrictive element is not set off with commas.

> **RESTRICTIVE** For camp the children needed clothes *that were washable.*

If you remove a restrictive element from a sentence, the meaning changes significantly, becoming more general than you intended. The writer of the example sentence does not mean that the children needed clothes in general. The intended meaning is more limited: the children needed *washable* clothes.

A *nonrestrictive* element describes a noun or pronoun whose meaning has already been clearly defined or limited. Because it contains nonessential or parenthetical information, a nonrestrictive element is set off with commas.

> **NONRESTRICTIVE** For camp the children needed sturdy shoes, *which were expensive.*

If you remove a nonrestrictive element from a sentence, the meaning does not change dramatically. Some meaning is lost, to be sure, but the defining characteristics of the person or thing described remain the same as before. The children needed *sturdy shoes,* and these happened to be expensive.

Word groups describing proper nouns are nearly always nonrestrictive: The Illinois River, *which flows through our town,* has reached flood stage. Word groups modifying indefinite pronouns such as *everyone* and *something* are nearly always restrictive: Joe whispered something *that we could not hear.*

Often it is difficult to tell whether a word group is restrictive or nonrestrictive without seeing it in context and considering your meaning. Should you write "The dessert made with fresh raspberries was delicious" or "The dessert, made with fresh raspberries, was delicious"? That depends. If the phrase *made with fresh raspberries* tells readers which of two or more desserts you're referring to, you should omit the commas. If the phrase merely adds information about the one dessert served with the meal, you should use the commas.

Adjective clauses

Adjective clauses are patterned like sentences, containing subjects and verbs, but they function within sentences as modifiers of nouns or pronouns. They always follow the word they modify, usually immediately. Adjective clauses begin with a relative pronoun (*who, whom, whose, which, that*) or with a relative adverb (*where, when*).

Nonrestrictive adjective clauses are set off with commas; restrictive adjective clauses are not.

NONRESTRICTIVE CLAUSE

▶ Ed's house, which is located on thirteen acres , was completely

furnished with bats in the rafters and mice in the kitchen.

The clause *which is located on thirteen acres* does not restrict the meaning of *Ed's house,* so the information is nonessential.

RESTRICTIVE CLAUSE

▶ An office manager for a corporation/ that had government

contracts/ asked her supervisor whether she could repri-

mand her co-workers for smoking.

Because the adjective clause *that had government contracts* iden-
tifies the corporation, the information is essential.

NOTE: Use *that* only with restrictive clauses. Many writers
prefer to use *which* only with nonrestrictive clauses, but
usage varies.

Phrases functioning as adjectives

Prepositional or verbal phrases functioning as adjectives may
be restrictive or nonrestrictive. Nonrestrictive phrases are set
off with commas; restrictive phrases are not.

NONRESTRICTIVE PHRASE

▶ The helicopter, with its 100,000-candlepower spotlight

illuminating the area, circled above.

The *with* phrase is nonessential because its purpose is not to
specify which of two or more helicopters is being discussed.

RESTRICTIVE PHRASE

▶ One corner of the attic was filled with newspapers/ dating

from the turn of the century.

Dating from the turn of the century restricts the meaning of
newspapers, so the comma should be omitted.

Appositives

An appositive is a noun or noun phrase that renames a nearby noun. Nonrestrictive appositives are set off with commas; restrictive appositives are not.

NONRESTRICTIVE APPOSITIVE

▶ Norman Mailer's first novel **,** *The Naked and the Dead* **,** was a
best-seller.

The term *first* restricts the meaning to one novel, so the appositive *The Naked and the Dead* is nonrestrictive.

RESTRICTIVE APPOSITIVE

▶ The song **/**"Fire It Up****" was blasted out of amplifiers ten feet tall.

Once they've read *song,* readers still don't know precisely which song the writer means. The appositive following *song* restricts its meaning.

EXERCISE 32–3

Add or delete commas where necessary in the following sentences. If a sentence is correct, write "correct" after it. Answers to lettered sentences appear in the back of the book. Example:

My youngest sister **,** who plays left wing on the team **,** now
lives at The Sands **,** a beach house near Los Angeles.

a. B. B. King and Lucille, his customized black Gibson have electrified audiences all over the world.
b. The Scott Pack which is a twenty-five-pound steel bottle of air is designed to be worn on a firefighter's back.

c. The woman running for the council seat in the fifth district had a long history of community service.

d. Shakespeare's tragedy, *King Lear,* was given a splendid performance by the actor, Laurence Olivier.

e. Douglass's first autobiography, *Narrative of the Life of Frederick Douglass, An American Slave,* was published in 1845.

1. I had the pleasure of talking to a woman who had just returned from India where she had lived for ten years.

2. The Irish students knew by heart the exploits of Cuchulain a legendary Irish warrior but they knew nothing about Freud or Marx or any religion but their own.

3. The gentleman waiting for a prescription is Mr. Rhee.

4. *Where the Wild Things Are,* the 1964 Caldecott Medal winner, is my nephew's favorite book.

5. Going on an archeological dig which has always been an ambition of mine seems out of the question this year.

32f Use commas to set off transitional and parenthetical expressions, absolute phrases, and elements expressing contrast.

Transitional expressions

Transitional expressions serve as bridges between sentences or parts of sentences. They include conjunctive adverbs such as *however, therefore,* and *moreover* and transitional phrases such as *for example, as a matter of fact,* and *in other words.* (For more complete lists, see 34b.)

When a transitional expression appears between independent clauses in a compound sentence, it is preceded by a semicolon and is usually followed by a comma. (See 34b.)

▶ Minh did not understand our language; moreover, he was
unfamiliar with our customs.

▶ Natural foods are not always salt free; for example⌄celery

contains more sodium than most people would imagine.

When a transitional expression appears at the beginning of a sentence or in the middle of an independent clause, it is usually set off with commas.

▶ As a matter of fact⌄American football was established by fans

who wanted to play a more organized game of football.

▶ The prospective babysitter looked very promising; she was

busy⌄ however ⌄throughout the month of January.

EXCEPTION: If a transitional expression blends smoothly with the rest of the sentence, calling for little or no pause in reading, it does not need to be set off with a comma. Expressions such as *also, at least, certainly, consequently, indeed, of course, moreover, no doubt, perhaps, then,* and *therefore* do not always call for a pause.

> Alice's bicycle is broken; *therefore* you will need to borrow Sue's.

NOTE: The conjunctive adverb *however* always calls for a pause, but it should not be confused with *however* meaning "no matter how," which does not: *However hard Bill tried, he could not match his previous record.*

Parenthetical expressions

Expressions that are distinctly parenthetical should be set off with commas. Providing supplemental information, they interrupt the flow of a sentence or appear at the end as afterthoughts.

▶ Evolution ‸ as far as we know ‸ doesn't work this way.

▶ The bass weighed about twelve pounds ‸ give or take a few

ounces.

Absolute phrases

An absolute phrase, which modifies the whole sentence, usually consists of a noun followed by a participle or participial phrase. (See 59e.) Absolute phrases may appear at the beginning or at the end of a sentence. Wherever they appear, they should be set off with commas.

▶ Her tennis game at last perfected ‸ Krista won the cup.

▶ Brian was forced to rely on public transportation ‸ his car

having been wrecked the week before.

In the first example, the absolute phrase appears at the beginning of the sentence; in the second example, it appears at the end.

CAUTION: Do not insert a comma between the noun and participle of an absolute construction.

▶ The next day / being a school day, we turned down the

invitation.

Contrasted elements

Sharp contrasts beginning with words such as *not, never,* or *unlike* are set off with commas.

▶ Celia⌄unlike Robert⌄ had no loathing for dance contests.

▶ Jane talks to me as an adult and friend⌄ not as her little sister.

32g Use commas to set off nouns of direct address, the words *yes* and *no*, interrogative tags, and mild interjections.

▶ Forgive us⌄Dr. Spock ⌄for reprimanding Jason.

▶ Yes⌄the loan will probably be approved.

▶ The film was faithful to the book⌄ wasn't it?

▶ Well⌄ cases like these are difficult to decide.

32h Use commas with expressions such as *he said* to set off direct quotations. (See also 37f.)

▶ Naturalist Arthur Cleveland Bent remarked⌄ "In part the peregrine declined unnoticed because it is not adorable."

▶ "Convictions are more dangerous foes of truth than lies⌄ " wrote philosopher Friedrich Nietzsche.

32i Use commas with dates, addresses, titles, and numbers.

Dates

In dates, the year is set off from the rest of the sentence with a pair of commas.

▶ On December 12 ^,^ 1890 ^,^ orders were sent out for the arrest of Sitting Bull.

EXCEPTIONS: Commas are not needed if the date is inverted or if only the month and year are given.

The recycling plan goes into effect on 15 April 1994.

January 1990 was an extremely cold month.

Addresses

The elements of an address or place name are followed by commas. A zip code, however, is not preceded by a comma.

▶ John Lennon was born in Liverpool ^,^ England ^,^ in 1940.

▶ Please send the package to Greg Tarvin at 708 Spring Street ^,^ Washington ^,^ Illinois 61571.

Titles

If a title follows a name, separate it from the rest of the sentence with a pair of commas.

▶ Sandra Belinsky ^,^ M.D. ^,^ has been appointed to the board.

Numbers

In numbers more than four digits long, use commas to separate the numbers into groups of three, starting from the right. In numbers four digits long, a comma is optional.

        3,500 [*or* 3500]
      100,000
    5,000,000

EXCEPTIONS: Do not use commas in street numbers, zip codes, telephone numbers, or years.

32j Use a comma to prevent confusion.

In certain contexts, a comma is necessary to prevent confusion. If the writer has omitted a word or phrase, for example, a comma may be needed to signal the omission.

▶ To err is human; to forgive⌄divine.

If two words in a row echo each other, a comma may be needed for ease of reading.

▶ All of the catastrophes that we had feared might happen⌄

happened.

Sometimes a comma is needed to prevent readers from grouping words in ways that do not match the writer's intention.

▶ Patients who can⌄walk up and down the halls several times a

day.

EXERCISE 32–4: Major uses of the comma

This exercise covers the major uses of the comma listed in the chart on page 367. Add or delete commas where necessary. If a sentence is correct, write "correct" after it. Answers to lettered sentences appear in the back of the book. Example:

Although we invited him to the party⌄Gerald decided to

spend another late night in the computer room.

a. The whiskey stills which were run mostly by farmers and fishermen were about twenty miles from the nearest town.
b. At the sound of a starting pistol the horses surged forward toward the first obstacle, a sharp incline three feet high.
c. Each morning the seventy-year-old woman cleans the barn, shovels manure and spreads clean hay around the milking stalls.
d. The students of Highpoint are required to wear dull green, polyester pleated skirts.
e. Beauty is in the eye of the beholder but glamour is for anyone who can afford it.

1. After the passage of the Civil Rights Act of 1964 the Ku Klux Klan went underground for a few years but the group's racist views did not change.
2. Jan's costume was completed with bright red, snakeskin sandals.
3. As the summer slowly passed and we came to terms with Mike's death we visited the grave site less frequently.
4. The lawyer fully explained the contract, but we weren't certain we understood all of its implications.
5. While hunting with a relative Greg was accidentally shot in the back.
6. I called my pup Pawnee meaning "water" in our Indian dialect, simply because we lived on the banks of a large river.
7. Aunt Emilia was an impossible demanding guest.
8. The French Mirage, the fastest airplane in the Colombian air force, was an astonishing machine to fly.
9. There I was with a shiny, nickel-plated .45-caliber handgun, an object that no kid could resist.
10. Siddhartha decided to leave his worldly possessions behind and live in the forest by a beautiful river.

EXERCISE 32–5: All uses of the comma

Add or delete commas where necessary in the following sentences. If a comma is correct, write "correct" after it. Answers to lettered sentences appear in the back of the book. Example:

"Yes ,Virginia, there is a Santa Claus," said the editor.

Major uses of the comma

BEFORE A COORDINATING CONJUNCTION JOINING INDEPENDENT CLAUSES (32a)

No grand idea was ever born in a conference, but a lot of foolish ideas have died there. — F. Scott Fitzgerald

AFTER AN INTRODUCTORY CLAUSE OR PHRASE (32b)

If thought corrupts language, language can also corrupt thought. — George Orwell

BETWEEN ALL ITEMS IN A SERIES (32c)

All the things I really like to do are either immoral, illegal, or fattening. — Alexander Woollcott

BETWEEN COORDINATE ADJECTIVES (32d)

There is a mighty big difference between good, sound reasons and reasons that sound good. — Burton Hillis

TO SET OFF NONRESTRICTIVE ELEMENTS (32e)

Silence, which will save me from shame, will also deprive me of fame. — Igor Stravinsky

---

a. April 13, 1995 is the final deadline for all applications.
b. The coach having bawled us out thoroughly, we left the locker room with his last harsh words ringing in our ears.
c. Good technique does not guarantee however, that the power you develop will be sufficient for Kyok Pa competition.
d. We all piled into Sadiq's car which we affectionately referred to as the Blue Goose.
e. Please make the check payable to David Kerr D.D.S., not David Kerr M.D.

1. Mr. Mundy was born on July 22, 1939 in Arkansas, where his family had lived for four generations.
2. It has been reported that the Republican who suggested Eisenhower as a presidential candidate meant Milton not Ike.
3. One substitute for CFC's has environmentalists concerned because it contains chlorine which is also damaging to the ozone layer.
4. We pulled into the first apartment complex we saw, and slowly patrolled the parking lots.
5. Eating raw limpets, I found out, is like trying to eat art gum erasers.
6. Cobbled streets too narrow for two cars to pass, were lined with tiny houses leaning so close together they almost touched.
7. We wondered how our overweight grandmother could have been the slim bride in the picture, but we kept our wonderings to ourselves.
8. "The last flight" she said with a sigh "went out five minutes before I arrived at the airport."
9. The Rio Grande, the border between Texas and Mexico lay before us. It was a sluggish mud-filled meandering stream that gave off an odor akin to sewage.
10. Pittsburgh, Pennsylvania is the home of several fine colleges and universities.

33

Unnecessary commas

Many common misuses of the comma result from an incomplete understanding of the major comma rules presented in 32. In particular, writers frequently form misconceptions about rules 32a–32e, either extending the rules inappropriately or misinterpreting them. Such misconceptions can lead to the errors described in 33a–33e; rules 33f–33h list other common misuses of the comma.

33a Do not use a comma between compound elements that are not independent clauses.

Though a comma should be used before a coordinating conjunction joining independent clauses (see 32a), this rule should not be extended to other compound word groups.

▶ Jake still doesn't realize that his illness is serious/and that

he will have to alter his diet to improve.

And links two subordinate clauses, each beginning with *that.*

▶ The director led the cast members to their positions/and

gave an inspiring last-minute pep talk.

And links the two parts of a compound predicate: *led . . . and gave.*

33b Do not use a comma after a phrase that begins an inverted sentence.

Though a comma belongs after most introductory phrases (see 32b), it does not belong after phrases that begin an inverted sentence. In an inverted sentence, the subject follows the verb, and a phrase that ordinarily would follow the verb is moved to the beginning (see 58c).

▶ At the bottom of the sound/lies a ship laden with treasure.

33c Do not use a comma before the first or after the last item in a series.

Though commas are required between items in a series (32c), do not place them either before or after the whole series.

▶ Other causes of asthmatic attacks are/ stress, change in

temperature, humidity, and cold air.

▶ Ironically, this job that appears so glamorous, carefree, and

easy/ carries a high degree of responsibility.

33d Do not use a comma between cumulative adjectives, between an adjective and a noun, or between an adverb and an adjective.

Commas are required between coordinate adjectives (those that can be separated with *and*), but they do not belong between cumulative adjectives (those that cannot be separated with *and*). (For a full discussion, see 32d.)

▶ In the corner of the closet we found an old/ maroon hatbox

from Sears.

A comma should never be used to separate an adjective from the noun that follows it.

▶ It was a senseless, dangerous/ mission.

Nor should a comma be used to separate an adverb from an adjective that follows it.

▶ The Hurst Home is unsuitable as a mental facility for

severely/disturbed youths.

33e Do not use commas to set off restrictive or mildly parenthetical elements.

Restrictive elements are modifiers or appositives that restrict the meaning of the nouns they follow. Because they are essential to the meaning of the sentence, they are not set off with commas. (For a full discussion of both restrictive and nonrestrictive elements, see 32e.)

▶ Drivers/who think they own the road/make cycling a

dangerous sport.

The modifier *who think they own the road* restricts the meaning of *Drivers* and is therefore essential to the meaning of the sentence. Putting commas around the *who* clause falsely suggests that all drivers think they own the road.

▶ Margaret Mead's book/*Coming of Age in Samoa*/stirred up

considerable controversy when it was published.

Since Mead wrote more than one book, the appositive contains information essential to the meaning of the sentence.

Although commas should be used with distinctly parenthetical expressions (see 32f), do not use them to set off elements that are only mildly parenthetical.

▶ As long as patients are treated in a professional yet compassionate manner, most/eventually/learn to deal with their

illness.

33f Do not use a comma to set off a concluding adverb clause that is essential to the meaning of the sentence.

When adverb clauses introduce a sentence, they are nearly always followed by a comma (see 32b). When they conclude a sentence, however, they are not set off by commas if their content is essential to the meaning of the earlier part of the sentence. Adverb clauses beginning with *after, as soon as, before, because, if, since, unless, until,* and *when* are usually essential.

▶ Don't visit Paris at the height of the tourist season/ unless

   you have booked hotel reservations.

   Without the *unless* clause, the meaning of the sentence would be broader than the writer intended.

When a concluding adverb clause is nonessential, it should be preceded by a comma. Clauses beginning with *although, even though, though,* and *whereas* are usually nonessential.

   The lecture seemed to last only a short time, although the clock said it had gone on for more than an hour.

33g Do not use a comma to separate a verb from its subject or object.

A sentence should flow from subject to verb to object without unnecessary pauses. Commas may appear between these major sentence elements only when a specific rule calls for them.

▶ Zoos large enough to give the animals freedom to roam,/are

becoming more popular.

▶ Francesca explained to him,/that she was busy and would see

him later.

In the first sentence, the comma should not separate the subject, *Zoos*, from the verb, *are becoming*. In the second sentence, the comma should not separate the verb, *explained*, from its object, the subordinate clause *that she was busy and would see him later*.

33h Avoid other common misuses of the comma.

Do not use a comma in the following situations.

AFTER A COORDINATING CONJUNCTION (*AND, BUT, OR, NOR, FOR, SO, YET*)

▶ Occasionally soap operas are performed live, but,/more often

they are taped.

AFTER *SUCH AS* OR *LIKE*

▶ Many shade-loving plants, such as,/begonias, impatiens, and

coleus, can add color to a shady garden.

BEFORE *THAN*

▶ Touring Crete was more thrilling for us,/than visiting the

Greek islands frequented by the jet set.

AFTER *ALTHOUGH*

▶ Although/ the air was balmy, the water was too cold for swimming.

BEFORE A PARENTHESIS

▶ At MCI Sylvia began at the bottom/ (with only three and a half walls and a swivel chair), but within five years she had been promoted to supervisor.

TO SET OFF AN INDIRECT (REPORTED) QUOTATION

▶ Samuel Goldwyn once said/ that a verbal contract isn't worth the paper it's written on.

WITH A QUESTION MARK OR AN EXCLAMATION POINT

▶ "Why don't you try it?/" she coaxed. "You can't do any worse than the rest of us."

EXERCISE 33–1

Delete commas where necessary in the following sentences. If a sentence is correct, write "correct" after it. Answers to lettered sentences appear in the back of the book. Example:

> Loretta Lynn has paved the way for artists such as/ Reba
>
> McEntire and Wynonna Judd.

a. We'd rather spend our money on blue-chip stocks, than speculate on porkbellies.

LOOKING AT YOURSELF AS A WRITER
The comma and unnecessary commas

It is not necessary to learn all of the comma rules in 32 and 33; just know where to find them. If commas cause you considerable difficulty, however, you may want to consider some common causes and cures.

CAUSE   You insert a comma whenever you take a breath.
CURE   The "breath" method is too unreliable; learn to punctuate by grammatical structure instead.

CAUSE   You oversimplify the rules by focusing on words. For example, because a comma goes before *and* some of the time, you conclude that it belongs before *and* all of the time.
CURE   Make a conscious effort to unlearn oversimplified rules. If the word *and* gives you problems, for example, consult 32a and 33a to see whether you need the comma.

CAUSE   Two of the most important comma rules (32a and 32b) refer to two different kinds of clauses—independent and subordinate—and you've never really understood clauses.
CURE   You can probably grasp the rules by focusing on the examples in 32a and 32b, together with the brief definitions of clauses that are given in those sections. If not, turn to 59b and 60a for a quick review of clauses.

CAUSE   You are confused about the difference between restrictive and nonrestrictive word groups (32e and 33e).
CURE   You are not alone. Most writers find this distinction tricky because it requires us to think carefully about our intended meaning. When in doubt, ask two or three "test readers" to tell you how the presence or absence of commas affects your meaning.

b. Being prepared for the worst, is one way to escape disappointment.
c. When he heard the groans, he opened the door, and ran out.
d. My father said, that he would move to California, if I would agree
   to transfer to UCLA.
e. I quickly accepted the fact that I was, literally, in third-class
   quarters.

1. As a child growing up in Jamaica, I often daydreamed about life
   in the United States.
2. He wore a thick, black, wool coat over army fatigues.
3. Often public figures, (Michael Jackson is a good example) go to
   great lengths to guard their private lives.
4. She loved early spring flowers such as, crocuses, daffodils, for-
   sythia, and irises.
5. On Pam's wrist, was a tattoo of a dragon chasing a tiger.
6. Mesquite, the hardest of the softwoods, grows primarily in the
   Southwest.
7. Male supremacy was assumed by my father, and accepted by my
   mother.
8. The kitchen was covered with black soot, that had been depos-
   ited by the wood-burning stove, which stood in the middle of the
   room.
9. Captain Edward Spurlock observed, that the vast majority of
   crimes in our city are committed by repeat offenders.
10. Many abusive parents were themselves abused children, so they
    have no history of benevolent experiences, and lack appropriate
    healthy role models after which to pattern their behavior as
    parents.

34

The semicolon

The semicolon is used between major sentence elements of
equal grammatical rank.

34a   Use a semicolon between closely related independent clauses not joined by a coordinating conjunction.

When related independent clauses appear in one sentence, they are ordinarily linked with a comma and a coordinating conjunction (*and, but, or, nor, for, so, yet*). The coordinating conjunction signals the relation between the clauses. If the clauses are closely related and the relation is clear without a conjunction, they may be linked with a semicolon instead.

> Injustice is relatively easy to bear; what stings is justice.
> — H. L. Mencken

> Wit has truth in it; wisecracking is simply calisthenics with words.   — Dorothy Parker

> When I was a boy, I was told that anybody could become President; I'm beginning to believe it.   — Clarence Darrow

A semicolon must be used whenever a coordinating conjunction has been omitted between independent clauses. To use merely a comma creates an error known as a comma splice. (See 20.)

▶ Some of the inmates were young and strung out on drugs,/;

others looked as if they might kill at any moment.

▶ Grandmother's basement had walls of Mississippi clay,/;to

me it looked like a dungeon.

CAUTION: Do not overuse the semicolon as a means of revising comma splices. For other revision strategies, see 20a, 20c, and 20d.

34b Use a semicolon between independent clauses
linked with a conjunctive adverb or transitional phrase.

The following conjunctive adverbs and transitional phrases
frequently link independent clauses appearing in one sentence.

> **CONJUNCTIVE ADVERBS**
> accordingly, also, anyway, besides, certainly, consequently,
> conversely, finally, furthermore, hence, however, incidentally,
> indeed, instead, likewise, meanwhile, moreover, nevertheless,
> next, nonetheless, otherwise, similarly, specifically, still,
> subsequently, then, therefore, thus
>
> **TRANSITIONAL PHRASES**
> after all, as a matter of fact, as a result, at any rate, at the
> same time, even so, for example, for instance, in addition, in
> conclusion, in fact, in other words, in the first place, on the
> contrary, on the other hand

When a conjunctive adverb or transitional phrase appears between independent clauses, it is preceded by a semicolon and usually followed by a comma.

▶ I learned all the rules and regulations/; however, I never really

   learned to control the ball.   ∧

When a conjunctive adverb or transitional phrase appears in the middle or at the end of the second independent
clause, the semicolon goes *between the clauses.*

> Most singers gain fame through hard work and dedication;
> Evita, however, found other means.

Conjunctive adverbs and transitional phrases should not
be confused with the coordinating conjunctions *and, but, or,*

nor, for, so, and *yet,* which are preceded by a comma when they link independent clauses. (See 32a.)

34c Use a semicolon between items in a series containing internal punctuation.

▶ Classic science fiction sagas are *Star Trek*, with Mr. Spock

and his large pointed ears/; *Battlestar Galactica*, with its

Cylon Raiders/; and *Star Wars*, with Han Solo, Luke

Skywalker, and Darth Vader.

Without the semicolons, the reader would have to sort out the major groupings, distinguishing between important and less important pauses according to the logic of the sentence. By inserting semicolons at the major breaks, the writer does this work for the reader.

34d Avoid common misuses of the semicolon.

Do not use a semicolon in the following situations.

BETWEEN A SUBORDINATE CLAUSE AND THE REST OF THE SENTENCE

▶ Unless you brush your teeth within ten or fifteen minutes

after eating/, brushing does almost no good.

BETWEEN AN APPOSITIVE AND THE WORD IT REFERS TO

▶ Another delicious dish is the chef's special/, a roasted duck

rubbed with spices and stuffed with wild rice.

TO INTRODUCE A LIST

▶ Some of my favorite artists are featured on *Red, Hot, and Blue/*: the Neville Brothers, Sinead O'Connor, Kirsty MacColl, Annie Lennox, and Neneh Cherry.

BETWEEN INDEPENDENT CLAUSES JOINED BY *AND*, *BUT*, *OR*, *NOR*, *FOR*, *SO*, OR *YET*

▶ Five of the applicants had worked with spreadsheets/, but only one was familiar with database management.

EXCEPTIONS: If at least one of the independent clauses contains internal punctuation, you may use a semicolon even though the clauses are joined with a coordinating conjunction.

> As a vehicle [the model T] was hard-working, commonplace, and heroic; and it often seemed to transmit those qualities to the person who rode in it.   —E. B. White

Although a comma would also be correct in this sentence, the semicolon is more effective, for it indicates the relative weights of the pauses.

Occasionally, a semicolon may be used to emphasize a sharp contrast or a firm distinction between clauses joined with a coordinating conjunction.

> We hate some persons because we do not know them; and we will not know them because we hate them.
>   —Charles Caleb Colton

EXERCISE 34–1

Add commas or semicolons where needed in the following well-known quotations. If a sentence is correct, write "correct" after it. Answers to lettered sentences appear in the back of the book. Example:

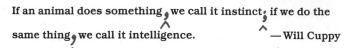

If an animal does something **‸** we call it instinct **;** if we do the
same thing **‸** we call it intelligence. **‸** —Will Cuppy

a. When a woman behaves like a man why doesn't she behave like
a nice man? —Edith Evans
b. No amount of experimentation can ever prove me right a single
experiment can prove me wrong. —Albert Einstein
c. Don't talk about yourself it will be done when you leave.
—Wilson Mizner
d. The only sensible ends of literature are first the pleasurable toil
of writing second the gratification of one's family and friends and
lastly the solid cash. —Nathaniel Hawthorne
e. When men talk about defense they always claim to be protecting
women and children but they never ask the women and children
what they think. —Pat Schroeder

1. Everyone is a genius at least once a year a real genius has his
[or her] original ideas closer together. —G. C. Lichtenberg
2. When choosing between two evils I always like to try the one I've
never tried before. —Mae West
3. Once the children were in the house the air became more vivid
and more heated every object in the house grew more alive.
—Mary Gordon
4. America is a country that doesn't know where it is going but is
determined to set a speed record getting there.
—Lawrence J. Peter
5. I've been rich and I've been poor rich is better.
—Sophie Tucker

EXERCISE 34–2

Edit the following sentences to correct errors in the use of the comma
and the semicolon. If a sentence is correct, write "correct" after it.
Answers to lettered sentences appear in the back of the book.
Example:

Love is blind **;** envy has its eyes wide open.
‸

a. Many people believe that ferrets are vicious little rodents, in fact,
ferrets are affectionate animals that tend to bite only out of fear.

b. America has been called a country of pragmatists; although the American devotion to ideals is legendary.
c. The first requirement is honesty, everything else follows.
d. I am not fond of opera, I must admit; however, that I was greatly moved by *Les Misérables.*
e. Deaf-REACH runs a group home, which prepares residents to live independently; a daytime activity center, where walk-in clients receive job training; and a community service center, which provides counseling and legal representation.

1. When Chao Neng joined the police force in 1991; he had no idea how hard it would be to bury a fellow officer.
2. Martin Luther King, Jr. had not intended to be a preacher, initially, he had planned to become a lawyer.
3. Severe, unremitting pain is a ravaging force; especially when the patient tries to hide it from others.
4. I entered this class feeling jittery and incapable, I leave feeling poised and confident.
5. Some educators believe that African American history should be taught in separate courses, others prefer to see it integrated into survey courses.

35

The colon

The colon is used primarily to call attention to the words that follow it.

35a Use a colon after an independent clause to direct attention to a list, an appositive, or a quotation.

A LIST
The daily routine should include at least the following: twenty knee bends, fifty sit-ups, fifteen leg lifts, and five minutes of running in place.

AN APPOSITIVE
My roommate is guilty of two of the seven deadly sins: gluttony and sloth.

A QUOTATION
Consider the words of John F. Kennedy: "Ask not what your country can do for you; ask what you can do for your country."

For other ways of introducing quotations, see 37f.

35b Use a colon between independent clauses if the second summarizes or explains the first.

Faith is like love: It cannot be forced.

NOTE: When an independent clause follows a colon, it may begin with a lowercase or a capital letter.

35c Use a colon after the salutation in a formal letter, to indicate hours and minutes, to show proportions, between a title and subtitle, and between city and publisher in bibliographic entries.

Dear Sir or Madam:

5:30 P.M. (or p.m.)

The ratio of women to men was 2:1.

The Glory of Hera: Greek Mythology and the Greek Family

Boston: Bedford, 1994

NOTE: In biblical references, a colon is ordinarily used between chapter and verse (Luke 2:14). The Modern Language Association recommends a period instead (Luke 2.14).

35d Avoid common misuses of the colon.

A colon must be preceded by a full independent clause. Therefore, avoid using it in the following situations.

BETWEEN A VERB AND ITS OBJECT OR COMPLEMENT

▶ Some important vitamins found in vegetables are/ vitamin A,

thiamine, niacin, and vitamin C.

BETWEEN A PREPOSITION AND ITS OBJECT

▶ The areas to be painted consisted of/ three gable ends, trim

work, sixteen windows, and a front and back porch.

AFTER *SUCH AS, INCLUDING,* OR *FOR EXAMPLE*

▶ The trees on our campus include many fine Japanese

specimens such as/ black pines, ginkgos, and weeping

cherries.

EXERCISE 35–1

Edit the following sentences to correct errors in the use of the comma,
the semicolon, or the colon. If a sentence is correct, write "correct"
after it. Answers to lettered sentences appear in the back of the book.
Example:

> Smiling confidently, the young man stated his major goal in
>
> life/: to be secretary of agriculture before he was thirty.
>   /\

a. The second and most memorable week of survival school consisted of five stages: orientation; long treks; POW camp; escape
   and evasion; and return to civilization.
b. Among the canceled classes were: calculus, physics, advanced
   biology, and English 101.
c. There are only three seasons here: winter, July, and August.
d. For example: Teddy Roosevelt once referred to the wolf as "the
   beast of waste and desolation."
e. In his introduction to Katharine White's book on gardening,
   E. B. White describes her writing process: "The editor in her

fought the writer every inch of the way; the struggle was felt all through the house. She would write eight or ten words, then draw her gun and shoot them down."

1. The patient survived for one reason, the medics got to her in time.
2. While traveling through France, Fiona visited: the Loire Valley, Chartres, the Louvre, and the McDonald's stand at the foot of the Eiffel Tower.
3. Minds are like parachutes, they function only when open.
4. Historian Robert Kee looks to the past for the source of the political troubles in Ireland: "If blame is to be apportioned for today's situation in Northern Ireland, it should be laid not at the door of men today but of history."
5. Robin sorts the crabs into three groups: males, females, and crabs about to molt.

36

The apostrophe

36a Use an apostrophe to indicate that a noun is possessive.

Possessive nouns usually indicate ownership, as in *Tim's hat* or *the lawyer's desk*. Frequently, however, ownership is only loosely implied: *the tree's roots, a day's work*. If you are not sure whether a noun is possessive, try turning it into an *of* phrase: *the roots of the tree, the work of a day*.

When to add -'s

1. If the noun does not end in -s, add -'s.

Roy managed to climb out on the driver's side.

Thank you for refunding the children's money.

2. If the noun is singular and ends in *-s*, add *-'s*.

Lois's sister spent last year in India.

EXCEPTION: If pronunciation would be awkward with the added *-'s*, some writers use only the apostrophe. Either use is acceptable.

Sophocles' plays are among my favorites.

When to add only an apostrophe

If the noun is plural and ends in *-s*, add only an apostrophe.

Both diplomats' briefcases were stolen.

Joint possession

To show joint possession, use *-'s* or (*-s'*) with the last noun only; to show individual possession, make all nouns possessive.

Have you seen Joyce and Greg's new camper?

John's and Marie's expectations of marriage couldn't have been more different.

In the first sentence, Joyce and Greg jointly own one camper. In the second sentence, John and Marie individually have different expectations.

Compound nouns

If a noun is compound, use *-'s* (or *-s'*) with the last element.

My father-in-law's sculpture won first place.

36b Use an apostrophe and *-s* to indicate that an indefinite pronoun is possessive.

Indefinite pronouns refer to no specific person or thing: *everyone, someone, no one, something.* (See 57b.)

> Someone's raincoat has been left behind.
>
> This diet will improve almost anyone's health.

36c Use an apostrophe to mark omissions in contractions and numbers.

In contractions the apostrophe takes the place of missing letters.

> It's a shame that Frank can't go on the tour.

It's stands for *it is, can't* for *cannot.*

The apostrophe is also used to mark the omission of the first two digits of a year (the class of '95) or years (the '60s generation).

> We'll never forget the blizzard of '78.

36d Use an apostrophe and *-s* to pluralize numbers mentioned as numbers, letters mentioned as letters, words mentioned as words, and abbreviations.

> Margarita skated nearly perfect figure 8's.
>
> The bleachers in our section were marked with large red *J*'s.
>
> We've heard enough *maybe*'s.
>
> You must ask to see their I.D.'s.

Notice that the *-s* is not italicized when used with an italicized number, letter, or word.

EXCEPTION: An *-s* alone is often added to the years in a decade: *the 1980s.*

MLA NOTE: The Modern Language Association recommends no apostrophe in plurals of numbers and abbreviations: figure 8s, VCRs.

36e Avoid common misuses of the apostrophe.

Do not use an apostrophe in the following situations.

WITH NOUNS THAT ARE NOT POSSESSIVE

> Some ~~outpatient's~~ *outpatients* are given special parking permits.

IN THE POSSESSIVE PRONOUNS *ITS, WHOSE, HIS, HERS, OURS, YOURS,* AND *THEIRS*

> Each area has ~~it's~~ *its* own conference room.

It's means *it is.* The possessive pronoun *its* contains no apostrophe despite the fact that it is possessive.

> This course was taught by a professional florist ~~who's~~ *whose*

technique was oriental.

Who's means *who is.* The possessive pronoun is *whose.*

EXERCISE 36–1

Edit the following sentences to correct errors in the use of the apostrophe. If a sentence is correct, write "correct" after it. Answers to lettered sentences appear in the back of the book. Example:

Marietta lived above the only bar in town, Smiling ~~Jacks.~~ Jack's.

a. In a democracy anyones vote counts as much as mine.
b. He received two A's, three B's, and a C.
c. The puppy's favorite activity was chasing it's tail.
d. After we bought J.J. the latest style pants and shirts, he decided that last years faded, ragged jeans were perfect for all occasions.
e. A crocodiles' life span is about thirteen years.

1. The snow does'nt rise any higher than the horses' fetlocks. [*more than one horse*]
2. For a bus driver, complaints, fare disputes, and robberies are all part of a days work.
3. Each day the menu features a different European countries' dish.
4. We cleared four years accumulation of trash out of the attic; its amazing how much junk can pile up.
5. Booties are placed on the sled dogs feet to protect them from sharp rocks and ice. [*more than one dog*]
6. Sue and Ann went to a party for a friend of theirs'.
7. Three teenage son's can devour about as much food as four full-grown field hands. The only difference is that they dont do half as much work.
8. Ethiopians's meals were served on fermented bread.
9. Luck is an important element in a rock musicians career.
10. My sister-in-law's quilts are being shown at the Fendrick Gallery.

37

Quotation marks

37a Use quotation marks to enclose direct quotations.

Direct quotations of a person's words, whether spoken or written, must be in quotation marks.

In a husky voice Muhammad Ali bragged, "My opponent will be on the floor in round four. He'll take a dive in round five. In round nine he'll be all mine."

"A foolish consistency is the hobgoblin of little minds," wrote Ralph Waldo Emerson.

CAUTION: Do not use quotation marks around indirect quotations. An indirect quotation reports someone's ideas without using that person's exact words.

Ralph Waldo Emerson believed that consistency for its own sake is the mark of a small mind.

NOTE: In dialogue, begin a new paragraph to mark a change in speaker.

"Mom, his name is Willie, not William. A thousand times I've told you, it's *Willie*."

"Willie is a derivative of William, Lester. Surely his birth certificate doesn't have Willie on it, and I like calling people by their proper names."

"Yes, it does, ma'am. My mother named me Willie K. Mason."
— Gloria Naylor

If a single speaker utters more than one paragraph, introduce each paragraph with quotation marks, but do not use closing quotation marks until the end of the speech.

37b Set off long quotations of prose or poetry by indenting.

When a quotation of prose runs to more than four typed lines in your paper, set if off by indenting ten spaces from the left margin. Quotation marks are not required because the indented format tells readers that the quotation is taken word for word from a source. Long quotations are ordinarily introduced by a sentence ending with a colon.

After making an exhaustive study of the historical record, James Horan, evaluates Billy the Kid like this:

> The portrait that emerges of [the Kid] from the thousands of pages of affidavits, reports, trial transcripts, his letters, and his testimony is neither the mythical Robin Hood nor the stereotyped adenoidal moron and pathological killer. Rather Billy appears as a disturbed, lonely young man, honest, loyal to his friends, dedicated to his beliefs, and betrayed by our institutions and the corrupt, ambitious, and compromising politicians of his time. (158)

The number in parentheses is a citation handled according to the Modern Language Association style. (See 50a.)

NOTE: When you quote two or more paragraphs from the source, indent the first line of each paragraph an additional three spaces.

When you quote more than three lines of a poem, set the quoted lines off from the text by indenting ten spaces from the left margin. Use no quotation marks unless they appear in the poem itself. (To punctuate two or three lines of poetry, see 39e.)

Although many anthologizers "modernize" her punctuation, Emily Dickinson relied heavily on dashes, using them, perhaps, as a musical device. Here, for example, is the original version of the opening stanza from "The Snake":

> A narrow Fellow in the Grass
> Occasionally rides--
> You may have met Him--did you not
> His notice sudden is--

37c   Use single quotation marks to enclose a quotation within a quotation.

> According to Paul Eliott, Eskimo hunters "chant an ancient magic song to the seal they are after: 'Beast of the sea! Come and place yourself before me in the early morning!' "

37d   Use quotation marks around the titles of short works: newspaper and magazine articles, poems, short stories, songs, episodes of television and radio programs, and chapters or subdivisions of books.

> Katherine Mansfield's "The Garden Party" provoked a lively discussion in our short-story class last night.

NOTE: Titles of books, plays, and films and names of magazines and newspapers are put in italics or underlined. See 42a.

37e   Quotation marks may be used to set off words used as words.

Although words used as words are ordinarily underlined, to indicate italics (see 42d), quotation marks are also acceptable. Just be sure to follow consistent practice throughout a paper.

> The words "flaunt" and "flout" are frequently confused.
>
> The words *flaunt* and *flout* are frequently confused.

37f   Use punctuation with quotation marks according to convention.

This section describes the conventions used by American publishers in placing various marks of punctuation inside or outside quotation marks. It also explains how to punctuate when introducing quoted material.

Periods and commas

Always place periods and commas inside quotation marks.

> "This is a stick-up," said the well-dressed young couple. "We want all your money."

This rule applies to single quotation marks as well as double quotation marks. (See 37c.) It also applies to all uses of quotation marks: for quoted material, for titles of works, and for words used as words.

EXCEPTION: In the Modern Language Association's style of parenthetical in-text citations (see 50a), the period follows the citation in parentheses.

> James M. McPherson acknowledges that the Whigs "were not averse to extending the blessings of American liberty, even to Mexicans and Indians" (48).

Colons and semicolons

Put colons and semicolons outside quotation marks.

> Harold wrote, "I regret that I am unable to attend the fundraiser for AIDS research"; his letter, however, came with a substantial contribution.

Question marks and exclamation points

Put question marks and exclamation points inside quotation marks unless they apply to the whole sentence.

> Contrary to tradition, bedtime at my house is marked by "Mommy, can I tell you a story now?"

> Have you heard the old proverb "Do not climb the hill until you reach it"?

In the first sentence, the question mark applies only to the quoted question. In the second sentence, the question mark applies to the whole sentence.

NOTE: Modern Language Association parenthetical citations create a special problem. According to MLA, the question mark or exclamation point should appear before the quotation mark, and a period should follow the parenthetical citation: *Rosie Thomas asks, "Is nothing in life ever straight and clear, the way children see it?" (77).* But because the question mark and period look rather odd so close together, perhaps it is best to restructure such a sentence: *"Is nothing in life ever straight and clear, the way children see it?" asks Rosie Thomas (77).*

Introducing quoted material

After a word group introducing a quotation, choose a colon, a comma, or no punctuation at all, whichever is appropriate in context.

If a quotation is formally introduced, a colon is appropriate. A formal introduction is a full independent clause, not just an expression such as *he said* or *she remarked.*

> Morrow views personal ads in the classifieds as an art form: "The personal ad is like a haiku of self-celebration, a brief solo played on one's own horn."

If a quotation is introduced with an expression such as *he said* or *she remarked*—or if it is followed by such an expression—a comma is needed.

> Robert Frost said, "You can be a little ungrammatical if you come from the right part of the country."

> "You can be a little ungrammatical if you come from the right part of the country," Robert Frost said.

When a quotation is blended into the writer's own sentence, either a comma or no punctuation is appropriate, depending on the way in which the quotation fits into the sentence structure.

> The future champion could, as he put it, "float like a butterfly and sting like a bee."

> Charles Hudson noted that the prisoners escaped "by squeezing through a tiny window eighteen feet above the floor of their cell."

If a quotation appears at the beginning of a sentence, set it off with a comma unless the quotation ends with a question mark or an exclamation point.

> "We shot them like dogs," boasted Davy Crockett, who was among Jackson's troops.

> "What is it?" I asked, bracing myself.

If a quoted sentence is interrupted by explanatory words, use commas to set off the explanatory words.

> "A great many people think they are thinking," wrote William James, "when they are merely rearranging their prejudices."

If two successive quoted sentences from the same source are interrupted by explanatory words, use a comma before the explanatory words and a period after them.

> "I was a flop as a daily reporter," admitted E. B. White. "Every piece had to be a masterpiece — and before you knew it, Tuesday was Wednesday."

37g Avoid common misuses of quotation marks.

1. Do not use quotation marks to draw attention to familiar slang, to disown trite expressions, or to justify an attempt at humor.

▶ Between Thanksgiving and Super Bowl Sunday, many

American wives become ~~"~~football widows~~."~~

2. Do not use quotation marks around indirect quotations. (See also 37a.)

▶ After leaving the scene of the domestic quarrel, the officer

said that ~~"~~he was due for a coffee break.~~"~~

3. Do not use quotation marks around the title of your own essay.

EXERCISE 37–1

Add or delete quotation marks as needed and make any other necessary changes in punctuation in the following sentences. If a sentence is correct, write "correct" after it. Answers to lettered sentences appear in the back of the book. Example:

Bill Cosby once said ∧**"** I don't know the key to success, but the

key to failure is trying to please everyone.∧**"**

a. My commanding officer said, "If we wanted you to have children, we would have issued them to you."
b. As Emerson wrote in 1849, I hate quotations. Tell me what you know.
c. Andrew Marvell's most famous poem, To His Coy Mistress, is a tightly structured argument.
d. "Ladies and gentlemen," said the emcee, "I am happy to present our guest speaker."
e. Historians Segal and Stineback tell us that the English settlers considered these epidemics "the hand of God making room for His followers in the "New World"."

1. The dispatcher's voice cut through the still night air: "Scout 41, robbery in progress, alley rear of 58th and Blaine.

2. Dean Romero's letter warned me that "if I didn't drop the class I would receive a failing grade."

3. Kara looked hopelessly around the small locked room. "If only I were a flea," she thought, "I could get out of here."

4. My skiing instructor promised us that "we would all be ready for the intermediate slope in one week."

5. After the movie Vicki said, "The reviewer called this flick "trash of the first order." I guess you can't believe everything you read."

6. Gloria Steinem once twisted an old proverb like this, "A woman without a man is like a fish without a bicycle."

7. Joan was a self-proclaimed "rabid Blue Jays fan"; she went to every home game and even flew to Atlanta for the World Series.

8. As David Anable has written: "The time is approaching when we will be able to select the news we want to read from a pocket computer."

9. "Even when freshly washed and relieved of all obvious confections," says Fran Lebowitz, "children tend to be sticky."

10. Have you heard the Cowboy Junkies' rendition of Hank Williams's "I'm So Lonesome I Could Cry?"

38

End punctuation

38a   The period

1. Use a period to end all sentences except direct questions or genuine exclamations.

Everyone knows that a period should be used to end most sentences. The only problems that arise concern the choice between a period and a question mark or between a period and an exclamation point.

If a sentence reports a question instead of asking it directly, it should end with a period, not a question mark.

Celia asked whether the picnic would be canceled.

If a sentence is not a genuine exclamation, it should end with a period, not an exclamation point.

After years of working her way through school, Pat finally graduated with high honors.

2. Use periods in abbreviations according to convention.

A period is conventionally used in abbreviations such as the following:

Mr.	B.A.	B.C.	i.e.	A.M. (or a.m.)
Mrs.	M.A.	B.C.E.	e.g.	P.M. (or p.m.)
Ms.	Ph.D.	A.D.	etc.	
Dr.	R.N.	C.E.		

A period is not used with U.S. Postal Service abbreviations for states: MD, TX, CA.

Ordinarily a period is not used in abbreviations of organization names:

NATO	UNESCO	AFL-CIO	FCC
TVA	IRS	SEC	IBM
USA	NAACP	PUSH	FTC
(or U.S.A.)	UCLA	NBA	NIH

Usage varies, however. When in doubt, consult a dictionary, a style manual, or a publication by the agency in question. Even the yellow pages can help.

NOTE: If a sentence ends with a period marking an abbreviation, do not add a second period.

38b The question mark

1. Use a question mark after a direct question.

Obviously a direct question should be followed by a question mark.

What is the horsepower of a 747 engine?

If a polite request is written in the form of a question, it too is usually followed by a question mark.

Would you please send me your catalog of lilies?

CAUTION: Do not use a question mark after an indirect question, one that is reported rather than asked directly. Use a period instead.

He asked me who was teaching the mythology course.

2. Questions in a series may be followed by question marks even when they are not complete sentences:

We wondered where Calamity had hidden this time. Under the sink? Behind the furnace? On top of the bookcase?

38c The exclamation point

1. Use an exclamation point after a word group or sentence that expresses exceptional feeling or deserves special emphasis.

The medic shook me and kept yelling, "He's dead! He's dead! Can't you see that?"

2. Do not overuse the exclamation point.

▶ In the fisherman's memory the fish lives on, increasing in

length and weight with each passing year, until at last it is big

enough to shade a fishing boat!⁄.
　　　　　　　　　　　　　　　　　∧

This sentence doesn't need to be pumped up with an exclamation
point. It is emphatic enough without it.

▶ Whenever I see Steffi lunging forward to put away an overhead

smash, it might as well be me!⁄.She does it just the way that I
　　　　　　　　　　　　　∧

would!

The first exclamation point should be deleted so that the second
one will have more force.

EXERCISE 38–1

Add appropriate end punctuation in the following paragraph.

　　Although I am generally rational, I am superstitious I
never walk under ladders or put shoes on the table If I spill the
salt, I go into frenzied calisthenics picking up the grains and
tossing them over my left shoulder As a result of these curious
activities, I've always wondered whether knowing the roots of
superstitions would quell my irrational responses Superstition
has it, for example, that one should never place a hat on the
bed This superstition arises from a time when head lice were
quite common and placing a guest's hat on the bed stood a
good chance of spreading lice through the host's bed Doesn't
this make good sense And doesn't it stand to reason that if I
know that my guests don't have lice I shouldn't care where
their hats go Of course it does It is fair to ask, then, whether I
have changed my ways and place hats on beds Are you kidding
I wouldn't put a hat on a bed if my life depended on it

39

Other punctuation marks: the dash, parentheses, brackets, the ellipsis mark, the slash

39a The dash

When typing, use two hyphens to form a dash (--). Do not put spaces before or after the dash.

1. Use dashes to set off parenthetical material that deserves emphasis.

> Everything that went wrong—from the peeping Tom at her window to my head-on collision—was blamed on our move.

2. Use dashes to set off appositives that contain commas.

An appositive is a noun or noun phrase that renames a nearby noun. Ordinarily most appositives are set off with commas (32e), but when the appositive contains commas, a pair of dashes helps readers see the relative importance of all the pauses.

> In my hometown the basic needs of people—food, clothing, and shelter—are less costly than in Los Angeles.

3. Use a dash to prepare for a list, a restatement, an amplification, or a dramatic shift in tone or thought.

> Along the wall are the bulk liquids—sesame seed oil, honey, safflower oil, and that half-liquid "peanuts only" peanut butter.

> Consider the amount of sugar in the average person's diet—104 pounds per year, 90 percent more than that consumed by our ancestors.

Everywhere we looked there were little kids — a box of Cracker Jacks in one hand and mommy or daddy's sleeve in the other.

Kiere took a few steps back, came running full speed, kicked a mighty kick — and missed the ball.

In the first two examples, the writer could also use a colon. (See 35a.) The colon is more formal than the dash, and not quite as dramatic.

4. Do not overuse the dash.

Unless there is a specific reason for using the dash, avoid it. Unnecessary dashes create a choppy effect.

▶ Insisting that students use computers as instructional tools

for information retrieval makes good sense. Herding

them sheeplike into computer technology does not.

39b Parentheses

1. Use parentheses to enclose supplemental material, minor digressions, and afterthoughts.

After taking her temperature, pulse, and blood pressure (routine vital signs), the nurse made Becky as comfortable as possible.

The weights James was first able to move (not lift, mind you) were measured in ounces.

2. Use parentheses to enclose letters or numbers labeling items in a series.

Regulations stipulated that only the following equipment could be used on the survival mission: (1) a knife, (2) thirty feet of parachute line, (3) a book of matches, (4) two ponchos, (5) an *E* tool, and (6) a signal flare.

3. Do not overuse parentheses.

Rough drafts are likely to contain more afterthoughts than necessary. As writers head into a sentence, they often think of additional details, occasionally working them in as best they can with parentheses. Usually such sentences should be revised so that the additional details no longer seem to be afterthoughts.

▶ Tucker's Restaurant serves homestyle breakfasts with fresh eggs, ∧buttered toast ⟂(which is still warm),∧ sausage, bacon,
   warm

   waffles, pancakes, and even kippers.

▶ Researchers have said that ten million (estimates run as high as fifty million) Americans have hypoglycemia.
   from ten to fifty million

39c Brackets

Use brackets to enclose any words or phrases that you have inserted into an otherwise word-for-word quotation.

> *Audubon* reports that "if there are not enough young to balance deaths, the end of the species [California condor] is inevitable."

The sentence quoted from the *Audubon* article did not contain the words *California condor* (since the context made clear what species was meant), so the writer in this example needed to add the name in brackets.

The Latin word *sic* in brackets indicates that an error in a quoted sentence appears in the original source.

> According to the review, Darcy Kistler's performance was brilliant, "exceding [*sic*] the expectations of even her most loyal fans."

Do not overuse *sic,* however, since calling attention to others' mistakes can appear snobbish. The preceding quotation, for example, might have been paraphrased instead: *According to the review, even Darcy Kistler's most loyal fans were surprised by the brilliance of her performance.*

39d The ellipsis mark

The ellipsis mark consists of three spaced periods. Use an ellipsis mark to indicate that you have deleted words from an otherwise word-for-word quotation.

> Reuben reports that "when the amount of cholesterol circulating in the blood rises over . . . 300 milligrams per 100, the chances of a heart attack increase dramatically."

If you delete a full sentence or more in the middle of a quoted passage, use a period before the three ellipsis dots.

> "Most of our efforts," writes Dave Erikson, "are directed toward saving the bald eagle's wintering habitat along the Mississippi River. . . . It's important that the wintering birds have a place to roost, where they can get out of the cold wind and be undisturbed by man."

CAUTION: Do not use the ellipsis mark at the beginning of a quotation; do not use it at the end of a quotation unless you have cut some words from the final sentence quoted. (See also 49e.)

In quoted poetry, use a full line of dots to indicate that you have dropped a line or more from the poem:

Had we but world enough, and time,
This coyness, lady, were no crime.

. . . .

But at my back I always hear
Time's wingèd chariot hurrying near;   —Andrew Marvell

The ellipsis mark may also be used to mark a hesitation
or interruption in speech or to suggest unfinished thoughts.

Before falling into a coma, the victim whispered,
"It was a man with a tattoo on his. . . ."

39e The slash

Use the slash to separate two or three lines of poetry that have
been run in to your text. Add a space both before and after
the slash.

In the opening lines of "Jordan," George Herbert pokes gentle
fun at popular poems of his time: "Who says that fictions only
and false hair / Become a verse? Is there in truth no beauty?"

More than three lines of poetry should be handled as an indented quotation. See 37b.

The slash may occasionally be used to separate paired
terms such as *pass/fail* and *producer/director.* Do not use a
space before or after the slash.

Roger, the producer/director, announced a casting change.

Be sparing, however, in this use of the slash. In particular,
avoid use of *and/or, he/she,* and *his/her.*

EXERCISE 39–1

Edit the following sentences to correct errors in punctuation, focusing
especially on appropriate use of the dash, parentheses, brackets,

ellipsis mark, and slash. If a sentence is correct, write "correct" after it. Answers to lettered sentences appear in the back of the book. Example:

Social insects/→bees, for example/→are able to communicate
            ∧   ∧

quite complicated messages to their fellows.

a. We lived in Iowa (Davenport, to be specific) during the early years of our marriage.
b. Every night — after her jazzercise class — Elizaveta bragged about how invigorated she felt, but she always looked exhausted.
c. *Infoworld* reports that "customers without any particular aptitude for computers can easily learn to use it [the Bay Area Teleguide] through simple, three-step instructions located at the booth."
d. Every person there — from the youngest toddler to the oldest great-grandparent, was expected to sit through the three-hour sermon in respectful silence.
e. The class stood, faced the flag, placed hands over hearts, and raced through "I pledge allegiance — liberty and justice for all" in less than sixty seconds.

1. Of the three basic schools of detective fiction, the tea-and-crumpet, the hardboiled detective, and the police procedural, I find the quaint, civilized quality of the tea-and-crumpet school the most appealing.
2. In *Lifeboat*, Alfred Hitchcock appears (some say without his knowledge) in a newspaper advertisement for weight loss.
3. There are three points of etiquette in poker: 1. always allow someone to cut the cards, 2. don't forget to ante up, and 3. never stack your chips.
4. When he was informed that fewer than 20 percent of the panelists scheduled for the 1986 PEN conference were women, Norman Mailer gave this explanation: "There are more men who are deeply interested in intellectual matters than women . . . [If we put more women on the panel] all we'd be doing is lowering the level of discussion."
5. The old Valentine verse we used to chant said it all: "Roses are red, / Violets are blue, / Sugar is sweet, / And so are you."

PART VIII

Editing for Mechanics

40

Abbreviations

40a Use standard abbreviations for titles immediately before and after proper names.

TITLES BEFORE PROPER NAMES	TITLES AFTER PROPER NAMES
Mr. Rafael Zabala	William Albert, Sr.
Ms. Nancy Linehan	Thomas Hines, Jr.
Mrs. Edward Horn	Anita Lor, Ph.D.
Dr. Margaret Simmons	Robert Simkowski, M.D.
the Rev. John Stone	William Lyons, M.A.
St. Joan of Arc	Margaret Chin, LL.D.
Prof. James Russo	Polly Stein, D.D.S.

Do not abbreviate a title if it is not used with a proper name.

▶ My history ~~prof.~~ *professor* was an expert on America's use of the atomic bomb in World War II.

Avoid redundant titles such as *Dr. Susan Hasselquist, M.D.* Choose one title or the other: *Dr. Susan Hasselquist* or *Susan Hasselquist, M.D.*

40b Use familiar abbreviations for the names of organizations, corporations, and countries.

Familiar abbreviations, often written without periods, are acceptable:

CIA	FBI	AFL-CIO	NAACP
IBM	UPI	NEA	IRS
YMCA	CBS	USA (or U.S.A.)	

While in Washington the schoolchildren toured the FBI.

The YMCA has opened a new gym close to my office.

NOTE: When using an unfamiliar abbreviation (such as CBE for Council of Biology Editors) throughout a paper, write the full name followed by the abbreviation in parentheses at the first mention of the name. Then use the abbreviation throughout the rest of the paper.

40c   Use B.C., A.D., A.M., P.M., No., and $ only with specific dates, times, numbers, and amounts.

The abbreviation B.C. ("before Christ") follows a date, and A.D. ("*anno Domini*") precedes a date. Acceptable alternatives are B.C.E. ("before the common era") and C.E. ("common era").

40 B.C. (or B.C.E.)	4:00 A.M. (or a.m.)	No. 12 (or no. 12)
A.D. 44 (or C.E.)	6:00 P.M. (or p.m.)	$150

Avoid using A.M., P.M., No., or $ when not accompanied by a specific figure.

▶ We set off for the lake early in the ~~A.M.~~ *morning.*
^

▶ There were a ~~no.~~ *number* of old hats in the trunk.
^

40d   Be sparing in your use of Latin abbreviations.

Latin abbreviations are acceptable in footnotes and bibliographies and in informal writing for comments in parentheses.

cf. (Latin *confer,* "compare")
e.g. (Latin *exempli gratia,* "for example")
et al. (Latin *et alii,* "and others")

etc. (Latin *et cetera*, "and so forth")
i.e. (Latin *id est*, "that is")
N.B. (Latin *nota bene*, "note well")

Harold Simms et al., *The Race for Space*

She hated the slice-and-dice genre of horror movies (e.g., *Happy Birthday to Me, Psycho, Friday the 13th*).

In formal writing use the appropriate English phrases.

▶ Many obsolete laws remain on the books, ~~e.g.~~ *for example,* a law in Vermont forbidding an unmarried man and woman to sit closer than six inches apart on a park bench.

40e Avoid inappropriate abbreviations.

In formal writing, abbreviations for the following are not commonly accepted: personal names, units of measurement, days of the week, holidays, months, courses of study, divisions of written works, states and countries (except in addresses and except Washington, D.C.). Do not abbreviate *Company* and *Incorporated* unless their abbreviated forms are part of an official name.

PERSONAL NAME Charles (not Chas.)

UNITS OF MEASUREMENT pound (not lb.)

DAYS OF THE WEEK Monday (not Mon.)

HOLIDAYS Christmas (not Xmas)

MONTHS January, February, March (not Jan., Feb., Mar.)

COURSES OF STUDY political science (not poli. sci.)

DIVISIONS OF WRITTEN WORKS chapter, page (not ch., p.)

STATES AND COUNTRIES Massachusetts (not MA or Mass.)

PARTS OF A BUSINESS NAME Adams Lighting Company (not Adams Lighting Co.); Kim and Brothers, Inc. (not Kim and Bros., Inc.)

▶ Eliza promised to buy me one ~~lb.~~ *pound* of Godiva chocolate for my birthday, which was last ~~Fri.~~ *Friday.*

EXERCISE 40–1

Edit the following sentences to correct errors in abbreviations. If a sentence is correct, write "correct" after it. Answers to lettered sentences appear in the back of the book. Example:

This year ~~Xmas~~ *Christmas* will fall on a ~~Fri.~~ *Friday.*

a. Audrey Hepburn was a powerful spokesperson for UNICEF for many years.
b. Denzil spent all night studying for his psych. exam.
c. "Mahatma" Gandhi has inspired many modern leaders, including Martin Luther King, Jr.
d. The first discovery of America was definitely not in 1492 A.D.
e. Turning to p. 195, Marion realized that she had finally reached the end of ch. 22.

1. Many girls fall prey to a cult worship of great entertainers—e.g., in my mother's generation, girls worshiped the Beatles.
2. Three interns were selected to assist the chief surgeon, Dr. Enrique Derenzo, M.D., in the hospital's first heart-lung transplant.
3. Some historians think that the New Testament was completed by A.D. 100.
4. My soc. prof. spends most of his lecture time talking about political science.
5. Since its inception, the BBC has maintained a consistently high standard of radio and television broadcasting.

41

Numbers

41a Spell out numbers of one or two words or those that begin a sentence. Use figures for numbers that require more than two words to spell out.

▶ Now, some ~~8~~ *eight* years later, Muffin is still with us.

▶ I counted ~~one hundred seventy-six~~ *176* CD's on the shelf.

If a sentence begins with a number, spell out the number or rewrite the sentence.

▶ ~~150~~ *One hundred fifty* children in our program need expensive dental treatment.

Rewriting the sentence will also correct the error and may be less awkward if the number is long: *In our program are 150 children who need expensive dental treatment.*

EXCEPTIONS: In technical and some business writing, figures are preferred even when spellings would be brief, but usage varies.

When several numbers appear in the same passage, many writers choose consistency rather than strict adherence to the rule.

When one number immediately follows another, spell out one and use figures for the other: three 100-meter events, 125 four-poster beds.

41b   Generally, figures are acceptable for dates, addresses, percentages, fractions, decimals, scores, statistics and other numerical results, exact amounts of money, divisions of books and plays, pages, identification numbers, and the time.

DATES   July 4, 1776, 56 B.C., A.D. 30

ADDRESSES   77 Latches Lane, 519 West 42nd Street

PERCENTAGES   55 percent (or 55%)

FRACTIONS, DECIMALS   ½, 0.047

SCORES   7 to 3, 21–18

STATISTICS   average age 37, average weight 180

SURVEYS   4 out of 5

EXACT AMOUNTS OF MONEY $105.37, $106,000

DIVISIONS OF BOOKS   volume 3, chapter 4, page 189

DIVISIONS OF PLAYS   act III, scene iii (or act 3, scene 3)

IDENTIFICATION NUMBERS   serial number 10988675

TIME OF DAY   4:00 P.M., 1:30 A.M.

▶ Several doctors put up ~~two hundred fifty-five thousand dollars~~ $255,000 for the construction of a golf course.

▶ Though I was working on a ~~nineteen thirty-nine~~ *1939* sewing machine, my costume turned out well.

NOTE: When not using A.M. or P.M., write out the time in words (*four o'clock in the afternoon, twelve noon, seven in the morning*).

EXERCISE 41–1

Edit the following sentences to correct errors in the use of numbers. If a sentence is correct, write "correct" after it. Answers to lettered sentences appear in the back of the book. Example:

> By the end of the evening Ashanti had only ~~three dollars and six cents~~ left.
>
> $3.06 ∧

a. We have ordered 4 azaleas, 3 rhododendrons, and 2 mountain laurels for the back area of the garden.
b. Venezuelan independence from Spain was declared on July 5, 1811.
c. The score was tied at 5–5 when the momentum shifted and carried the Standards to a decisive 12–5 win.
d. We ordered three four-door sedans for company executives.
e. The Vietnam Veterans Memorial in Washington, D.C., had fifty-eight thousand one hundred thirty-two names inscribed on it when it was dedicated in 1982.

1. One of my favorite scenes in Shakespeare is the property division scene in act I of *King Lear.*
2. The botany lecture will begin at precisely 3:30 P.M.
3. 90 of the firm's employees signed up for the insurance program.
4. After her 5th marriage ended in divorce, Melinda decided to give up her quest for the perfect husband.
5. With 6 students and 2 teachers, the class had a 3:1 student-teacher ratio.

42

Italics (underlining)

In handwritten or typed papers, <u>underlining</u> represents *italics,* a slanting typeface used in printed material.

42a   Underline the titles of works according to convention.

Titles of the following works are underlined to indicate italics:

TITLES OF BOOKS   *The Great Gatsby, A Distant Mirror*

MAGAZINES   *Time, Scientific American*

NEWSPAPERS   the *St. Louis Post-Dispatch*

PAMPHLETS   *Common Sense, Facts about Marijuana*

LONG POEMS   *The Waste Land, Paradise Lost*

PLAYS   *King Lear, A Raisin in the Sun*

FILMS   *Malcolm X, The Crying Game*

TELEVISION PROGRAMS   *Murphy Brown, 60 Minutes*

RADIO PROGRAMS   *All Things Considered*

MUSICAL COMPOSITIONS   Gershwin's *Porgy and Bess*

CHOREOGRAPHIC WORKS   Twyla Tharp's *Push Comes to Shove*

WORKS OF VISUAL ART   Rodin's *The Thinker*

COMIC STRIPS   *Calvin and Hobbes*

SOFTWARE   *WordPerfect*

The titles of other works, such as short stories, essays, songs, and short poems, are enclosed in quotation marks. (See 37d.)

NOTE: Do not underline the Bible or the titles of books in the Bible (Genesis, not *Genesis*); the titles of legal documents (the Constitution, not the *Constitution*); or the titles of your own papers.

42b Underline the names of spacecraft, aircraft, ships, and trains.

> *Challenger, Spirit of St. Louis, Queen Elizabeth II, Silver Streak*

▶ The success of the Soviets' <u>Sputnik</u> galvanized the U.S. space

program.

42c Underline foreign words used in an English sentence.

▶ Although Joe's method seemed to be successful, I decided to

establish my own <u>modus operandi</u>.

EXCEPTION: Do not underline foreign words that have become part of the English language—"laissez-faire," "fait accompli," "habeus corpus," and "per diem," for example.

42d Underline words mentioned as words, letters mentioned as letters, and numbers mentioned as numbers.

▶ Tim assured us that the howling probably came from his

bloodhound, Hill Billy, but his <u>probably</u> stuck in our minds.

▶ Sarah called her father by his given name, Johnny, but she

was unable to pronounce <u>J</u>

▶ A big <u>3</u> was painted on the door.

NOTE: Quotation marks may be used instead of underlining to set off words mentioned as words. (See 37e.)

42e   Avoid excessive underlining for emphasis.

Underlining to emphasize words or ideas is distracting and should be used sparingly.

▶ Tennis is a sport that has become an ~~addiction~~.

EXERCISE 42–1

Edit the following sentences to correct errors in the use of italics. If a sentence is correct, write "correct" after it. Answers to lettered sentences appear in the back of the book. Example:

> <u>Leaves of Grass</u> by Walt Whitman was quite controversial
>
> when it was published a century ago.

a. Howard Hughes commissioned the Spruce Goose, a beautifully built but thoroughly impractical wooden aircraft.

b. Pulaski was so *exhausted* he could barely lift his foot the six inches to the elevator floor.

c. Even though it is almost always hot in Mexico in the summer, you can usually find a cool spot on one of the park benches in the town's zócalo.

d. Cinema audiences once gasped at hearing the word *damn* in *Gone With the Wind.*

e. "The City and the Pillar" was an early novel by Gore Vidal.

1. Bernard watched as Eileen stood transfixed in front of Vermeer's Head of a Young Girl.

2. The monastery walls were painted with scenes described in the book of Genesis.

3. I learned the Latin term ad infinitum from an old nursery rhyme about fleas: "Great fleas have little fleas upon their back to bite 'em, / Little fleas have lesser fleas and so on ad infinitum."

4. Redford and Newman in the movie "The Sting" were amateurs compared with the seventeen-year-old con artist who lives at our house.
5. I find it impossible to remember the second *l* in *llama*.

43

Spelling

You learned to spell from repeated experience with words in both reading and writing, but especially writing. Words have a look, a sound, and even a feel to them as the hand moves across the page. As you proofread, you can probably tell if a word doesn't look quite right. In such cases, the solution is obvious: Look up the word in the dictionary.

A word processor equipped with a spelling checker is a useful alternative to a dictionary, but only up to a point. A spelling checker will not tell you how to spell words not listed in its dictionary; nor will it help you catch words commonly confused, such as *accept* and *except,* or common typographical errors, such as *own* for *won.* You will still need to proofread, and for some words you may need to turn to the dictionary.

43a Become familiar with your dictionary.

A good desk dictionary — such as *The American Heritage Dictionary of the English Language, The Random House College Dictionary,* or *Merriam-Webster's Collegiate Dictionary* or *New World Dictionary of the American Language* — is an indispensable writer's aid. By reading or at least skimming your dictionary's guide to its use, which usually appears at the front of the book, you will discover many new reasons for turning to the dictionary for help.

A sample dictionary entry, taken from *The American Heritage Dictionary,* appears below. Labels show where various kinds of information about a word can be found in that dictionary.

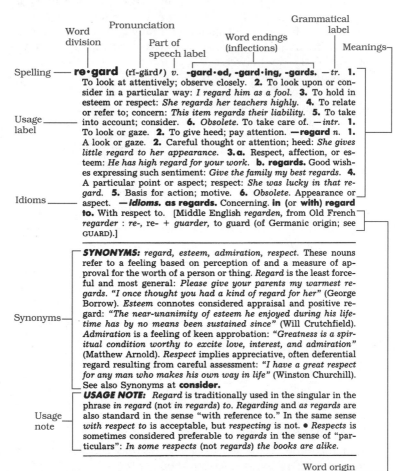

Word division | Pronunciation | Part of speech label | Word endings (inflections) | Grammatical label | Meanings

Spelling — **re·gard** (rĭ-gärd′) *v.* **-gard·ed, -gard·ing, -gards.** —*tr.* **1.** To look at attentively; observe closely. **2.** To look upon or consider in a particular way: *I regard him as a fool.* **3.** To hold in esteem or respect: *She regards her teachers highly.* **4.** To relate or refer to; concern: *This item regards their liability.* **5.** To take into account; consider. **6.** *Obsolete.* To take care of. —*intr.* **1.** To look or gaze. **2.** To give heed; pay attention. —**regard** *n.* **1.** A look or gaze. **2.** Careful thought or attention; heed: *She gives little regard to her appearance.* **3.a.** Respect, affection, or esteem: *He has high regard for your work.* **b. regards.** Good wishes expressing such sentiment: *Give the family my best regards.* **4.** A particular point or aspect; respect: *She was lucky in that regard.* **5.** Basis for action; motive. **6.** *Obsolete.* Appearance or aspect. —*idioms.* **as regards.** Concerning. **in** (or **with**) **regard to.** With respect to. [Middle English *regarden,* from Old French *regarder* : *re-,* re- + *guarder,* to guard (of Germanic origin; see GUARD).]

Usage label · Idioms

SYNONYMS: *regard, esteem, admiration, respect.* These nouns refer to a feeling based on perception of and a measure of approval for the worth of a person or thing. *Regard* is the least forceful and most general: *Please give your parents my warmest regards.* "*I once thought you had a kind of regard for her*" (George Borrow). *Esteem* connotes considered appraisal and positive regard: "*The near-unanimity of esteem he enjoyed during his lifetime has by no means been sustained since*" (Will Crutchfield). *Admiration* is a feeling of keen approbation: "*Greatness is a spiritual condition worthy to excite love, interest, and admiration*" (Matthew Arnold). *Respect* implies appreciative, often deferential regard resulting from careful assessment: "*I have a great respect for any man who makes his own way in life*" (Winston Churchill). See also Synonyms at **consider.**

Synonyms

USAGE NOTE: *Regard* is traditionally used in the singular in the phrase *in regard* (not *in regards*) *to. Regarding* and *as regards* are also standard in the sense "with reference to." In the same sense *with respect to* is acceptable, but *respecting* is not. • *Respects* is sometimes considered preferable to *regards* in the sense of "particulars": *In some respects* (not *regards*) *the books are alike.*

Usage note

Word origin (etymology)

Spelling, word division, pronunciation

The main entry (*re·gard* in the sample entry) shows the correct spelling of the word. When there are two correct spellings of a word (as in *collectible, collectable*, for example), both are given, with the preferred spelling usually appearing first.

The main entry also shows how the word is divided into syllables. The dot between *re* and *gard* separates the word's two syllables. When a word is compound, the main entry shows how to write it: as one word (*crossroad*), as a hyphenated word (*cross-stitch*), or as two words (*cross section*).

The word's pronunciation is given just after the main entry. The accents indicate which syllables are stressed; the other marks are explained in the dictionary's pronunciation key. In some dictionaries this key appears at the bottom of every page or every other page.

Word endings and grammatical labels

When a word takes endings to indicate grammatical functions (called *inflections*), the endings are listed in boldface, as with *-garded, -garding,* and *-gards* in the sample entry.

Labels for the parts of speech and for other grammatical terms are abbreviated. The most commonly used abbreviations are these:

n.	noun	adj.	adjective
pl.	plural	adv.	adverb
sing.	singular	pron.	pronoun
v.	verb	prep.	preposition
tr.	transitive verb	conj.	conjunction
intr.	intransitive verb	interj.	interjection

Meanings, word origin, synonyms, and antonyms

Each meaning for the word is given a number. Occasionally a word's use is illustrated in a quoted sentence.

Sometimes a word can be used as more than one part of speech (*regard*, for instance, can be used as either a verb or a noun). In such a case, all the meanings for one part of speech are given before all the meanings for another, as in the sample entry. The entry also gives idiomatic uses of the word.

The origin of the word, called its *etymology*, appears in brackets after all the meanings (in some dictionaries it appears before the meanings).

Synonyms, words similar in meaning to the main entry, are frequently listed. In the sample entry, the dictionary draws distinctions in meaning among the various synonyms. Antonyms, which do not appear in the sample entry, are words having a meaning opposite from that of the main entry.

Usage

Usage labels indicate when, where, or under what conditions a particular meaning for a word is appropriately used. Common labels are *informal* (or *colloquial*), *slang, nonstandard, dialect, obsolete, archaic, poetic,* and *British.* In the sample entry, two meanings of *regard* are labeled *obsolete* because they are no longer in use.

Dictionaries sometimes include usage notes as well. In the sample entry, the dictionary offers advice on several uses of *regard* not specifically covered by the meanings. Such advice is based on the opinions of many experts and on actual usage in current magazines, newspapers, and books.

43b Discriminate between words that sound alike but have different meanings.

Words that sound alike or nearly alike but have different meanings and spellings are called homophones. The following homophones are so commonly confused that a good proof-reader will double-check their every use.

affect (verb: "to exert an influence")
effect (verb: "to accomplish"; noun: "result")

its (possessive pronoun: "of or belonging to it")
it's (contraction for "it is")

loose (adjective: "free, not securely attached")
lose (verb: "to fail to keep, to be deprived of")

principal (adjective: "most important"; noun: "head of a school")
principle (noun: "a general or fundamental truth")

their (possessive pronoun: "belonging to them")
they're (contraction for "they are")
there (adverb: "that place or position")

who's (contraction for "who is")
whose (possessive form of "who")

your (possessive form of "you")
you're (contraction of "you are")

To check for correct use of these and other homophones, consult the Glossary of Usage, which begins on page 689. There you will find definitions and examples for all of the following sets of words.

HOMOPHONES IN THE GLOSSARY OF USAGE

accept, except	censor, censure
adapt, adopt	cite, site
adverse, averse	climactic, climatic
advice, advise	coarse, course
affect, effect	complement, compliment
all ready, already	conscience, conscious
all together, altogether	continual, continuous
allusion, illusion	disinterested, uninterested
amoral, immoral	elicit, illicit
anyone, any one	eminent, imminent
awhile, a while	everyone, every one
beside, besides	explicit, implicit
capital, capitol	farther, further

HOMOPHONES IN THE GLOSSARY OF USAGE

imply, infer
ingenious, ingenuous
its, it's
lead, led
loose, lose
maybe, may be
media, medium
nauseated, nauseous
passed, past
precede, proceed
principal, principle

relation, relationship
respectfully, respectively
sensual, sensuous
sometime, some time,
   sometimes
than, then
there, their, they're
to, too, two
weather, whether
who's, whose
your, you're

43c Become familiar with the major spelling rules.

1. Use *i* before *e* except after *c* or when sounded like the
letter *a*, as in *neighbor* and *weigh*.

i **BEFORE** *e*	relieve, believe, sieve, frieze
e **BEFORE** *i*	receive, deceive, sleigh, freight, eight
EXCEPTIONS	seize, either, weird, height, foreign, leisure

2. Generally, drop a final silent *-e* when adding a suffix
that begins with a vowel. Keep the final *-e* if the suffix begins
with a consonant.

desire, desiring; remove, removable

achieve, achievement; care, careful

Words such as *argument, truly,* and *changeable* are exceptions.

3. When adding *-s* or *-d* to words ending in *-y,* ordinarily
change the *y* to *ie* when the *y* is preceded by a consonant but
not when it is preceded by a vowel.

comedy, comedies; dry, dried

monkey, monkeys; play, played

With proper names ending in *y*, however, do not change the *y* to *i* even if it is preceded by a consonant: *Dougherty, the Doughertys.*

4. If a final consonant is preceded by a single vowel *and* the consonant ends a one-syllable word or a stressed syllable, double the consonant when adding a suffix beginning with a vowel.

bet, betting; commit, committed; occur, occurrence

5. Add *-s* to form the plural of most nouns; add *-es* to singular nouns ending in *-s*, *-sh*, *-ch*, and *-x*.

table, tables; paper, papers

church, churches; dish, dishes

Ordinarily add *-s* to nouns ending in *-o* when the *o* is preceded by a vowel. Add *-es* when it is preceded by a consonant.

radio, radios; video, videos

hero, heroes; tomato, tomatoes

To form the plural of a hyphenated compound word, add the *-s* to the chief word even if it does not appear at the end.

mother-in-law, mothers-in-law

NOTE: English words derived from other languages such as Latin or French sometimes form the plural as they would in their original language.

medium, media; criterion, criteria; chateau, chateaux

ESL NOTE: Spelling may vary slightly among English-speaking countries. This can prove particularly confusing for ESL students, who may have learned British or Canadian English. Following is a list of some common words spelled differently in American and British English. Consult a dictionary for others.

AMERICAN	BRITISH
canceled, traveled	cancelled, travelled
color, humor	colour, humour
judgment	judgement
check	cheque
realize, apologize	realise, apologise
defense	defence
anemia, anesthetic	anaemia, anaesthetic
theater, center	theatre, centre
fetus	foetus
mold, smolder	mould, smoulder
civilization	civilisation
connection, inflection	connexion, inflexion
licorice	liquorice

43d Be alert to the following commonly misspelled words.

absence	address	answer	association
academic	aggravate	apology	athlete
accidentally	all right	apparently	athletics
accommodate	almost	appearance	attendance
accomplish	although	appropriate	audience
accumulate	altogether	arctic	bachelor
achievement	always	argument	basically
acknowledge	amateur	arising	beginning
acquaintance	among	arithmetic	believe
acquire	analyze	arrangement	benefited
across	annual	ascend	brilliant

Britain
bureau
business
cafeteria
calendar
candidate
category
cemetery
changeable
changing
characteristic
chosen
column
coming
commitment
committed
committee
comparative
competitive
conceivable
conference
conferred
conqueror
conscience
conscientious
conscious
convenient
courteous
criticism
criticize
curiosity
dealt
decision
definitely
descendant
describe
description
despair
desperate
develop

dictionary
dining
disagree
disappear
disappoint
disastrous
dissatisfied
eighth
eligible
eliminate
embarrass
eminent
emphasize
entirely
entrance
environment
equivalent
especially
exaggerated
exhaust
existence
experience
explanation
extraordinary
extremely
familiar
fascinate
February
foreign
forty
fourth
friend
government
grammar
guard
guidance
harass
height
humorous
illiterate

imaginary
imagination
immediately
incidentally
incredible
indefinitely
indispensable
inevitable
infinite
intelligence
interesting
irrelevant
irresistible
knowledge
laboratory
legitimate
license
lightning
literature
loneliness
maintenance
maneuver
marriage
mathematics
mischievous
necessary
nevertheless
noticeable
obstacle
occasion
occasionally
occur
occurred
occurrence
optimistic
original
outrageous
pamphlet
parallel
particularly

pastime
perform
performance
permissible
perseverance
perspiration
phenomenon
physically
picnicking
playwright
politics
practically
precede
precedence
preference
preferred
prejudice
preparation
prevalent
primitive
privilege
probably
proceed
professor
prominent
pronunciation
quantity
quiet
quite
quizzes
receive
recognize
recommend
reference
referred
regard
religion
repetition
restaurant
rhythm

rhythmical	several	succeed	unnecessarily
ridiculous	siege	surprise	until
roommate	similar	temperature	usually
sandwich	sincerely	thorough	vacuum
schedule	soliloquy	tragedy	vengeance
secretary	sophomore	transferred	villain
seize	specimen	tries	weird
separate	strictly	truly	whether
sergeant	subtly	unanimous	writing

LOOKING AT YOURSELF AS A WRITER
Spelling

If spelling is a problem for you, consider possible sources of your difficulties. Here are some causes and cures.

CAUSE You have trouble with a few commonly misspelled words, and because these words occur so often, your spelling problem seems worse than it is.

CURE Ask someone to dictate words from the list of commonly misspelled words on pages 425–27, and write the words as they are read to you. Once you have identified your "spelling demons," practice writing the words correctly.

CAUSE You tend to confuse words that sound alike.

CURE Keep a list of the commonly confused words that give you trouble. When they occur in a draft, consult the Glossary of Usage at the back of this book.

CAUSE Your handwriting is so poor that the words don't flow smoothly onto the paper. (Spelling is to some extent kinesthetic — a matter of how a word "feels" as you form it.)

CURE Try typing your drafts. The words may flow more smoothly as you type, reducing your misspellings.

Another advantage of typing—if you use a word processor—is that you'll have access to a spelling checker.

CAUSE   You have a learning disability. Maybe you have trouble distinguishing between sounds, or perhaps your eyes scramble or reverse letters.

CURE   If possible, consult an expert on learning disabilities. With the expert's help, you can diagnose the cause of your problem and devise ways to overcome it—or work around it. Almost certainly the expert will advise you to type your writing on a word processor equipped with a spelling checker.

44

The hyphen

44a   Consult the dictionary to determine how to treat a compound word.

The dictionary will tell you whether to treat a compound word as a hyphenated compound (*water-repellent*), one word (*waterproof*), or two words (*water table*). If the compound word is not in the dictionary, treat it as two words.

▶ The prosecutor chose not to cross—examine any witnesses.
                                          ∧

▶ Grandma kept a small notebook in her apron pocket.

▶ Alice walked through the looking/glass into a backward world.

44b Use a hyphen to connect two or more words functioning together as an adjective before a noun.

▶ Mrs. Douglas gave Toshiko a seashell and some newspaper—
wrapped fish to take home to her mother.

▶ Priscilla Hobbes is not yet a well-known candidate.

Newspaper-wrapped and *well-known* are adjectives used before the nouns *fish* and *candidate*.

Generally, do not use a hyphen when such compounds follow the noun.

▶ After our television campaign, Priscilla Hobbes will be well/
known.

Do not use a hyphen to connect *-ly* adverbs to the words they modify.

▶ A slowly/moving truck tied up traffic.

NOTE: In a series, hyphens are suspended.

Do you prefer first-, second-, or third-class tickets?

44c Hyphenate the written form of fractions and of compound numbers from twenty-one to ninety-nine.

▶ One—fourth of my income goes to pay off the national debt.
    ∧

44d Use a hyphen with the prefixes *all-*, *ex-* (meaning "former"), and *self-* and with the suffix *-elect*.

▶ The charity is funneling more money into self—help projects.
                                                        ∧

▶ Anne King is our club's president—elect.
                                     ∧

44e A hyphen is used in some words to avoid ambiguity or to separate awkward double or triple letters.

Without the hyphen there would be no way to distinguish between words such as *re-creation* and *recreation.*

> Bicycling in the country is my favorite recreation.

> The film was praised for its astonishing re-creation of nineteenth-century London.

Hyphens are sometimes used to separate awkward double or triple letters in compound words (*anti-intellectual, cross-stitch*). Always check a dictionary for the standard form of the word.

44f If a word must be divided at the end of a line, divide it correctly.

1. Divide words between syllables.

▶ When I returned from overseas, I didn't ~~reco~~ recognize
~~gnize~~ one face on the magazine covers.
          ∧

2. Never divide one-syllable words.

▶ He didn't have the courage or the ~~stren~~
strength
~~gth~~ to open the door.
∧

3. Never divide a word so that a single letter stands alone
at the end of a line or fewer than three letters begin a line.

▶ She'll bring her brother with her when she comes ~~a~~
again.
~~gain.~~

▶ As audience to *The Mousetrap,* Hamlet is a ~~watch~~
watcher
~~er~~ watching watchers.
∧

4. When dividing a compound word at the end of a line,
either make the break between the words that form the compound or put the whole word on the next line.

▶ My niece is determined to become a long-~~dis~~
distance
~~tance~~ runner when she grows up.
∧

EXERCISE 44–1

Edit the following sentences to correct errors in hyphenation. If a sentence is correct, write "correct" after it. Answers to lettered sentences
appear in the back of the book. Example:

Zola's first readers were scandalized by his slice—of—life
                                                        ∧ ∧
novels.

a. Gold is the seventy-ninth element in the periodic table.
b. The quietly-purring cat cleaned first one paw and then the other before curling up under the stove.
c. The Moche were a pre-Columbian people who established a sophisticated culture in ancient Peru.
d. Your dog is well-known in our neighborhood.
e. Dmitri did fifty push-ups in two minutes and then collapsed.

1. We knew we were driving too fast when our tires skidded over the rain slick surface.
2. The Black Death reduced the population of some medieval villages by two thirds.
3. The flight attendant asked us to fasten our seat belts before lift-off.
4. One-quarter of the class signed up for the debate on U.S. foreign aid to Latin America.
5. Joan had been brought up to be independent and self reliant.

45

Capital letters

In addition to the following rules, you can use a good dictionary to tell you when to use capital letters.

45a Capitalize proper nouns and words derived from them; do not capitalize common nouns.

Proper nouns are the names of specific persons, places, and things. All other nouns are common nouns. The following types of words are usually capitalized: names for the deity, religions, religious followers, sacred books; words of family relationship used as names; particular places; nationalities and their languages, races, tribes; educational institutions, departments, degrees, particular courses; government departments, organizations, political parties; and historical movements, periods, events, documents.

PROPER NOUNS	COMMON NOUNS
God (used as a name)	a god
Book of Jeremiah	a book
Uncle Pedro	my uncle
Father (used as a name)	my father
Lake Superior	a picturesque lake
the Capital Center	a center for advanced studies
the South	a southern state
Japan, a Japanese garden	an ornamental garden
University of Wisconsin	a good university
Geology 101	geology
Environmental Protection Agency	a federal agency
Phi Kappa Psi	a fraternity
a Democrat	an independent
the Enlightenment	the eighteenth century
the Declaration of Independence	a treaty

Months, holidays, and days of the week are treated as proper nouns; the seasons and numbers of the days of the month are not.

Our academic year begins on a Tuesday in early September, right after Labor Day.

My mother's birthday is in early summer, on the thirteenth of June.

Names of school subjects are capitalized only if they are names of languages. Names of particular courses are capitalized.

This semester Austin is taking math, geography, geology, French, and English.

Professor Anderson offers Modern American Fiction 501 to graduate students.

CAUTION: Do not capitalize common nouns to make them seem important: *Our company is currently hiring computer programmers* (not *Company, Computer Programmers*).

45b Capitalize titles of persons when used as part of a proper name but usually not when used alone.

Professor Margaret Barnes; Dr. Harold Stevens; John Scott Williams, Jr.; Anne Tilton, LL.D.

District Attorney Marshall was reprimanded for badgering the witness.

The district attorney was elected for a two-year term.

Usage varies when the title of an important public figure is used alone: *The president* (or *President*) *vetoed the bill.*

45c Capitalize the first, last, and all major words in titles and subtitles of works such as books, articles, and songs.

In both titles and subtitles, major words such as nouns, pronouns, verbs, adjectives, and adverbs should be capitalized. Minor words such as articles, prepositions, and coordinating conjunctions are not capitalized unless they are the first or last word of a title or subtitle. Capitalize the second part of a hyphenated term in a title if it is a major word but not if it is a minor word.

The Country of the Pointed Firs
The Impossible Theater: A Manifesto
The F-Plan Diet

Capitalize chapter titles and the titles of other major divisions of a work following the same guidelines used for titles of complete works.

"Work and Play" in Santayana's *The Nature of Beauty*

45d Capitalize the first word of a sentence.

Obviously the first word of a sentence should be capitalized.

When lightning struck the house, the chimney collapsed.

When a sentence appears within parentheses, capitalize its first word unless the parentheses appear within another sentence.

Early detection of breast cancer significantly increases survival rates. (See table 2.)

Early detection of breast cancer significantly increases survival rates (see table 2).

45e Capitalize the first word of a quoted sentence unless it is blended into the sentence that introduces it.

In *Time* magazine Robert Hughes writes, "There are only about sixty Watteau paintings on whose authenticity all experts agree."

Russell Baker has written that in our country "it is sport that is the opiate of the masses."

If a quoted sentence is interrupted by explanatory words, do not capitalize the first word after the interruption. (See 37f.)

"If you wanted to go out," he said sharply, "you should have told me."

When quoting poetry, copy the poet's capitalization exactly. Many poets capitalize the first word of every line of poetry; a few contemporary poets dismiss capitalization altogether.

When I consider everything that grows
Holds in perfection but a little moment   —Shakespeare

it was the week   that
i felt the city's narrow breezes rush about
me   —Don L. Lee

45f Do not capitalize the first word after a colon unless it begins an independent clause, in which case capitalization is optional.

Most of the bar's patrons can be divided into two groups: the occasional after-work socializers and the nothing-to-go-home-to regulars.

This we are forced to conclude: the [*or* The] federal government is needed to protect the rights of minorities.

45g Capitalize abbreviations for departments and agencies of government, other organizations, and corporations; capitalize trade names and the call letters of radio and television stations.

EPA, FBI, OPEC, IBM, Xerox, WCRB, KNBC-TV

EXERCISE 45–1

Edit the following sentences to correct errors in capitalization. If a sentence is correct, write "correct" after it. Answers to lettered sentences appear in the back of the book. Example:

On our trip to the West we visited the grand canyon and the great salt desert.

a. District attorney Johnson was disgusted when the jurors turned in a verdict of not guilty after only one hour of deliberation.
b. My mother has begun to research the history of her indian ancestors in North Carolina.
c. W. C. Fields's epitaph reads, "On the whole, I'd rather be in Philadelphia."
d. Refugees from central America are finding it more and more difficult to cross the rio Grande into the United States.
e. I want to take Environmental Biology 103, one other Biology course, and one English course.

1. "O Liberty," cried madame Roland from the scaffold, "What crimes are committed in thy name!"
2. The grunion is an unremarkable fish except for one curious habit: it comes ashore to spawn.
3. Does your Aunt still preach in local churches whenever she's asked?
4. Historians have described Robert E. Lee as the aristocratic south personified.
5. My brother is a Doctor and my sister-in-law is an Attorney.

PART IX

Research Guide

46

Conducting research

College research assignments are an opportunity for you to contribute to an intellectual inquiry or debate. Most college assignments ask you to pose a question worth exploring, to read widely in search of possible answers, to interpret what you read, to draw reasoned conclusions, and to support those conclusions with valid and well-documented evidence. Such assignments may at first seem overwhelming, but if you pose a question that intrigues you and approach it like a detective, with genuine curiosity, you will soon learn how rewarding doing research can be.

Admittedly, the process takes time: time for researching and time for drafting, revising, and documenting the paper in the style recommended by your instructor (see 50 or 51). Before beginning a research project, you should set a realistic schedule of deadlines. For example, before she began researching the paper that appears on pages 514–38, Karen Shaw constructed the following schedule. She received her assignment on October 1, and the due date was November 1.

SCHEDULE	FINISHED BY
1. Take the college's library tour.	October 2
2. Choose a topic and plan a search strategy.	4
3. Compile a bibliography.	8
4. Read and take notes.	15
5. Decide on a tentative thesis and outline.	17
6. Draft the paper.	22
7. Visit the writing center to get help with ideas for revision.	25
8. Revise the paper.	26
9. Prepare a list of works cited.	27
10. Type and proofread the final draft.	28

Notice that Shaw built some extra time into her schedule to allow for unexpected delays. Although the due date for the paper was November 1, her schedule called for completing the paper by October 28.

46a Pose possible questions worth exploring.

Working within the guidelines of your assignment, jot down a few questions that seem worth researching. Here, for example, are some preliminary questions jotted down by students who were asked to write about a significant political or scholarly issue:

Should the use of lie detectors be banned?

What was Marcus Garvey's contribution to the fight for racial equality?

What are the hazards of fad diets?

Does investing in wind energy make economic sense?

Have gorillas and chimpanzees demonstrated significant language skills?

Why was amateur archeologist Heinrich Schliemann such a controversial figure in his own time?

Which geological formations are the safest repositories for nuclear waste?

How can governments and zoos help preserve China's endangered giant panda?

If you have trouble coming up with a list of questions, you can browse through certain library references for ideas. For example, *Opposing Viewpoints Series* compiles recent articles on controversial social issues and current events, and *CQ Researcher* contains digests of recent articles and editorials on contemporary issues. You can discover other possible lines of inquiry by skimming through current magazines such as *Newsweek, Harper's, Science News,* and *Smithsonian* or by consulting specialized periodicals in your academic discipline. Scholarly controversies encountered in college courses are yet another potential source of ideas; ask your professors for suggestions.

Once you have come up with a list of possible questions, choose the question that intrigues you the most and do a bit of preliminary research to see where your line of inquiry might lead. If it seems to be leading to a dead end—maybe because you can't find a variety of sources on the subject or because the information is too technical for you to understand—turn to another question on your list, which may prove more promising.

Once you have settled on a question that looks promising, check to see if it is too broad, given the length of the paper you plan to write. If you suspect it is—and most writers' initial questions are—look for ways to narrow your focus as you begin researching.

Narrowing your focus

Even before you visit the library, you may be able to limit the scope of your investigation. For instance, if initially you asked "Should the use of lie detectors be banned?" you might restrict your inquiry to the use of lie detectors *in the military.* Or if at first you asked "What are the hazards of fad diets?" you might narrow your focus to the hazards of *liquid* diets. (Also see the chart on page 7.)

Once inside the library, you can use reference tools to help narrow your topic. For example, by scanning encyclopedia articles, you can get a sense of your subject's natural subdivisions. For current topics you can check the headings and subheadings in periodical indexes such as the computerized *General Periodicals Ondisc* or *Academic Index.* One of these subheadings might help you restrict your topic even before you have read a single article.

As you begin reading books and articles and become more knowledgeable, you may be able to restrict your focus even further and at the same time decide what approach you will take in your paper—or even decide on a tentative main point. The main point of your paper, known as a *thesis,* will be an answer to the central question that you finally decide to pose. (See 49a.)

46b Become familiar with your library.

If you have not already done so, explore your library to find out what it's like. Most libraries provide maps and handouts that describe their services; many conduct orientation programs or have cassette walking tours or slide-cassette shows.

As you explore your library, seek out answers to at least the following questions.

— Are the stacks (the shelves on which books are stored) open or closed? In other words, can you go to the books directly, or must you request them at a desk?

— Are some books, periodicals, and reference materials located in special rooms or even special buildings?

— Where is the reference section?

— Does the library have a computerized catalog to lead you to books? If so, will it also lead you to other materials, such as videotapes? How are locations of different kinds of materials identified?

— Where are the periodical indexes? Which ones are available in CD-ROM or other computer form?

— How and where are periodicals stored? Where are the photocopiers and microfilm or microfiche reader-printers located?

— Which computer search services does the library offer? Some libraries offer dial-in services so that students can search from their homes or dormitories.

As you get to know your library, don't forget the library staff. Librarians are information specialists who can save you time by helping you define what you are looking for and then telling you where to find it. Librarians, especially those in college and university libraries, are educators. You can usually find librarians in the reference section, or you can inquire at the information desk. Feel free to tell them about your information needs, not just to ask where to find the encyclopedias.

46c   Follow a search strategy.

A search strategy is a systematic plan for tracking down source materials. To create a search strategy, you'll need to ask yourself two questions:

What kinds of source materials should I consult?

In what order should I consult them?

A good search strategy moves from sources that give you an overview of your subject to those that supply you with more specialized information. For a historical subject you might begin with general reference works such as encyclopedias and then move to books and finally to scholarly articles. For a current subject, you might begin with magazines of general interest and end with specialized articles in scholarly journals.

To research the topic of apes and language, Karen Shaw, whose paper appears on pages 514–38, decided to turn to magazines for an overview of her subject. Her librarian recommended *Periodical Abstracts Ondisc* as the fastest way to locate magazine articles on her topic. Working at a computer terminal, Shaw typed the keywords *apes* and *language* to call up abstracts of articles of possible interest. The abstracts helped Shaw decide which articles would give her an overview of her subject.

Once Shaw had located and read several magazine articles, she became intrigued by current research with pygmy chimpanzees at Yerkes Primate Center in Atlanta. At this point she realized that her search strategy should focus mainly on periodicals, since books would be too dated to supply her with information about such recent studies. Using *Periodical Abstracts Ondisc* again, Shaw located several articles about pygmy chimpanzees in magazines, newspapers, and scholarly journals.

Shaw didn't overlook books entirely, however, because she needed a historical overview of ape language studies. In particular, she was interested to learn about the scholarly battles that had been waged over the past twenty-five years, especially between two key researchers, Herbert Terrace and Francine Patterson. The computer catalog led Shaw to several books, including one by Terrace and one by Patterson. Shaw didn't have time to read the books cover to cover, so she used the table of contents and the index of each book to lead her to relevant chapters and pages: those that focused on the scholarly controversies surrounding the early years of the ape language studies.

Because Shaw had planned her search strategy carefully, most of her reading was relevant to her final approach to the topic. As you survey the possible sources of information listed on the following pages, try to develop an organized search strategy appropriate to your topic. Remember that if you run into problems, a reference librarian will be glad to help.

Reference works

Often you'll want to begin by reading background information in a general encyclopedia, a specialized encyclopedia, or a biographical reference. Later you may need to turn to other reference works such as atlases, almanacs, or unabridged dictionaries.

GENERAL ENCYCLOPEDIAS Articles in general encyclopedias introduce a topic to you, give you a sense of how broad or narrow it is, and often end with a bibliography of books for further reading. In most encyclopedias, the last volume provides a subject index to the entire set. Here are four general encyclopedias frequently used on the college level.

Academic American Encyclopedia
Collier's Encyclopedia
Encyclopedia Americana
The New Encyclopaedia Britannica

Although general encyclopedias are a good place to begin your research, do not rely too heavily on them in your finished paper. No doubt you will find more specific information later during your search.

SPECIALIZED ENCYCLOPEDIAS   For topics that fall within a particular academic discipline, turn to a specialized encyclopedia for an overview. As you read, look for areas in which experts take different positions or in which trends, attitudes, beliefs, or circumstances are changing; your finished paper could demonstrate your support for one of the positions or explain the causes or effects of the changes.

Following is a list of specialized encyclopedias covering a number of disciplines.

The Cambridge Encyclopedia of Human Evolution
The Dance Encyclopedia
Dictionary of Asian American History
Education Encyclopedia
Encyclopedia of Anthropology
Encyclopedia of Associations
Encyclopedia of Banking and Finance
The Encyclopedia of Biological Sciences
Encyclopedia of Computers and Data Processing
Encyclopedia of Crime and Justice
The Encyclopedia of Management
The Encyclopedia of Philosophy
Encyclopedia of Psychology
Encyclopedia of World Architecture
Encyclopedia of World Art

An Encyclopedia of World History
Encyclopedia of World Literature in the 20th Century
Grzimek's Animal Life Encyclopedia
Guide to American Law: Everyone's Legal Encyclopedia
Handbook of North American Indians
Harvard Encyclopedia of American Ethnic Groups
Harvard Guide to American History
International Encyclopedia of Education
International Encyclopedia of the Social Sciences
McGraw-Hill Encyclopedia of Environmental Science and Engineering
McGraw-Hill Dictionary of Modern Economics
McGraw-Hill Encyclopedia of Science and Technology
McGraw-Hill Encyclopedia of World Drama
The New Grove Dictionary of Music and Musicians
The Oxford Companion to American Literature
The Oxford Companion to English Literature
Reference Encyclopedia of the American Indian

BIOGRAPHICAL REFERENCES If your subject is a person, a good place to begin is with a biographical reference. Before consulting any of the following books, you will save time if you check your library's catalog for *Biography and Genealogy Master Index*. This index tells you which biographical reference books contain information on the person you are researching. If your library does not have it, try *Biography Index* or go directly to the books listed here.

African American Biographies
Contemporary Architects
Contemporary Artists
Contemporary Authors
Contemporary Photographers
Current Biography
Dictionary of American Biography
Dictionary of Contemporary American Artists
Dictionary of Literary Biography
Dictionary of Scientific Biography
McGraw-Hill Encyclopedia of World Biography

Macmillan Encyclopedia of Architects
Notable American Women
Reader's Companion to American History
Webster's New Biographical Dictionary
Who's Who among Black Americans
Who's Who among Hispanic Americans
Who's Who in America
Who's Who of American Women

ATLASES   An atlas is a bound collection of maps. For current topics, make sure that you are working with an up-to-date atlas. For historical topics, consult an atlas that covers the particular period you are interested in. Following is a brief list of commonly used atlases.

Atlas of American History
Atlas of the 1990 Census
Atlas of the Third World
Atlas of World Cultures: A Geographical Guide to Ethno-
    graphic Literature
The Economist Atlas of the New Europe
Historical Atlas
National Geographic Atlas of the World
1993 Commercial Atlas and Marketing Guide
Rand McNally Cosmopolitan World Atlas
The New York Times Atlas of the World
We the People: An Atlas of America's Diversity

ALMANACS AND YEARBOOKS   Almanacs and yearbooks are annual publications that record information about a year, often in the form of lists, charts, and tables. The information covers a range of subjects such as politics, world events, sports, economics, and even the weather. Here is a brief list of almanacs and yearbooks.

Almanac of American Politics
Americana Annual
Britannica Book of the Year
Business One Irwin Business and Investment Almanac

CQ Washington Information Directory
Education Almanac
The Europe World Yearbook
Facts on File
The Hispanic-American Almanac
The Negro Almanac: A Reference Work on the African American
Statistical Abstract of the United States
Statistical Handbook on U.S. Hispanics
Statistical Record of Black America
The Timetables of History
World Almanac and Book of Facts
World Directory of Minorities

UNABRIDGED DICTIONARIES   An unabridged dictionary such as one of the following is more comprehensive than an ordinary college or desk dictionary.

The Oxford English Dictionary
The Random House Dictionary of the English Language
Webster's Third New International Dictionary

Books

Your library may have a computer catalog, a card catalog, a microform catalog, or some combination of these. Most libraries now have computer catalogs that allow you to search for information on books and often other materials through a terminal or personal computer.

THE COMPUTER CATALOG   A computer catalog is a database that contains bibliographic and location information about a library's books. Often other materials—such as government documents, pamphlets, and audiovisuals—are cataloged as well. The computer catalog can be searched by subject, author, or title.

While computer catalogs vary from library to library, most are easy to use, and a reference librarian will be available to help you if you get stuck. Look for instructions on the computer terminal's menu display or look for a help key. Instructions may also be available in a handout or display next to the computer. To begin a search, you will usually respond to a direction such as "Type in an author" or "Enter your subject." The computer will then display either a list of books under that author's name or subject heading or a list of subcategories from which you can choose the one closest to your topic.

Searching by subject involves the use of keywords or subject headings, which prompt the computer to retrieve the relevant information. The keywords may be used alone, such as *diabetes* or *blindness,* or sometimes they may be combined. In some systems, for example, you can use the connector *and* to narrow a subject search: *diabetes and blindness.* Occasionally you may want to narrow your search by using *but not.* For example, if you are interested in diabetes but do not want articles focusing on blindness, you could eliminate them by typing *diabetes but not blindness.* (If you need help identifying a keyword or subject heading, you might consult *The Library of Congress Subject Headings,* two large volumes usually placed near the catalog that list the subject headings used by most catalog systems.)

If searching for the subject *human animal communication,* you might see a screen like the one at the top of page 451. The computer has provided a list containing the overall subject category as well as four subcategories.

Once you select an entry from the list, the computer displays a list of books related to the subject category. At the bottom of page 451 is the display resulting from choosing the first subject category: "1 HUMAN ANIMAL COMMUNICATION." If a title looks useful, you can command the computer to print or display the complete record for the work, which includes the bibliographic information and call number. The call number on the last line of the record leads you to the book on the shelf. You will need the bibliographic information — author, title, publisher, and place and date of publication —

SUBJECT SEARCH: SCREEN 1

```
HU GUIDE: SUBJECT HEADING LIST              18 items retrieved by your search:
FIND SU HUMAN ANIMAL COMMUNICATION
-----------------------------------------------------------------------------
   1 HUMAN ANIMAL COMMUNICATION
  15 HUMAN ANIMAL COMMUNICATION --CONGRESSES
  16 HUMAN ANIMAL COMMUNICATION --DATA PROCESSING
  17 HUMAN ANIMAL COMMUNICATION --FOLKLORE
  18 HUMAN ANIMAL COMMUNICATION --RESEARCH --CONGRESSES




-----------------------------------------------------------------------------
OPTIONS: INDEX (or I 5 etc) to see list of items         HELP
                                                         START - search options
         REDO - edit search                              QUIT - exit database
COMMAND?
```

SUBJECT SEARCH: SCREEN 2

```
HU INDEX: LIST OF ITEMS RETRIEVED           18 items retrieved by your search:
FIND SU HUMAN ANIMAL COMMUNICATION
-----------------------------------------------------------------------------
HUMAN ANIMAL COMMUNICATION
   1 adams task calling animals by name /hearne vicki 1946/ 1986  bks
   2 animals are equal an exploration of animal conciousn /hall rebec/ 1980  bks
   3 apes men and language /linden eugene/ 1976  bks
   4 aping language /wallman joel/ 1992  bks
   5 butterfly revelations /swanson henry f 1923/ 1979  bks
   6 communication between man and dolphin the possibilit /lilly john/ 1987  bks
   7 education of koko /patterson francine/ 1981  bks
   8 gavagai or the future history of the animal language /premack da/ 1986  bks
   9 hund und mensch eine semiotische analyse ihrer kommu /fleischer/ 1987  bks
  10 language in primates perspectives and implications/ 1983  bks
  11 nim /terrace herbert s 1936/ 1979  bks
  12 silent partners the legacy of the ape language exper /linden eug/ 1986  bks
  13 speaking of apes a critical anthology of two way com/ 1980  bks
  14 teaching sign language to chimpanzees/ 1989  bks
----------------------------------------------------- (CONTINUES) ------------
OPTIONS: DISPLAY 1 (or D 5 etc) to see a record          HELP
         GUIDE                    MORE - next page        START - search options
         REDO - edit search                               QUIT - exit database
COMMAND?
```

SUBJECT SEARCH: SCREEN 3

```
HU LONG DISPLAY    page 1 of 1      Item 7 of 18 retrieved by your search:
FIND SU HUMAN ANIMAL COMMUNICATION
-----------------------------------------------------------HU HOLLIS# AEK5177 /bks
         AUTHOR: Patterson, Francine.
          TITLE: The education of Koko / Francine Patterson and Eugene Linden.
        EDITION: 1st ed.
      PUB. INFO: New York : Holt, Rinehart and Winston, c1981.
    DESCRIPTION: xiv, 224 p. : ill. ; 24 cm.
          NOTES: Includes index.
                 Bibliography: p. 215-216.

       SUBJECTS: *S1 Gorilla--Psychology.
                 *S2 Human-animal communication.
                 *S3 Sign language.
        AUTHORS: *A1 Patterson, Francine.
                 *A2 Linden, Eugene.

       LOCATION: Gutman Education: QL737.P96 P37

----------------------------------------------------------------------
OPTIONS: DISPLAY SHORT                            NEXT - next item      HELP
         LOCATION                                 PREVIOUS - prev item  INDEX
         HELP COMMANDS       TRACE *S1 (etc)      QUIT - exit database  REDO
COMMAND?
```

---

if you decide to use the book in your paper (see 50 and 51). Above is the complete record for title number 7 on the preceding screen.

THE CARD OR MICROFORM CATALOG   The card catalog lists books alphabetically in three ways: by author's last name, by title, and by subject. Most libraries no longer have a card catalog.

In some libraries, catalogs are presented on rolls of microfilm or on microfiche, 4″ × 6″ pieces of film. The microfilm or microfiche is viewed on a machine called a *reader.* Some readers allow you to print a copy of the titles that appear on the screen.

OTHER INDEXES TO BOOKS   *Books in Print* and *Paperbound Books in Print* list books by author, title, and subject; *Cumulative Book Index* lists books by author and subject.

These indexes are available in print form and on CD-ROM (compact disc–read-only memory), a database accessed by a computer terminal and keyboard.

You may also want to consult bibliographies, which are lists of books on specific topics. You can look for bibliographies on your topic in your library's catalog by using the relevant keyword or subject heading and the word *bibliography.* You also may use *Bibliography Index* for citations to bibliographies in both books and magazine articles.

Periodicals

Periodicals are publications issued at regular intervals, such as magazines, newspapers, and scholarly or technical journals. Articles in periodicals are useful reference tools because they often contain more up-to-date information than books and because they usually discuss in detail a specific aspect of a subject.

To track down useful articles, consult a magazine index, a newspaper index, or one of the many specialized indexes to scholarly or technical journals. Most libraries provide, in a conspicuous spot close to these indexes or in the catalog, a list of the periodicals they own. This list tells you the form in which the periodical has been preserved: on microfilm, on microfiche, in bound volumes, or in unbound files. It also tells you which years and volumes of the periodical the library owns.

Some periodical indexes are in print form; others are stored as databases in a computer. The latter indexes use CD-ROM (compact disc–read-only memory) technology, in which information is stored on compact discs and accessed through a computer terminal. Most commonly, college libraries have a number of CD-ROM indexes loaded into the computer network (either the same network the catalog is on or a different one) for access by students through a menu on the screen.

COMPUTER INDEX MENU

MultiPlatter   Main Menu

To Select:
use ↑ or ↓ to position the highlight bar and press Enter.

Press F1 for Help.

    MORE SELECTIONS
Medline 1989
Medline 1988
Medline 1987
PAIS 1972 to present
PsycLIT 1987 to present
PsycLIT 1974 to 1988
Readers' Guide 1983 to present
Test CD-ROM Drives (requires password)
Quit
    END OF SELECTIONS

You search for articles in the CD-ROM database just as you look for books in the library's catalog, by typing the author, title, or subject keywords. Bibliographic records appear on the screen; sometimes an abstract or even the full text of an article can be printed. All or part of these records, abstracts, or text can be printed out from the computer or put on a formatted diskette (a process called *downloading*). You can take the disk back to your own computer or one in the computer lab and view the information on your screen and print out what you need.

If your library does not have an index you need in either print or CD-ROM form, your reference librarian may be able to do an online database search using a computer and a telephone line. Librarians often charge a fee for this service, so it is usually a last resort if you need the most up-to-date information or cannot find the information in any other way.

COMPUTER INDEX RECORD WITH ABSTRACT

SilverPlatter 3.1   Journal Articles (1/74−12/86)

TI: Can an ape create a sentence?
AU: Terrace,-H.-S.; Petitto,-L.A.; Sanders,-R.J.; Bever,-T.G.
IN: Columbia U
JN: Science; 1979 Nov Vol 206(4421) 891−902
AB: Recent demonstrations that chimpanzees and gorillas can communicate with humans via arbitrary "words" raise the issue of whether the ability to create and understand sentences is uniquely human. To answer this question, more than 19,000 multisign utterances of an infant chimpanzee (Nim) were analyzed for syntactic and semantic regularities. Lexical regularities were observed in the case of 2-sign combinations: particular signs (e.g., more) tended to occur in a particular position. These regularities could not be attributed to memorization or to position habits, suggesting that they were structurally constrained. That conclusion, however, was invalidated by videotape analyses, which showed that most of Nim's utterances were prompted by his teacher's prior utterance and that Nim interrupted his teachers to a much larger extent than a child interrupts an adult's speech. Signed utterances of other apes (as shown on films) showed similar non-human patterns of discourse.
AN: 65-00553

GENERAL PERIODICAL INDEXES   Some general periodical indexes list articles in general-interest magazines such as *Time, Popular Mechanics, Science,* and *Fortune* as well as scholarly and professional journals. Others list articles in major newspapers such as the *New York Times,* the *Washington Post,* and the *Christian Science Monitor.*

Most college libraries subscribe to at least one of the following computer services, which index general periodicals.

Periodical Abstracts Ondisc. Indexes and abstracts articles in more than one thousand general reference periodicals and scholarly journals in the humanities, sciences, social sciences, business, and current affairs from 1986 to the present. New titles added yearly. Updated monthly or quarterly.

Newspaper Abstracts Ondisc. Indexes and abstracts articles in eight major newspapers. Updated monthly or quarterly.

General Periodicals Ondisc. Provides the full text of each article for more than two hundred journals and magazines and indexes and abstracts four hundred more. Updated monthly.

Readers' Guide to Periodical Literature. Indexes articles in two hundred popular general-interest magazines. No abstracts. Updated monthly.

Academic Index (InfoTrac). Indexes articles in nearly four hundred scholarly and general-interest journals plus articles for the past six months of the *New York Times.* Updated monthly.

National Newspaper Index. Indexes selected articles from five newspapers for the past three to four years: the *New York Times,* the *Christian Science Monitor,* the *Wall Street Journal,* the *Washington Post,* and the *Los Angeles Times.* Updated monthly.

Newsbank CD News. Indexes selected articles from more than one hundred newspapers representing a cross section of regional issues and events from across the United States. This index is now available with full text. Earlier articles are on microfiche.

NEXIS/LEXIS. An online (telephone-connected) database of full texts or abstracts. It includes mainly U.S. but also international magazines and newspapers and other information, generally from the mid-1980s up to the previous day. Especially useful for business and political science as well as general interest. LEXIS covers federal and state laws and other information.

If you are looking for periodical articles that appeared before the mid-1980s, you will need to turn to a print index such as the *Readers' Guide to Periodical Literature* or the *New York Times Index.*

> *Readers' Guide to Periodical Literature.* 1900–present. A print index to articles in nearly two hundred general-interest magazines.
>
> *New York Times Index.* 1851–present. A print index to all the articles in the *New York Times.* Other major newspapers — the *Washington Post,* the *Christian Science Monitor,* the *Wall Street Journal,* the London *Times* — publish similar indexes.

SPECIALIZED PERIODICAL INDEXES   To locate articles in technical and scholarly journals such as *Computer World* and *Art in America,* you can consult a specialized index. The following specialized indexes, formerly available only in print form, are available as databases on computers.

> *Applied Science and Technology Index.* Computer: 1983–present. Print: 1958–present. (Formerly *Industrial Arts Index,* 1913–1957.)
>
> *Art Index.* Computer: 1984–present. Print: 1929–present.
>
> *Biological and Agricultural Index.* Computer: 1983–present. Print: 1965–present. (Formerly *Agricultural Index,* 1916–1964.)
>
> *Business Periodicals Index.* Computer: 1982–present. Print: 1958–present. (Formerly *Industrial Arts Index,* 1913–1957.)
>
> *Education Index.* Computer: 1983–present. Print: 1929–present.
>
> *General Science Index.* Computer: 1984–present. Print: 1978–present.
>
> *Humanities Index.* Computer: 1984–present. Print: 1975–present. (Formerly *International Index to Periodicals,* 1907–1965, and *Social Sciences and Humanities Index,* 1965–1974.)

Social Sciences Index. Computer: 1983–present. Print:
1975–present. (Formerly *International Index to Periodicals*,
1907–1965, and *Social Sciences and Humanities Index*,
1965–1974.)

*CINAHL (Cumulative Index to Nursing and Allied Health
Literature).* Abstracts nearly all English-language nursing
journals and important journals in allied health disciplines. Updated monthly. Computer: 1983–present. Print:
1956–present.

PAIS (Public Affairs Information Service). Abstracts international
journals, government documents, reports, and statistics
on public policy in business, economics, government, law,
and international relations. Computer: 1972–present.
Print: *PAIS Bulletin*, 1915–present.

ERIC (Educational Resources Information Center). Abstracts
the journal and research literature in education. Updated
quarterly or annually. Computer: 1966–present. Print:
Current Index to Journals in Education, 1969–present;
Resources in Education, 1966–present.

PsycLIT. Abstracts more than 1,300 journals in psychology and
the behavioral sciences. Updated quarterly. Computer:
1974–present (book chapters included, 1987–present).
Print: *Psychological Abstracts*, 1919–present.

Sociofile. Abstracts professional articles in sociology and
related disciplines from 1,600 journals as well as from
Dissertations Abstracts International. Computer:
1974–present. Print: *Sociological Abstracts*, 1952–present.

*MLA International Bibliography of Books and Articles in the
Modern Languages and Literature.* Computer:
1981–present. Print: 1921–present.

Other library sources

A library's holdings are not limited to reference works, books,
and periodicals. Your library may have pamphlets, usually
located in a large file cabinet known as the *vertical file*, or rare
and unpublished manuscripts in a special collection. Holdings might also include records, tapes, and compact discs;
films, filmstrips, videos, and interactive videodiscs; drawings,
paintings, engravings, and slides.

If your research topic is especially complex or unusual, you may need greater resources than your library offers. In such cases, talk to a librarian about interlibrary loan, a process in which one library borrows materials from another. This procedure can take several weeks for books, but magazine articles are commonly sent by fax in less than a week.

Sources beyond the library

For some topics, you may want to look beyond the library for information. Many organizations, both public and private, willingly mail literature in response to a phone call or a letter. The *Encyclopedia of Associations* lists organizations by their special interests, such as environment or family planning, and provides titles of their publications. Consider also the possibility of learning more about your subject through interviews or experiments that you conduct yourself.

Interviews can often shed new light on a topic. Look for experts who have firsthand knowledge of the subject or for individuals whose personal experience provides an enlightening perspective on your topic. Look too for sources with alternative or underrepresented viewpoints to balance the perspectives of conventional authorities.

When asking for an interview, be clear about who you are, what the purpose of the interview is, whether you plan to tape it, and approximately how long it will take. If you succeed in getting an appointment, plan for the interview by writing down a series of questions and arranging them in a logical order. Try to avoid questions with yes or no answers or those that encourage vague rambling; instead, phrase your questions to elicit facts, anecdotes, and opinions that will add a meaningful dimension to your paper.

Accuracy is important in an interview. If you cannot tape the interview, take careful notes, and if a point is unclear, ask your subject to explain it. When quoting your source in your paper, you should of course be as accurate and as fair as possible. For instance, if you interviewed a record store owner about the popularity of a particular rap group and she told you, "Their CDs don't sell as well as two or three other groups' recordings," it would be misrepresenting your source to write, "Their CDs don't sell well."

For some topics you may want to supplement others' research with your own experiments. Most academic disciplines have specific guidelines for conducting experiments and reporting results; if you are unsure of the appropriate method in your discipline, consult a style manual (see 51c) or ask your instructor.

47

Reading critically

When you read in search of answers to a research question, you must read critically. Critical readers do not just process information or follow the plot lines of a story; they assess what they read. With their research questions in mind, they seek the truth. And this often means questioning an author's expertise or objectivity, looking for possible flaws in an author's reasoning, and weighing the evidence of one author against evidence presented by others.

You can exercise your critical intelligence at two points: when selecting sources and when doing the actual reading.

47a   Read selectively.

As you consult the library's catalog and its periodical indexes, take down bibliographic information only for sources that seem promising (see pages 462–64 for the exact information to take down). Be alert for clues that indicate whether a book or article is worth tracking down. Many of the CD-ROM indexes for magazines and newspapers provide abstracts — brief summaries of articles — that can help you choose which ones to use. Here are some questions to guide you as you make your choices.

DECIDING WHETHER TO TRACK DOWN A SOURCE

— How relevant to your research question is the work's title?
— How recent is the source? For current topics, some books or articles may be outdated.
— How long is the source? A very short article may be too general to be helpful.
— Is the source available in your library?

Once you have tracked down a source, preview it quickly to see how much of your attention, if any, it is worth. Techniques for previewing a book and an article are a bit different.

PREVIEWING A BOOK

— Glance through the table of contents, keeping your research question in mind.
— Skim the preface in search of a statement of the author's purposes.
— Using the index, look up a few words related to your research question.
— If a chapter seems useful, read its opening and closing paragraphs and skim any headings.
— Consider the author's style, level, and tone. Does the style invite further reading? Is the level appropriate (neither above nor below your ability to comprehend)? Does the tone suggest a balanced approach?
— If the author's credentials are given on the cover or dust jacket, how relevant are they to the book and your research question?

PREVIEWING AN ARTICLE

— For magazine and journal articles, look for a statement of purpose in the opening paragraphs; look for a possible summary in the closing paragraph.
— For newspaper articles, focus on the headline and the opening sentences, known as the *lead.*
— Skim any headings and take a look at any charts, graphs, diagrams, or illustrations that might indicate the article's focus and scope.

47b Maintain a working bibliography.

Keep a record of any sources that you decide to consult. You will need this record, called a *working bibliography,* when you compile the list of works cited that will appear at the end of your paper. (See page 536 for an example.) This list of works cited will almost certainly be shorter than your working bibliography, since it will include only the sources that you actually cite in your paper.

You may record bibliographic information about sources in a notebook or on separate 3″ × 5″ cards. The advantage of 3″ × 5″ cards is that you can easily arrange them in alphabetical order when you type the list of works cited. (If you have used a computer catalog or index that prints bibliographic information, you can use the printouts as your working bibliography.) For books, you will need the following bibliographic information:

Call number

All authors; any editors or translators

Title and subtitle

Edition (if not the first)

Publishing information: city, publishing company, and date

SAMPLE BIBLIOGRAPHY CARD FOR A BOOK

> QL 737.P96 L57 1986
>
> Linden, Eugene. <u>Silent Partners:</u>
> <u>The Legacy of the Ape Language</u>
> <u>Experiments</u>. New York: Times,
> 1986.

SAMPLE BIBLIOGRAPHY CARD FOR A PERIODICAL

> Lewin, Roger. "Look Who's Talking
> Now." <u>New Scientist</u> 29 April
> 1991: 49-52.

For periodical articles you need this information:

> All authors of the article
>
> Title and subtitle of the article
>
> Title of the magazine, journal, or newspaper
>
> Date and page numbers
>
> Volume and issue numbers, if relevant

NOTE: For the exact bibliographic form to be used in the final paper, see 50b.

47c Read with a critical eye.

When you read critically, you are not necessarily judging an author's work harshly; you are simply examining its assumptions, assessing its evidence, and weighing its conclusions.

Distinguishing between primary and secondary sources

As you begin assessing the evidence in a text, consider whether you are reading a primary or a secondary source. Primary sources are original documents such as speeches, diaries, novels, legislative bills, laboratory studies, field research reports, or eyewitness accounts. Secondary sources are commentaries on primary sources.

A primary source for Karen Shaw, whose research paper appears beginning on page 514, was an article by Patricia Marks Greenfield and E. Sue Savage-Rumbaugh reporting experiments with the pygmy chimpanzee Kanzi. Shaw also consulted Flora Davis's book *Eloquent Animals*, a secondary source that reports on the studies of several researchers.

Although a primary source is not necessarily more reliable than a secondary source, it has the advantage of being a firsthand account. Naturally, you can better evaluate what a secondary source says if you have first read the primary source and are familiar with it.

Being alert for signs of bias

As you are no doubt aware, some publishers are more objective than others. If you were exploring the conspiracy theories surrounding the Kennedy assassination, for example, you wouldn't look to a supermarket tabloid such as the *National Enquirer* for answers. You would rely instead on newspapers and magazines with a national reputation for fair and objective reporting.

Like publishers, some authors are more objective than others. Few authors are altogether objective, of course, since they are human beings with their own life experiences, values, and beliefs. But if you have reason to believe that an author is particularly biased, you will want to assess his or her arguments with special care.

Here are some questions to ask yourself as you look for possible signs of bias in an author or a publisher.

— Do the author and publisher have reputations for accurate and balanced reporting?
— Does the author or publisher have political leanings or religious views that could affect objectivity?
— Is the author or publisher associated with a special-interest group, such as the National Rifle Association, that tends to see only one side of an issue?
— How fairly does the author treat those with opposing views?
— Does the author's language show signs of bias? (See 52f.)

Assessing the author's argument

In nearly all subjects worth writing about, there is some element of argument, so don't be surprised to encounter experts who disagree. When you encounter areas of disagreement, you will want to read your sources' arguments with special care, testing them with your own critical intelligence. Questions such as the following can help you weigh the strengths and weaknesses of each author's argument.

—What is the author's central claim or thesis?
—How does the author support this claim—with relevant and sufficient evidence or with just a few anecdotes or emotional examples?
—Are statistics accurate? Have they been used fairly? (It is possible to "lie" with statistics by using them selectively or by omitting mathematical details.)
—Are any of the author's assumptions questionable?
—Does the author consider opposing arguments and refute them persuasively? (See pages 578–80.)

48

Taking notes

48a   As you read, take notes systematically.

Taking systematic notes as you read will help you remember later, as you are drafting your paper, just which words and phrases belong to your sources and which are your own. This is a crucial matter, for if any language from your sources finds its way into your final draft without quotation marks and proper documentation, you will be guilty of plagiarism, a serious academic offense. (See 49d.)

Many researchers use the note card system for taking notes. If you decide to use note cards, purchase a large stack of 3″ × 5″ or 4″ × 6″ cards. Write one note on each card so you can shuffle and reshuffle the cards in different orders later as you experiment with the organization of your paper. Put the last name of the author of your source in the upper right corner of the card, and put a subject label in the upper left corner. If you have read enough to form a preliminary outline, use the subdivisions of the outline as subject headings on your cards.

Not every researcher uses note cards. For short research projects, some writers prefer to photocopy important material and underline or highlight key ideas, sometimes color coding the highlighted passages to reflect subdivisions of the topic. In the margins they may write personal comments or cross-references to other sources. Photocopying has the obvious advantage of saving time and labor. For extensive research projects, however, the technique is of limited value since there is no way of physically sorting the highlighted passages into separate batches of information.

A second alternative to note cards, the use of computer software, overcomes this disadvantage. With the appropriate software, you can type notes as you read, coding them to reflect the divisions of your outline. You can then print the notes in sorted batches. For example, Karen Shaw might have printed one batch of notes on the apes' sign language vocabularies, another on their creative uses of language, another on their mastery of grammar, and so on.

Although software programs can be time savers, their advantages should not be oversold. Any style of note taking demands that you read carefully, analyze what you read, and record information with care.

48b As you take notes, avoid unintentional plagiarism.

You will discover that it is amazingly easy to borrow too much language from a source as you take notes. Do not allow this to happen. You are guilty of the academic offense known as *plagiarism* if you half-copy the author's sentences—either by mixing the author's phrases with your own without using quotation marks or by plugging your synonyms into the author's sentence structure. (For examples of this kind of plagiarism, see 49d.)

To prevent unintentional borrowing, resist the temptation to look at the source as you take notes—except when you are quoting. Keep the source close by so you can check for accuracy, but don't try to put ideas in your own words with the source's sentences in front of you. You should also follow this advice while drafting your paper. (See the chart on pages 486–87.)

There are four kinds of note taking: summarizing, paraphrasing, quoting, and writing personal comments. When you summarize, paraphrase, or quote, be sure to include exact page references, since you will need the page numbers later if you use the information in your paper.

Notes that summarize

Summarizing is the best kind of preliminary note taking because it is the fastest. A summary condenses information, perhaps reducing a chapter to a short paragraph or a paragraph to a single sentence. A summary should be written in your own words; if you use phrases from the source, put them in quotation marks.

Here is a passage from an original source read by Karen Shaw in researching her essay on apes and language. Following the passage is Shaw's note card summarizing it.

ORIGINAL SOURCE

Public and scientific interest in the question of apes' ability to use language first soared some 15 years ago when Washoe, a chimpanzee raised like a human child by R. Allen Gardner and Beatrice Gardner of the University of Nevada, learned to make hand signs for many words and even seemed to be making short sentences.

Since then researchers have taught many chimpanzees and a few gorillas and orangutans to "talk" using the sign language of deaf humans, plastic chips or, like Kanzi, keyboard symbols. Washoe, Sarah, a chimpanzee trained by David Premack of the University of Pennsylvania, and Koko, a gorilla trained by the psychologist Francine Patterson, became media stars.   —Eckholm, "Pygmy," p. B7

SUMMARY

> *Types of languages*   Eckholm, "Pygmy"
>
> *The ape experiments began about 20 years ago with Washoe, who learned sign language. In later experiments some apes learned to communicate using plastic chips or symbols on a keyboard. (p. B7)*

Notes that paraphrase

Like a summary, a paraphrase is written in your own words; but whereas a summary reports significant information in fewer words than the source, a paraphrase retells the information in roughly the same number of words. If you retain occasional choice phrases from the source, use quotation marks so you'll know later which phrases are your own.

As you read the note card on page 470, which paraphrases the first paragraph of Shaw's original source (see page 468), notice that the language is significantly different from that in the original. Working with this note card, Shaw was in no danger of unintentional plagiarism.

Notes that quote

A quotation consists of the exact words from a source. In your notes, put all quoted material in quotation marks; do not trust yourself to remember later which words, phrases, and passages you have quoted and which are your own. When

PARAPHRASE

Washoe   Eckholm, "Pygmy"

A chimpanzee named Washoe, trained
20 years ago by U. of Nevada professors
R. Allen and Beatrice Gardner, learned
words in the sign language of the deaf
and may even have created short
sentences. (p. B7)

QUOTATION

Washoe   Eckholm, "Pygmy"

Washoe, trained by R. Allen and Beatrice
Gardner, "learned to make hand signs
for many words and even seemed to
be making short sentences."
(p. B7)

you quote, be sure to copy the words of your source exactly, including punctuation and capitalization.

Quotations should be reserved for special purposes: to use a writer's especially vivid or expressive wording, to allow an expert to explain a complex matter clearly, or to let critics of an opinion object in their own words. If you find yourself quoting a great deal in your notes, you are probably wasting time, because your final essay should not contain excessive quotations. (Scc 49e.)

At the bottom of page 470 is an example of a note card with a quotation from Shaw's original source (page 468).

Personal notes

At unexpected moments in your reading, you will experience the lucky accidents typical of the creative process: flashes of insight, connections with other reading, sharp questions, a

PERSONAL COMMENT

Types of training

Washoe (and I think Koko) were raised almost like children, not in a laboratory setting. Does the setting affect the apes' performance? What about scientific objectivity?

more restricted topic, ways to set up the arguments of two opposing positions, a vivid scenario. Write these inspirations down before you forget them. An example of such a personal note appears on page 471.

49

Writing the research paper

49a Form a tentative thesis and construct a preliminary outline.

A look through your notes will probably suggest many ways to focus and organize your material. Before you begin writing, you should decide on a tentative thesis and construct a preliminary outline or you will flounder among the possibilities. Remain flexible, however, because you may need to revise your approach later. Writing about a subject is a way of learning about it; as you write, your understanding of your subject will almost certainly deepen.

Forming a tentative thesis

A thesis is a sentence asserting the main point of your essay (see 2b). If you are writing on a clearly argumentative topic, such as some aspect of the problem of nuclear waste, your thesis should state your informed opinion: that seabed disposal is not as safe as has been claimed, for example, or that because of politics and economics certain states have become dumping grounds for nuclear waste. You should avoid writing a paper that reports information for no apparent purpose. Few instructors want to read a paper that simply lists and describes the methods for disposing of nuclear waste. Most instructors want their students to take a stand.

Even if your subject is not so obviously controversial as nuclear waste, you can still assert a thesis. Nearly all subjects worth writing about contain some element of controversy; that is why scholars so often engage in polite — and sometimes not so polite — arguments.

In researching the topic of apes and language, Karen Shaw, whose paper appears on pages 514–38, encountered a number of scholarly arguments. Some early researchers, such as Herbert Terrace, discounted the linguistic abilities of gorillas and chimpanzees, arguing that the apes were being cued by their trainers and that they could not form even simple sentences. Other early researchers, such as Francine Patterson, insisted that the apes used language spontaneously (without being cued) and suggested that apes could form primitive sentences. After looking at the evidence, Shaw reached a conclusion: Patterson was right in insisting that the apes had used language spontaneously; Terrace was right in claiming that the apes' ability to form a sentence had not been proved in the early studies. More recent studies, however, convinced Shaw that pygmy chimpanzees may well have the ability to understand and create sentences. Shaw's thesis articulates her assessment of the evidence:

> The great apes resemble humans in language abilities more than researchers once believed, and evidence is mounting that pygmy chimpanzees can understand and perhaps even create sentences.

Constructing a preliminary outline

Before committing yourself to a detailed outline, experiment with alternatives. Shuffle and reshuffle your note cards or rearrange your computer notes to get a feeling for the possibilities. After some experimenting, Karen Shaw sorted her notes into three large batches: early ape language studies, recent studies, and the philosophical implications of the ape language research. Then she drafted the following simple outline.

> Thesis: The great apes resemble humans in language abilities
>   more than researchers once believed, and evidence is
>   mounting that pygmy chimpanzees can understand
>   and perhaps even create sentences.
>   I. Early ape language studies showed that apes could
>   acquire significant language skills but failed to prove
>   they could create sentences.
>   II. Recent research demonstrates that pygmy chimpanzees
>   can understand and perhaps even create sentences.
>   III. Evidence suggests that linguistic abilities in humans and
>   apes are part of a continuum.

It is a good idea to keep your preliminary outline simple, as Shaw did, since a simple outline is easier to adjust as you gain new insights about your topic while writing the paper. As she drafted each of the three parts of her paper, Shaw sorted her information into smaller batches, which became the basis for her final outline (see pages 516–17).

49b Draft the paper in your own voice.

With a restricted thesis, a preliminary outline, and plenty of notes, you are ready to write a first draft. Keep it rough and keep it moving. Don't let your wish for perfect sentences stall you at this stage. First write down your ideas and their supporting details; polish your sentences later. Writing rapidly usually produces a more natural, individual voice and helps you avoid echoing the language of your sources.

A chatty, breezy voice is usually not welcome in academic papers, but neither is a stuffy, pretentious style or a timid, unsure one. If you believe in your main point and are interested in your subject, try to communicate that sense of conviction.

Many researchers find that writing only from their outlines (rather than directly from their note cards) allows them to write in their own voices without mimicking the style of their sources. In writing their first draft, they refer to their notes only for direct quotations and specific statistics. Other writers prefer to work more closely with their notes, consulting them frequently as they write. Whichever method you use, make sure that your sentences are written in your own words, not half-copied from your sources. (See 49d.)

Writing an introduction

In a research paper that refers to many other writers, it is especially important to establish your own voice in the introduction. Your opening paragraphs introduce you as well as your ideas to the reader.

One or two paragraphs are usually enough introduction for most papers in undergraduate courses. Most readers don't want a great deal of background; they want you to get right to the point.

Readers are accustomed to seeing the thesis statement— a one-sentence summary of the main point of the essay — at the beginning or at the end of the introduction. The advantage of beginning with the thesis is that readers can immediately grasp your purpose. The advantage of delaying the thesis is that you can provide a context for your point. You may first want to establish the importance of your topic, then review various attitudes toward it, and finally point to your view in your thesis statement.

In addition to stating the thesis and showing its importance, an introduction should hook readers. (See 2b.) Sometimes you can connect your topic to something recently in the news or bring your readers up to date about changing ideas. Other strategies are to pose a puzzling problem or to open with a startling statistic. Karen Shaw's paper (pages 514–38) begins with a series of vivid examples leading up to her thesis.

49c As you write, document sources using a consistent system. (See 50 and 51 for important details.)

In a research paper, you will be drawing on the work of other writers, and you must document their contributions. Documentation is required when you quote from a source, when you summarize or paraphrase a source, and when you borrow facts and ideas from a source (except for common knowledge). (See also 49d.)

The various academic disciplines use their own editorial styles for documenting sources. Most English professors prefer the Modern Language Association's system of in-text citations. Here, very briefly, is how an MLA in-text citation usually works:

1. The source is introduced by a signal phrase that names its author.
2. The material being cited is followed by a page number in parentheses.
3. At the end of the paper, a list of works cited (arranged alphabetically according to the authors' last names) gives complete publishing information about the source.

SAMPLE IN-TEXT CITATION

According to Eugene Linden, some psychologists have adopted the oddly unscientific attitude that "the idea of the language capacity of apes is so preposterous that it should not be investigated at all" (11).

SAMPLE ENTRY IN THE LIST OF WORKS CITED

Linden, Eugene. Silent Partners: The Legacy of the Ape
    Language Experiments. New York: Times, 1986.

Handling an MLA citation is not always this simple. For a detailed discussion of possible variations, see 50a. Section

50 is easy to find because its pages are marked with a vertical band in color.

If your instructor has asked you to use footnotes (also acceptable to MLA) or the American Psychological Association (APA) style of in-text citation, consult 51, where you will also find a list of style manuals used in various disciplines.

49d Do not plagiarize: Document all quotations and borrowed ideas; avoid paraphrases that closely resemble your sources.

Your research paper is a collaboration between you and your sources. To be fair and ethical, you must acknowledge your borrowing of another writer's ideas and language by documenting the source, as explained in 49c. To borrow without proper documentation is a form of dishonesty known as plagiarism. (See also 48b.)

The academic, business, and legal communities take plagiarism very seriously. Universities have been known to withdraw graduate degrees from students who have plagiarized. Professional writers sue for (and often get) thousands of dollars when they discover that someone has plagiarized their work.

Two different acts are considered plagiarism: (1) borrowing someone's ideas, information, or language without documenting the source and (2) documenting the source but paraphrasing the source's language too closely, without using quotation marks to indicate that language has been borrowed.

Documenting quotations and borrowed ideas

You must of course document all direct quotations. You must also document any ideas borrowed from a source: paraphrases of sentences, summaries of paragraphs or chapters, statistics and little-known facts, and tables, graphs, or diagrams.

The only exception is common knowledge — information that your readers could find in any number of general sources because it is commonly known. For example, the current population of the United States is common knowledge in such fields as sociology and economics; Freud's theory of the unconscious is common knowledge in the field of psychology.

As a rule, when you have seen certain information repeatedly in your reading, you don't need to document it. However, when information has appeared in only one or two sources or when it is controversial, you should document it. If a topic is new to you and you are not sure what is considered common knowledge or what is a matter of controversy, ask someone with expertise. When in doubt, document the source.

Avoiding close paraphrases

Close paraphrases are the most common form of plagiarism because if a researcher is sloppy at the note-taking stage, unacceptable borrowings can occur unintentionally (see 48b). When you paraphrase, it is not enough to name the source; you must restate the source's meaning completely in your own words. The following is an example of plagiarizing an author's wording even though the source is cited.

ORIGINAL VERSION
If the existence of a signing ape was unsettling for linguists, it was also startling news for animal behaviorists.
— Davis, *Eloquent Animals*, p. 26

UNACCEPTABLE BORROWING OF WORDING
The existence of a signing ape unsettled linguists and startled animal behaviorists (Davis 26).

Notice that the phrase "the existence of a signing ape" has been lifted from the source without quotation marks. Notice, too, that "unsettled linguists and startled animal behaviorists" closely resembles the wording of the source.

It is also plagiarism to borrow the source's sentence structure but substitute your own synonyms, even though the source is cited, as illustrated here.

UNACCEPTABLE BORROWING OF STRUCTURE

If the presence of a sign-language-using chimp was disturbing for scientists studying language, it was also surprising to scientists studying animal behavior (Davis 26).

To avoid plagiarizing an author's wording, close the book, write from memory, and then open the book to check for accuracy. (See also 48b.) This technique prevents you from being captivated by the words on the page; it encourages you to write naturally, in your own voice, without plagiarizing. These two paraphrases were written with the book closed.

ACCEPTABLE PARAPHRASES

According to Flora Davis, linguists and animal behaviorists were unprepared for the news that a chimp could communicate with its trainers through sign language (26).

When they learned of an ape's ability to use sign language, both linguists and animal behaviorists were taken by surprise (Davis 26).

49e **Limit quotations and integrate them as smoothly as possible.**

It is tempting to insert many long quotations in your paper and to use your own words only for connecting passages. This is an especially strong temptation if you feel that the authors of your sources are better writers than you are. But do not quote excessively. Long series of quotations give readers the impression that you cannot think for yourself.

Use direct quotations only when the source is particularly clear or expressive or when it is important to let the debaters of an issue explain their positions in their own words. Except for this infrequent need for direct quotations, use your own words to summarize and paraphrase your sources and to explain your own ideas.

Integrating quotations

Integrate quotations smoothly enough for readers to move from your words to the words of a source without feeling a jolt. Avoid dropping quotations into the text without warning; instead, provide clear signal phrases, usually including the author's name, to prepare readers for the quotation.

DROPPED QUOTATION

Although the bald eagle is still listed as an endangered species, its ever-increasing population is very encouraging. "The bald eagle seems to have stabilized its population, at the very least, almost everywhere" (Sheppard 96).

QUOTATION WITH SIGNAL PHRASE

Although the bald eagle is still listed as an endangered species, its ever-increasing population is very encouraging. According to ornithologist Jay Sheppard, "The bald eagle seems to have stabilized its population, at the very least, almost everywhere" (96).

To avoid monotony, try to vary your signal phrases. The following models suggest a range of possibilities:

In the words of researcher Herbert Terrace, " . . . "

As Flora Davis has noted, " . . . "

The Gardners, Washoe's trainers, point out that " . . . "

" . . . ," claims linguist Noam Chomsky.

> Psychologist H. S. Terrace offers an odd argument for this view: " . . . "

> Terrace answers these objections with the following analysis: " . . . "

When your signal phrase includes a verb, choose one that is appropriate in the context. Is your source arguing a point, making an observation, reporting a fact, drawing a conclusion, refuting an argument, or stating a belief? By choosing an appropriate verb, such as one on the following list, you can make your source's stance clear.

acknowledges	comments	endorses	reasons
adds	compares	grants	refutes
admits	confirms	illustrates	rejects
agrees	contends	implies	reports
argues	declares	insists	responds
asserts	denies	notes	suggests
believes	disputes	observes	thinks
claims	emphasizes	points out	writes

It is not always necessary to quote full sentences from a source. At times you may wish to borrow only a phrase or to weave part of a source's sentence into your own sentence structure:

> Brian Millsap claims that the banning of DDT in 1972 was "the major turning point" leading to the eagles' comeback (2).

> The ultrasonography machine takes approximately 250 views of each breast, step by step. Mary Spletter likens the process to "examining an entire loaf of bread, one slice at a time" (40).

Handling long quotations

When you quote more than four typed lines, set off the quotation by indenting it ten spaces from the left margin. Use the normal right margin and do not single-space. This format displays your source's words more obviously than a set of widely separated quotation marks.

Long quotations should be introduced by an informative sentence, usually followed by a colon. Quotation marks are unnecessary because the indented format tells readers that the words are taken directly from the source.

> Desmond describes how Washoe tried signing to the other
> apes when the Gardners returned her to an ape colony in
> Oklahoma:
>
> > One particularly memorable day, a snake spread
> > terror through the castaways on the ape island,
> > and all but one fled in panic. This male sat
> > absorbed, staring intently at the serpent. Then
> > Washoe was seen running over signing to him
> > "come, hurry up." (42)

Notice that at the end of a block quotation the parenthetical citation goes outside the final period.

Using the ellipsis mark and brackets

Two useful marks of punctuation, the ellipsis mark and brackets, allow you to keep quoted material to a minimum and to integrate it smoothly into your text.

THE ELLIPSIS MARK   To condense a quoted passage, you can use the ellipsis mark (three periods, with spaces between) to indicate that you have omitted words. What remains must be grammatically complete.

> In a recent <u>New York Times</u> article, Erik Eckholm reports
> that "a 4-year-old pygmy chimpanzee . . . has demonstrated

what scientists say are the most humanlike linguistic skills
ever documented in another animal" (A1).

The writer has omitted the words *at a research center near
Atlanta,* which appeared in the original.

On the rare occasions when you want to omit a full sentence or more, use a period before the three ellipsis dots.

> According to Wade, the horse Clever Hans "could apparently
> count by tapping out numbers with his hoof. . . . Clever Hans
> owes his celebrity to his master's innocence. Von Osten sin-
> cerely believed he had taught Hans to solve arithmetical
> problems" (1349).

Ordinarily, do not use an ellipsis mark at the beginning
or at the end of a quotation. Your readers will understand that
the quoted material is taken from a longer passage, so such
ellipsis marks are not necessary. The only exception occurs
when words at the end of the final quoted sentence have been
dropped.

Obviously you should not use an ellipsis mark to distort
the meaning of your source.

BRACKETS   Brackets (square parentheses) allow you to
insert words of your own into quoted material. You can insert
words in brackets to explain a confusing reference or to keep
a sentence grammatical in your context.

> Robert Seyfarth reports that "Premack [a scientist at the
> University of Pennsylvania] taught a seven-year-old chim-
> panzee, Sarah, that the word for 'apple' was a small, plastic
> triangle" (13).

If your typewriter has no brackets, you should ink them in by
hand.

Reviewing your use of quotations

AVOIDING PLAGIARISM; BEING ACCURATE

1. Have you placed each quotation in quotation marks (except long quotations that have been set off from the text)? To use another writer's words as if they were your own is a form of dishonesty known as plagiarism. (See 49d.)
2. Is each quotation word-for-word accurate? If you added a word, did you place it in brackets? If you deleted part of the quotation, did you use an ellipsis mark? (See 49e.)
3. Have you documented each quotation with a combination of a signal phrase and a parenthetical citation? (See numbers 4 and 5.)

DOCUMENTING QUOTATIONS

4. Have you introduced each quotation with a clear signal phrase? Usually the signal phrase should name the author. Here are some examples of commonly used signal phrases:

   According to Jane Doe, " . . . "

   In the words of researcher Jane Doe, " . . . "

   As biologist Jane Does puts it, " . . . "

Quotations (continued)

Jane Doe points out that " . . . "

    argues that " . . . "

    admits that " . . . "

    has concluded that " . . . "

    reports that " . . ."

    writes that " . . . "

    stated in an interview that " . . . "

" . . . ," remarks Jane Doe, " . . . "

" . . . ," claims attorney Jane Doe.

Jane Doe offers an intriguing argument: " . . . "

Jane Doe's language is biased. Consider, for example, the following passage: " . . . "

5. Have you placed a parenthetical citation after each quotation? As a rule, if the author has been named in the signal phrase, only a page number goes in the parentheses. (See 50a.)

    Flora Davis reports that a chimp at the Yerkes Primate Research Center "has combined words into new sentences that she was never taught" (67).

Reviewing your use of summaries and paraphrases

AVOIDING PLAGIARISM

1. Did you write summaries and paraphrases from memory, without looking at the source as you wrote? (If not, you may have borrowed too much language from the source. See number 2.) Did you then reread the source to check for accuracy?

2. Are you certain you have not borrowed too much language from your sources? It is plagiarism to borrow strings of words without putting them in quotation marks or to borrow sentence structures and simply plug in synonyms. (For examples of plagiarism, see pages 478–79.)

3. Have you documented each summary and paraphrase (except for common knowledge) with a citation? (See number 4.)

DOCUMENTING SUMMARIES AND PARAPHRASES

4. Have you introduced most summaries and paraphrases with a clear signal phrase and followed them with a page number in parentheses? The signal phrase lets readers know where the summarized or paraphrased material begins. In the following example, the signal phrase is underlined.

Summaries and paraphrases (continued)

CITATION PRECEDED BY SIGNAL PHRASE

In the past, many researchers have been skeptical about whether the apes were really learning signs or merely imitating their trainers or responding to cues. Psychologist H. S. Terrace, the chief trainer of a chimp named Nim, was one of the most formidable of the skeptics because he was once a believer. Ultimately Terrace concluded that most of Nim's signs were responses to deliberate or nondeliberate cues by trainers (Terrace et al. 891).

NOTE: If readers will understand from the context precisely what information comes from the source, the signal phrase may be omitted. In such cases, put the name of the author in the parentheses along with the page number.

CITATION WITH NAME OF AUTHOR IN PARENTHESES

The most dramatic instances of spontaneous signing have involved Washoe. When Washoe had a baby in 1976, although the baby chimp lived only a few hours, Washoe signed to it before it died (Davis 42).

49f Revise the paper.

When you are revising any paper, it is a good idea to concentrate first on the larger elements of writing—content, focus, organization, paragraphing, and coherence—and then to turn to matters of style and correctness. With the research paper, this strategy is especially important because reviewing your use of sources requires considerable attention to detail.

The following checklist will help you review your draft for issues other than your use of sources. To review your use of sources (quotations, summaries, and paraphrases), consult the charts on pages 484–87.

CONTENT, FOCUS, AND ORGANIZATION

— Is your topic restricted?
— Is your thesis or purpose clearly stated in the introduction?
— Does the body of the paper support the thesis with appropriate evidence such as facts, statistics, reasons, and expert testimony?
— Can readers follow the organization? Are the ideas effectively arranged?

PARAGRAPHING AND COHERENCE

— Does each paragraph have a clear topic sentence stating a central idea related to the thesis?
— Does each paragraph fully support its topic sentence?
— Do the paragraphs read smoothly? Can readers move from one paragraph to another without feeling lost?

STYLE AND CORRECTNESS

— Are the sentences clear, emphatic, and varied?
— Is your style formal without being inflated?
— Is the paper free of errors in grammar, punctuation, and mechanics?
— Have sources been properly documented with in-text citations?

Once you have revised and edited your draft, type the final copy according to your instructor's guidelines and proofread it carefully. Then only one task remains: compiling the list of works cited.

49g Prepare a list of works cited.

On a separate page at the end of your paper you must provide a list of the works you have cited in your paper. The purpose of this list is to acknowledge your sources and to help your readers track down a source should they be interested in doing so.

Rules for preparing the list of works cited are quite strict, and they are complex. Fortunately, however, there is no need to memorize these rules. If you are using the MLA style of documentation, consult 50b; if you are using APA style, consult 51a.

50

Using the MLA system for documenting sources

The various academic disciplines use their own editorial styles for citing sources and for listing the works that have been cited. The style described in this section is that of the Modern Language Association (MLA), contained in the *MLA Handbook for Writers of Research Papers* (3rd ed., 1988), which recommends that citations be given in the text of the paper rather than in footnotes or endnotes. If your instructor prefers footnotes or endnotes (also acceptable to MLA) or the American Psychological Association (APA) style of in-text citation, consult 51, where you will also find a list of style manuals used in various disciplines.

Directory to the MLA system

50a: MLA in-text citations

MLA INFORMATION NOTES, 497

50b: MLA list of works cited

BOOKS

NOTE: For a sample paper documented with the MLA system,
see pages 514–38.

50a   MLA in-text citations

The MLA's in-text citations are made with a combination of signal phrases and parenthetical references. A signal phrase indicates that something taken from a source (such as a quotation, summary, or paraphrase) is about to be used; usually the signal phrase includes the author's name. The parenthetical reference includes at least a page number.

Citations in parentheses should be as concise as possible but complete enough so that readers can find the source in the list of works cited at the end of the paper, where works are listed alphabetically by authors' last names. The following models illustrate the form for the MLA style of citation.

AUTHOR NAMED IN A SIGNAL PHRASE   Ordinarily, you should introduce the material being cited with a signal phrase that includes the author's name. In addition to preparing readers for the source, the signal phrase allows you to keep the parenthetical citation brief.

> Flora Davis reports that a chimp at the Yerkes Primate Research Center "has combined words into new sentences that she was never taught" (67).

The signal phrase — "Flora Davis reports" — provides the name of the author; the parenthetical citation gives the page number where the quoted sentence may be found. By looking up the author's last name in the list of works cited, readers will find complete information about the work's title, publisher, and place and date of publication.

Notice that the period follows the parenthetical citation. For the MLA technique for handling quotations that end in a question mark or an exclamation point, see page 394.

AUTHOR NOT NAMED IN A SIGNAL PHRASE   If the signal phrase does not include the author's name (or if there is no signal phrase), the author's last name must appear in parentheses along with the page number.

> Although the baby chimp lived only a few hours, Washoe
> signed to it before it died (Davis 42).

Use no punctuation between the name and the page number.

TWO OR MORE WORKS BY THE SAME AUTHOR   If your list of works cited includes two or more works by the same author, include the title of the work either in the signal phrase or in abbreviated form in the parenthetical reference.

> In <u>Eloquent Animals,</u> Flora Davis reports that a chimp at the
> Yerkes Primate Research Center "has combined words into
> sentences that she was never taught" (67).

> Flora Davis reports that a chimp at the Yerkes Primate Re-
> search Center "has combined words into sentences that she
> was never taught" (<u>Eloquent</u> 67).

The title of a book should be underlined, as in the examples. The title of an article from a periodical should be put in quotation marks. In the rare case when both the author and a short title must be given in parentheses, the citation should appear as follows:

> Although the baby chimpanzee lived only for a few hours,
> Washoe signed to it before it died (Davis, <u>Eloquent</u> 42).

TWO OR THREE AUTHORS   If your source has two or three authors, name them in the signal phrase or include them in the parenthetical reference.

> Patterson and Linden agree that the gorilla Koko acquired
> language more slowly than a normal speaking child
> (83-90).

FOUR OR MORE AUTHORS   If your source has four or more authors, include only the first author's name followed by "et al." (Latin for "and others") in the signal phrase or in the parenthetical reference.

> The study was extended for two years, and only after results were duplicated on both coasts did the authors publish their results (Doe et al. 137).

CORPORATE AUTHOR   Either name the corporate author in the signal phrase or include a shortened version in the parentheses.

> The Internal Revenue Service warns businesses that deductions for "lavish and extravagant entertainment" are not allowed (43).

UNKNOWN AUTHOR   If the author is not given, either use the complete title in a signal phrase or use a short form of the title in the parentheses.

> The UFO reported by the crew of a Japan Air Lines flight remains a mystery. Radar tapes did not confirm the presence of another craft ("Strange Encounter" 26).

AUTHORS WITH THE SAME LAST NAME   If your list of works cited includes works by two or more authors with the same last name, include the first name of the author you are citing in the signal phrase or parenthetical reference.

> Both Lucy and Koko have been reported to lie (Adrian Desmond 201).

> Adrian Desmond has reported that Lucy was clever enough to see through the lies of her trainers (102).

A MULTIVOLUME WORK   If your paper cites more than one volume of a multivolume work, indicate in the parentheses the volume you are referring to, followed by a colon.

> Terman's studies of gifted children reveal a pattern of accelerated language acquisition (2: 279).

If your paper cites only one volume of a multivolume work, you will include the volume number in the list of works cited at the end of the paper and will not need to include it in the parentheses.

A NOVEL, A PLAY, OR A POEM   In citing literary sources, include information that will enable readers to find the passage in various editions of the work. For a novel, put the page number first and then, if possible, indicate the part or chapter in which the passage can be found.

> Fitzgerald's narrator captures Gatsby in a moment of isolation: "A sudden emptiness seemed to flow now from the windows and the great doors, endowing with complete isolation the figure of the host" (56; ch. 3).

For a verse play, list the act, scene, and line numbers, separated by periods. Use arabic numerals unless your instructor prefers roman numerals.

> In his famous advice to the players, Hamlet defines the purpose of theater, "whose end, both at the first and now, was and is, to hold, as 'twere, the mirror up to nature" (3.2.21-23).

For a poem, cite the part (if there are a number of parts) and the line numbers, separated by periods.

> When Homer's Odysseus came to the hall of Circe, he found his men "mild / in her soft spell, fed on her drug of evil" (10.209-11).

A WORK IN AN ANTHOLOGY   Put the name of the author of the work (not the editor of the anthology) in the signal phrase or in the parentheses.

> At the end of Kate Chopin's "The Story of an Hour," Mrs. Mallard drops dead upon learning that her husband is alive. In the final irony of the story, doctors report that she has died of a "joy that kills" (25).

INDIRECT SOURCE   When a writer's or speaker's quoted words appear in a source written by someone else, begin the citation with the abbreviation "qtd. in."

> "We only used seven signs in his presence," says Fouts.   "All of his signs were learned from the other chimps at the laboratory" (qtd. in Toner 24).

AN ENTIRE WORK   To cite an entire work, use the author's name in a signal phrase or a parenthetical reference.

> Patterson and Linden provide convincing evidence for the speech-making abilities of nonhuman primates.

TWO OR MORE WORKS   To cite more than one source to document a particular point, separate the citations with a semicolon.

> With intensive training, the apes in this study learned more than two hundred signs or signals (Desmond 229; Linden 173).

Multiple citations can be distracting to readers, however, so the technique should not be overused. If you want to alert readers to several sources that discuss a particular topic, consider using an information note instead (discussed next).

MLA information notes

Researchers who use the MLA system of parenthetical documentation may also use information notes for one of two purposes:

1. to provide additional material that might interrupt the flow of the paper yet is important enough to include;
2. to refer readers to sources not discussed in the paper.

Information notes may be either footnotes or endnotes. Footnotes appear at the foot of the page; endnotes appear on a separate page at the end of the paper, just before the list of works cited. (See page 534 for an example.) For either style, the notes are numbered consecutively throughout the paper. The text of the paper contains a raised arabic numeral that corresponds to the number of the note.

TEXT

The apes' achievements cannot be explained away as the simple results of conditioning or unconscious cuing by trainers.[1]

NOTE

[1] For a discussion of the cuing of animals, see Wade 1349-51.

Information notes should not be confused with notes used as an alternative to parenthetical documentation (see 51b).

50b MLA list of works cited

A list of works cited, which appears at the end of your research paper, gives publishing information for each of the sources you have cited in the paper. Start on a new page and title your list "Works Cited." Then, working from your bibliography cards (see 47b), list in alphabetical order all the sources that you have cited in the paper. Unless your instructor asks for them, do not give sources not actually cited in the paper, even if you read them.

Alphabetize the list by the last names of the authors (or editors); if a work has no author or editor, alphabetize by the first word of the title other than *a, an,* or *the.*

Do not indent the first line of each bibliography entry, but indent any additional lines five spaces. This technique highlights the names by which the list has been alphabetized (see, for example, the list of works cited at the end of Karen Shaw's paper on page 536 and 538).

The following models illustrate the form that the Modern Language Association (MLA) recommends for bibliographic entries.

Books

BASIC FORMAT FOR A BOOK   For most books, arrange the information into three units, each followed by a period: (1) the author's name, last name first; (2) the title and subtitle, underlined; and (3) the place of publication, the publisher, and the date.

> Tompkins, Jane.   West of Everything: The Inner Life of
>   Westerns.   New York: Oxford UP, 1992.

The information is taken from the title page of the book and from the reverse side of the title page (the copyright page), not from the outside cover. The complete name of the publisher (in this case Oxford University Press) need not be given. You may use a short form as long as it is easily identifiable; omit terms such as *Press, Inc.,* and *Co.* except when naming university presses (Harvard UP, for example). The date to use in your bibliographic entry is the most recent copyright date.

TWO OR THREE AUTHORS Name the authors in the order in which they are presented on the title page; reverse the name of only the first author.

> Rico, Barbara, and Sandra Mano. <u>American Mosaic:</u>
>   <u>Multicultural Readings in Context</u>. Boston: Houghton,
>   1991.

The names of three authors are separated by commas.

> Kagan, Donald, Steven Ozment, and Frank M. Turner. <u>The</u>
>   <u>Western Heritage since 1300</u>. New York: Macmillan,
>   1987.

FOUR OR MORE AUTHORS Cite only the first author, name reversed, followed by "et al." (Latin for "and others").

> Medhurst, Martin J., et al. <u>Cold War Rhetoric: Strategy,</u>
>   <u>Metaphor, and Ideology</u>. New York: Greenwood, 1990.

EDITORS An entry for an editor is similar to that for an author except that the name is followed by a comma and the abbreviation "ed." for "editor." If there is more than one editor, use the abbreviation "eds." for "editors."

> Anaya, Rodolfo, and Francisco Lomeli, eds. <u>Aztlán: Essays</u>
>   <u>on the Chicano Homeland</u>. Albuquerque: Academia–
>   El Norte, 1989.

AUTHOR WITH AN EDITOR Begin with the author and title, followed by the name of the editor. In this case the abbreviation "Ed." means "edited by," so it is the same for one or multiple editors.

> Franklin, Benjamin. <u>The Autobiography and Other</u>
>   <u>Writings.</u> Ed. Kenneth Silverman. New York: Penguin,
>   1986.

TRANSLATION   List the entry under the name of the author, not the translator. After the title, write "Trans." (for "translated by") and the name of the translator.

Eco, Umberto. Foucault's Pendulum. Trans. William
  Weaver. San Diego: Harcourt, 1989.

CORPORATE AUTHOR   List the entry under the name of the corporate author, even if it is also the name of the publisher.

Fidelity Investments. Fidelity Brokerage Services
  Handbook. Boston: Fidelity Investments, 1993.

UNKNOWN AUTHOR   Begin with the title. Alphabetize the entry by the first word of the title other than *a, an,* or *the.*

The Times Atlas of the World. 9th ed. New York: Times,
  1992.

TWO OR MORE WORKS BY THE SAME AUTHOR   If your list of works cited includes two or more works by the same author, use the author's name only for the first entry. For subsequent entries use three hyphens followed by a period. The three hyphens must stand for exactly the same name or names as in the preceding entry. List the titles in alphabetical order.

Gordon, Mary. Good Boys and Dead Girls and Other Essays.
  New York: Viking, 1991.
---. The Other Side. New York: Viking, 1989.

EDITION OTHER THAN THE FIRST   If you are citing an edition other than the first, include the number of the edition after the title: 2nd ed., 3rd ed., and so on.

Lindemann, Erika. A Rhetoric for Writing Teachers.
  2nd ed. New York: Oxford UP, 1987.

MULTIVOLUME WORK   Include the number of volumes before the city and publisher, using the abbreviation "vols."

> Mark Twain: Collected Tales, Sketches, Speeches, and Essays.
>
>   2 vols.   New York: Library of America, 1992.

If your paper cites only one of the volumes, write the volume number before the city and publisher and write the total number of volumes in the work after the date.

> Mark Twain: Collected Tales, Sketches, Speeches, and
>
>   Essays.   Vol. 2.   New York: Library of America, 1992.
>
>   2 vols.

ENCYCLOPEDIA OR DICTIONARY   Articles in well-known dictionaries and encyclopedias are handled in abbreviated form. Simply list the author of the article (if there is one), the title of the article, the title of the reference work, the edition number, if any, and the date of the edition.

> "Croatia."   The New Encyclopaedia Britannica: Micropaedia.
>
>   1991.

Volume and page numbers are not necessary because the entries are arranged alphabetically and therefore are easy to locate.

   If a reference work is not well known, provide full publishing information as well.

WORK IN AN ANTHOLOGY   Present the information in this order, with each item followed by a period: author of the selection; title of the selection; title of the anthology; editor of the anthology, preceded by "Ed."; city, publisher, and date; page numbers on which the selection appears.

> Synge, J. M.   "On an Anniversary."   The New Oxford Book
>
>   of Irish Verse.   Ed. Thomas Kinsella.   Oxford: Oxford
>
>   UP, 1986.   318.

If an anthology gives the original publishing information for a selection and if your instructor prefers that you use it, cite that information first. Follow with "Rpt. in," the title, editor, and publishing information for the anthology, and the page numbers in the anthology on which the selection appears.

> Rodriguez, Richard. "Late Victorians." <u>Harper's</u> Oct. 1990:
>
> 57-66. Rpt. in <u>The Best American Essays 1991</u>. Ed.
>
> Joyce Carol Oates. New York: Ticknor, 1991.
>
> 119-34.

TWO OR MORE WORKS FROM THE SAME ANTHOLOGY If you wish, you may cross-reference two or more works from the same anthology. Provide a separate entry for the anthology with complete publication information.

> Kinsella, Thomas, ed.   <u>The New Oxford Book of Irish Verse</u>.
>
> Oxford: Oxford UP, 1986.

Then list an entry for each selection from the anthology by author and title of the selection with a cross-reference to the anthology. The cross-reference should include the last name of the editor of the anthology and the page numbers in the anthology on which the selection appears.

> Colum, Padraic. "An Old Woman of the Roads." Kinsella
>
> 321-22.

> Synge, J. M. "On an Anniversary." Kinsella 318.

FOREWORD, INTRODUCTION, PREFACE, OR AFTERWORD If in your paper you quote from one of these elements, begin with the name of the writer of that element. Then identify the element being cited, neither underlined nor in quotation marks, followed by the title of the complete book, the book's author, and the book's editor, if any. After the publishing information, give the page numbers on which the foreword, introduction, preface, or afterword appears.

Murray, Charles. Foreword. <u>Unfinished Business: A Civil
  Rights Strategy for America's Third Century</u>. By
  Clint Bolick. San Francisco: Pacific Research Inst.
  for Public Policy, 1990. ix-xiii.

BOOK WITH A TITLE WITHIN ITS TITLE If the book title
contains a title normally underlined, neither underline the
internal title nor place it in quotation marks.

Abbott, Keith. <u>Downstream from</u> Trout Fishing in
  America: <u>A Memoir of Richard Brautigan</u>. Santa
  Barbara: Capra, 1989.

If the title within the title is normally enclosed within quotation marks, retain the quotation marks and underline the entire title.

Faulkner, Dewey R. <u>Twentieth Century Interpretations
  of "The Pardoner's Tale."</u> Englewood Cliffs: Spectrum-
  Prentice, 1973.

BOOK IN A SERIES Before the publishing information, cite
the series name as it appears on the title page followed by the
series number, if any.

Laughlin, Robert M. <u>Of Cabbages and Kings: Tales from
  Zinacantán</u>. Smithsonian Contributions to Anthropology 23. Washington: Smithsonian, 1977.

REPUBLISHED BOOK After the title of the book, cite the
original publication date followed by the current publishing
information. If the republished book contains new material,
such as an introduction or afterword, include that information after the original date.

McClintock, Walter. <u>Old Indian Trails</u>. 1926. Foreword
  William Least Heat Moon. Boston: Houghton, 1992.

PUBLISHER'S IMPRINT   If a book was published by an imprint of a publishing company, cite the name of the imprint followed by a hyphen and the publisher's name. An imprint name usually precedes the publisher's name on the title page.

> Oates, Joyce Carol. (Woman) Writer: Occasions and Oppor-
>
>   tunities. New York: Abrahams-Dutton, 1988.

Articles in periodicals

ARTICLE IN A MONTHLY MAGAZINE   In addition to the author, the title of the article, and the title of the magazine, list the month and year and the page numbers on which the article appears. Abbreviate the names of months except May, June, and July.

> Lukacs, John. "The End of the Twentieth Century."
>
>   Harper's Jan. 1993: 39-58.

If the article had appeared not on consecutive pages but on, say, pages 39–41 and 91–96, you would write "39+" (not "39–96").

ARTICLE IN A WEEKLY MAGAZINE   Handle articles in weekly (or biweekly) magazines as you do those for monthly magazines, but give the exact date of the issue, not just the month and year.

> Schiff, Stephen. "Muriel Spark between the Lines."
>
>   New Yorker 24 May 1993: 36-43.

ARTICLE IN A JOURNAL PAGINATED BY VOLUME   Many professional journals continue page numbers throughout the year instead of beginning each issue with page 1; at the end of the year, all of the issues are collected in a volume. Interested readers need only the volume number, the year, and the page numbers to find an article.

Segal, Gabriel. "Seeing What Is Not There." Philosophical
Review 98 (1989): 189-214.

ARTICLE IN A JOURNAL PAGINATED BY ISSUE If each issue
of the journal begins with page 1, you need to indicate the
number of the issue. Simply place a period after the number
of the volume, followed by the number of the issue.

Johnson, G. J. "A Distinctiveness Model of Serial Learning."
Psychological Review 98.2 (1991): 204-17.

ARTICLE IN A DAILY NEWSPAPER Begin with the author,
if there is one, followed by the title of the article. Next give the
name of the newspaper, the date, the section letter or number,
and the page number.

Sun, Lena H. "Chinese Feel the Strain of a New Society."
Washington Post 13 June 1993: A1+.

If the section is marked with a number rather than a letter,
handle the entry as follows:

Greenhouse, Linda. "Justices Plan to Delve Anew into Race
and Voting Rights." New York Times 11 July 1993,
sec. 1: 1+.

If an edition of the newspaper is specified on the masthead,
name the edition after the date and before the page reference:
eastern ed., late ed., natl. ed., and so on.

UNSIGNED ARTICLE IN A NEWSPAPER OR MAGAZINE Use
the same form you would use for an article in a newspaper or
a weekly or monthly magazine, but begin with the title of the
article.

"Radiation in Russia." U.S. News and World Report 9 Aug.
1993: 40-42.

EDITORIAL IN A NEWSPAPER   Cite an editorial as you would an unsigned article, adding the word "Editorial" after the title.

> "Gays and the Military." Editorial. Boston Globe 13 July
> 1993: 14.

LETTER TO THE EDITOR   Cite the writer's name, followed by the word "Letter" and the publishing information for the newspaper or magazine in which the letter appears.

> Benston, Graham. Letter. Opera Now May 1993: 12.

BOOK OR FILM REVIEW   Cite first the reviewer's name and the title of the review, if any, followed by the words "Rev. of" and the title and author or director of the work reviewed. Add the publishing information for the publication in which the review appears.

> Kermode, Frank. "Criticism without Machinery." Rev. of
> Literary Reflections, by R. W. B. Lewis. New York
> Times Book Review 11 July 1993: 16.

> Holden, Stephen. "A Union of Convenience across a Cul-
> tural Divide." Rev. of The Wedding Banquet, dir. Ang
> Lee. With Winston Chao, May Chin, and Mitchell Lich-
> tenstein. Goldwyn, 1993. New York Times 4 Aug.
> 1993: C18.

Other sources

GOVERNMENT PUBLICATION   Treat the government agency as the author, giving the name of the government followed by the name of the agency.

> United States. Natl. Endowment for the Humanities. Study
> Grants for College and University Teachers. Washington:
> GPO, 1993.

PAMPHLET   Cite a pamphlet as you would a book.

United States.   Dept. of the Interior.   Natl. Park Service.
 <u>Ford's Theatre and the House Where Lincoln Died</u>.   Washington: GPO, 1989.

PUBLISHED DISSERTATION   Cite a published dissertation as you would a book, underlining the title and giving the place of publication, the publisher, and the year of publication. After the title, add the word "Diss.," the institution name, and the year the dissertation was written.

Healey, Robert F.   <u>Eleusinian Sacrifices in the Athenian Law
 Code</u>.   Diss.   Harvard U, 1961.   New York: Garland,
 1990.

UNPUBLISHED DISSERTATION   Begin with the author's name, followed by the dissertation title in quotation marks, the word "Diss.," the name of the institution, and the year it was written.

Fedorko, Kathy Anne.   "Edith Wharton's Haunted House: The
 Gothic in Her Fiction."   Diss.   Rutgers U, 1987.

ABSTRACT OF A DISSERTATION   Give the author's name, the dissertation title in quotation marks, and the abbreviation *DA* or *DAI* (for *Dissertation Abstracts* or *Dissertation Abstracts International*), followed by the volume number, date, and page number. Add the name of the institution at the end.

Berkman, Anne Elizabeth.   "The Quest for Authenticity: The
 Novels of Toni Morrison."   <u>DAI</u> 48 (1988): 2059A.
 Columbia U.

PUBLISHED PROCEEDINGS OF A CONFERENCE   Cite published conference proceedings as you would a book, adding information about the conference after the title.

> Howell, Benita J., ed. <u>Cultural Heritage Conservation in the
> American South</u>. Proc. of Southern Anthropological
> Soc. Tampa, 1988. Athens: U of Georgia P, 1990.

WORK OF ART   Cite the artist's name, followed by the title of the artwork, usually underlined, and the institution and city in which the artwork can be found.

> Constable, John. <u>Dedham Vale</u>. Victoria and Albert Museum,
> London.

MUSICAL COMPOSITION   Cite the composer's name, followed by the title of the work. Underline the title of an opera, ballet, or a composition identified by name, but do not underline or use quotation marks around a composition identified by number or form.

> Copland, Aaron. <u>Appalachian Spring.</u>

> Shostakovich, Dmitri. Quartet no. 1 in C, op. 49.

PERSONAL LETTER   To cite a letter you have received, begin with the writer's name and add the phrase "Letter to the author," followed by the date.

> Cipriani, Karen. Letter to the author. 25 April 1993.

LECTURE OR PUBLIC ADDRESS   Cite the speaker's name, followed by the title of the lecture (if any) in quotation marks, the organization sponsoring the lecture, the location, and date.

> Quinn, Karen. "John Singleton Copley's <u>Watson and the
> Shark</u>." Museum of Fine Arts. Boston, 1 July 1993.

PERSONAL INTERVIEW   To cite an interview that you conducted, begin with the name of the person interviewed. Then write "Personal interview," followed by the date of the interview.

Harrison, Patricia.   Personal interview.   19 Feb. 1993.

PUBLISHED INTERVIEW   Name the person interviewed, followed by the word "Interview" and the publication in which the interview was printed. If the interview has a title, put it in quotation marks after the interviewee's name and do not use the word "Interview."

Quindlen, Anna.   Interview.   Commonweal 14 Feb. 1992:
    9-13.

RADIO OR TELEVISION INTERVIEW   Name the person interviewed, followed by the word "Interview." Then give the title of the program, underlined, and identifying information about the broadcast.

Holm, Celeste.   Interview.   Fresh Air.   Natl. Public Radio.
    WBUR, Boston.   28 June 1990.

COMPUTER SOFTWARE   Begin with the author of the program (if known), the title of the program, underlined, and the words "Computer software." Then name the distributor and the year of publication. At the end of the entry you may add other pertinent information, such as the computer for which the program is designed or the form of the program.

Encarta.   Computer software.   Microsoft, 1992.   PC-DOS
    3.1, Windows, 386SX, CD-ROM.

MATERIAL FROM INFORMATION SERVICE OR DATABASE
Cite the material as you would any other material, including all publishing information. At the end of the citation add the name of the service (such as ERIC, for Educational Resources Information Center) and the number the service assigns to the material.

Horn, Pamela.   "The Victorian Governess."   History of Edu-
    cation 18 (1989): 333-44.   ERIC EJ 401 533.

Trueheart, Charles. "Graham Greene's Private Heart."
    Washington Post 4 Apr. 1991. NewsBank, People,
    Apr. 1991, fiche 14, grids F5-7.

FILM OR VIDEOTAPE   Begin with the title. For a film, cite
the director and the names of the lead actors or narrator; for
a videotape, give the word "Videotape" followed by the director
and the names of the lead actors or narrator. End with the
distributor and year and any other pertinent information,
such as running time.

Much Ado about Nothing. Dir. Kenneth Branagh. With
    Emma Thompson, Kenneth Branagh, Denzel Washing-
    ton, Michael Keaton, and Keanu Reeves. Goldwyn,
    1993.

Through the Wire. Videotape. Dir. Nina Rosenblum. Narr.
    Susan Sarandon. Fox/Lorber Home Video, 1990.
    77 min.

RADIO OR TELEVISION PROGRAM   List the information
about the program in this order: the title of the program, underlined; the writer ("By"), director ("Dir."), narrator ("Narr."),
producer ("Prod."), or main actors ("With"), if relevant; the
network; the local station on which you heard or saw the program and the city; and the date the program was broadcast.
If a television episode or radio segment has a title, the order
is as follows: episode or segment title in quotation marks;
writer, director, narrator, and so on; title of the program, underlined; network; local station and city; and date of broadcast.

Coração Brasileiro. WMBR, Boston. 1 Aug. 1993.

"This Old Pyramid." With Mark Lehner and Roger Hopkins.
    Nova. PBS. WGBH, Boston. 4 Aug. 1993.

LIVE PERFORMANCE OF A PLAY   Begin with the title of the play, followed by the author. Then include specific information about the live performance: the director, the major actors, the theater company and its location, and the date of the performance.

> The Sisters Rosensweig. By Wendy Wasserstein. Dir.
>   Daniel Sullivan. With Jane Alexander, Christine
>   Estabrook, and Madeline Kahn. Barrymore, New York.
>   11 July 1993.

RECORDS, TAPES, AND CDs   Begin with the composer (or author, if the recording is spoken), followed by the title of the piece. Next list pertinent artists (for instance, the conductor, the pianist, or the reader). End with the company label, the catalog number, and the date.

> Verdi, Giuseppe. Falstaff. With Tito Gobbi, Elisabeth
>   Schwarzkopf, Nan Merriman, and Fedora Barbieri.
>   Cond. Herbert von Karajan. Philharmonia Orch. and
>   Chorus. EMI, 7 49668 2, 1988.

CARTOON   Begin with the cartoonist's name, the title of the cartoon (if it has one) in quotation marks, the word "Cartoon," and the publishing information for the publication in which the cartoon appears.

> Chast, Roz. "Are You All Right?" Cartoon. New Yorker
>   5 July 1993: 65.

MAP OR CHART   Cite a map or chart as you would a book with an unknown author. Underline the title of the map or chart and add the word "Map" or "Chart" following the title.

> Spain/Portugal. Map. Paris: Michelin, 1992.

SAMPLE STUDENT RESEARCH PAPER (WITH MLA DOCUMENTATION)

On the following pages is a research paper written by Karen Shaw, a student in a first-semester composition class. Shaw's paper is documented with the MLA style of in-text citations and list of works cited.

Numbered comments on the pages opposite Shaw's paper draw your attention to features of special interest. (A corresponding number appears in the margins of the paper.) Here is a directory of those numbered comments:

TITLE PAGE, OUTLINE, FORMAT
1. Title page format
2. Outline
3. Paper format

COMPOSITION PRINCIPLES
5. Thesis
9. Importance of statistics and other specific evidence
12. Addressing opposing arguments
14. Variety in signal phrases
17. Effective use of evidence
21. Transition paragraph
22. Use of anecdotal evidence
25. Importance of topic sentences
26. Transition
28. A balanced approach

HANDLING SOURCE MATERIAL; CITATIONS
4. Summarizing without plagiarizing
6. Author named in parentheses
7. Author named in signal phrase
8. Two authors
10. Use of information notes

11. Use of "et al."
13. Use of information notes
15. Indented quotations, ellipsis marks, and brackets
16. No page number in parentheses
18. Sample note cards
19. Short title in parentheses
20. Interview
23. Short title in parentheses
24. Paraphrasing without plagiarizing
27. Indirect source

INFORMATION NOTES
29. Format of information notes
30. Use of information notes
31. Format of the bibliographic reference

BIBLIOGRAPHIC FORMAT (LIST OF WORKS CITED)
32. Format of the list of works cited
33. Book by a single author
34. Article in a newspaper
35. Two works by the same author
36. Article in a journal paginated by volume
37. Book by two authors
38. Work in an anthology
39. Interview
40. Journal article with four or more authors
41. Article in a magazine

Somewhere Between the Word and the Sentence: 1
The Great Apes and the Acquisition of Language

Karen Shaw

English 101, Section 30
Dr. Robert Barshay
1 November 1993

1. *Title page format.* Shaw uses a separate title page. She types the title about one-third down the page. One inch below the title Shaw types her name, and one inch below that she types the name and section number of the course, her instructor's name, and the date. Each item is on a separate line, and the lines are double-spaced. All the information is centered between the left and right margins.

   If your instructor does not require a title page, see pages 629–30. (See also pages 603 and 608.)

Pages 516–17

2. *Outline.* Shaw begins the outline with her thesis, the main point of the paper. Shaw's outline is presented in standard form, with roman numerals for the major categories, capital letters indented for the next level, and arabic numerals indented further for the third level (see 1d).

   Shaw decided that a sentence outline was necessary to reflect the complexity of the ideas in her paper. She keeps the sentences as parallel and as simple as possible to make the relationships between and among ideas clear.

   The pages of the outline are numbered with small roman numerals: *i, ii.*

Outline

Thesis: The great apes resemble humans in language abil-   2
ities more than researchers once believed, and evidence is mounting that pygmy chimpanzees can
understand and perhaps even create sentences.

I.   Early ape language studies showed that apes could acquire significant language skills, but researchers
failed to prove that apes could create sentences.

    A.   Apes acquired impressive vocabularies in sign
language and in artificial languages.

    B.   Despite charges that they were responding to
cues, apes were using language spontaneously.

        1.   They performed well in experiments that
eliminated the possibility of cuing.

        2.   They learned signs and symbols from each
other and initiated conversations on their
own.

    C.   Apes were using language creatively.

        1.   They invented creative names.

        2.   They may even have lied and joked.

    D.   There was once little evidence that apes could or-
der symbols grammatically to form sentences.

        1.   The apes' sequences of signs were often con-
fusing and repetitious.

        2.   Evidence of meaningful sequences was incon-
clusive.

II.   Recent research with Kanzi demonstrates that pygmy
      chimpanzees can understand and perhaps even create
      grammatical patterns.

    A.   Kanzi can understand grammatically complex
           spoken English.

    B.   Kanzi has picked up simple grammatical patterns
           from his caretakers.

    C.   Kanzi appears to have developed his own pat-
           terns.

III. Evidence suggests that linguistic abilities in humans
      and apes are part of a continuum.

    A.   The skeptics tend to apply a double standard: one
           for very young human children, another for
           apes.

    B.   In our human ancestors, the ability to communi-
           cate in language must have preceded language
           itself.

Shaw 1

Somewhere Between the Word and the Sentence:
The Great Apes and the Acquisition of Language   3
One afternoon, Koko the gorilla, who was often bored with
language lessons, stubbornly and repeatedly signaled "red" in
American Sign Language when asked the color of a white towel.
She did this even though she had correctly identified the color
white many times before. At last the gorilla plucked a bit of red
lint from the towel and showed it to her trainer (Patterson and
Linden 80-81). At Yerkes Primate Center, chimpanzees Sher-   4
man and Austin, who had been taught symbols for foods and
tools, were put in separate rooms. To obtain food in different
containers, one chimp had to ask the other for a tool, such as a
key or a wrench, by projecting symbols onto a screen using a
computer. After some experimentation, the chimpanzees suc-
ceeded 97 percent of the time (Marx 1333). More recently, a
pygmy chimpanzee named Kanzi has learned to understand
spoken English and is responding correctly 90 percent of the time
to such complex instructions as "Go to the colony room and get
the orange," even when another orange has been placed in front
of him (Lewin 51). These and hundreds of similar scenes played   5
out over the last twenty-five years demonstrate that the great
apes (gorillas, orangutans, chimpanzees, and pygmy chimpanzees) resemble humans in language abilities far more than researchers once thought. And evidence is mounting, despite
opposition from some linguists and psychologists, that the most
intelligent of the apes--pygmy chimpanzees--can understand and
perhaps even create grammatical patterns.

3. *Paper format.* The writer's last name and the page number appear in the upper right-hand corner, about a half-inch from the top of the page. The title is centered, all text is double-spaced, and there is a margin of one inch at the top, bottom, and sides of the paper.

4. *Summarizing without plagiarizing.* When summarizing, Shaw avoids plagiarism by using her own language, not that of the source. Here, for instance, is the passage from Marx that Shaw has summarized.

ORIGINAL SOURCE

In one of the experiments, Sherman and Austin were put in separate rooms, both of which were equipped with the computer terminals with which the animals communicate. Food was then placed in Sherman's room in such a way that he needed one of six tools to retrieve it. Although Sherman knew the location of the food, only Austin, who did not see where it was hidden, had access to the tools. In order for Sherman to get at the food, he had to ask Austin for the right tool. The animals had previously been trained in the use of the tools, which included a key for unlocking a box and a stick for pushing food out of a long, narrow tube, and had learned the symbols for them.

After a few false starts, in which Sherman unsuccessfully asked the human experimenter for the tool, he caught on to the fact that he had to ask Austin. When asked for a tool, Austin would pick out the right one and give it to Sherman, who would retrieve the food and then share it with his buddy.

The animals learned this process very quickly, Rumbaugh says, and completed the task successfully 97 percent of the time if the computer terminals were turned on.

—Marx, p. 1333

5. *Thesis.* Shaw uses two sentences to express her thesis because her conclusions about the ape language experiments are complex. The thesis sentence that appears in Shaw's outline presents the main point more succinctly.

Though apes lack the vocal ability to produce human sounds, they have acquired fairly large vocabularies in American Sign Language (Ameslan) and in artificial languages. Washoe, trained by psychologists Alan and Beatrice Gardner from 1966 to 1970, learned 160 signs in Ameslan as measured by a strict criterion (Davis 21).   According to H. Lyn White Miles, an orangutan under her supervision "learned to use a vocabulary of 140 signs and invented additional signs of his own" (511).   The largest Ameslan vocabulary claimed for an ape, 600 signs, is that of Francine Patterson's gorilla Koko.   This figure has been attacked because it is based on a simple count, but Patterson and her coauthor Eugene Linden have responded with a chart showing that Koko has mastered nearly 200 signs as measured by the Gardners' criterion (83-84).

Apes using artificial languages have mastered impressive vocabularies as well.   David Premack's chimpanzee Sarah learned to use more than 100 symbols in a language of plastic tokens; and Duane Rumbaugh's Lana, Sherman, and Austin learned to manipulate more than 100 symbols on a computer.   Kanzi, trained by a team headed by Sue Savage-Rumbaugh, has the largest vocabulary in an artificial language.   In 1991, Roger Lewin reported that the ten-year-old pygmy chimp had learned to communicate about 200 symbols on the computerized board that he carries with him (51).

In the past, many researchers have been skeptical about whether the apes were really learning signs or merely imitating their trainers or responding to cues.[1] Psychologist H. S. Terrace, the chief trainer of a chimp named Nim, was one of the most formidable of the skeptics because he was once a believer.

6. *Author named in parentheses.* Because the author's name (Davis) does not appear in a signal phrase, it appears in the parenthetical reference along with the page number.

7. *Author named in signal phrase.* Quotations must be introduced with a signal phrase. Shaw includes the author's name (Miles) in the signal phrase, so it does not appear in the parentheses.

8. *Two authors.* When a work has two authors, both authors' names must appear either in the signal phrase or in the parentheses. Shaw includes Patterson's and Linden's names in the signal phrase, so only a page number is needed in the parentheses.

9. *Importance of statistics and other specific evidence.* Throughout her paper, Shaw uses statistics and other specific evidence to support her assertions.

10. *Use of information notes.* The number at the end of this sentence refers to an information note at the end of Shaw's paper. Shaw's rough draft contained a long discussion of cuing and the subtle ways it can occur, but the material had to be cut because Shaw was losing her focus on the thesis. She preserved a short passage by putting it in the note. (See page 497.)

Ultimately Terrace concluded that "most of Nim's utterances were prompted by his teacher's prior utterance" (Terrace et al. 891).   **11**
Terrace and his colleagues argued that cuing played a large role in the training of other apes, including Washoe and Koko.

In the early ape language studies, it is possible that a high   **12**
percentage of the apes' signs were in response to cues, but Terrace and other critics failed to prove that all of them were. Even as early as 1979, the Gardners were performing double-blind experiments that prevented any possibility of cuing.[2]   **13**

Perhaps the most convincing evidence that the apes have not been simply responding to cues is that they have used signs or symbols spontaneously among themselves, often without a trainer present. Patterson's gorillas Koko and Michael sign to one another, with Michael occasionally using signs that he could have learned only from Koko. "Even more intriguing," write Patterson and Linden, "is his variation of the <u>tickle</u> sign depending on whom he is conversing with" (176).   **14**

When the Gardners returned Washoe to an ape colony in Oklahoma, she desperately signaled to humans from whom she was separated by a moat, and from the start she signed to the other apes. Adrian Desmond vividly describes Washoe's efforts to converse:

> Frustrated by lack of conversationalists, she [Washoe]   **15**
> even tried talking to dogs. . . . One particularly memorable day, a snake spread terror through . . . the ape island, and all but one fled in panic. This male sat absorbed, staring intently at the serpent. Then Washoe was seen running over signing to him "come, hurry up."
> (42)

11. *Use of "et al."* When a source has four or more authors, the last name of the first author is followed by "et al.," meaning "and others." Shaw names Terrace in the signal phrase, but since Terrace was not the sole author of the article being quoted, this fact must be indicated in the parentheses.

12. *Addressing opposing arguments.* Shaw wisely addresses her opponents' arguments throughout the paper, showing that she knows both sides and believes that her arguments stand up against the opposition. Here she counters Terrace's conclusion and offers evidence from concrete experiments to support her assertion.

13. *Use of information notes.* The number at the end of this sentence refers to an information note at the end of Shaw's paper. Shaw does not have the space to discuss the double-blind experiments but thinks some readers may want to read about them. The note suggests an article included in the list of works cited.

14. *Variety in signal phrases.* For variety, Shaw puts her signal phrase between parts of the quotation.

15. *Indented quotations, ellipsis marks, and brackets.* Quotations longer than four typed lines should be indented ten spaces from the left margin and typed double-spaced. Quotation marks are not used to enclose indented quotations because the format tells readers that the material is a quotation.

    It is a sacred rule of research that material should be quoted *exactly* as it appears in a source. Often, however, it is necessary to insert or omit material in a quoted passage. Brackets are used to insert words not in the original source, in this case the name Washoe. Bracketed information often clarifies the quotation or makes it fit grammatically within your text. Ellipsis dots indicate that words have been deleted. The first ellipsis mark in the quotation consists of a period (indicating the end of a sentence) and three dots. The second ellipsis mark appears

Shaw 4

The most dramatic instances of spontaneous signing have involved Washoe. When Washoe had a baby in 1976, although the
baby chimp lived only a few hours, Washoe signed to it before it
died (Davis 42). Later, another baby chimpanzee placed in
Washoe's care mastered more than 50 signs in Ameslan without
help from humans (Toner).   16

In addition to learning signs and using them spontaneously,   17
apes have used language creatively. Koko has signed "finger
bracelet" to describe a ring and "bottle match" for a cigarette
lighter (Patterson and Linden 146). The Gardners' Lucy is re-   18
ported to have called an onion "cry fruit" and a radish "cry hurt
food" (Desmond 40). An orangutan named Chantek has signed
"eye-drink" for his caregiver's contact lens fluid (Miles 535).
And Kanzi has punched lexigrams for "campfire" and "TV" to request to see Quest for Fire, a film about early primates discovering fire (Eckholm, "Kanzi" C3).   19

Apes who invent creative names are not simply learning by
rote. They are adapting language for their own purposes. And
those purposes, it turns out, may even include lying and joking.
In a recent interview, Professor Esther Robbins, who worked with
Francine Patterson's gorilla Michael for seven months, pointed
out how difficult it is to verify such uses of language quantita-
tively. What counts as language is "a very gray area," she says. 20
"But you know that animal, and there is very definitely communication, even lying and joking."

Although the great apes have demonstrated significant lan-   21
guage skills, one central question remains: Can they be taught to
use that uniquely human language tool we call grammar, to learn
the difference, for instance, between "ape bite human" and "human bite ape"? In other words, can an ape create a sentence?

within a sentence, so it consists simply of three dots. (See 49e.) Notice that the parenthetical reference for an indented quotation, unlike that for an in-text citation, appears after the last sentence period of the quotation and contains no punctuation of its own.

16. *No page number in parentheses.* Because Toner's article is only one page long, no page number is needed in the parenthetical reference.

17. *Effective use of evidence.* Shaw draws on different sources for evocative examples of creative names. Each example is followed by a parenthetical reference to its source.

18. *Sample note cards*

> *Creative naming*   *Desmond*
>
> *p. 40 Lucy: "cry fruit" (onion)*
>   *"cry hurt food" (radish)*
>
> *Not all researchers accept these and other examples, but Desmond says, "Personally, I give the apes the benefit of the doubt." (p. 40)*

> *Creative naming*   *Patterson and Linden*
>
> *p. 146 Koko: "elephant baby" (Pinocchio*
>   *doll)*
>   *"finger bracelet" (ring)*
>   *"white tiger" (toy zebra)*
>   *"bottle match" (cigarette*
>   *lighter)*
>   *"eye hat" (mask)*
>   *Washoe: "smoke string food"*
>   *(chewing tobacco)*
>   *Lucy: "cry hurt food" (radish)*

Apes have used multisign sequences, but until recently there was little convincing evidence that the combinations displayed a grasp of grammar. Many of the sequences seemed confusing and repetitious, such as Nim's longest sequence: "give orange me give eat orange me eat orange give me eat orange give me you" (Terrace et al. 895). Francine Patterson's gorillas Koko and Michael **22** have strung together numerous sequences, but whether one can conclude much from this behavior seems doubtful. For example, when Michael was asked what "bird" meant, he signed, "bird good cat chase eat red trouble cat eat bird." Patterson believes that Michael had seen a cat catch a bird and was trying to describe the scene (Patterson and Linden 173). It is certainly possible, but, as Patterson herself might admit, hardly proved.

Currently, however, Sue Savage-Rumbaugh's studies on Kanzi are making even the skeptics take notice. Young Kanzi had played in the lab while his mother was being tutored in lexigrams, and when he was two and a half, his mother was sent away for breeding. "To the scientists' amazement," writes Eric Eckholm, "he had been learning symbols out of the corner of his eye. He hit the sign for apple, then proved he knew what he was saying by picking an apple from an assortment of foods" ("Kanzi" **23** C2).

Impressed by Kanzi's ability to pick up language without ex- **24** plicit training, Savage-Rumbaugh decided to replace rote learning with "a more naturalistic approach": Kanzi would learn language much the way human children do (Lewin 50). Consequently, Kanzi's linguistic development has taken place not in a laboratory but in a fifty-five-acre forest, which he roams in the company of his caregivers. During games of tag and hide-and-seek and other

19. *Short title in parentheses.* There are two works by Eckholm in Shaw's list of works cited at the end of her paper, so Shaw uses a short title of the newspaper article in the parenthetical reference.

20. *Interview.* An in-text citation is not needed when quoting from an oral interview, since there is no page number. Shaw mentioned Robbins's name and qualifications in the text of the paper, and she includes her interview with Robbins in the list of works cited at the end of the paper.

21. *Transition paragraph.* Shaw uses a brief transition paragraph that alludes to the ideas in the previous paragraphs (significant language skills) and prepares readers for a discussion of whether apes use grammar.

22. *Use of anecdotal evidence.* The example in this paragraph is anecdotal evidence that many researchers would discount. Shaw finds the example intriguing enough to include, but she does make clear at the end of her paragraph that such evidence is not the result of a controlled scientific experiment.

23. *Short title in parentheses.* A short title of the newspaper article appears in the parentheses because there are two works by Eckholm in Shaw's list of works cited at the end of the paper. The author does not need to be named in the parentheses because he is mentioned in a signal phrase.

24. *Paraphrasing without plagiarizing.* When paraphrasing, Shaw avoids plagiarism by using her own words and sentence structures, not those of the source, and by putting any borrowed phrases in quotation marks. Here is the passage from Lewin that Shaw is paraphrasing.

ORIGINAL SOURCE
Instead of putting the chimpanzees through rote learning of symbols, gradually building up the vocabulary a symbol at a time, [Savage-Rumbaugh] decided to take a more naturalistic approach. She set out to employ a large vocabulary of symbols from the beginning, using them as language is used around human children. —Lewin, p. 50

childhood activities, Kanzi communicates with his caregivers on a computerized keyboard equipped with a voice synthesizer. A word is spoken each time Kanzi touches a symbol on the board.

Evidence of Kanzi's linguistic progress was published in 1991, when Kanzi was ten. The results show that he can understand grammatically complex spoken English and that he seems to be developing a primitive grammar. In their studies of Kanzi and his half-sister Mulika, Savage-Rumbaugh and members of her team have taken great care to avoid any cuing. Lewin reports that spoken instructions to Kanzi were "delivered by someone out of his sight" and that the other team members wore earphones so they "could not hear the instructions and so could not cue Kanzi, even unconsciously" (51). When Kanzi correctly responded to sentences like "Can you put the raisins in the bowl?" his caretakers made the instructions more difficult. For example, in response to the question "Can you go to the colony room and get the telephone?" Kanzi brought back the telephone even though there were other objects in the room (Lewin 51).

Most surprising is Kanzi's apparent grasp of grammar. The first grammatical rule that Kanzi began to display was to put action before object (as in "hide peanut" and "grab Kanzi"), a pattern probably picked up from his caregivers. In 1985, Eric Eckholm reported that Kanzi's "two and three word statements are often made without prompting, systematically add useful information and represent his own creative responses to novel situations" ("Pygmy" B7). In the first month of study, Kanzi showed no understanding of grammatical ordering, but gradually he began to pick it up. Greenfield and Savage-Rumbaugh point out that this developmental trend "was also found for human children at the two-word stage" (559).

25. *Importance of topic sentences.* Like this paragraph, almost every one of Shaw's paragraphs opens with a clear topic sentence that focuses the reader's attention on the paragraph's main point. Notice that many of Shaw's topic sentences also clarify the paragraph's connection with ideas that have gone before. In this topic sentence, for example, the phrase "Most surprising" links the paragraph to the previous paragraph describing Kanzi's accomplishments.

At times Kanzi deviated from the grammar of his keepers and began to develop his own patterns, an ability that may be more impressive than picking up rules from keepers. Kanzi began to combine gestures and lexigrams, usually pointing to the lexigram first. Gibbons reports, for instance, that "when he wanted to see the lab's dog, he would point to the symbol for dog, then make a gesture for 'go' " (1561).

Perhaps even more significant is the pattern that Kanzi developed on his own in combining various lexigrams. According to Ann Gibbons, "When he gave an order combining two symbols for action--such as 'chase' and 'hide'--it was important to him that the first action--'chase'--be done first" (1561). Lewin suggests that there is a rationale for such a pattern: "Lexigrams that appear first represent an invitation to play, while those in second place represent the content of the play" (52).

If Kanzi and other pygmy chimpanzees continue to develop **26** grammatical patterns, the implications for the study of human evolution could be quite profound. Anthropologist Richard Leakey and coauthor Roger Lewin pose the issue like this: "Is spoken language merely an extension and enhancement of cognitive capacities to be found among our ape relatives? Or is spoken language a unique human characteristic completely separate from any cognitive abilities in apes?" (240).

Leakey believes that there is a continuity in linguistic ability between apes and humans. Linguist Noam Chomsky believes the opposite. Chomsky describes the entire ape language field as gripped by "sentimental confusion" and dismisses the studies on Kanzi with a flippant analogy: "To maintain that Kanzi has language ability is like saying a man can fly because he can jump in

26. *Transition.* Shaw provides readers with a smooth transi-
    tion between the second and third parts of her paper
    (parts II and III of her outline).

Shaw 8

the air" (qtd. in Booth). This is certainly strong language from a 27
man who, in the words of Ann Gibbons, has not even "seen the
new data--and doesn't care to" (1562).

Skeptics such as Chomsky seem to be applying a double stan- 28
dard when they compare apes' linguistic abilities to those of
young human children. As Sue Savage-Rumbaugh puts it, "When
children make up novel words it is called lexical innovation, but
when chimpanzees do the same thing it is called ambiguous" (qtd.
in Lewin 51). The double standard issue is unlikely to be resolved any time soon, however, because the methodologies used
in studies of human children are different from those used in the
ape language studies. Greenfield and Savage-Rumbaugh suggest
that methodologies in studies of human children may need to be
more rigorous, and they look forward to a time when comparisons can be made in a fair and impartial manner (571).

Certainly no one expects any chimpanzee to perform linguis-
tically far beyond the level of a very young human child. After
all, a chimpanzee's brain is only one-third the size of our own.
But the brains of the ancestors of <u>Homo sapiens</u> at some point
were of similar size. Surely it makes more sense that an animal
with whom we share 99 percent of our genetic makeup would at
least have the inklings in its brain of the ability to communicate
in language. No doubt even Chomsky would admit that the
<u>ability</u> to communicate in language in our human ancestors came
before language itself. Maybe I am "sentimental," to use Chomsky's word, but when I read about Kanzi's amazing achievements, it is difficult not to believe that there is some commonality
of abilities.

27. *Indirect source.* The quotation by Chomsky appeared in a book by Booth, so Shaw must begin her citation with "qtd. in." (meaning "quoted in"). (See page 496.) The signal phrase introducing the quotation is in Shaw's words, not Booth's.

28. *A balanced approach.* Shaw is critical of Chomsky's apparent lack of objectivity. In her own writing, Shaw weighs the evidence more objectively; she sides with Greenfield and Savage-Rumbaugh but acknowledges that it is difficult to compare the linguistic abilities of apes with those of young children.

Shaw 9

Notes   29

[1] The most famous example of cuing involves a horse named 30
Clever Hans whose owner sincerely thought the horse could solve
mathematical problems, tapping out the answers with his foot. It
was demonstrated that the horse was in fact responding to the in-
voluntary jerks of the owner's head at the point when the correct
number of taps had been reached.

[2] For a description of the Gardners' double-blind experi-   31
ments, see Thomas A. Sebeok and Jean Umiker-Sebeok.

29. *Format of information notes.* If your paper has information notes, begin them on a separate page. Type the heading "Notes" one inch from the top of the page and centered between the left and right margins. Double-space to the first note. Double-space the notes and indent the first line of each note five spaces from the left margin. The number of the note (corresponding to the number used in the text of the paper) should be raised slightly above the note and separated from it by one space. The number should not be followed by a period or enclosed in parentheses.

30. *Use of information notes.* Information notes are optional; not every research paper has them. Shaw's first note discusses interesting information that did not fit gracefully into the text of her paper. Her second note mentions a source that may be of interest to her readers. This source appears in Shaw's list of works cited.

31. *Format of the bibliographic reference.* Unlike in the list of works cited, the authors' names are all in normal order in an information note.

Shaw 10

Works Cited 32

Booth, William. "Monkeying with Language: Is Chimp Using Words or Merely Aping Handlers?" Washington
Post 29 Oct. 1990: A3.

Davis, Flora. Eloquent Animals: A Study in Animal Com- 33
munication. New York: Coward, 1978.

Desmond, Adrian. The Ape's Reflexion. New York:
Wade-Dial, 1979.

Eckholm, Erik. "Kanzi the Chimp: A Life in Science." 34
New York Times 25 June 1985, local ed.: C1+.

---. "Pygmy Chimp Readily Learns Language Skill." New 35
York Times 24 June 1985, local ed.: A1+.

Gibbons, Ann. "Déjà Vu All Over Again: Chimp-Language 36
Wars." Science 251 (1991): 1561-62.

Greenfield, Patricia Marks, and E. Sue Savage-Rumbaugh.
"Grammatical Combination in Pan paniscus: Processes of Learning and Invention in the Evolution and
Development of Language." "Language" and Intelligence in Monkeys and Apes: Comparative Developmental Perspectives. Ed. Sue Taylor Parker and
Kathleen Rita Gibson. Cambridge: Cambridge UP,
1990. 540-78.

Leakey, Richard, and Roger Lewin. Origins Reconsidered: 37
In Search of What Makes Us Human. New York:
Doubleday, 1992.

Lewin, Roger. "Look Who's Talking Now." New Scientist
29 Apr. 1991: 49-52.

Marx, Jean L. "Ape-Language Controversy Flares Up."
Science 207 (1980): 1330-33.

32. *Format of the list of works cited.* Begin the list of works cited on a separate page. Type the heading "Works Cited" one inch from the top of the page, centered between the left and right margins and double-spaced to the first entry. Double-space every entry, with the first line of each entry beginning at the left margin; indent subsequent lines in an entry five spaces from the left margin. Begin each entry with the author's name in inverted order and any additional authors' names in normal order. Alphabetize the entire list by the authors' names. Anonymous works should be alphabetized by title.

    The heading "Works Cited" tells readers that the list includes only the works that have been cited in the paper. If your instructor prefers a list of all the works you consulted, title the list "Works Consulted."

33. *Book by a single author.* Author's name; title of book; place of publication; publisher; date of publication. (See also page 498.)

34. *Article in a newspaper.* Author's name; title of article; name of newspaper; date; page number. (See also page 505.)

35. *Two works by the same author.* Author's name for first work; three hyphens and a period in place of the author's name for the second work. (See also page 500.)

36. *Article in a journal paginated by volume.* Author's name, title of article; name of journal; volume number; year; page numbers of article. (See also page 504.)

37. *Book by two authors.* First author's name, last name first; second author's name, first name first; title of book; place of publication; publisher; date of publication. (See also page 499.)

Miles, H. Lyn White. "The Cognitive Foundations for Ref-   **38**
    erence in a Signing Orangutan." "Language" and
    Intelligence in Monkeys and Apes: Comparative
    Developmental Perspectives. Ed. Sue Taylor Parker
    and Kathleen Rita Gibson. Cambridge: Cambridge
    UP, 1990. 511-39.

Patterson, Francine, and Eugene Linden. The Education of
    Koko. New York: Holt, 1981.

Robbins, Esther. Personal interview. 17 May 1993.   **39**

Sebeok, Thomas A., and Jean Umiker-Sebeok. "Perform-
    ing Animals: Secrets of the Trade." Psychology
    Today Nov. 1979: 78-91.

Terrace, H. S., et al. "Can an Ape Create a Sentence?"   **40**
    Science 206 (1979): 891-902.

Toner, Mike. "Loulis, the Talking Chimp." National Wild-   **41**
    life Feb.-Mar. 1986: 24.

38. *Work in an anthology.* Author of article; title of article; title of anthology; editors of anthology; place of publication; publisher; date of publication; page numbers of article. (See also page 501.)

39. *Interview.* Name of person interviewed; type of interview; date of interview. (See also page 508.)

40. *Journal article with four or more authors.* Name of first author, followed by "et al."; title of article; name of journal; volume of journal; date; page numbers. (See also pages 499 and 504.)

41. *Article in a magazine.* Author's name; title of article; name of magazine; date; page number or numbers. (See also page 504.)

51

Alternative systems for documenting sources

Most English classes use the Modern Language Association (MLA) style of in-text citation that is described in 50. This section surveys two alternative systems of documentation commonly required by professors in other disciplines. In the social sciences, you will usually be asked to use the American Psychological Association (APA) style of in-text citation, which refers the reader to a list of references at the end of the paper. (See 51a and 51b.) In history and the humanities, you may be asked to use footnotes or endnotes. (See 51c.) For a list of style manuals in a variety of disciplines, see 51d.

Always use the style of documentation recommended by your instructor.

51a   APA in-text citations (used in the social sciences)

The American Psychological Association (APA) recommends an author/date style of in-text citations. These citations refer readers to a list of references at the end of the paper.

APA in-text citations provide at least the author's last name and the date of publication. For direct quotations, a page number is given as well.

BASIC FORMAT FOR A QUOTATION   Ordinarily, introduce the quotation with a signal phrase that includes the author's last name followed by the date of publication in parentheses. Put the page number (preceded by "p.") in parentheses at the end of the quotation.

As Davis (1978) reports, "If the existence of a signing ape was unsettling for linguists, it was also startling news for animal behaviorists" (p. 26).

When the author's name does not appear in the signal phrase, place the author's name, the date, and the page number in parentheses at the end of the quotation. Use commas between items in the parentheses: (Davis, 1978, p. 26).

BASIC FORMAT FOR A SUMMARY OR A PARAPHRASE For a summary or a paraphrase, include the author's last name and the date either in a signal phrase or in parentheses at the end. A page number is not required.

According to Davis (1978), when they learned of an ape's ability to use sign language, both linguists and animal behaviorists were taken by surprise.

When they learned of an ape's ability to use sign language, both linguists and animal behaviorists were taken by surprise (Davis, 1978).

A WORK WITH TWO AUTHORS Name both authors in the signal phrase or parentheses each time you cite the work. In the parentheses, use "&" between the authors' names; in the signal phrase, use "and."

Patterson and Linden (1981) agree that the gorilla Koko acquired language more slowly than a normal speaking child.

Koko acquired language more slowly than a normal speaking child (Patterson & Linden, 1981).

A WORK WITH THREE TO FIVE AUTHORS Identify all authors in the signal phrase or the parentheses the first time you cite the source.

Directory to the APA system

NOTE: For a sample APA paper, see pages 551–59.

Directory to footnotes or endnotes

51c: Footnotes or endnotes (an MLA alternative)

NOTE: For a list of style manuals for various disciplines, see pages 566–68.

The study noted a fluctuating divorce rate in Middletown between the 1920s and the 1970s (Caplow, Bahr, Chadwick, Hill, & Williamson, 1982).

In subsequent citations, use the first author's name followed by "et al." in either the signal phrase or the parentheses.

While the incidence of wife abuse may not be higher than in the past, the researchers found that women are more willing to report it (Caplow et al., 1982).

A WORK WITH SIX OR MORE AUTHORS Use only the first author's name followed by "et al." in all citations.

Communes in the late 1960s functioned like extended families, with child-rearing responsibilities shared by all adult members (Berger et al., 1971).

UNKNOWN AUTHOR If the author is not given, either use the complete title in a signal phrase or use the first two or three words of the title in the parenthetical citation.

The UFO reported by the crew of a Japan Air Lines flight remains a mystery. Radar tapes did not confirm the presence of another craft ("Strange Encounter," 1987).

If "Anonymous" is specified as the author, treat it as if it were a real name: (Anonymous, 1987). In the bibliographic references, also use the name Anonymous as author.

CORPORATE AUTHOR If the author is a government agency or other corporate organization with a long and cumbersome name, spell out the name the first time you use it in a citation followed by an abbreviation in brackets. In later citations, simply use the abbreviation.

First citation: (National Institute of Mental Health [NIMH], 1981)

Later citations: (NIMH, 1981)

TWO OR MORE WORKS IN THE SAME PARENTHESES When your parenthetical citation names two or more works, put them in the same order that they appear in the bibliography, separated by semicolons.

Some researchers claim that the experimental design was flawed (Berger et al., 1971; Smith, 1990).

AUTHORS WITH THE SAME LAST NAME To avoid confusion, use initials with the last names if your bibliography lists two or more authors with the same last name.

Research by J. A. Smith (1987) revealed that . . .

PERSONAL COMMUNICATION Conversations, memos, letters, and similar unpublished person-to-person communications should be cited by initials, last name, and precise date.

L. Smith (personal communication, October 12, 1987) predicts that government funding of this type of research will end soon.

Do not include personal communications in the bibliographic references at the end of your paper.

51b APA references (bibliographic list)

In APA style, the alphabetical list of works cited is called "References." The general principles are as follows.

1. Invert *all* authors' names, and use initials instead of first names. With two or more authors, use an ampersand (&)

rather than the word *and*. Separate the names with commas. Alphabetize the list by authors' names.

2. Use all authors' names; do not use *et al.*

3. Place the date of publication in parentheses immediately after the last author's name.

4. Underline titles and subtitles of books; capitalize only the first word of the title and subtitle (as well as all proper nouns).

5. Do not place titles of articles in quotation marks, and capitalize only the first word of the title and subtitle (and all proper nouns). Capitalize names of periodicals as you would capitalize them ordinarily (see 45c). Underline the volume number of periodicals.

6. Use the abbreviation "p." (or "pp." for plural) before page numbers of magazine and newspaper articles and works in anthologies, but do not use it before page numbers of articles appearing in scholarly journals.

7. You may use a short form of the publisher's name as long as it is easily identifiable.

8. Alphabetize your list by the last name of the author (or editor); if there is no author or editor, alphabetize by the first word of the title other than *a, an,* or *the.*

9. Do not indent the first line of an entry but indent any additional lines three spaces.

Books

BASIC FORMAT FOR A BOOK

Shaller, G. B. (1993). <u>The last panda</u>. Chicago: University of Chicago Press.

TWO OR MORE AUTHORS

Eggan, P. D., & Kauchall, D. (1992). <u>Educational psychology: Classroom connections</u>. New York: Merrill.

Caplow, T., Bahr, H. M., Chadwick, B. A., Hill, R., & Williamson, M. H. (1982). <u>Middletown families: Fifty years of</u>

change and continuity.   Minneapolis: University of Minnesota Press.

CORPORATE AUTHOR   When the author is an organization, the publisher is often the same organization. In such a
case, give the publisher's name as "Author."

National Head Start Association.   (1990).   Head Start: The
nation's pride, a nation's challenge.   Report of the Silver
Ribbon Panel.   Alexandria, VA: Author.

UNKNOWN AUTHOR

The Times Atlas of the World (9th ed.).   (1992).   New York:
Times Books.

EDITORS

Fox, R. W., & Lears, T. J. J. (Eds.).   (1993).   The power of
culture: Critical essays in American history.   Chicago:
University of Chicago Press.

TRANSLATION

Miller, A.   (1990).   The untouched key: Tracing childhood
trauma in creativity and destructiveness (H. and H. Han-
num, Trans.).   New York: Doubleday.

EDITION OTHER THAN THE FIRST

Cavanaugh, J. C.   (1993).   Adult development and aging
(2nd ed.).   Pacific Grove, CA: Brooks/Cole.

WORK IN AN ANTHOLOGY

Ochs, E., & Schieffelin, B.   (1984).   Language acquisition
and socialization: Three developmental stories.   In R.
Schweder and R. Levine (Eds.), Culture theory: Essays in
mind, self, and emotion (pp. 276-320).   New York: Cambridge University Press.

TWO OR MORE WORKS BY THE SAME AUTHOR   Use the author's name for first and subsequent entries. Arrange the entries by date, the earliest first.

Davis, F.   (1973).   Inside intuition: What we know about
    nonverbal communication.   New York: McGraw-Hill.
Davis, F.   (1978).   Eloquent animals: A study in animal
    communication.   New York: Coward, McCann & Geoghe-
    gan.

Articles in periodicals

ARTICLE IN A JOURNAL PAGINATED BY VOLUME
Block, N.   (1992).   Begging the question: Against phenome-
    nal consciousness.   Behavioral and Brain Sciences, 15,
    205-206.

ARTICLE IN A JOURNAL PAGINATED BY ISSUE
Searle, J.   (1990).   Is the brain a digital computer?   Pro-
    ceedings of the American Philosophical Association,
    64(3), 21-37.

ARTICLE IN A MAGAZINE
Caputo, R.   (1993, August).   Tragedy stalks the Horn of
    Africa.   National Geographic, pp. 88-121.

ARTICLE IN A NEWSPAPER
Goleman, D.   (1993, July 13).   New treatments for autism
    arouse hope and skepticism.   The New York Times,
    pp. C1, C11.

LETTER TO THE EDITOR
Fuller, K. S.   (1993).   The issue of ivory [Letter to the edi-
    tor].   Audubon, 95(4), 12.

REVIEW

Blaut, J. M. (1993). [Review of Global capitalism: Theories of societal development]. Science and Society, 57(1), 106-107.

TWO OR MORE WORKS BY THE SAME AUTHOR IN THE SAME YEAR   Cite the works according to the usual style, and arrange them alphabetically by title. Add lowercase letters beginning with "a," "b," and so on, within the parentheses immediately following the year.

Eckholm, Erik. (1985a, June 25). Kanzi the chimp: A life in science. The New York Times, pp. C1, C3.

Eckholm, Erik. (1985b, June 24). Pygmy chimp readily learns language skill. The New York Times, pp. A1, B7.

Other sources

MATERIAL FROM A DATABASE

Seefeldt, R. W., & Lyon, M. A. (1990, March). Personality characteristics of adult children of alcoholics: Fact or fiction? Paper presented at the annual meeting of the American Association for Counseling and Development, Cincinnati, OH. (ERIC Document Reproduction Service No. ED 316 784)

DISSERTATION ABSTRACT

Pellman, J. L. (1988). Community integration: Its influence on the stress of widowhood (Doctoral dissertation, University of Missouri, 1988). Dissertation Abstracts International, 49, 2367.

GOVERNMENT DOCUMENT

U.S. Bureau of the Census. (1989). Statistical abstract of the United States. (109th ed.). Washington, DC: U.S. Government Printing Office.

PROCEEDINGS OF A CONFERENCE

Waterhouse, L. H. (1982). Maternal speech patterns and differential development. In C. E. Johnson & C. L. Thew (Eds.), Proceedings of the Second Annual International Study of Child Language (pp. 442-454). Washington, DC: University Press of America.

COMPUTER PROGRAM

Notebuilder [Computer program]. (1993). Palo Alto, CA: Pro/Tem.

VIDEOTAPE

National Geographic Society (Producer). (1987). In the shadow of Vesuvius [Videotape]. Washington, DC: National Geographic Society.

A SAMPLE STUDENT PAPER:
APA STYLE

On the following pages is a research paper written by Karen Shaw, a student in a psychology class. Shaw's assignment was to write a "review of the literature" paper documented with the APA style of citations and references. Shaw received permission from her instructor to review the literature written by psychologists studying the linguistic abilities of apes, a topic she had previously investigated in an English class (see pages 514–39). Shaw's two papers are quite different both in approach and in their styles of documentation.

Apes and Language:
A Review of the Literature

Karen Shaw

Psychology 110, Section 2
Professor Verdi
April 4, 1994

Apes and Language:

A Review of the Literature

Over the past twenty-five years, researchers have demonstrated that the great apes (chimpanzees, gorillas, and orangutans) resemble humans in language abilities more than had been thought possible. Just how far that resemblance extends, however, has been a matter of some controversy. Researchers agree that the apes have acquired fairly large vocabularies in American Sign Language and in artificial languages, but they have drawn quite different conclusions in addressing the following questions:

1. How spontaneously have apes used language?
2. How creatively have apes used language?
3. Have apes learned to conceptualize?
4. Can apes create sentences?
5. What are the implications of the research?

This review of the literature on apes and language focuses on these five questions.

How Spontaneously Have Apes Used Language?

In an influential article, Terrace, Petitto, Sanders, and Bever (1979) argue that apes in language experiments were not using language spontaneously, but were merely imitating their trainers, responding to conscious or unconscious cues. Terrace and his colleagues at Columbia University had trained a chimpanzee, Nim, in American Sign Language, so their skepticism about the apes' abilities received much attention. In fact, funding for ape language research was sharply reduced following publication of their 1979 article "Can an Ape Create a Sentence?"

Apes and Language

3

In retrospect, the conclusions of Terrace et al. seem to have been premature. Although some of the early ape language studies had not been rigorously controlled to eliminate cuing, even as early as 1979 R. A. Gardner and B. T. Gardner were conducting double-blind experiments that prevented any possibility of cuing (Sebeok & Umiker-Sebeok, 1979). Since 1979, researchers have diligently guarded against cuing. For example, Lewin (1991) reports that instructions for pygmy chimpanzee Kanzi were "delivered by someone out of his sight," with other team members wearing earphones so that they "could not hear the instructions and so could not cue Kanzi, even unconsciously" (p. 51).

There is considerable evidence that apes have signed to one another spontaneously, without trainers present. Like many of the apes studied, gorillas Koko and Michael signed to one another when alone (Patterson & Linden, 1981). At Central Washington University the baby chimpanzee Loulis, placed in the care of an older, signing chimpanzee, mastered more than fifty signs in American Sign Language without help from humans. "We only used seven signs in his presence," says psychologist Roger Fouts. "All of his signs were learned from the other chimps in the laboratory" (Toner, 1986, p. 24).

The extent to which chimpanzees spontaneously use language may depend on their training. Terrace trained Nim using the behaviorist technique of operant conditioning, so it is not surprising that many of Nim's signs were cued. R. A. Gardner and B. T. Gardner and many other researchers have used a conversational approach that parallels the process by which human children acquire language. In an experimental study, C. O'Sullivan and C. P. Yeager (1989) contrasted the two techniques, using Terrace's Nim as their subject. They found that Nim's use of language was significantly more spontaneous under conversational conditions.

How Creatively Have Apes Used Language?

Although creative uses of language are difficult to prove, there is considerable evidence that apes have invented creative names. One of the earliest and most controversial examples involves the Gardners' chimpanzee Washoe. Washoe, who knew the signs for "water" and "bird," once signed "water bird" when in the presence of a swan. Terrace et al. (1979) suggest that there is "no basis for concluding that Washoe was characterizing the swan as a 'bird that inhabits water.' " Washoe may simply have been "identifying correctly a body of water and a bird, in that order" (p. 895).

Other examples are not so easily explained away. The pygmy chimpanzee Kanzi has requested particular films by combining symbols in a creative way. For instance, to ask for Quest for Fire, a film about early primates discovering fire, Kanzi began to use symbols for "campfire" and "TV" (Eckholm, 1985). An orangutan, Chantek, signed "eye-drink" to refer to his caretaker's contact lens fluid (Miles, 1990). And the gorilla Koko has a long list of creative names to her credit: "elephant baby" to describe a Pinocchio doll, "finger bracelet" to describe a ring, "bottle match" to describe a cigarette lighter, and so on. If Terrace's analysis of the "water bird" example were applied to the examples just mentioned, it would not hold. Surely Koko did not

Apes and Language

5

first see an elephant and then a baby before signing "elephant baby"--or a bottle and a match before signing "bottle match."

Have Apes Learned to Conceptualize?

Conceptualization is the process through which a human child realizes that words can be used to refer to classes of things. For example, a child comes to realize that "dog," first learned for the family dachshund, can be applied to other dogs. Many chimpanzees have gone through a similar process. Gardner, Van Cantfort, and Gardner (1992) report that Washoe "used DOG to refer to live dogs and pictures of dogs of many breeds, sizes, and colors, as well as the sound of barking by an unseen dog" (p. 30). The orangutan Chantek also learned to conceptualize with his signs, using "cat" for cat noises, cats, and "meow" sounds made by his keepers. Even his mistakes, such as applying the sign "cat" to an opossum, were appropriate (Miles, 1990).

Can Apes Create Sentences?

The early ape language studies offered little proof that apes could combine symbols into grammatically ordered sentences. Apes strung together various signs, but the sequences were often random and repetitious. Nim's series of sixteen signs is a case in point: "give orange me give eat orange me eat orange give me eat orange give me you" (Terrace et al., 1979, p. 895). The Gardners were impressed by Washoe's multisign sequences, seeing in them the beginnings of some grasp of grammar, but their findings have been disputed. In one frequently cited film sequence, Washoe's teacher placed a baby doll in a cup. Washoe signed "baby in baby in my drink," a series of signs that seemed to make grammatical sense. Terrace et al. point out, however, that

Washoe had previously been drilled in similar patterns and that
the teacher had pointed to the objects.

Recent studies with pygmy chimpanzees at the Yerkes Primate Center in Atlanta are breaking new ground. Kanzi, a
pygmy chimpanzee trained by E. S. Savage-Rumbaugh, seems to
understand simple grammatical rules about lexigram order. For
instance, Kanzi learned from his caregivers that in two-word utterances action precedes object, an ordering also used by human
children at the two-word stage. In a major new article reporting
on their research, Greenfield and Savage-Rumbaugh (1990) write
that Kanzi rarely "repeated himself or formed combinations that
were semantically unrelated" (p. 556).

More important, Kanzi began on his own to create certain
patterns that may not exist in English but can be found among
deaf children and in other human languages. For example,
Kanzi used his own rules when combining action symbols. Lexigrams that involved an invitation to play such as "chase" would
appear first; lexigrams that indicated what was to be done during
play ("hide") would appear second. Kanzi also created his own
rules when combining gestures and lexigrams. He would use the
lexigram first and then gesture, a practice often followed by
young deaf children (Greenfield & Savage-Rumbaugh, 1990).

What Are the Implications of the Research?

Kanzi's linguistic abilities are so impressive that they may
help us understand how humans came to acquire language.
Pointing out that 99 percent of our genetic material is held in
common with the chimpanzees, Greenfield and Savage-Rumbaugh
(1990) suggest that something of the "evolutionary root of hu-

man language" can be found in the "linguistic abilities of the great apes" (p. 540). Anthropologist R. Leakey agrees. Noting that apes' brains are similar to those of our human ancestors, Leakey and Lewin (1992) write that in ape brains "the cognitive foundations on which human language could be built are already present" (p. 244).

The suggestion that there is a continuity in the linguistic abilities of apes and humans has created much controversy. Linguist Noam Chomsky remains firmly convinced that language is a unique human characteristic (cited in Booth, 1990). Gibbons (1991) points out, however, that "Chomsky hasn't seen the new data--and doesn't care to see it" (p. 1562). Terrace continues to be skeptical of the claims made for the apes, as are Petitto and Bever, coauthors of the 1979 article that caused such skepticism earlier (Gibbons, 1991). On the other hand, according to Lewin (1991), "Many psychologists are extremely impressed with Kanzi and the implications of the observations" (p. 52).

Although the ape language studies continue to generate controversy, researchers have shown over the past twenty-five years that the gap between the linguistic abilities of apes and humans is far less dramatic than was once believed.

References

Booth, W. (1990, October 29). Monkeying with language: Is chimp using words or merely aping handlers? The Washington Post, p. A3.

Eckholm, E. (1985, June 25). Kanzi the chimp: A life in science. The New York Times, pp. C1, C3.

Gardner, R. A., Van Cantfort, T. E., & Gardner, B. T. (1992). Categorical replies to categorical questions by cross-fostered chimpanzees. American Journal of Psychology, 105, 27-57.

Gibbons, A. (1991). Déjà vu all over again: Chimp-language wars. Science, 251, 1561-1562.

Greenfield, P. M., & Savage-Rumbaugh, E. S. (1990). Grammatical combination in Pan paniscus: Processes of learning and invention in the evolution and development of language. In S. T. Parker & K. R. Gibson (Eds.), "Language" and intelligence in monkeys and apes: Comparative developmental perspectives (pp. 540-578). Cambridge: Cambridge University Press.

Leakey, R., & Lewin, R. (1992). Origins reconsidered: In search of what makes us human. New York: Doubleday.

Lewin, R. (1991, April 29). Look who's talking now. New Scientist, pp. 49-52.

Miles, H. L. W. (1990). The cognitive foundations for reference in a signing orangutan. In S. T. Parker & K. R. Gibson (Eds.), "Language" and intelligence in monkeys and apes: Comparative developmental perspectives (pp. 511-539). Cambridge: Cambridge University Press.

O'Sullivan, C., & Yeager, C. P. (1989). Communicative context and linguistic competence: The effect of social setting on a chimpanzee's conversational skill. In R. A. Gardner, B. T. Gardner, & T. E. Van Cantfort (Eds.), Teaching sign language to chimpanzees (pp. 269-279). Albany: SUNY Press.

Patterson, F., & Linden, E. (1981). The education of Koko. New York: Holt, Rinehart and Winston.

Sebeok, T. A., & Umiker-Sebeok, J. (1979, November). Performing animals: Secrets of the trade. Psychology Today, pp. 78-91.

Terrace, H. S., Petitto, L. A., Sanders, R. J., & Bever, T. G. (1979). Can an ape create a sentence? Science, 206, 891-902.

Toner, M. (1986, February-March). Loulis, the talking chimp. National Wildlife, p. 24.

51c Footnotes or endnotes (an MLA alternative)

Although the *MLA Handbook* treats in-text citations as its preferred style (see 50), it also lists traditional notes as an acceptable alternative.

Notes provide complete publishing information, either at the bottom of the page (footnotes) or at the end of the paper (endnotes). A raised arabic numeral in the text indicates that a quotation, paraphrase, or summary has been borrowed from a source; to find the publishing information for that source, readers consult the footnote or endnote with the corresponding number. Notes are numbered consecutively throughout the paper.

TEXT

For instance, Lana once described a cucumber as "banana which-is green."[9]

NOTE

[9] Flora Davis, <u>Eloquent Animals: A Study in Animal Communication</u> (New York: Coward, 1978) 300.

The first time you cite a source in your paper, give the full publication information for that work as well as the page number of the specific quotation, paraphrase, or summary. The following examples cover the formats that are most frequently encountered.

Books

BASIC FORMAT FOR A BOOK

[1] Jane Tompkins, <u>West of Everything: The Inner Life of Westerns</u> (New York: Oxford UP, 1992) 22.

TWO OR THREE AUTHORS

2 Barbara Rico and Sandra Mano, American Mosaic: Multicultural Readings in Context (Boston: Houghton, 1991) 121.

FOUR OR MORE AUTHORS

3 Martin J. Medhurst et al., Cold War Rhetoric: Strategy, Metaphor, and Ideology (New York: Greenwood, 1990) 52.

CORPORATE AUTHOR

4 Fidelity Investments, Fidelity Brokerage Services Handbook (Boston: Fidelity Investments, 1993) 5.

UNKNOWN AUTHOR

5 The Times Atlas of the World, 9th ed. (New York: Times, 1992) 135.

TRANSLATION

6 Umberto Eco, Foucault's Pendulum, trans. William Weaver (San Diego: Harcourt, 1989) 234.

EDITORS

7 Rodolfo Anaya and Francisco Lomeli, eds., Aztlán: Essays on the Chicano Homeland (Albuquerque: Academia-El Norte, 1989) 65.

EDITION OTHER THAN THE FIRST

8 Erika Lindemann, A Rhetoric for Writing Teachers, 2nd ed. (New York: Oxford UP, 1987) 23.

MULTIVOLUME WORK

[9] Mark Twain: Collected Tales, Sketches, Speeches, and Essays, vol. 2 (New York: Library of America, 1992) 98.

WORK IN AN ANTHOLOGY

[10] J. M. Synge, "On an Anniversary," The New Oxford Book of Irish Verse, ed. Thomas Kinsella (Oxford: Oxford UP, 1986) 318.

ENCYCLOPEDIA OR DICTIONARY

[11] "Croatia," The New Encyclopaedia Britannica: Micropaedia, 1991.

Periodicals

ARTICLE IN A MAGAZINE

[12] John Lukacs, "The End of the Twentieth Century," Harper's Jan. 1993: 41.

ARTICLE IN A JOURNAL PAGINATED BY VOLUME

[13] Gabriel Segal, "Seeing What Is Not There," Philosophical Review 98 (1989): 200.

ARTICLE IN A JOURNAL PAGINATED BY ISSUE

[14] G. J. Johnson, "A Distinctiveness Model of Serial Learning," Psychological Review 98.2 (1991): 208.

ARTICLE IN A NEWSPAPER

[15] Lena H. Sun, "Chinese Feel the Strain of a New Society," Washington Post 13 June 1993: A1.

UNKNOWN AUTHOR

[16] "Radiation in Russia," U.S. News and World Report 9 Aug.
1993: 41.

EDITORIAL

[17] "Gays and the Military," editorial, Boston Globe 13 July
1993: 14.

LETTER TO THE EDITOR

[18] Graham Benston, letter, Opera Now May 1993: 12.

BOOK OR FILM REVIEW

[19] Frank Kermode, "Criticism without Machinery," rev. of
Literary Reflections, by R. W. B. Lewis, New York Times
Book Review 11 July 1993: 16.

Other sources

MATERIAL FROM AN INFORMATION SERVICE OR DATABASE

[20] Pamela Horn, "The Victorian Governess," History of
Education 18 (1989): 335 (ERIC EJ 401 533).

GOVERNMENT PUBLICATION

[21] United States, Natl. Endowment for the Humanities, Study
Grants for College and University Teachers (Washington:
GPO, 1993) 3.

PAMPHLET

[22] United States, Dept. of the Interior, Natl. Park Service,
Ford's Theatre and the House Where Lincoln Died (Washington: GPO, 1989) 1.

PUBLISHED DISSERTATION

[23] Robert F. Healey, <u>Eleusinian Sacrifices in the Athenian Law Code</u>, diss., Harvard U, 1961 (New York: Garland, 1990) 36.

UNPUBLISHED DISSERTATION

[24] Kathy Anne Fedorko, "Edith Wharton's Haunted House: The Gothic in Her Fiction," diss., Rutgers U, 1987, 59.

ABSTRACT OF A DISSERTATION

[25] Anne Elizabeth Berkman, "The Quest for Authenticity: The Novels of Toni Morrison," <u>DAI</u> 48 (1988): 2059A (Columbia U).

COMPUTER SOFTWARE

[26] <u>Encarta</u>, computer software, Microsoft, 1992, PC-DOS 3.1, Windows, 386SX, CD-ROM.

TELEVISION OR RADIO PROGRAM

[27] "This Old Pyramid," with Mark Lehner and Roger Hopkins, <u>Nova</u>, PBS, WGBH, Boston, 4 Aug. 1993.

FILM OR VIDEOTAPE

[28] <u>Through the Wire</u>, videotape, dir. Nina Rosenblum, narr. Susan Sarandon, Fox/Lorber Home Video, 1990 (77 min.).

LIVE PERFORMANCE OF A PLAY

[29] <u>The Sisters Rosensweig</u>, by Wendy Wasserstein, dir. Daniel Sullivan, with Jane Alexander, Christine Estabrook, and Madeline Kahn, Barrymore, New York, 11 July 1993.

RECORDING

[30] Giuseppe Verdi, <u>Falstaff</u>, with Tito Gobbi, Elisabeth
    Schwarzkopf, Nan Merriman, and Fedora Barbieri, cond.
    Herbert von Karajan, Philharmonia Orch. and Chorus,
    EMI, 7 49668 2, 1988.

LECTURE OR PUBLIC ADDRESS

[31] Karen Quinn, "John Singleton Copley's <u>Watson
    and the Shark</u>," Museum of Fine Arts, Boston, 1 July
    1993.

PERSONAL INTERVIEW

[32] Patricia Harrison, personal interview, 19 Feb.
    1993.

PUBLISHED INTERVIEW

[33] Anna Quindlen, interview, <u>Commonweal</u> 14 Feb.
    1992: 10.

Subsequent references to the same source

Subsequent references to a work that has already been cited
in a note should be given in shortened form. You need to give
only enough information so that the reader can identify which
work you are referring to—usually the author's last name and
a page number. The abbreviations *ibid.* and *op. cit.* are no
longer used.

[34] Tompkins 85.

[35] Rico and Mano 23.

[36] <u>Times Atlas</u> 99.

If you are using more than one work by one author or two
works by authors with the same last name, cite the author's
last name and a shortened title.

[37] Gordon, <u>Good</u> 135.

[38] Gordon, <u>Other</u> 34.

When you use notes as your method of documentation, you may not need a list of works cited, since complete publishing information is given in the notes themselves. Many professors prefer, however, that you include an alphabetized list of the works cited in the paper or a bibliography of the works you consulted, whether or not they were cited. If you do include a list of works cited or a bibliography, use the MLA style described in 50b.

51d A list of style manuals for various disciplines

The *Bedford Handbook for Writers* describes three commonly used systems of documentation: MLA in-text citations, used in English and the humanities (see 50); APA in-text citations, used in psychology and the social sciences (see 51a and 51b); and footnotes or endnotes, an MLA alternative (see 51c). Following is a list of style manuals used in a variety of disciplines.

BIOLOGY
Council of Biology Editors. *CBE Style Manual: A Guide for Authors, Editors, and Publishers in the Biological Sciences.* 5th ed. Bethesda, 1983.

CHEMISTRY
Dodd, Janet S., ed. *The ACS Style Guide: A Manual for Authors and Editors.* Washington: American Chemical Soc., 1986.

ENGLISH AND THE HUMANITIES (SEE **50.**)
Gibaldi, Joseph, and Walter S. Achtert. *MLA Handbook for Writers of Research Papers.* 3rd ed. New York: Modern Language Association of America, 1988.

GEOLOGY

Cochran, Wendell, Peter Fenner, and Mary Hills, eds.
  *Geowriting: A Guide to Writing, Editing, and Printing in
  Earth Science.* Alexandria, VA: American Geological Inst.,
  1984.

GOVERNMENT DOCUMENTS

Garner, Diane L. *The Complete Guide to Citing Government
  Information Resources: A Manual for Writers and
  Librarians.* Rev. ed. Bethesda: Congressional Information
  Service, 1993.
United States. Government Printing Office. *Style Manual.*
  Washington: GPO, 1984.

JOURNALISM

Associated Press Staff. *Associated Press Stylebook and Libel
  Manual.* Reading, MA: Addison, 1992.

LAW

The Bluebook: A Uniform System of Citation. Comp. editors of
  Columbia Law Review et al. 15th ed. Cambridge: Harvard
  Law Review, 1991.

LINGUISTICS

Linguistic Society of America. "LSA Style Sheet." Published
  annually in the December issue of the *LSA Bulletin.*

MATHEMATICS

American Mathematical Society. *A Manual for Authors of
  Mathematical Papers.* Rev. ed. Providence: AMS, 1990.

MEDICINE

Iverson, Cheryl, et al. *American Medical Association Manual of
  Style.* 8th ed. Baltimore: Williams and Wilkins, 1989.

MUSIC

Holoman, D. Kern, ed. *Writing about Music: A Style Sheet from
  the Editors of* 19th-Century Music. Berkeley: U of
  California P, 1988.

PHYSICS

American Institute of Physics. *AIP Style Manual.* 4th ed. New
York: AIP, 1990.

**PSYCHOLOGY AND THE SOCIAL SCIENCES (SEE 51A
AND 51B.)**

American Psychological Association. *Publication Manual of the
American Psychological Association.* 3rd ed. Washington,
DC: APA, 1983.

SCIENCE AND TECHNICAL WRITING

Rubens, Philip, ed. *Science and Technical Writing: A Manual of
Style.* New York: Holt, 1992.

PART X

Special Types of Writing

52

Writing arguments

In argumentative writing, you take a stand on a debatable issue. The issue being debated might be a matter of public policy: Should religious groups be allowed to meet on school property? What is the least dangerous way to dispose of nuclear waste? Should a state enact laws rationing medical care? On such questions, reasonable persons can disagree.

Reasonable men and women also disagree about many scholarly issues. Psychologists debate the validity of behaviorism; historians interpret the causes of the Civil War quite differently; biologists conduct genetic experiments to challenge the conclusions of other researchers.

Your goal, in argumentative writing, is to change the way your readers think about a subject or to convince them to take an action that they might not otherwise be inclined to take. Do not assume that your audience already agrees with you; instead, envision skeptical readers who will make up their minds after listening to both sides of the debate. To convince such readers, you will need to build arguments strong enough to stand up to the arguments put forward by your opponents (sometimes called *the opposition*).

52a   Plan a strategy.

Although thinking critically about your topic is an important first step in all writing, it is especially important in argumentative writing. Planning a strategy for an argumentative essay is much like planning a debate for a speech class. A good way to begin is to list your arguments and the arguments of the opposition and then consider the likely impact of these arguments on your audience. If the arguments of the opposition look very powerful, you may want to rethink your position. By modifying your initial position—perhaps by claiming less or by proposing a less radical solution to a problem — you may have a greater chance of persuading readers to change their views.

Listing your arguments

Let's say that your tentative purpose (which may change as you think about your audience and the opposition) is to argue in favor of lowering the legal drinking age from twenty-one to eighteen. Here is a list of possible arguments in favor of this point of view.

—Society treats eighteen-year-olds as mature for most purposes.

—They can vote.

—They can go away to college.

—At eighteen, men must register with Selective Service and be available for a possible draft.

—Age is not necessarily an indication of maturity.

—The current drinking age is unfair, since many older Americans were allowed to drink at eighteen.

—An unrealistic drinking age is almost impossible to enforce, and it breeds disrespect for the law.

—In European countries that allow eighteen-year-olds to drink, there is less irresponsible teenage drinking than in our country.

Listing the arguments of the opposition

The next step is to list the key arguments of the opposition. Here are some possible arguments *against* lowering the drinking age to eighteen.

—Teenage drinking frequently leads to drunk driving, which in turn leads to many deaths.

— Teenage drinking sometimes leads to date rape and gang violence.

— Alcoholism is a serious problem in our society, and a delayed drinking age can help prevent it.

— If the legal age were eighteen, many fifteen- and sixteen-year-olds would find a way to purchase alcohol illegally.

If possible, you should talk to someone who disagrees with your view or read some articles that are critical of your position. By familiarizing yourself with the views of the opposition, you can be reasonably sure you have not overlooked an important argument that might be used against you.

Considering your audience

Once you have listed the major arguments on both sides, think realistically about the impact they are likely to have on your intended audience. If your audience is the voting age population in the United States, for example, consider how you might assess some of the arguments of each side of the drinking age question.

Looking at your list, you would see that your audience, which includes many older Americans, might not be impressed by the suggestion that age is no sign of maturity or by the argument that because eighteen-year-olds are old enough to attend college they should be allowed to drink. You would decide to emphasize your other arguments instead. Americans who remember a time when young men were drafted, for example, might be persuaded that it is unfair to ask a man to die for his country but not allow him to drink. And anyone who has heard of Prohibition might be moved by the argument that an unrealistic drinking regulation can breed disrespect for the law.

As for the arguments of the opposition, clearly the first one on the list is the most powerful. Statistics show that drunk driving by teenagers causes much carnage on our highways and that teenagers themselves are frequently the victims. To have any hope of convincing your audience, you would need to take this argument very seriously; it would be almost impossible to argue successfully that reducing highway deaths is not important.

Rethinking your position

After exploring both sides of an argument, you may decide to modify your initial position. Maybe your first thoughts about the issue were oversimplified, too extreme, or mistaken in some other respect. Or maybe, after thinking more about your readers, you see little hope of persuading them of the truth or wisdom of your position.

If you were writing about the drinking age, for example, you might decide to modify your position in light of your audience. To have a better chance of convincing the audience, you could argue that eighteen-year-olds *in the military* should be allowed to drink. Or you could argue that eighteen-year-olds should be allowed to drink beer and wine, not hard alcohol. Or you could link your proposal to new tough laws against drunk driving.

52b Frame a thesis and state your major arguments.

A thesis is a sentence that expresses the main point of an essay. (See 2b.) In argumentative writing, your thesis should clearly state your position on the issue you have chosen to write about. Let's say your issue is the high insurance rates that most companies set for young male drivers. After thinking carefully about your own views, the arguments of the opposition, and your audience (the general public), you might state your position like this:

> Although young male drivers have a high accident rate, insurance companies should not be allowed to discriminate against anyone who has driven for the past two years without a traffic violation.

Notice that this is a debatable point, one about which reasonable persons can disagree. It is not merely a fact (for example, that companies do set higher rates for young males). Nor is it a statement of belief (for example, that differing rates are always unfair). Neither facts nor beliefs can be substantiated by reasons, so they cannot serve as a thesis for an argument.

Once you have framed a thesis, try to state your major arguments, preferably in sentence form. Together, your thesis and your arguments will give you a rough outline of your essay. Consider the following rough outline of an essay written by Julian L. Simon, a business professor at the University of Maryland. Simon argues for an easing of restrictions on immigration into the United States. His thesis frames the issue in economic terms, and his major arguments are economic reasons that support his thesis.

Thesis: Despite claims that increased immigration would hurt the economy, the evidence strongly suggests that new immigrants strengthen the economy in a variety of ways.

— Immigrants do not cause native unemployment, even among low-paid and minority groups.
— Immigrants do not overuse welfare services.
— Immigrants bring high-tech skills that the economy needs badly.
— Immigration is lower than it was in the peak years at the turn of the century.
— Natural resources and the environment are not at risk from immigration.
— Immigration reduces the social costs of the elderly, which can't be cut.

Some of the sentences in your rough outline might become topic sentences of paragraphs in your final essay. (See 5a.)

52c Draft an introduction that states your position without alienating readers.

In argumentative writing, your introduction should state your position on an issue in a clear thesis sentence (see 2b and 52b), and it should do this without needlessly alienating the audience whom you hope to convince. Where possible, try to establish common ground with readers who may not be in initial agreement with your views.

One student, who argued against allowing prayer in public schools, established common ground with readers who disagreed with her by explaining that she once shared their views. Her introduction ends with a clear thesis that states her current position on the issue.

> During most of my school years, the Lord's Prayer was a part of our opening exercises. I never gave it a second thought, and I never heard anyone complain about it. So when prayer in the schools became an issue in the courts, I was surprised to hear that anyone viewed it as a threat to individual rights or as a violation of the division between church and state. But now that I've thought about it, I would not like to see the practice of prayer in the schools reinstituted.

In her first draft, the student began the introduction like this: "I do not think prayer should be allowed in schools." This sentence clearly stated her position, but its blunt tone was likely to alienate readers who favor school prayer. The student wisely decided to establish common ground with her readers before stating her position. Notice that her new thesis statement, at the end of the introduction, is as clear as her original thesis but has a much more reasonable tone.

One way to establish common ground with readers who disagree with your position is to show that you share common values. If your subject is school prayer, for instance, you might show that even though you oppose allowing prayer in schools, you believe in the value of prayer. The writer of the following introduction successfully used this strategy.

> Although the Supreme Court has ruled against prayer in public schools on First Amendment grounds, many people still feel that prayers should be allowed. These people, most of whom hold strong religious beliefs, are well intentioned. What they fail to realize is that the Supreme Court decision, although it was made on legal grounds, makes good sense on religious grounds as well. Prayer is too important to be trusted to our public schools.

Like the writer of the other introduction about school prayer, this writer sounds reasonable. He states his position clearly and firmly in a thesis at the end of the paragraph, but because he takes into consideration the values of those who disagree with him, readers are likely to approach his essay with an open mind.

52d Support each argument with specific evidence.

When presenting the arguments for your position, you will of course need to back them up with evidence: facts, statistics, examples and illustrations, expert opinion, and so on. Depending on the issue you have chosen to write about, you may or may not need to do some reading to gather evidence. Some argumentative topics, such as whether class attendance should be required at your college or university, can be developed through personal experience and maybe questionnaires or interviews. Other debatable topics, such as the extent to which apes can learn language, require library research.

If any of your evidence is based on reading, you will need to document your sources. Documentation gives credit to your sources and shows readers how to track down the source in case they want to assess its credibility or explore the issue further. The style of documentation used in most English classes is described in 50; two other styles are described in 51. Always find out from your instructor which style he or she prefers.

Using facts and statistics

A fact is something that is known with certainty because it has been objectively verified: The capital of Wyoming is Cheyenne. Carbon has an atomic weight of 12. John F. Kennedy was assassinated on November 22, 1963. Statistics are collections of numerical facts: One-half of U.S. households currently own a VCR. North America holds only 4 percent of the world's proven oil reserves; together, Iraq, Kuwait, and Saudi Arabia own 44 percent.

Most arguments are supported at least to some extent by facts and statistics. For example, if you were arguing against mandatory class attendance, you might include facts about the attendance policies of professors in several disciplines; you could also report statistics on the views of students.

Karen Shaw, the student who wrote the MLA research essay on apes and language that is printed in Part IX, gathered facts and statistics from printed sources. When she included them in her essay, she documented them, as in the following example.

The gorilla Koko has mastered nearly 200 signs as measured by

the Gardners' criterion (Patterson and Linden 83-84).

Shaw got this statistic from *The Education of Koko,* a book by Francine Patterson and Eugene Linden. The parenthetical citation at the end of the sentence includes the last names of the authors and the page numbers on which the information appears. (See 50 for more about documentation.)

Using examples and anecdotes

Examples and anecdotes (illustrative stories) alone rarely prove a point, but when used in combination with other forms of evidence, they flesh out an argument and bring it to life. In an essay arguing against mandatory class attendance, you might give examples of class sessions that were obviously a waste of time, maybe because the professor simply read from the textbook or because you were asked to play games that had nothing to do with the subject.

In her research essay, Karen Shaw used several examples from a variety of sources to show that apes are capable of using language creatively (see page 524).

Citing expert opinion

Although they are no substitute for careful reasoning of your own, the views of an expert can contribute to the force of your argument. You might interview an educational psychologist on learning styles, for example, to help support your argument that class attendance is not the only way to learn. Or, if you were arguing in favor of mandatory class attendance, you might interview a dean to learn about academic goals (such as increased tolerance for persons from other cultures) that can be accomplished only through class attendance.

When you rely on expert opinion, you must document your sources. You can summarize or paraphrase the expert's opinion (see 49d) or you can quote the expert's exact words (see 49e). For important advice on appropriate use of written sources, see the charts on pages 484–87.

52e Anticipate objections; refute opposing arguments.

Readers who already agree with you need no convincing, although a well-argued case for their own point of view is always welcome. But indifferent and skeptical readers may resist your arguments because they have minds of their own. To give up a position that seems reasonable, a reader has to see that there is an even more reasonable one. In addition to presenting your own case, therefore, you should review the chief arguments of the opposition and explain what you think is wrong with them.

There is no best place in an essay to deal with the opposition. Often it is useful to summarize the opposing position early in your essay. After stating your thesis but before developing your own arguments, you might have a paragraph beginning "Critics of this view argue that. . . ." But sometimes a better plan is to anticipate objections as you develop your case paragraph by paragraph. Wherever you decide to deal with opposing arguments, do your best to refute them. Show that those who oppose you are not as persuasive as they claim because their arguments are flawed or because your arguments to the contrary have greater weight.

As you refute opposing arguments, try to establish common ground with readers who are not in initial agreement with your views. If you can show that you share your readers' values, they may be able to switch to your position without giving up what they feel is important. For example, to persuade people opposed to shooting deer, a state wildlife commission would have to show that it too cares about preserving deer and does not want them to die needlessly. Having established these values in common, the commission might be able to persuade critics that a carefully controlled hunting season is good for the deer population because it prevents starvation caused by overpopulation. Likewise, if those opposed to hunting want to persuade the commission to ban the hunting season, they would need to show that the commission could achieve its goals by some other feasible means, such as expanding the deer preserve or increasing the food supply to support an increased herd.

People believe that intelligence and decency support their side of an argument. To change sides, they must continue to feel intelligent and decent. Otherwise they will persist in their opposition.

52f Avoid common mistakes in reasoning.

Certain errors in reasoning occur frequently enough to deserve special attention. In both your reading and your writing, you will want to be alert to common mistakes in inductive and deductive reasoning and to certain mistakes known as logical fallacies.

Using inductive reasoning with care

When you reason inductively, you draw a conclusion from an array of facts. For example, you might conclude that a professor is friendly because he or she smiles frequently and talks to students after class or that fifty-five miles per hour is a safer speed limit than sixty-five miles per hour because there are fewer deaths per accident at that speed.

Inductive reasoning deals in probability, not certainty. For a conclusion based on inductive reasoning to be highly probable, the evidence must be sufficient, representative, and relevant. Consider, for example, how you would decide whether to trust the following conclusion, drawn from evidence gathered in a survey.

> **CONCLUSION** The majority of households in our city would subscribe to cable television if it were available.
>
> **EVIDENCE** In a recent survey, 356 of the 500 households questioned say they would subscribe to cable television.

Is the evidence sufficient? That depends. In a city of 10,000, the 500 households are a 5 percent sample, sufficient for the purposes of marketing research. But in a city of 2 million, the households would amount to one-fortieth of 1 percent of the population, an inadequate sample on which to base an important decision.

Is the evidence representative? Again, that depends. The cable company would trust the survey if it knew that the sample had been carefully constructed to reflect the age, sex, geographic distribution, and income of the city's population as a whole. If, however, the 500 households were concentrated in one wealthy neighborhood, the company would be wise to question the survey's conclusion.

Is the evidence relevant? The answer is a cautious yes. The survey question is directly linked to the conclusion. A question about the number of hours spent watching television, by contrast, would not be relevant, because it would not be about *subscribing* to *cable* television. In addition, a cautious interpreter of the evidence would want to know whether people who *say* they would subscribe tend to subscribe *in fact.* By looking at marketing research done in other cities, the cable television company could determine — through a new round of inductive reasoning— how many of the 356 households who say they would subscribe are likely in fact to subscribe.

Using deductive reasoning with care

When you reason deductively, you draw a conclusion from two or more assertions (called premises).

> The police do not give speeding tickets to people driving less than five miles per hour over the limit. Sam is driving fifty-nine miles per hour in a fifty-five-mile-per-hour zone. Therefore, the police will not give Sam a speeding ticket.

The conclusion is true only if the premises are true. If the police sometimes give tickets for less than five-mile-per-hour violations or if the speedometer is inaccurate, Sam cannot safely conclude that he will avoid a ticket.

Deductive reasoning can often be structured in a three-step argument called a *syllogism*. The three steps are the major premise, the minor premise, and the conclusion:

1. Anything that increases radiation in the environment is dangerous to public health. (Major premise)
2. Nuclear reactors increase radiation in the environment. (Minor premise)
3. Therefore, nuclear reactors are dangerous to public health. (Conclusion)

The major premise is a generalization. The minor premise is a specific case. The conclusion follows from applying the generalization to the specific case.

Many deductive arguments do not state one of the premises but rather leave the reader to infer it. In the preceding example, the conclusion would still sound plausible without the major premise: *Nuclear reactors increase radiation in the environment; therefore, they are dangerous to public health.* A careful reader, however, will see the missing premise and will question the whole argument if the premise is debatable.

Deductive arguments break down if one of the premises is not true or if the conclusion does not logically follow from them. For example, consider this argument:

The deer population in our state should be preserved. During hunting season hundreds of deer are killed. Therefore, the hunting season should be discontinued.

To challenge this argument, the state's wildlife commission might agree with both the major and minor premises but question whether the conclusion follows logically from them. True, the deer population should be preserved; true, deer are killed during hunting season. However, in an area where deer have no natural enemies, herds become too large for the forest vegetation to support them. The overpopulated herds strip the leaves and bark from the young trees, killing the trees before dying of starvation themselves. The commission might conclude, therefore, that a limited hunting season helps preserve a healthier and more stable population of deer.

Avoiding logical fallacies

Some errors in reasoning are so common that writers and readers call them by name: hasty generalization, non sequitur, false analogy, and so on. Such errors are known as *logical fallacies*.

HASTY GENERALIZATION   A hasty generalization is a conclusion based on insufficient or unrepresentative evidence.

> Deaths from drug overdoses in Metropolis have doubled in the past three years. Therefore, more Americans than ever are dying from drug abuse.

Data from one city do not justify a conclusion about the whole United States.

Many hasty generalizations contain words like *all, every, always,* and *never,* when qualifiers such as *most, many, usually,* and *seldom* would be more accurate. Go over your writing carefully for such general statements and make sure that you have enough data to verify your position or that you qualify the statements.

A *stereotype* is a hasty generalization (usually derogatory) about a group. Examples: Women are bad bosses; politicians are corrupt; people without children are self-centered. Stereotyping is common because of our human tendency to perceive selectively. We tend to see what we want to see; that is, we notice evidence confirming our already formed opinions and fail to notice evidence to the contrary. For example, if you have concluded that politicians are corrupt, your stereotype will be confirmed by occasional news reports of legislators being indicted—even though every day the newspapers describe conscientious officials serving the public honestly and well. Generalizations about people must be based on numerous typical cases and not contradicted by many exceptions. And even conclusions that are generally valid — that Americans tend to place a high value on individual rights, for example— will have significant exceptions because what is generally true about groups of people will not be true of all individuals within those groups.

NON SEQUITUR   A non sequitur (Latin for "does not follow") is a conclusion that does not follow logically from preceding statements or that is based on irrelevant data.

> Mary loves good food; therefore, she will be an excellent chef.

Mary's love of good food does not guarantee that she will be able to cook it well.

FALSE ANALOGY   An analogy points out a similarity between two things that are otherwise dissimilar. Analogies can be an effective means of illustrating a point (see 6b), but they are not proof. In a false analogy, a writer falsely assumes that because two things are alike in one respect, they must be alike in others.

> If we can put humans on the moon, we should be able to find a cure for the common cold.

Putting humans on the moon and finding a cure for the common cold are both scientific challenges, but the technical problems confronting medical researchers are quite different from those solved by space scientists.

***EITHER . . . OR* FALLACY**   The *either . . . or* fallacy is the suggestion that only two alternatives exist when in fact there are more.

> Either learn how to operate a computer or you won't be able to get a decent job after college.

In fact, many occupations do not require knowledge of computers.

FAULTY CAUSE-AND-EFFECT REASONING   Careless thinkers often assume that because one event follows another, the first is the cause of the second. This common fallacy is known as *post hoc,* from the Latin *post hoc, ergo propter hoc,* meaning "after this, therefore because of this." Like a non sequitur, it is a leap to an unjustified conclusion.

> Since Governor Smith took office, unemployment of minorities in the state has decreased by 7 percent. Governor Smith should be applauded for reducing unemployment among minorities.

The writer must show that Governor Smith's policies are responsible for the decrease in unemployment; it is not enough to show merely that the decrease followed the governor's taking office.

Demonstrating the connection between causes and effects is rarely a simple matter. For example, to explain why an introductory chemistry course has a very high failure rate, you would begin by listing possible causes: inadequate preparation of students, poor teaching, large class size, unavailability of qualified tutors, and so on. Next you would need to investigate each possible cause by gathering statistical data. For example, to see whether inadequate preparation of students contributes to the high failure rate, you might do a statistical comparison of the math and science backgrounds of successful and failing students. Or to see whether large class size is a contributing cause, you might run a pilot program of small classes and then compare grades in the small classes with those in the larger ones. Only after thoroughly investigating all of the possible causes would you be able to weigh the relative impact of each cause and then suggest appropriate remedies.

CIRCULAR REASONING AND BEGGING THE QUESTION   Suppose you go to see a doctor about a rash you suddenly developed. "I have a rash," you say to the doctor. "What is your diagnosis?" The doctor answers, "You have allergitis." When you ask, "What's that?" the doctor replies, "It's a rash." This is an example of circular reasoning: No real information has been introduced; by a trick of semantics you have wound up back where you started.

Like circular reasoning, begging the question is a way of ducking the issue. Instead of supporting the conclusion with evidence and logic, the writer simply restates the conclusion in different language.

> Faculty and administrators should not be permitted to come to student council meetings because student council meetings should be for students only.

The writer has given no reason for this position but has merely repeated the point.

APPEALS TO EMOTION   Many of the arguments we see in the media strive to win our sympathy rather than our intelligent agreement. A TV commercial suggesting that you will be thin and sexy if you drink a certain diet beverage is making a pitch to emotions. So is a political speech that recommends electing John D'Eau because he is a devoted husband and father who fought for his country in Vietnam.

The following passage illustrates several types of emotional appeals.

> This progressive proposal to build a large ski resort in the state park has been carefully researched by Fidelity, the largest bank in the state; furthermore, it is favored by a majority of the local merchants. The only opposition comes from narrow-minded, do-gooder environmentalists who care more about trees than they do about people; one of their leaders was actually arrested for disturbing the peace several years ago.

Words with strong positive or negative connotations, such as *progressive* and *do-gooders,* are examples of *biased language.* Attacking the persons who hold a belief (environmentalists) rather than refuting their argument is called *ad hominem,* a Latin term meaning "to the man." Associating a prestigious name (Fidelity) with the writer's side is called *transfer.* Claiming that an idea should be accepted because a large number of people are in favor (the majority of merchants) is called the *bandwagon appeal.* Bringing in irrelevant issues (the arrest) is a *red herring,* named after a trick used in fox hunts to mislead the dogs by dragging a smelly fish across the trail.

In examining your own and other people's writing for errors of logic, you will find that logical fallacies are frequently not so clear-cut that a casual reader can spot them immediately. Often they show up in combination. To recognize such fallacies in your own writing takes discipline, but you can do it if you train yourself to become a skeptical and demanding reader—the kind of person who measures all claims against the evidence.

EXERCISE 52–1

Explain what is illogical in the following brief arguments. It may be helpful to identify the logical fallacy or fallacies by name. Answers to lettered sentences appear in the back of the book.

a. All of my blind dates have been embarrassing disasters, so I know this one will be too.

b. If you're old enough to vote, you're old enough to drink. Therefore, the drinking age should be lowered to eighteen.

c. This country has been run too long by old, out-of-date, out-of-touch, entrenched politicians protecting the special interests that got them elected.

d. It was possible to feed a family of four on $70 a week before Governor Leroy took office and drove up food prices.

e. If you're not part of the solution, you're part of the problem.

1. Whenever I wash my car, it rains. I have discovered a way to end all droughts — get all the people to wash their cars.
2. Our current war on drugs has not worked. Either we should legalize drugs or we should turn the drug war over to our armed forces and let them fight it.
3. College professors tend to be sarcastic. Three of my five professors this semester make sarcastic remarks.
4. Although Ms. Bell's book on Joe DiMaggio was well researched, I doubt that an Australian historian can contribute much to our knowledge of an American baseball player.
5. Self-righteous nonsmoking fanatics have eroded our basic individual freedoms by railroading the passage of oppressive antismoking laws that interfere with our natural right to make our own decisions.
6. If professional sports teams didn't pay athletes such high salaries, we wouldn't have so many kids breaking their legs at hockey and basketball camps.
7. Ninety percent of the students oppose a tuition increase; therefore, the board of trustees should not pass the proposed increase.
8. If the president had learned the lesson of Vietnam, he would realize that sending U.S. troops into a foreign country can only end in disaster.
9. A mandatory ten-cent deposit on bottles and cans will eliminate litter because everyone I know will return the containers for the money rather than throw them away.
10. Soliciting money to save whales and baby seals is irresponsible when thousands of human beings can't afford food and shelter.

53

Writing about literature

Most of us know how to read and respond to literature—novels, stories, poems, and plays—in an informal way. "I like it," we say. "What was it about?" we ask. "What made it so powerful?" we might want to know. The purpose of the literary paper is to take our informal judgments about a work and, through reflection and analysis, transform them into reasoned, compelling arguments.

All good writing about literature attempts to answer a question, spoken or unspoken, about the text: "Is Huckleberry Finn a hero?" "Why doesn't Hamlet kill his uncle sooner?" "What makes Emily Dickinson's poems so popular?" The goal of a literary essay should be to answer such questions with a meaningful interpretation, presented forcefully and persuasively.

53a   Get involved in the work; be an active reader.

Read the work closely and carefully. Think of the work as speaking to you: What is it telling you? Asking you? Trying to make you feel?

If the work provides an introduction and footnotes, read them attentively. They may be a source of important information. Use the dictionary to look up words unfamiliar to you or words with subtle nuances that may affect the work's meaning.

Rereading is a central part of the process. You should read short works several times, first to get an overall impression and then again to focus on meaningful details. With longer works, such as novels or three-act plays, read the most important chapters or scenes more than once while keeping in mind the work as a whole.

As you read and reread, interact with the work by posing questions and looking for answers. The chart on pages 594–95 suggests some questions about literature that may help you become a more active reader.

Annotating the work and taking notes

Annotating the work is a way to focus your reading. The first time through, you may want to pencil a check mark next to passages you find particularly significant. On a more careful rereading, pay particular attention to these passages and jot down your ideas and reactions in a notebook or (if the book is your own) in the margins of the page.

Here is one student's annotation of the opening paragraphs of a short story by Charlotte Perkins Gilman.

The Yellow Wallpaper   *first-person narrate*

It is very seldom that mere ordinary people like John and (myself)

secure ancestral halls for the summer.

Ominous—
or is she
just joking?

A colonial mansion, a hereditary estate, I would say (a) (haunted house) and reach the height of romantic felicity—but that would be asking too much of fate!   *Can mean "happiness" or "an appropriate and pleasing*

Sounds like
the beginning
of a ghost story.
Foreshadowing?

Still I will proudly declare that (there is something queer) *manner, or style.*

(about it.) Else, why should it be let so cheaply? And why have stood so long untenanted?   *Not sure what "romantic felicity" means here. Ask in class.*

(John) laughs at me, of course, but one expects that.   *↗ Why?*   *Tension? Narrator*

(John) is practical in the extreme. He has no patience with *thinks husband*
faith, an intense horror of superstition, and he scoffs openly at *too*
any talk of things not to be felt and seen and put down in figures.   *Practical*

She keeps
repeating
his name,
but we
don't even
know hers.

(John) is a physician, and *perhaps*—(I would not say it to a *she's*
dead because it can't hear her?   *writing*
living soul, of course, but this is (dead) paper and a great relief to *this*
my mind)—*perhaps* that is one reason I do not get well faster.   *down in private.*

So the narrator is sick!   *Needs to tell story for herself.*

Notice how the student has responded to unfamiliar words, raised questions, and commented on the narrator. These annotations may lead the student to an interpretation based on the narrator's mental state.

Note taking is also an important part of rereading a work of literature. In your notes you can try out ideas and develop your perspective on the work. Here are some notes one student took on a story by Edgar Allan Poe:

"The Fall of the House of Usher"

House of Usher has two meanings—the building and the family

seeing the building has an emotional impact on the narrator: "with the first glimpse of the building, a sense of insufferable gloom pervaded my spirit"

narrator uses descriptive language that evokes his feelings— "dull," "dark," "soundless," "dreary," "melancholy," "insufferable gloom"

produces feeling of depression in reader too

Who is this narrator? What is his relationship to the Ushers?

Such notes, consisting of observations and questions to yourself, are the raw material out of which you will build an interpretation.

Forming an interpretation

After getting a clearer understanding of the work through rereading and jotting notes, you are ready to start forming an interpretation. Look through your notes and annotations for recurring insights about some aspect of the work, perhaps about its characters, theme, pattern of imagery, or central conflict. Look for insights that reveal meanings in the work that were not obvious to you on a first reading, and make sure you have plenty of details and examples to support your interpretation.

In forming an interpretation, it is important to focus on a central issue. You should avoid trying to do several things at once. You may think, for example, that *Huckleberry Finn* is a great book because it contains brilliant descriptions of scenery, has a lot of humorous moments, but also tells a serious story of one boy's development. This is an interesting, complex response to the work, but your job in writing an essay will be to close in on one issue that you can develop into a sustained, in-depth argument. Your essay's focus might be on how Mark Twain uses humor to make a point or on why Huck's emotional growth is important to the novel's theme or even on how the long passages of scenic description break up the story's action.

53b   Plan your essay.

Think ahead about your essay's purpose, length, and scope. What will you be trying to accomplish? Most short essays necessarily deal with either a broad question about a short work (How does language function in Gwendolyn Brooks's "We Real Cool"? How does James Joyce's "The Dead" confront traditions of love and romance? What might the moth symbolize in Virginia Woolf's "The Death of the Moth"?) or a narrow question about a long work (How does Dickens portray lawyers in *Great Expectations?* How is Hell depicted in *Paradise Lost?* What is the purpose of the comic scenes in *Macbeth?*). Don't take on more than you can handle; you cannot give an exhaustive explanation of the significance of a six-hundred-page novel in a five-page essay.

In addition to thinking about your essay's purpose, length, and scope, spend some time planning its focus and shape. As with any piece of writing, you can best do this by drafting a tentative thesis and sketching an outline. (See also 1c and 1d.)

Drafting a tentative thesis

Your thesis statement should be a strong, assertive summary of your interpretation. Consider, for example, the following successful thesis statements taken from student essays.

In Stephen Crane's gripping tale "The Open Boat," four men lost at sea discover not only that nature is indifferent to their fate but that their own particular talents make little difference as they struggle for survival.

Although Medea professes great love for her children, Euripides gives us reason to suspect her sincerity: Medea does not hesitate to use the children as weapons in her bloody battle with Jason, and from the outset she displays little real concern for their fate.

In Eudora Welty's "Why I Live at the P.O.," the plot, the point of view, and the characterization all contribute to the theme of family as theater.

As in other writing, the thesis of a literary paper cannot be too factual ("As a runaway slave, Jim is in danger from the law"), too broad ("One major theme of American literature is discovery"), or too vague ("Shakespeare was a brilliant man"). (See also 2b.)

In a literary essay, your thesis should usually appear in your introductory paragraph. In the following example, the student writer's thesis is italicized.

> In *Electra*, Euripides depicts two women who have had too little control over their lives. Electra, ignored by her mother, Clytemnestra, has been married off to a farmer and treated more or less like a slave. Clytemnestra has fared even worse. Her husband, Agamemnon, has slashed the throat of their daughter Iphigenia as a sacrifice to the gods. *The experience of powerlessness has taught mother and daughter two very different lessons: Electra has learned the value of traditional, conservative sex roles for women, but Clytemnestra has learned just the opposite.*

Sketching an outline

Your thesis may strongly suggest a method of organization, in which case you will have little difficulty jotting down your

Questions to ask about literature

GENRE

What kind of work is it? Is it a novel, a short story, a play, a film, a poem? Is it a specialized genre that has conventions of its own, such as a mystery novel, a tragedy, a western, or a sonnet?

PLOT

What happens? Are events revealed in chronological order or are there flashbacks? What patterns do you find in the plot's development? Is there a central conflict? When do events come to a climax? Are there any subplots? Which events are foreshadowed, and which take the reader by surprise? Are any events ironic?

SETTING

When and where do events take place? Does the setting create an atmosphere that reinforces the plot, gives an insight into a character, or hints at the theme of the work?

CHARACTER

Who are the central characters? What seems to motivate them? Which characters change significantly, and what, if anything, have they learned from their experiences? Which characters are well rounded and which are relatively "flat" or stereotypical? How are conflicts between characters resolved?

POINT OF VIEW

In a story or novel, who is the narrator and from what point of view does he or she relate the action? In fiction, the most common points of view are *first person* (the narrator is a character in the story who uses the word *I*), *omniscient* (the narrator is the author, who knows things no character possibly could), and *limited omniscient* (the narrator is the author but views most of the action from the perspective of one of the characters). Is the narrator perhaps innocent or naive or self-deceptive?

In a poem, who is the speaker? The speaker may be the poet, but often it is a *persona,* a voice or role that the poet assumes, possibly for dramatic effect. To whom, if anyone, is the voice in the poem speaking?

THEME

What is the overall meaning of the work — the central insight about people or the truth about life that it illustrates?

IMAGERY

What sensory images does the writer evoke most often? How do such images contribute to the work's meaning? Do any recurring images seem symbolic?

NOTE: For more technical matters, such as rhyme and meter in poetry, consult a literature textbook or a reference work on literature.

essay's key points. For example, one of the thesis statements given earlier, based on Eudora Welty's "Why I Live at the P.O.," suggested this informal outline. (The student paper based on this outline appears on pages 608–14.)

> Thesis: In Eudora Welty's "Why I Live at the P.O.," the plot, the point of view, and the characterization all contribute to the theme of family as theater.

> — The plot is arranged in theatrical scenes.
> — The first-person point of view reveals the narrator as a self-centered woman who enjoys picking fights and provoking melodramatic scenes.
> — All of the central characters escape boredom by bickering and upstaging one another.

After checking through his notes to make sure he had enough material to develop the points listed in his informal outline, the student was ready to begin drafting his essay.

If your thesis does not by itself suggest a method of organization, turn to your notes and begin putting them into categories that relate to the thesis. The student who drafted the tentative thesis based on Euripides' play *Medea* (see page 593) constructed the following formal outline from her notes:

> Thesis: Although Medea professes great love for her children, Euripides gives us reason to suspect her sincerity: Medea does not hesitate to use the children as weapons in her bloody battle with Jason, and from the outset she displays little real concern for their fate.

> I. From the very beginning of the play, Medea is a less than ideal mother.
>   A. Her first words about the children are hostile.
>   B. Her first actions suggest indifference.

> II. In three scenes Medea appears to be a loving mother, but in each of these scenes we have reason to doubt her sincerity.

III. Throughout the play, as she plots her revenge, Medea's overriding concern is not her children but her reputation.
   A. Fearing ridicule, she is proud of her reputation as one who can "help her friends and hurt her enemies."
   B. Her obsession with reputation may stem from the Greek view of reputation as a means of immortality.

IV. After she kills her children, Medea reveals her real concern.
   A. She shows no remorse.
   B. She revels in Jason's agony over their death.

Whether to use a formal or an informal outline is to some extent a matter of personal preference. For most purposes, you will probably find that an informal outline is sufficient, perhaps even preferable. (See 1d.)

53c Support your interpretation with specific evidence from the text.

Although anyone can express an opinion about a literary work, your task in literary analysis is to find examples in the text that confirm the validity of your interpretation and to cite them forcefully enough to convince others of the worth of your interpretation.

As a rule, each paragraph in the body of your essay should begin with a topic sentence that is clearly interpretive; often it will state one of the points listed in your outline. The rest of the paragraph should consist of details and perhaps quotations in support of your interpretation. Consider, for example, the following student paragraph, which develops one of the points in the preceding outline.

> A woman rejected by the man she loves, Medea is highly sensitive to ridicule. She fears that unless she is hard-boiled, unless she commits the most hideous of crimes in vengeance for Jason's treatment of her, people will laugh at her. Early in the play she says that if she should die in the course of her

revenge plot, she would give her enemies "cause for laughter" (line 383). A bit later she tells herself, "Never/Shall you be mocked by Jason's Corinthian wedding,/Whose father was noble, grandfather Helius" (404–06). Her first explanation for her plan to kill the children is "For it is not bearable to be mocked by enemies" (797). When later she is debating whether to kill the children, she asks herself, "Do I want to let go/My enemies unhurt and be laughed at for it?/I must face this thing" (1049–51). Finally, facing Jason after she has killed the children, Medea proclaims, "No, it was not to be that you should scorn my love,/And pleasantly live your life through, laughing at me" (1354–55).

Notice that although the examples in this paragraph are given in chronological order, the student is not simply summarizing the story's plot. Instead, she uses the examples to support an interpretation: that Medea, as portrayed by Euripides, is indeed "highly sensitive to ridicule."

Avoiding simple plot summary

In a literary essay, it is tempting to rely heavily on plot summary and avoid interpretation. You can resist this temptation by paying special attention to your topic sentences. If the opening sentence of a paragraph in the body of your essay states a fact instead of announcing an interpretation, you probably need to rethink your approach. The following rough-draft topic sentence, for instance, led to a plot summary rather than an interpretation.

As they drift down the river on a raft, Huck and the runaway slave Jim have many philosophical discussions.

The student's revised topic sentence, which announces an interpretation, is much better:

This theme of dawning moral awareness is reinforced by the many philosophical discussions between Huck and Jim, the runaway slave, as they drift down the river on a raft.

Usually a little effort is all that is needed to make the difference between a plot summary that goes nowhere and a focused, forceful interpretation. As with all forms of writing, revision is key.

53d Observe the conventions of literary papers.

When you are writing a literary paper, it is important to observe certain conventions so that your readers' attention will be focused directly on your argument, not on the details of your presentation.

Referring to authors and titles

The first time you make reference to authors, refer to them by their first and last names: "Virginia Woolf was one of England's most important novelists." In subsequent references, use their last names only: "Woolf's early work was largely overlooked." Do not refer to the author by his or her first name; as a rule, do not use titles such as Mr. or Ms. or Dr.

Titles of short stories, essays, and most poems are put in quotation marks: "The Dead" by James Joyce; "The Death of the Moth" by Virginia Woolf; "High Windows" by Philip Larkin. (See 37d.) Titles of novels, nonfiction books, plays, and epics or other long poems are underlined to indicate italics: *Heart of Darkness* by Joseph Conrad; *I Know Why the Caged Bird Sings* by Maya Angelou; *Macbeth* by William Shakespeare; *Howl* by Allen Ginsberg. (See 42a.)

Referring to characters and events

Refer to each character by the name most often used for him or her in the work. If, for instance, a character's name is Lambert Strether and he is always referred to as "Strether," do not call him "Lambert" or "Mr. Strether." Similarly, write "Lady Macbeth," not "Mrs. Macbeth."

When describing fictional events in a work of literature, use the present tense: "Octavia *demands* blind obedience from James and from all of her children. When James and Ty *catch* two redbirds in their trap, they *want* to play with them; Octavia, however, *has* other plans for the birds." (See also 13b and 28a.)

Referring to parts of works

Be as accurate as possible when referring to subdivisions of a literary work. Avoid using phrases like "the part where." Instead give specific references by using the appropriate descriptive terms: "the final stanza," "the scene in which Hamlet confronts his mother," "the passage that refers to Jane Austen," and so on.

When referring to a specific sentence or paragraph in prose (a novel, story, or nonfiction work), use a page number in a parenthetical notation: "It seemed as if this were the Loom of Time," says Ishmael (185). With poems, refer to specific lines: "Shall I compare thee to a summer's day?" asks Shakespeare (line 1). When discussing a play, give the act number, scene number, and line number, if there is one, separated by periods: Early in *Hamlet*, the stage is set for the appearance of the ghost (1.1.1–12). "Everything that matters in this town has fallen into the hands of a few bureaucrats," says Hovstad in Ibsen's *An Enemy of the People* (1.2). (See also 50a.)

Formatting quotations

If a prose quotation takes up fewer than four typed lines, put it in quotation marks and run it into the text of your essay. If it is four lines or longer, set it off from your text by indenting ten spaces from the left margin; when a quotation has been set off from the text, quotation marks are not needed. (See 37b.)

Enclose quotations of three or fewer lines of poetry in quotation marks within your text, and indicate line breaks by a slash. (See 39e.) When you quote more than three lines of poetry, set the quotation off from the text and omit the quotation marks. (See 37b.)

53e If you use secondary sources, document them appropriately and avoid plagiarism.

Many literary essays do not rely on secondary sources — works other than the literary text under discussion. For an example of an essay without secondary sources, see pages 603–06.

Other literary essays use some ideas from sources such as articles or books of literary criticism, biographies of the author, the author's own essays and autobiography, and histories of the era in which the work was written. (For an example of a paper that uses secondary sources, see pages 608–14.) Even if you use secondary sources, your main goal should always be to develop your own understanding and interpretation of the literary work.

Whenever you use secondary sources, you must document them and you must avoid plagiarism. Plagiarism is unacknowledged borrowing — whether intentional or unintentional — of a source's words or ideas. (See 49d.)

Documenting sources

Most literary essays are documented with the system recommended by the Modern Language Association (MLA). This system of documentation is discussed in detail in 50, which is easy to find because its pages have a vertical band in color. For other systems of documentation, see 51.

An MLA in-text citation usually combines a signal phrase with a page number in parentheses:

SAMPLE MLA IN-TEXT CITATION

Arguing that fate has little to do with the tragedy that befalls Oedipus, Bernard Knox writes that "the catastrophe of

Oedipus is that he discovers his own identity; and for his discovery he is first and last responsible" (6).

The signal phrase prepares readers for the quotation and names the author; the number in parentheses is the page on which the quotation appears.

The in-text citation is used in combination with a list of works cited at the end of the paper. Anyone interested in knowing the other publishing information about the source can consult the list of works cited. Here, for example, is the works cited entry for the work referred to in the sample in-text citation:

SAMPLE ENTRY IN THE LIST OF WORKS CITED

Knox, Bernard. <u>Oedipus at Thebes: Sophocles' Tragic Hero and His Time</u>. New York: Norton, 1971.

As you document sources with in-text citations, consult 50a; as you construct your list of works cited, consult 50b.

Avoiding plagiarism

The rules about plagiarism are the same for literary papers as for other research writing. It is wrong to use other writers' ideas or language without giving credit to your source. If an interpretation was suggested to you by another critic's work or if an obscure point was clarified by someone else's research, it is your responsibility to cite the source. If you have borrowed any phrases or sentences from your source, you must put them in quotation marks and credit the author.

For important tips on avoiding plagiarism, see 49d and the charts on pages 484–87.

Following are two sample essays. The first, by Margaret Peel, has no secondary sources. (Langston Hughes's "Ballad of the Landlord," the poem on which the essay is based, appears on page 607.) The second essay, by Jim Dixon, is an example of a paper that has used secondary sources.

SAMPLE ESSAY (WITHOUT SECONDARY SOURCES)

Margaret Peel

Professor Welch

English 102

2 February 1994

Opposing Voices in "Ballad of the Landlord"

Langston Hughes's "Ballad of the Landlord" is narrated through four voices, each with its own perspective on the poem's action. These opposing voices -- of a tenant, a landlord, the police, and the press -- dramatize a black man's experience in a society dominated by whites.

The main voice in the poem is that of the tenant, who, as the last line tells us, is black. The tenant is characterized by his informal, nonstandard speech. He uses slang ("Ten Bucks"), contracted words ('member, more'n), and nonstandard grammar ("These steps is broken down"). This colloquial English suggests the tenant's separation from the world of convention, represented by the formal voices of the police and the press, which appear later in the poem.

Although the tenant uses nonstandard English, his argument is organized and logical. He begins with a reasonable complaint and a gentle reminder that the complaint is already a week old: "My roof has sprung a leak. / Don't you 'member I told you about it / Way last week?" (lines 2-4). In the second stanza, he appeals diplomatically to the landlord's self-interest: "These steps is broken down. / When you come up yourself / It's a wonder you don't fall down" (6-8). In the third stanza, when the landlord has responded to his complaints with a demand for rent money, the tenant becomes more forceful, but his voice is still reasonable: "Ten Bucks you say is due? / Well, that's Ten Bucks more'n I'll pay you / Till you fix this house up new" (10-12).

The fourth stanza marks a shift in the tone of the argument. At this point the tenant responds more emotionally, in reaction to the landlord's threats to evict him. By the fifth stanza, the tenant has unleashed his anger: "Um-huh! You talking high and mighty" (17). Hughes uses an exclamation point for the first time; the tenant is raising his voice at last. As the argument gets more heated, the tenant finally resorts to the language of violence: "You ain't gonna be able to say a word / If I land my fist on you" (19-20).

These are the last words the tenant speaks in the poem. Perhaps Hughes wants to show how black people who threaten violence are silenced. When a new voice is introduced--the landlord's--the poem shifts to italics:

> Police! Police!
> Come and get this man!
> He's trying to ruin the government
> And overturn the land! (21-24)

This response is clearly an overreaction to a small threat. Instead of dealing with the tenant directly, the landlord shouts for the police. His hysterical voice--marked by repetitions and punctuated with exclamation points--reveals his disproportionate fear and outrage. And his conclusions are equally excessive: This black man, he claims, is out to "ruin the government" and "overturn the land." Although the landlord's overreaction is humorous, it is sinister as well, because the landlord knows that, no matter how excessive his claims are, he has the police and the law on his side.

In line 25, the regular meter and rhyme of the poem break down, perhaps showing how an arrest disrupts everyday life. The "voice" in lines 25–29 has two parts: the clanging sound of the police ("Copper's whistle! / Patrol bell!") and, in sharp contrast, the unemotional, factual tone of a police report ("Arrest. / Precinct Station. / Iron cell").

The last voice in the poem is the voice of the press, represented in newspaper headlines: "MAN THREATENS LANDLORD / TENANT HELD NO BAIL / JUDGE GIVES NEGRO 90 DAYS IN COUNTY JAIL" (31-33). Meter and rhyme return here, as if to show that once the tenant is arrested, life can go on as usual. The language of the press, like that of the police, is cold and distant, and it gives the tenant less and less status. In line 31, he is a "man"; in line 32, he has been demoted to a "tenant"; and in line 33, he has become a "Negro," or just another statistic.

By using four opposing voices in "Ballad of the Landlord," Hughes effectively dramatizes different views of minority assertiveness. To the tenant, assertiveness is informal and natural, as his language shows; to the landlord, it is a dangerous threat, as his hysterical response suggests. The police response is, like the language that describes it, short and sharp. Finally, the press's view of events, represented by the headlines, is distant and unsympathetic.

By the end of the poem, we understand the predicament of the black man. Exploited by the landlord, politically oppressed by those who think he's out "to ruin the government," physically restrained by the police and the judicial system, and denied his

Peel 4

individuality by the press, he is saved only by his own sense of
humor. The very title of the poem suggests his--and Hughes's--
sense of humor. The tenant is singing a ballad to his oppressors,
but this ballad is no love song. It portrays the oppressors,
through their own voices, in an unflattering light: the landlord as
cowardly and ridiculous, the police and press as dull and soulless.
The tenant may lack political power, but he speaks with vitality,
and no one can say he lacks dignity or the spirit to survive.

Ballad of the Landlord

Landlord, landlord,
My roof has sprung a leak.
Don't you 'member I told you about it
Way last week?

Landlord, landlord,
These steps is broken down.
When you come up yourself
It's a wonder you don't fall down.

Ten Bucks you say I owe you?
Ten Bucks you say is due?
Well, that's Ten Bucks more'n I'll pay you
Till you fix this house up new.

What? You gonna get eviction orders?
You gonna cut off my heat?
You gonna take my furniture and
Throw it in the street?

Um-huh! You talking high and mighty.
Talk on — till you get through.
You ain't gonna be able to say a word
If I land my fist on you.

Police! Police!
Come and get this man!
He's trying to ruin the government
And overturn the land!

Copper's whistle!
Patrol bell!
Arrest.

Precinct Station.
Iron cell.
Headlines in press:

MAN THREATENS LANDLORD

TENANT HELD NO BAIL

JUDGE GIVES NEGRO 90 DAYS IN COUNTY JAIL

— Langston Hughes

SAMPLE ESSAY (WITH SECONDARY SOURCES)

Jim Dixon

Professor Goldsmith

Literature 110

12 October 1993

Family as Theater in

Eudora Welty's "Why I Live at the P.O."

The outspoken narrator of Eudora Welty's "Why I Live at the P.O.," known to us only as "Sister," intends to convince us--the world at large--that her family has "turned against" her, led on by her sister, Stella-Rondo. To escape her family, she explains, she has left home and now lives at the P.O., where she is postmistress. As she delivers her monologue, the narrator reveals more about herself than she intends. We see her as a self-centered young woman who enjoys picking fights and provoking melodramatic scenes in which she is the center of attention. Not too far into the story, we realize that others in the family behave the same way, and we begin to wonder why. The story's setting may provide the answer: In a small town in Mississippi, long before television, entertainment is scarce. The members of this family cope with isolation and boredom by casting themselves in a continuing melodrama, with each person stealing as many scenes as possible. Eudora Welty has carefully constructed the story's plot, its point of view, and its characterization to reinforce this theme of the family as theater.

Plot

The plot is arranged in scenes, almost as if it were a theatrical performance, with Sister playing the starring role. Each scene focuses on a family member "turning against" her. Scene 1 begins like this: "So the first thing Stella-Rondo did at the table was turn Papa-Daddy against me" (Welty, "Why" 47). To announce scene 2, Sister uses similar phrasing: "Papa-Daddy . . . tried to turn Uncle Rondo against me" (Welty, "Why" 48). Scene 3 concludes with another echo: "Stella-Rondo hadn't done a thing but turn [Mama] against me" (Welty, "Why" 51). And the final echo, at the end of scene 4, marks the dramatic climax: "There I was with the whole entire house on Stella-Rondo's side and turned against me" (Welty, "Why" 52).

That the story is arranged in dramatic scenes is no accident. Such stories impressed Eudora Welty as a child. Describing the stories told by one of her mother's friends, Welty writes, "What I loved about her stories was that everything happened in scenes. I might not catch on to what the root of the trouble was . . . but my ear told me it was dramatic" (One 14).

Point of View

Listening to her mother's friend, whose monologues revealed more about her than she knew, inspired Welty to use the first-person point of view in several stories. "Years later," writes Welty, "beginning with my story 'Why I Live at the P.O.,' I wrote reasonably often in the form of a monologue that takes possession of the speaker. How much more gets told besides!" (One 14).

The first-person point of view is crucial to the theme of Welty's story. It is both quicker and funnier to show that the narrator is self-centered and melodramatic than it would be to <u>tell</u> it. Sister is definitely the star in the melodrama. She begins her tale with "I," and every event is made to revolve around herself, even her sister's marriage:

> I was getting along fine with Mama, Papa-Daddy and
> Uncle Rondo until my sister Stella-Rondo just separated
> from her husband and came back home again. Mr.
> Whitaker! Of course I went with Mr. Whitaker first,
> when he first appeared here in China Grove, taking
> "Pose Yourself" photos, and Stella-Rondo broke us up.
> (Welty, "Why" 46)

Sister's monologue is, in the words of critic Ann Romines, "a highly elaborated weapon" (96). Consider, for example, the many catty remarks Sister makes about her enemies: She calls Stella-Rondo's Mr. Whitaker "this photographer with the pop-eyes," describes Papa-Daddy as someone who "sulks," and says that Mama "weighs two hundred pounds and has real tiny feet" (Welty, "Why" 46, 50). As for Stella-Rondo, the narrator tells us that she uses "cheap Kress tweezers," her kimono is "some terrible-looking flesh-colored contraption," and she has brought home "a peculiar-looking child" (Welty, "Why" 50, 49, 50).

Clearly the narrator's descriptions are exaggerated, and because of this we may be tempted to view her account of events with skepticism. On the whole, however, Sister seems to be right when she tells us that the entire family has "turned against" her. Much of the story is presented in dialogue that shows her family picking on her, and it is unlikely that Welty would have her completely fabricate the dialogue. In <u>The Eye of the Story</u>, Welty tells us that a story may mean what it says or it may mean more than it says, but "it is not all right, not in good faith, for things <u>not</u> to mean what they say" (160).

 This is not to suggest that the narrator's perceptions of things are always on the mark. She is probably kidding herself when she announces, at the beginning of the story, that everything was going well until Stella-Rondo arrived, because bickering is clearly a way of life in her family. Her self-deception is strongest, however, at the end of the story. "I want the world to know I'm happy," she proclaims, but we know this is not true. As she herself has just told us, her family makes up nearly the entire population of China Grove, and China Grove, whether she likes it or not, is her world. She cannot be happy apart from it. If she wants anyone to hear her monologue, she will have to return home. Even her curiosity will tempt her to return home, though she does not yet see this. "Stella-Rondo may be telling the most horrible tales in the world about Mr. Whitaker," she says, "but I haven't heard them" (Welty, "Why" 56). It is obvious to us that she very much wants to hear them.

 Because Sister is self-deceptive, a few critics have suggested that she is crazy. In her introduction to a collection of Welty's stories, Katherine Anne Porter describes Sister as "a terrifying case of <u>dementia praecox</u>," the Latin term for schizophrenia (xx). Travis Du Priest writes that Sister is "very likely paranoid" (46). And Charles E. May has called her an example of psychologist R. D. Laing's "unembodied self" (qtd. in Manning 59).

 These readings of the story strike me as going too far. Welty herself has stated that the narrator is excitable but sane:

> It never occurred to me while I was writing this story
> (and it still doesn't) that I was writing about someone in

serious mental trouble. I was trying to write about the
way people who live away off from nowhere have to
amuse themselves by dramatizing every situation that
comes along by exaggerating it. (Prenshaw 19)

Characterization

The narrator is not the only one in her family to exaggerate
a situation for dramatic effect. All of the other key players--
Papa-Daddy, Mama, Uncle Rondo, and Stella-Rondo--do so as well.
Papa-Daddy is eager to steal the first scene. Reacting to Stella-
Rondo's misrepresentation of a remark the narrator has made
about his beard, he plays the role of outraged victim and even
manufactures an insult to keep the attention on himself. " 'Bird's
nest'--is that what you call it?" he says, even though no one has
suggested that his beard resembles a bird's nest (Welty, "Why"
47). When Stella-Rondo's daughter, two-year-old Shirley T.,
finally grabs center stage, Papa-Daddy retreats to his hammock
in a fit of pique.

Mama views the return of her prodigal daughter, Stella-
Rondo, as a moment of high drama. As the narrator puts it,
"Mama said she like to made her drop dead for a second" (Welty,
"Why" 46). Although Mama claims to be "ashamed" of Stella-
Rondo for not writing to the family about Shirley T., she is so
effusive in her praise that we, like the narrator, feel she is play-
acting. And we know she is play-acting when she claims to believe that Shirley T. is adopted, because we learn from her later
comments that she knows very well whose child she is. Like others in the family, Mama is quick to pick a fight and provoke a
scene. When the narrator begins digging up her four-o'clocks to
replant at the P.O., Mama's response is theatrical. Raising the

window, she shouts, "Those happen to be my four-o'clocks. Every-thing planted in that star is mine. I've never known you to make anything grow in your life" (Welty, "Why" 53).

Like everyone else in the family, Uncle Rondo is not about to be ignored. Making a dramatic entrance in Stella-Rondo's flesh-colored kimono, he announces, "I'm poisoned." He has just drunk a bottle of medicine (the main ingredient being alcohol, no doubt), something he does every Fourth of July. Feeling dizzy and out of sorts, he plays the role of the invalid. Again like the other members of his family, Uncle Rondo enjoys a fight. When Stella-Rondo tells him that the narrator has said he looks like a fool in the flesh-colored negligee (a lie, since Stella-Rondo herself has said this), he responds with a temper tantrum. As if he hasn't already caused enough excitement, the next morning Uncle Rondo throws a package of firecrackers into the narrator's bed-room, getting--he thinks--just revenge for the perceived insult.

Stella-Rondo has gained everyone's attention simply by re-turning home, after a two-year absence, with Shirley T. in tow. This attention, however, is not enough. Perhaps better than any-one else at picking fights, Stella-Rondo stirs up trouble: fabricat-ing the story of Shirley T.'s being adopted, misrepresenting the narrator's words about Papa-Daddy's beard, reacting with an ex-aggerated sense of injury when she sees Uncle Rondo in her kimono, and lying to Uncle Rondo to get her sister into trouble.

The theme of family as theater is sustained throughout Welty's "Why I Live at the P. O." At the story's end, although Sister is still living in isolation at the P. O., readers can be fairly sure that things will soon be back to normal. The narrator will move home, and the family, welcoming the diversion, will no doubt find a way of turning her homecoming into a new round of excitement.

Works Cited

Du Priest, Travis. " 'Why I Live at the P. O.': Eudora Welty's
Epic Question." Christianity and Literature 31.4 (1982):
45–54.

Manning, Carol S. With Ears Opening like Morning Glories:
Eudora Welty and the Love of Storytelling. Westport, CT:
Greenwood, 1985.

Porter, Katherine Anne. Introduction. A Curtain of Green and
Other Stories. By Eudora Welty. New York: Harcourt,
1970. xi–xxiii.

Prenshaw, Peggy Whitman, ed. Conversations with Eudora
Welty. Jackson: UP of Mississippi, 1984.

Romines, Ann. "How Not to Tell a Story." Eudora Welty: Eye of
the Storyteller. Ed. Dawn Trouard. Kent: Kent State UP,
1989. 94-104.

Welty, Eudora. The Eye of the Story: Selected Essays and
Reviews. New York: Vintage, 1979.

---. One Writer's Beginnings. New York: Warner, 1984.

---. "Why I Live at the P.O." The Collected Stories of Eudora
Welty. New York: Harcourt, 1980. 46-56.

PART XI

Document Design

Well-designed documents—such as memos, résumés, newsletters, manuals, and sales brochures—have always been important in the business world, where writers must compete for the attention of readers. By using lists, headings, and a variety of visual cues, business writers make documents accessible to all segments of an audience: readers who want a quick overview, those who are scanning for specific information, those who need in-depth coverage of a topic, and so on.

Until recently, the academic world has paid more attention to the content of a piece of writing than to its presentation, the assumption being, perhaps, that scholars are motivated readers who can handle long stretches of unbroken text. While this may be true, many academics are now recognizing the potential of good document design. With the information explosion, academics too must compete for their readers' attention. The well-designed grant proposal, for example, has a better chance of being accepted than the poorly designed proposal, even if the content of both is excellent, because the people who read the proposals don't have time to read every word of every proposal. Professors too do not always have the time to read their students' work with great care. The student who designs a lab report or an essay so that the ideas are easily accessible therefore has a distinct advantage.

Interest in document design has been sparked, in part, by new technology. Increasingly sophisticated computers and printers provide writers with design strategies that were once prohibitively expensive. With access to various types of computer software, a psychology or sociology student can illustrate a report with bar graphs and flow charts, an accounting student can display columns of numbers, a history student can portray battlefield movements with line drawings, and so on.

54

Principles of document design

Good document design promotes readability, but what this means depends on your purpose and audience and perhaps on other elements of your writing situation, such as your subject and any length restrictions. (See the chart on pages 14–15.)

All of your design choices—format options, use of headings, use of displayed lists, and use of other visuals—should be made in light of your specific writing situation.

NOTE: In many writing situations, at least some design choices are dictated by convention. A corporation may require a specific format for all memos, for example. In college, too, essay formats must stay within certain guidelines (see 55). Always check to see which design elements are required and which you are free to create on your own.

54a   Select appropriate format options.

Most typewriters and word processors present you with several format options. Before you begin typing, you should make sure your margins, line spacing, and justification are set appropriately. If a number of fonts are available, you should also determine which is most appropriate for your purposes. For some projects, you may want to consider options such as double columns.

Margins, line spacing, and justification

For documents written on $8\frac{1}{2}'' \times 11''$ paper, you should leave a margin of between one and one and a half inches on all sides of the page. These margins leave enough white space so that the text won't seem crowded, and they allow room for annotations, such as a professor's comments or an editor's suggestions. Margins of this size serve another function as well: They ensure a reasonable line length, about ten to twelve words (less than 70 letters and spaces) per line. When a line of text is longer than this, the reader's eye cannot always stay on track when moving from one line to another.

Most manuscripts-in-progress are double-spaced to allow room for editing. Final copy is often double-spaced as well, since single-spacing is less inviting to read. But at times the advantages of double-spacing are offset by other considerations. In a business memo, for example, you may single-space to keep the memo to one easily scanned page. And in a long business report, you might single-space to save paper, for both ecological and financial reasons.

Word processors usually give you a choice between a justified and an unjustified (ragged) right margin. When the text is justified, all of the words line up against the right margin, as they do on a typeset page like the one you are now reading. Many writers like the look of a justified right margin, but text that has been justified on an ordinary word processor is often hard to read. The problem is that extra white space is added between words in some lines, creating "rivers" of white space that can be quite distracting. In addition, right-justified margins may create a need for excessive hyphenation at the ends of lines, again affecting readability. Unless you have technology that allows you to create the real look of a typeset page, you should turn off the justification feature.

Fonts

If you have a choice of fonts (typeface styles and sizes), for most purposes you should select a normal size (10 to 12 points, comparable to elite or pica on a typewriter) and a style that is not too offbeat. Although offbeat styles of type, such as those that look handwritten, may seem attractive, they slow readers down. We all read more efficiently when a text meets our usual expectations.

CAUTION: Never write a college essay or any other document in all capital letters. Research shows that readers experience much frustration when they are forced to read more than a few words in a row printed in all capital letters.

Columns

Most college and business writing is formatted in a single column, but in newsletters you may want to use double or multiple columns, like those in newspapers. Such columns invite readers to browse, and they give the writer flexibility in page layout — the placement of headings, photographs, and other visuals.

54b Consider using headings.

There is little need for headings in short informal essays, especially if the writer uses paragraphing and clear topic sentences to guide readers. In more complex documents, however, such as research papers, grant proposals, and business reports, headings can be a useful visual cue for readers.

Headings help readers see at a glance the organization of a document (for examples of college papers that use headings, see pages 551–59 and 608–14). If more than one level of heading is used, the headings also indicate the hierarchy of ideas — as they do throughout *The Bedford Handbook*. In the section you are now reading, for example, key advice is given in numbered and lettered headings printed in rust. Italic headings, also in rust, signal a lower level of organization.

Headings serve a number of functions, depending on the needs of different readers. When readers are simply looking up information, headings (along with a good table of contents and an index) will help them find it quickly. When readers are scanning, hoping to pick up the jist of things, headings will guide them. Even when readers are committed enough to read every word, headings can help. Efficient readers preview a document before they begin reading; when previewing and while reading they are guided by any visual cues that the writer provides.

CAUTION: Avoid using more headings (or more levels of headings) than you really need. Excessive use of headings can make a text choppy.

Phrasing headings

Headings should be as brief and as informative as possible. Certain styles of headings — the most common being -*ing* phrases, noun phrases, questions, and imperative sentences—work better for some purposes, audiences, and subjects than others.

Whatever style you choose, use it consistently for headings on the same level of organization. In other words, headings on the same level should be written in parallel structure (see 9).

-ING PHRASES Phrases beginning with verb forms ending in -*ing* suggest actions, so they are a good choice for manuals that show a person how to do something. In a word processing manual, for example, you may have encountered headings such as *Blocking text* and *Moving text.*

Again because they suggest actions, -*ing* verb forms are appropriate in documents that focus on solving problems. The following headings are drawn from an annual report written for World Resources Institute, an environmental think tank:

> Safeguarding the earth's atmosphere
>
> Charting the path to sustainable energy

Conserving global forests

Triggering technological revolution

Strengthening international institutions

It is a good idea to use colorful verb forms that suggest a fair amount of action. In the example just given, *Safeguarding, Charting, Conserving, Triggering,* and *Strengthening* underscore the report's central message: that with forceful action, the world's ecological problems can be solved.

NOUN PHRASES   Noun phrases, which are usually concise, work well as headings in a wide range of business and academic contexts. Business reports frequently use headings such as *Sales projections, Recommendations,* and *Executive summary.* Scientific reports often include headings such as *Materials and methods* and *Results.*

Noun phrases are especially appropriate in essays that survey a variety of persons, places, or things. The following headings, for example, have been drawn from a scholarly article surveying different methods of teaching a foreign language.

Grammar method

Direct method

Audiolingual method

Communicative method

For an example of an academic essay that uses noun phrases as headings, see pages 608–14.

QUESTIONS   Headings that are questions can generate interest in a document. For example, an article on diet and cholesterol might use commonly asked questions to motivate readers. Questions can also be used to help readers scan for information of interest to them, as with the following headings taken from a mutual fund brochure.

How do I buy shares?

How do I redeem shares?

What is the history of the fund's performance?

What are the tax consequences of investing in the fund?

Questions can be useful headings in research essays, since researchers usually pose questions that they hope to answer in their papers. For an example of a research paper that uses questions as headings, see pages 551–59.

IMPERATIVE SENTENCES Consider using imperative sentences if your purpose is to give direct advice to readers. An imperative sentence usually begins with a verb because its subject is an understood *You*. (See 58a.) The following imperative sentences appear as headings in a garden designer's newsletter. The writer is showing readers how to care for roses.

Fertilize roses in the fall.

Feed them again in the spring.

Prune roses when dormant and after flowering.

Spray roses during their growing season.

Placing and formatting headings

Headings on the same level of organization should be placed and formatted in a consistent way. For example, you might center your first-level headings and print them in boldface; then you might place the second-level headings flush left (against the left margin) and underline them to indicate italics, like this:

First-level heading

<u>Second-level heading</u>

Headings are usually centered or placed flush left, but at times you might decide to indent them five spaces from the left margin, like a paragraph indent. Or in a business document, you might choose to place headings in a column to the left of the text.

To highlight headings, consider using boldface, italics, all capital letters, color, larger or smaller typeface than the text, or some combination of these:

boldface

italics

<u>underlining</u> (to indicate italics)

ALL CAPITAL LETTERS

color

larger typeface

<small>smaller typeface</small>

On the whole, it is best to use restraint. Excessive highlighting results in a page that looks too busy, and it defeats its own purpose, since readers need to see which headings are more important than others.

Important headings can be highlighted by using a fair amount of white space around them. Less important headings can be downplayed by using less white space or even by running them in with the text (as with the small all-capitals headings on page 621 of this section).

54c Consider using displayed lists.

Lists are easy to read or scan when they are displayed, rather than run into your text. You might reasonably choose to display the following kinds of lists:

—steps in a process

—materials needed for a project

—parts of an object

—advice or recommendations

—items to be discussed

—criteria for evaluation (as in checklists)

Displayed lists should usually be introduced with an independent clause followed by a colon (see 35a), like the example just given. Periods are not used after items in a list unless the items are sentences.

Lists are most readable when they are presented in parallel grammatical form (see 9). In the sample list, for instance, the items are all noun phrases. As with headings (see 54b), some kinds of lists might be more appropriately presented as -*ing* phrases, as imperative sentences, or as questions.

To draw the reader's eye to a list, consider using bullets (circles or squares) or dashes if there is no need to number the items. If there is some reason to number the items, use an arabic number followed by a period for each item.

Although displayed lists can be a useful visual cue, they should not be overdone. Too many of them will give a document a choppy, cluttered look. And lists that are very long (sometimes called "laundry lists") should be avoided as well. Readers can hold only so many ideas in their short-term memory, so if a list grows too long, you should find some way of making it more concise or clustering similar items together.

54d Consider adding visuals.

Visuals such as charts, graphs, tables, diagrams, maps, and photographs convey information concisely and vividly. In a student essay not intended for publication, you can use another person's visuals as long as you credit the borrowing (see 49d). And with access to computer graphics, you can create your own visuals to enhance an essay or a report.

This section suggests when charts, graphs, tables, and diagrams might be appropriate for your purposes. It also discusses where you might place such visuals.

Using charts, graphs, tables, and diagrams

In documents that help readers follow a process or make a decision, flow charts can be useful; for an example, see page 155 of this book. Pie charts are appropriate for indicating ratios or apportionment, as in the following example.

PIE CHART

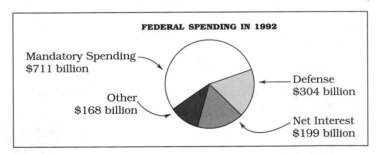

FEDERAL SPENDING IN 1992

Mandatory Spending $711 billion

Other $168 billion

Defense $304 billion

Net Interest $199 billion

Line graphs and bar graphs illustrate disparities in numerical data. Line graphs are appropriate when you want to illuminate trends over a period of time, such as trends in sales, in unemployment, or in population growth. Bar graphs can be used for the same purpose. In addition, bar graphs are useful for highlighting comparisons, such as vote totals for rival political candidates or the number of refugees entering the United States during different time periods.

LINE GRAPH

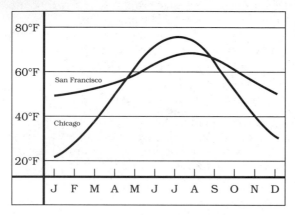

MONTHLY MEAN TEMPERATURE IN
SAN FRANCISCO AND CHICAGO

BAR GRAPH

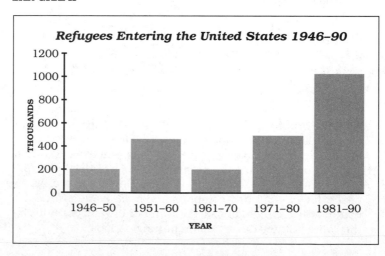

Tables are not as visually interesting as line graphs or charts, but they allow for inclusion of specific numerical data, such as exact percentages. The following table appears in one college's report of the results of a campus-wide questionnaire. Students and faculty, both white and minority, were responding to the question "Is American education based too much on European history and values?"

TABLE

Is American education based too much on European history and values?

	PERCENT		
	NO	UNDECIDED	YES
Nonwhite students	21	25	54
White students	55	29	16
Nonwhite faculty	15	19	65
White faculty	57	27	16

Diagrams are useful—and sometimes indispensable—in scientific and technical writing. It is more concise, for example, to use the following diagram than it would be to explain the chemical formula in words.

DIAGRAM

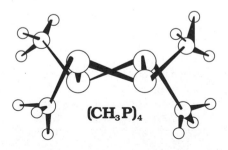

$(CH_3P)_4$

Placing visuals

A visual may be placed in the text of a document, close to a discussion of it, or it can be put in an appendix, labeled, and referred to in the text. In much college writing, the convention is to place visuals in an appendix; when in doubt, check with your professor.

Placing visuals in the text of an essay can be tricky. Usually you will want the visual to appear right after the sentences that prepare for it, but page breaks won't always allow this placement. At times, you may need to insert the visual at a later point and tell readers where it can be found or, with the help of software, you may be able to make the text flow around the visual.

In newsletters and in business or technical documents, page layout is both an art and a science. The best way to learn how to lay out pages is to work with colleagues who have had hands-on experience solving the many problems that can arise.

55

Academic essay formats

If your professor has provided you with guidelines for manuscript preparation, you should of course follow them. Otherwise, use one of the two standard academic essay formats discussed in this section.

In English and humanities classes, most professors prefer the Modern Language Association (MLA) guidelines in 55a; in social science classes, most professors prefer the American Psychological Association guidelines in 55b.

55a MLA guidelines

The following guidelines are based on advice given in the *MLA Handbook for Writers of Research Papers*, 3rd ed. (New York: MLA, 1988).

Materials

For a typed essay use 8½″ × 11″, 20-pound typing paper, not onionskin. A self-correcting typewriter or computer word processor will allow you to eliminate errors completely, but if you don't have access to such a typewriter or a computer, use white correction fluid. Some instructors will accept a line through the mistake with the correction neatly written or typed above. Use a caret (∧) to indicate where the correction should be inserted.

For an essay typed on a computer, make sure that the print quality and the paper quality meet your instructor's standards. If the paper emerges from the printer in a continuous sheet, separate the pages, remove the feeder strips from the sides of the paper, and assemble the pages in order.

Before you consider submitting a handwritten essay, be sure that your instructor will accept work that is not typewritten. Use 8½″ × 11″ wide-ruled white paper, and write in blue or black ink on one side of the paper only. Do not use sheets torn from a notebook. Obviously you should make your handwriting as clear as possible; if your handwriting is difficult to read, make an effort to type the essay or have it typed.

Title and identification

College essays normally do not require a separate title page. Unless instructed otherwise, against the left margin about one inch from the top of the paper, place on separate lines your name, the instructor's name, the course name and number, and the date. Double-space between lines.

Double-space after the heading and center the title of the essay. Capitalize the first and last words of the title and all other words except articles, prepositions, and coordinating conjunctions (see 45c). If there is a subtitle, separate it from the title with a colon and follow the capitalization rules for titles. Do not underline your title or put it in quotation marks, and do not use a period after it.

If you decide to use a title page, center the title and all elements of identification. Place the title about one-third down the page. About an inch below the title, write your name. About an inch below your name on separate lines, write the course name and number, your instructor's name, and the date; double-space between lines. For an example, see page 514.

Margins, spacing, and indentation

Leave margins of at least one inch but no more than an inch and a half at the top, bottom, and sides of the page.

Double-space between lines in a typewritten essay and indent the first line of each paragraph five spaces from the left margin.

For quotations of longer than four typed lines of prose or longer than three lines of verse, indent each line ten spaces from the left margin. Double-space between the body of the paper and the quotation, and double-space between the lines of the quotation. Quotation marks are not needed when a long quotation is set off from the text.

Pagination

Number all pages at the upper right corner, one-half inch below the top edge. (If you have a separate title page, the title page is uncounted and unnumbered.) Use arabic numerals (1, 2, 3, and so on), preceded by your last name. Do not put a period after the number and do not enclose the number in parentheses.

Punctuation and typing

In typing the essay, leave one space after words, commas, colons, and semicolons, and between the dots in ellipsis marks. Leave two spaces after periods, question marks, and exclamation points.

To form a dash, type two hyphens with no space between them. Do not put a space on either side of a dash.

Documentation

If in your essay you draw on written sources, you will need to document those sources. (See 50 for MLA documentation style.)

55b APA guidelines

The following guidelines are based on advice given in the *Publication Manual of the American Psychological Association*, 3rd edition (Washington, DC: American Psychological Association, 1983). Although much of the advice in the manual is intended for scholars submitting articles for professional publication, this section limits itself to the advice appropriate for undergraduate students.

Materials

Use 8½″ × 11″ heavy white bond typing paper, not onionskin. For an essay typed on a word processor, make sure that the print quality meets your instructor's standards. Avoid a typeface that is unusual or hard to read.

Title and identification

Begin your essay with a title page. Type a short title, consisting of the first two or three words of your title, flush right (at the right margin), about one-half inch from the top of the page. Double-space and type the arabic number 1 flush right. This is the page number.

About one-third down the page, type the title, centered. Then double-space and type your name, also centered. The APA manual does not provide guidelines for the placement of certain information necessary for college essays: the name and section number of the course, your instructor's name, and the date. Most instructors will want you to supply such information, using a title page format similar to the one on page 551.

Abstract

If your instructor requires one, include an abstract right after the title page. An abstract is a summary that provides readers with a quick overview of your essay. For most undergraduate essays, the abstract should be from 75 to 100 words long. It should express your thesis (or central idea) and your key points; it should also briefly suggest any implications or applications of the research you discuss in your paper.

Margins, spacing, and indentation

Use one-and-a-half-inch margins on all sides of the page. If you are working on a word processor, do not justify the right margin.

Double-space throughout the essay, and indent the first line of each paragraph five spaces from the left margin.

For quotations longer than forty words, indent each line five spaces from the left margin. Double-space between the body of the paper and the quotation, and double-space between lines in the quotation. Quotation marks are not needed when a long quotation is set off from the text.

Page numbers and short title

In the upper right-hand corner of each page, about one-half inch from the top of the page, type the short title that you typed on the title page, flush right (at the right margin). This will identify your essay in case pages get misplaced. Double-space and type the page number flush right. Number all pages, including the title page, using arabic numbers.

Punctuation and typing

Use one space after commas and semicolons and two spaces after end punctuation. Use two spaces after a colon, with the following exceptions: use no space in ratios (2:1), use one space in two-part titles, and use one space between the place of publication and the name of the publisher in entries in the reference list.

Although two spaces are used after a period that ends a sentence, use only one space after a period that follows a person's initial (B. F. Skinner).

To form a dash, type two hyphens with no space between them. Do not put a space on either side of a dash.

Headings

Although headings are not necessary, they are often useful cues for readers. For most undergraduate papers, use no more than one or two levels of headings. Major headings should be centered, with the first letter of important words capitalized. Subheadings should be typed flush left (against the left margin) and underlined, with the first letter of important words capitalized. (For an example of an APA paper that uses major headings, see pages 551–59.)

Documentation

If your essay draws on written sources, consult the APA documentation guidelines in 51a.

56

Business letters, résumés, and memos

56a Business letters

In writing a business letter, be direct, clear, and courteous, but do not hesitate to be firm if the situation calls for it. State your purpose or request at the beginning of the letter and include only pertinent information in the body. Follow conventions of form and usage, and avoid spelling errors.

Business letters usually follow one of three patterns: full block, block, and semiblock. In full block form, letterhead stationery, giving the return address of the writer (or of the writer's company), is used. Every element of the letter (including date, inside address, salutation, body, close, and signature) is typed flush with the left margin. In block form, the return address of the writer, the close, and the signature are moved to the right. Paragraphs are not indented but begin flush with the left margin. In semiblock form, considered the least formal of the three patterns, the return address, close, and signature are moved to the right, and the beginning of each paragraph is indented five spaces from the left margin.

Type business letters on letterhead stationery or on unlined paper that is at least 5½″ × 8½″. Type on only one side of the paper, single-spacing the body of the letter and double-spacing between paragraphs. The sample letter on the next page, in block form, illustrates the proper placement of each part of a business letter. The return address is followed by the date. (Note that the writer's name is not part of this heading.) The inside address includes the full name, title, and complete address of the person to whom the letter is written. (This information is repeated as the address on the envelope.) The inside address is typed flush left, a few lines below the return address heading. The salutation, or greeting, is typed two

BUSINESS LETTER IN BLOCK FORM

Return address —⌐ 121 Knox Road, #6
College Park, MD 20740
March 4, 1994

Linda Hennessee, Managing Editor ⌐
World Discovery
1650 K Street, NW
Washington, DC 20036 ⌐ Inside address

Dear Ms. Hennessee: ⌐— Salutation

I am applying for the summer editorial internship you
listed with the Career Development Center at the University
of Maryland. I am currently a junior at the University of
Maryland, with a double major in English and Latin American Studies.

Body

Over the past three years I have gained considerable
experience in newspaper and magazine journalism, as you
will see on my enclosed résumé. I am familiar with the
basic procedures of editing and photographic development,
but my primary interests lie in feature writing and landscape photography. My professional goal is to work as a
photojournalist with an international focus, preferably
for a major magazine. I cannot imagine a better introduction to that career than a summer at World Discovery.

I am available for an interview almost any time and can be
reached at 301-555-2651. I will be in Virginia from April 4
to April 12; if you want to contact me there, the number is
703-555-2006.

I look forward to hearing from you.

Close —⌐ Sincerely,

Signature—⌐ *Jeffrey Richardson*
Jeffrey Richardson

Enc.

lines below the inside address. A colon follows the salutation, and the body of the letter begins two lines below the greeting.

In the salutation use *Ms.* if you are writing to a woman whose title or marital status is unknown or if the woman prefers this form of address. If you are not writing to a particular person, you can use the salutation *Dear Sir or Madam* or you can address the company itself— *Dear Solar Technology.*

In block form the close is lined up with the return address and typed two lines below the end of the letter. Common closes are *Yours truly, Very truly yours,* and *Sincerely.* (Note that only the first word of the close is capitalized.) The name of the writer is typed four lines below the close, leaving room for the written signature between the close and the typed name. The name of the writer should not be prefaced by a title or followed by an abbreviation for a title or position. This information can be included in a separate line under the typed name (for example, *Director* or *Sales Manager*).

Other information can be included below the signature and flush with the left margin (for example: *Enc.*, indicating that something is enclosed with the letter; *cc: Mr. Theodore Jones*, indicating that a copy of the letter is being sent to Mr. Jones, a third party; or *JEF:njl*, indicating that JEF [the writer's initials] wrote the letter and njl typed it).

The name and return address of the writer is typed in the upper left-hand corner of the envelope. The addressee's name, title, and complete address are typed just right of the center of the envelope. The letter (which should be about the same width as the envelope) is folded in thirds.

56b Résumés

An effective résumé presents relevant information in a clear and concise form. Every résumé should include name, address, and telephone number; an employment objective; a list of relevant skills; a history of employment and education; additional activities; and information about how to obtain references. You may also include personal information such as date of birth or marital status, but such information is not necessary.

For an objective, you can name the specific position you are applying for or, if you are applying for a number of different positions, you can state an overall employment goal. When listing your skills, focus on your strongest work-related and personal skills and those that are most relevant to your objective. Under work experience, list your most recent job first and then work backward. Give the dates of employment and the company names and locations. You can also list your supervisors. Describe your responsibilities, highlighting those tasks or skills related to your objective. If you have experience that is not education- or work-related but that may be of interest to your prospective employer, list it separately. For your education history, begin with the institution you are currently attending and work backward to other colleges and universities, listing degrees and dates of attendance. Giving information about your high school education is optional. If you have won special honors or participated in relevant activities, include them. Instead of giving the names and addresses of references, you can state that references are available on request.

In a résumé, present yourself in the best possible light, but do not distort any of the facts about your experience or qualifications. Select details wisely and your résumé will be a valuable tool.

When you send your résumé, you should include a letter that tells what position you seek and where you learned about it. (See page 635.) The letter should also summarize your education and experience, relating them to the job you are applying for. You may want to highlight a specific qualification and refer the reader to your résumé for more information. End the letter with a suggestion for a meeting, and tell your prospective employer when you will be available.

RÉSUMÉ

Jeffrey Richardson
121 Knox Road, #6
College Park, MD 20740
301-555-2651

OBJECTIVE: To obtain an editorial internship with a magazine.

SKILLS

- Ability to write analytical stories, features, and interviews on deadline and under pressure.
- Strong background in photography: use of various types of cameras; darkroom procedures; landscape photography.
- Knowledge of copyediting and proofreading procedures.
- Languages: Spanish, French (reading).

WORK EXPERIENCE

The Diamondback (circulation 20,000), University of Maryland, College Park, Maryland, January 1992-present.
Photo editor for daily student newspaper.

Globe (circulation 80,000), Fairfax, Virginia, summers 1991-93.
Worked as intern on assignments from staff editors of this suburban Washington, DC, weekly paper: wrote stories about local issues and personalities; interviewed political candidates; performed editorial tasks (editing, proofreading, caption writing); coedited and took photographs for special supplement "The Landscapes of Northern Virginia: A Photoessay" (1993).

ADDITIONAL EXPERIENCE

Fairfax County Adult Education Program, Summer 1993.
Tutored Latino students in English as a Second Language.

EDUCATION

University of Maryland, College Park, Maryland. Bachelor of Arts expected June 1995, English and Latin American Studies.

Activities: Photographers' Workshop, Spanish Club.

References available on request.

56c Memos

Business memos (short for *memorandums*) are a form of communication used within a company or organization. Usually brief and to the point, a memo reports information, makes a request, or recommends an action. The format of a memo, which varies from company to company, is designed for easy distribution, quick reading, and efficient filing.

Most memos display the recipient, sender, date, and subject at the top of the page. Many also have a "cc" ("carbon copy") line to indicate additional people to receive a copy. Some companies have preprinted forms (similar to office stationery) for the first page of a memo.

The subject line should describe the subject as clearly and concisely as possible, and the introductory paragraph should get right to the point. The body of the memo should be well organized and easy to scan. To promote scanning, use headings where possible and display any items that deserve special attention by setting them off from the text.

Because readers of memos are busy people, you cannot always assume that they will read a memo word for word. Therefore, you should put important information first or highlight it in some way so that it cannot be missed.

In the sample memo that appears on page 640, headings are used to distinguish between information about a company's computer training program and information about the allocation and setup of new computers. The dates and times for each department's training program are broken out into a bulleted list so that they are easy to locate.

BUSINESS MEMO

Commonwealth Press

MEMORANDUM

To: Production, Promotion, and Editorial Assistants
cc: Stephen Chapman
From: Helen Brown
Date: February 28, 1994
Subject: New computers for staff

We will receive the new personal computers next week for the
assistants in production, promotion, and editorial. In preparation,
I would like you to take part in a training program and to
rearrange your work areas to accommodate the new equipment.

Training Program

A computer consultant will teach in-house workshops on how to
use our spreadsheet program. If you have already tried the
program, be prepared to discuss any problems you have
encountered.

Workshops for our three departments will be held in the training
room at the following times:

- Production: Monday, March 14, 10:00 a.m. to 2:00 p.m.
- Promotion: Wednesday, March 16, 10:00 a.m. to
  2:00 p.m.
- Editorial: Friday, March 18, 10:00 a.m. to 2:00 p.m.

Lunch will be provided in the cafeteria. If you cannot attend,
please let me know by March 4.

Allocation and setup

To give everyone access to a computer, the new computers will be
set up as follows: two in the assistants' work space in production;
two in the area outside the conference room for the promotion
assistants; and two in the library for the editorial assistants.

Assistants in all three departments should see me before the end
of the week to discuss preparation of the spaces to accommodate
the new equipment.

PART XII

Grammar Basics

57

Parts of speech

Traditional grammar recognizes eight parts of speech: noun, pronoun, verb, adjective, adverb, preposition, conjunction, and interjection. Many words can function as more than one part of speech. For example, depending on its use in a sentence, the word *paint* can be a noun (*The paint is wet*) or a verb (*Please paint the ceiling next*).

A quick-reference chart of the parts of speech appears on pages 656–58.

57a Nouns

As most schoolchildren can attest, a noun is the name of a person, place, or thing.

> The *cat* in *gloves* catches no *mice.*

In addition to the traditional definition of a noun, grammarians describe a noun as follows:

the kind of word that is often marked with an article (*a spoon, an apple, the newspaper*);

the kind of word that can usually be made plural (*one cat, two cats*) or possessive (*the cat's paw*);

the kind of word that when derived from another word typically takes one of these endings: play*er*, just*ice*, hap-pi*ness*, divis*ion*, guid*ance*, refer*ence*, pave*ment*, child*hood*, king*dom*, agen*cy*, tour*ist*, sincer*ity*, censor*ship*;

the kind of word that can fill one of these positions in a sentence: subject, direct object, indirect object, subject complement, object complement, object of the preposition. (See 58a and 58b.)

Nouns, in other words, may be identified as much by their form and function as by their meaning.

Nouns sometimes function as adjectives modifying other nouns. Because of their dual function, nouns used in this manner may be called *noun/adjectives.*

You can't make a *silk* purse out of a *sow's* ear.

Nouns are classified for a variety of purposes. When capitalization is the issue, we speak of *proper* versus *common nouns* (see 45a). If the problem is one of word choice, we may speak of *concrete* versus *abstract nouns* (see 18b). The distinction between *count nouns* and *noncount nouns* is useful primarily for nonnative speakers of English (see 30a, 30b). The term *collective noun* refers to a set of nouns that may cause problems with subject-verb or pronoun-antecedent agreement (see 21e and 22b).

EXERCISE 57–1

Underline the nouns (and noun/adjectives) in the following sentences. Answers to lettered sentences appear in the back of the book. Example:

Idle <u>hands</u> are the <u>devil's</u> <u>workshop.</u>

a. Clothe an idea in words, and it loses its freedom of movement.
                                              —Egon Freidell
b. Pride is at the bottom of all great mistakes.   —John Ruskin
c. The trouble with being in the rat race is that even if you win, you're still a rat.   —Lily Tomlin
d. The ultimate censorship is the flick of the dial.
                                              —Tom Smothers
e. Figures won't lie, but liars will figure.   —Anonymous

1. Conservatism is the worship of dead revolutions.
   —Clinton Rossiter
2. Luck is a matter of preparation meeting opportunity.
   —Oprah Winfrey
3. Problems are only opportunities in work clothes.
   —Henry Kaiser
4. A woman must have money and a room of her own.
   —Virginia Woolf
5. Prejudice is the child of ignorance.   —William Hazlitt

57b Pronouns

There are thousands of nouns, and new ones come into the language every year. This is not true of pronouns, which number about one hundred and are extremely resistant to change. Most of the pronouns in English are listed in this section.

A pronoun is a word used in place of a noun. Usually the pronoun substitutes for a specific noun, known as its *antecedent.*

When the *wheel* squeaks, *it* is greased.

Although most pronouns function as substitutes for nouns, some can function as adjectives modifying nouns.

This hanging will surely be a lesson to me.

Because they have the form of a pronoun and the function of an adjective, such pronouns may be called *pronoun/adjectives.*

Pronouns are classified as personal, possessive, intensive and reflexive, relative, interrogative, demonstrative, indefinite, and reciprocal.

PERSONAL PRONOUNS Personal pronouns refer to specific persons or things. They always function as noun equivalents.

Singular: I, me, you, she, her, he, him, it

Plural: we, us, you, they, them

POSSESSIVE PRONOUNS   Possessive pronouns indicate ownership.

Singular: my, mine, your, yours, her, hers, his, its

Plural: our, ours, your, yours, their, theirs

Some of these possessive pronouns function as adjectives modifying nouns: *my, your, his, her, its, our, their.*

INTENSIVE AND REFLEXIVE PRONOUNS   Intensive pronouns emphasize a noun or another pronoun (The senator *herself* met us at the door). Reflexive pronouns, which have the same form as intensive pronouns, name a receiver of an action identical with the doer of the action (Paula cut *herself*).

Singular: myself, yourself, himself, herself, itself

Plural: ourselves, yourselves, themselves

RELATIVE PRONOUNS   Relative pronouns introduce subordinate clauses functioning as adjectives (The man *who robbed us* was never caught). In addition to introducing the clause, the relative pronoun, in this case *who,* points back to a noun or pronoun that the clause modifies (*man*). (See 59b.)

who, whom, whose, which, that

Some grammarians also treat *whichever, whoever, whomever, what,* and *whatever* as relative pronouns. These words introduce noun clauses; they do not point back to a noun or pronoun. (See 59b.)

INTERROGATIVE PRONOUNS   Interrogative pronouns introduce questions (*Who* is expected to win the election?).

who, whom, whose, which, what

DEMONSTRATIVE PRONOUNS   Demonstrative pronouns identify or point to nouns. Frequently they function as adjectives (*This* chair is my favorite), but they may also function as noun equivalents (*This* is my favorite chair).

this, that, these, those

INDEFINITE PRONOUNS   Indefinite pronouns refer to nonspecific persons or things. Most are always singular (*everyone, each*); some are always plural (*both, many*); a few may be singular or plural (see 21d). Most indefinite pronouns function as noun equivalents (*Something* is burning), but some can also function as adjectives (*All* campers must check in at the lodge).

all	anything	everyone	nobody	several
another	both	everything	none	some
any	each	few	no one	somebody
anybody	either	many	nothing	someone
anyone	everybody	neither	one	something

RECIPROCAL PRONOUNS   Reciprocal pronouns refer to individual parts of a plural antecedent (By turns, we helped *each other* through college).

each other, one another

NOTE: Pronouns cause a variety of problems for writers. See Pronoun-antecedent agreement (22), Pronoun reference (23), Case of nouns and pronouns (24), and Case of *who* and *whom* (25).

EXERCISE 57–2

Underline the pronouns (and pronoun/adjectives) in the following sentences. Answers to lettered sentences appear in the back of the book. Example:

> Beware of persons <u>who</u> are praised by <u>everyone.</u>

a. Every society honors its live conformists and its dead trouble-makers. — Mignon McLaughlin
b. Watch the faces of those who bow low. — Polish proverb
c. I have written some poetry that I myself don't understand.
         — Carl Sandburg
d. I am firm. You are obstinate. He is a pig-headed fool.
         — Katherine Whitehorn
e. I must govern the clock, not be governed by it. — Golda Meir

1. Doctors can bury their mistakes, but architects can only advise their clients to plant vines. — Frank Lloyd Wright
2. Nothing is interesting if you are not interested.
         — Helen MacInness
3. We will never have friends if we expect to find them without fault.
         — Thomas Fuller
4. The gods help those who help themselves. — Aesop
5. You never find yourself until you face the truth. — Pearl Bailey

57c Verbs

The verb of a sentence usually expresses action (*jump, think*) or being (*is, become*). It is composed of a main verb possibly preceded by one or more helping verbs:

        MV
The best fish *swim* near the bottom.

        HV   **MV**
A marriage *is* not *built* in a day.

        HV **HV**   **MV**
Even God *has been defended* with nonsense.

Notice that words can intervene between the helping and the main verb (*is* not *built*).

Helping verbs

There are twenty-three helping verbs in English: forms of *have, do,* and *be,* which may also function as main verbs; and nine modals, which function only as helping verbs. The forms of *have, do,* and *be* change form to indicate tense; the nine modals do not.

> **FORMS OF *HAVE, DO,* AND *BE***
> have, has, had
>
> do, does, did
>
> be, am, is, are, was, were, being, been
>
> **MODALS**
> can, could, may, might, must, shall, should, will, would

The phrase *ought to* is often classified as a modal as well.

Main verbs

The main verb of a sentence is always the kind of word that would change form if put into these test sentences:

BASE FORM	Usually I (*walk, ride*).
PAST TENSE	Yesterday I (*walked, rode*).
PAST PARTICIPLE	I have (*walked, ridden*) many times before.
PRESENT PARTICIPLE	I am (*walking, riding*) right now.
-S FORM	Usually he/she/it (*walks, rides*).

If a word doesn't change form when slipped into these test sentences, you can be certain that it is not a main verb. For example, the noun *revolution*, though it may seem to suggest an action, can never function as a main verb. Just try to make it behave like one (*Today I revolution . . . Yesterday I revolutioned . . .*) and you'll see why.

When both the past-tense and the past-participle forms of a verb end in *-ed*, the verb is regular (*walked, walked*). Otherwise, the verb is irregular (*rode, ridden*). (See 27a).

The verb *be* is highly irregular, having eight forms instead of the usual five: the base form *be;* the present-tense forms *am, is,* and *are;* the past-tense forms *was* and *were;* the present participle *being;* and the past participle *been.*

Helping verbs combine with the various forms of main verbs to create tenses. For a survey of tenses, see 28a.

NOTE: Some verbs are followed by words that look like prepositions but are so closely associated with the verb that they are a part of its meaning. These words are known as *particles.* Common verb-particle combinations include *bring up, call off, drop off, give in, look up, run into,* and *take off.*

> A lot of parents *pack up* their troubles and *send* them *off* to camp.
> — Raymond Duncan

NOTE: Verbs cause many problems for writers. See Subject-verb agreement (21), Standard English verb forms (27), Verb tense, mood, and voice (28), and ESL problems with verbs (29).

EXERCISE 57–3

Underline the verbs in the following sentences, including helping verbs and particles. If a verb is part of a contraction (such as *is* in *isn't* or *would* in *I'd*), underline only the letters that represent the verb. Answers to lettered sentences appear in the back of the book. Example:

A full cup <u>must be carried</u> steadily.

a. Great persons have not commonly been great scholars.
— Oliver Wendell Holmes, Sr.

b. Without the spice of guilt, can sin be fully savored?
— Alexander Chase

c. One arrow does not bring down two birds.   — Turkish proverb

d. If love is the answer, could you please rephrase the question?
— Lily Tomlin

e. Don't scald your tongue in other people's broth.
— English proverb

1. Do not needlessly endanger your lives until I give you the signal.
— Dwight D. Eisenhower

2. The road to ruin is always kept in good repair.   — Anonymous

3. Love your neighbor, but don't pull down the hedge.
— Swiss proverb

4. I'd rather have roses on my table than diamonds around my neck.   — Emma Goldman

5. He is a fine friend. He stabs you in the front.
— Leonard Louis Levinson

57d Adjectives

An adjective is a word used to modify, or describe, a noun or pronoun. An adjective usually answers one of these questions: Which one? What kind of? How many?

the *lame* elephant [Which elephant?]

rare valuable old stamps [What kind of stamps?]

sixteen candles [How many candles?]

Grammarians also define adjectives according to their form and their typical position in a sentence, as follows:

the kind of word that usually comes before a noun in a noun phrase (a *frisky* puppy, an *amiable young* man);

the kind of word that can follow a linking verb and describe the subject (the ship was *unsinkable;* talk is *cheap*) (see 58b);

the kind of word that when derived from another part of speech typically takes one of these endings: wonder*ful,* court*eous,* luck*y,* fool*ish,* pleasur*able,* colon*ial,* help*less,* defens*ible,* urg*ent,* disgust*ing,* friend*ly,* spectacul*ar,* secret*ive.*

The definite article *the* and the indefinite articles *a* and *an* are also classified as adjectives.

Some possessive, demonstrative, and indefinite pronouns can function as adjectives: *their, its, this* (see 57b).

NOTE: Writers sometimes misuse adjectives (see 26b). Speakers of English as a second language may have trouble placing adjectives correctly (see 31d).

57e Adverbs

An adverb is a word used to modify, or qualify, a verb (or verbal), an adjective, or another adverb. It usually answers one of these questions: When? Where? How? Why? Under what conditions? To what degree?

Pull *gently* at a weak rope. [Pull how?]

Read the best books *first.* [Read when?]

Adverbs that modify a verb are also defined according to their form and their typical position in a sentence, as follows:

the kind of word that can appear nearly anywhere in a sentence and is often movable (he *sometimes* jogged after work; *sometimes* he jogged after work);

the kind of word that when derived from an adjective typically takes an *-ly* ending (nice, nice*ly;* profound, profound*ly*).

Adverbs modifying adjectives or other adverbs usually intensify or limit the intensity of the word they modify.

Be *extremely* good, and you will be *very* lonesome.

Adverbs modifying adjectives and other adverbs are not movable. We can't say "Be good *extremely*" or "*Extremely* be good."

The negators *not* and *never* are classified as adverbs. A word such as *cannot* contains the helping verb *can* and the adverb *not.* A contraction such as *can't* contains the helping verb *can* and a contracted form of the adverb *not.*

Adverbs can modify prepositions (Helen left *just* before midnight), prepositional phrases (The budget is *barely* on target), subordinate clauses (We will try to attend, *especially* if you will be there), or whole sentences (*Certainly* Joe did not intend to insult you).

NOTE: Writers sometimes misuse adverbs (see 26a). Speakers of English as a second language may have trouble placing adverbs correctly (see 31d).

EXERCISE 57–4

Underline the adjectives and circle the adverbs in the following sentences. If a word is a pronoun in form but an adjective in function, treat it as an adjective. Also treat the articles *a, an,* and *the* as adjectives. Answers to lettered sentences are in the back of the book. Example:

A wild goose (never) laid a tame egg.

a. General notions are generally wrong.

— Lady Mary Wortley Montagu

b. The American public is wonderfully tolerant.   — Anonymous
c. Gardening is not a rational act.   — Margaret Atwood
d. Hope is a very thin diet.   — Thomas Shadwell
e. Sleep faster. We need the pillows.   — Yiddish proverb

1. I'd rather be strongly wrong than weakly right.
   — Tallulah Bankhead
2. Their civil discussions were not interesting, and their interesting discussions were not civil.   — Lisa Alther
3. Money will buy a pretty good dog, but it will not buy the wag of its tail.   — Josh Billings
4. A little sincerity is a dangerous thing, and a great deal of it is absolutely fatal.   — Oscar Wilde
5. An old quarrel can be easily revived.   — Italian proverb

57f Prepositions

A preposition is a word placed before a noun or pronoun to form a phrase modifying another word in the sentence. The prepositional phrase nearly always functions as an adjective or as an adverb. (See 59a.)

The road *to hell* is usually paved *with good intentions*.

To hell functions as an adjective, modifying the noun *road;* *with good intentions* functions as an adverb, modifying the verb *is paved.*

There are a limited number of prepositions in English. The most common ones are included in the following list.

about	along	before	between	considering
above	among	behind	beyond	despite
across	around	below	but	down
after	as	beside	by	during
against	at	besides	concerning	except

for	of	past	throughout	unto
from	off	plus	till	up
in	on	regarding	to	upon
inside	onto	respecting	toward	with
into	opposite	round	under	within
like	out	since	underneath	without
near	outside	than	unlike	
next	over	through	until	

Some prepositions are more than one word long. *Along with, as well as, in addition to,* and *next to* are common examples.

NOTE: Except for certain idiomatic uses (see 18d), prepositions cause few problems for native speakers of English. For second-language speakers, however, prepositions can cause considerable difficulty (see 29d and 31f).

57g Conjunctions

Conjunctions join words, phrases, or clauses, and they indicate the relation between the elements joined.

COORDINATING CONJUNCTIONS A coordinating conjunction is used to connect grammatically equal elements. The coordinating conjunctions are *and, but, or, nor, for, so,* and *yet.*

Poverty is the parent of revolution *and* crime.

Admire a little ship, *but* put your cargo in a big one.

In the first sentence, *and* connects two nouns; in the second, *but* connects two independent clauses.

CORRELATIVE CONJUNCTIONS Correlative conjunctions come in pairs: *either . . . or; neither . . . nor; not only . . . but* *also; whether . . . or; both . . . and.* Like coordinating conjunctions, they connect grammatically equal elements.

> *Either* Jack Sprat *or* his wife could eat no fat.

SUBORDINATING CONJUNCTIONS   A subordinating conjunction introduces a subordinate clause and indicates its relation to the rest of the sentence. (See 59b.) The most common subordinating conjunctions are *after, although, as, as if, because, before, even though, if, in order that, rather than, since, so that, than, that, though, unless, until, when, where, whether,* and *while.*

> *If* you want service, serve yourself.

CONJUNCTIVE ADVERBS   A conjunctive adverb may be used with a semicolon to connect independent clauses; it usually serves as a transition between the clauses. The most common conjunctive adverbs are *consequently, finally, furthermore, however, moreover, nevertheless, similarly, then, therefore,* and *thus.* (See the chart on page 658 for a more complete list.)

> When we want to murder a tiger, we call it sport; *however,* when the tiger wants to murder us, we call it ferocity.

NOTE: When punctuating, writers sometimes confuse coordinating conjunctions and conjunctive adverbs. For punctuation with coordinating conjunctions, see 32a and 33a. For punctuation with conjunctive adverbs, see 34b and 32f.

57h Interjections

An interjection is a word used to express surprise or emotion (*Oh! Hey! Wow!*).

Parts of speech

A **NOUN** names a person, place, thing, or idea.

N   N   N

Repetition does not transform a *lie* into *truth*.

A **PRONOUN** substitutes for a noun.

PN PN   PN

When the gods wish to punish *us, they* heed *our* prayers.

Personal pronouns: I, me, you, he, him, she, her, it, we, us, they, them

Possessive pronouns: my, mine, your, yours, her, hers, his, its, our, ours, their, theirs

Intensive and reflexive pronouns: myself, yourself, himself, herself, itself, ourselves, yourselves, themselves

Relative pronouns: that, which, who, whom, whose (*also* what, whatever, whichever, whoever, whomever)

Interrogative pronouns: who, whom, whose, which, what

Demonstrative pronouns: this, that, these, those

Indefinite pronouns: all, another, any, anybody, anyone, anything, both, each, either, everybody, everyone, everything, few, any, neither, nobody, none, no one, nothing, one, several, some, somebody, someone, something

Reciprocal pronouns: each other, one another

A **HELPING VERB** comes before a main verb.

Modals: can, could, may, might, must, shall, should, will, would (*also* ought to)

Forms of be: be, am, is, are, was, were, being, been

Forms of have: have, has, had

Forms of do: do, does, did

(The forms of *be, have,* and *do* may also function as main verbs.)

A **MAIN VERB** asserts action, being, or state of being.

      MV   **HV**   **MV**

Charity *begins* at home but *should* not *end* there.

A main verb will always change form when put into these positions in sentences:

Usually I _____ .	(walk, ride)
Yesterday I _____ .	(walked, rode)
I have _____ many times before.	(walked, ridden)
I am _____ right now.	(walking, riding)
Usually he _____ .	(walks, rides)

There are eight forms of the highly irregular verb *be:* be, am, is, are, was, were, being, been.

An **ADJECTIVE** modifies a noun or pronoun, usually answering one of these questions: Which one? What kind of? How many? The articles *a, an,* and *the* are also adjectives.

ADJ   **ADJ**

Useless laws weaken *necessary* ones.

An **ADVERB** modifies a verb, adjective, or adverb, usually answering one of these questions: When? Where? Why? How? Under what conditions? To what degree?

ADV   **ADV**

People think *too historically.*

Parts of speech (continued)

A **PREPOSITION** indicates the relationship between the noun or pronoun that follows it and another word in the sentence.

     P   P

A journey *of* a thousand miles begins *with* a single step.

Common prepositions: about, above, across, after, against, along, among, around, as, at, before, behind, below, beside, besides, between, beyond, but, by, concerning, considering, despite, down, during, except, for, from, in, inside, into, like, near, next, of, off, on, onto, opposite, out, outside, over, past, plus, regarding, respecting, round, since, than, through, throughout, till, to, toward, under, underneath, unlike, until, unto, up, upon, with, without

A **CONJUNCTION** connects words or word groups.

Coordinating conjunctions: and, but, or, nor, for, so, yet

Subordinating conjunctions: after, although, as, as if, because, before, even though, how, if, in order that, once, rather than, since, so that, than, that, though, unless, until, when, where, whether, while, why

Correlative conjunctions: either . . . or, neither . . . nor, not only . . . but also, both . . . and, whether . . . or

Conjunctive adverbs: accordingly, also, anyway, besides, certainly, consequently, conversely, finally, furthermore, hence, however, incidentally, indeed, instead, likewise, meanwhile, moreover, nevertheless, next, nonetheless, otherwise, similarly, specifically, still, subsequently, then, therefore, thus

An **INTERJECTION** expresses surprise or emotion. (Oh! Wow! Hey! Hooray!)

58

Sentence patterns

Most English sentences flow from subject to verb to any objects or complements. The vast majority of sentences conform to one of these five patterns:

> subject / verb / subject complement
>
> subject / verb / direct object
>
> subject / verb / indirect object / direct object
>
> subject / verb / direct object / object complement
>
> subject / verb

Adverbial modifiers (single words, phrases, or clauses) may be added to any of these patterns, and they may appear nearly anywhere — at the beginning, the middle, or the end.

Predicate is the grammatical term given to the verb plus its objects, complements, and adverbial modifiers.

For a quick-reference chart of sentence patterns, see page 667.

58a Subjects

The subject of a sentence names who or what the sentence is about. The *complete subject* is usually composed of a *simple subject,* always a noun or pronoun, plus any words or word groups modifying the simple subject. To find the complete subject, ask Who? or What?, insert the verb, and finish the question. The answer is the complete subject.

┌── COMPLETE SUBJECT ──┐
The purity of a revolution usually lasts about two weeks.

Who or what lasts about two weeks? *The purity of a revolution.*

┌─────── **COMPLETE SUBJECT** ───────┐
Historical books that contain no lies are extremely tedious.

Who or what are extremely tedious? *Historical books that contain no lies.*

COMPLETE SUBJECT
┌─────────┐
In every country the sun rises in the morning.

Who or what rises in the morning? *The sun.* Notice that *In every country the sun* is not a sensible answer to the question. *In every country* is a prepositional phrase modifying the verb *rises.* Since sentences frequently open with such modifiers, it is not safe to assume that the subject must always appear first in a sentence.

To find the simple subject, strip away all modifiers in the complete subject. This includes single-word modifiers such as *the* and *historical*, phrases such as *of a revolution*, and subordinate clauses such as *that contain no lies.*

┌ **SS** ┐
The purity of a revolution usually lasts about two weeks.

┌ **SS** ┐
Historical books that contain no lies are extremely tedious.

┌ **SS** ┐
In every country *the sun* rises in the morning.

A sentence may have a compound subject containing two or more simple subjects joined with a coordinating conjunction such as *and, but,* or *or.*

┌── **SS** ──┐   ┌── **SS** ──┐
Much industry and little conscience make us rich.

Occasionally a verb's subject is understood but not present in the sentence. In imperative sentences, which give advice or commands, the subject is understood to be *you.*

[*You*] Hitch your wagon to a star.

Although the subject ordinarily comes before the verb, occasionally it does not. When a sentence begins with *There is* or *There are* (or *There was* or *There were*), the subject follows the verb. The word *There* is an expletive in such constructions, an empty word serving merely to get the sentence started.

┌── **ss** ──┐
There is *no substitute for victory.*

Occasionally a writer will invert a sentence for effect.

┌─ **ss** ─┐
Happy is *the nation that has no history.*

Happy is an adjective, so it cannot be the subject. Turn this sentence around and its structure becomes obvious: *The nation that has no history is happy.*

In questions, the subject frequently appears in an unusual position, sandwiched between parts of the verb.

┌ **ss** ┐
Do *married men* make the best husbands?

Turn the question into a statement, and the words will appear in their usual order: *Married men do make the best husbands.* (*Do make* is the verb.)

NOTE: The ability to recognize the subject of a sentence will help you edit for a variety of problems such as Sentence fragments (19), Subject-verb agreement (21), and Case of nouns and pronouns (24). If English is not your native language, see also 31a and 31b.

EXERCISE 58–1

In the following sentences, underline the complete subject and write *ss* above the simple subject(s). If the subject is an understood *you*, insert it in parentheses. Answers to lettered sentences appear in the back of the book. Example:

> *ss*   *ss*
> Fools and their money are soon parted.

  a. A spoiled child never loves its mother.   — Sir Henry Taylor
  b. To some lawyers, all facts are created equal.
                                      — Felix Frankfurter
  c. Speak softly and carry a big stick.   — Theodore Roosevelt
  d. There is nothing permanent except change.   — Heraclitus
  e. The only difference between a rut and a grave is their dimensions.   — Ellen Glasgow

  1. The secret of being a bore is to tell everything.   — Voltaire
  2. Don't be humble. You're not that great.   — Golda Meir
  3. In every country dogs bite.   — English proverb
  4. The wind and the waves are always on the side of the ablest navigators.   — Anonymous
  5. There are no signposts in the sea.   — Vita Sackville-West

58b Verbs, objects, and complements

Section 57c explains how to find the verb of a sentence, which consists of a main verb possibly preceded by one or more helping verbs. A sentence's verb is classified as linking, transitive, or intransitive, depending on the kinds of objects or complements the verb can (or cannot) take.

Linking verbs and subject complements

Linking verbs link the subject to a subject complement, a word or word group that completes the meaning of the subject by renaming or describing it. If the subject complement renames the subject, it is a noun or noun equivalent (sometimes called a *predicate noun*).

```
┌──────────── S ────────────┐┌─ V ─┐┌─ SC ─┐
The handwriting on the wall  may  be   a forgery.
```

If the subject complement describes the subject, it is an adjective or adjective equivalent (sometimes called a *predicate adjective*).

```
S   V   SC
Love is  blind.
```

Whenever they appear as main verbs (rather than helping verbs), the forms of *be* — *be, am, is, are, was, were, being, been*—usually function as linking verbs. In the preceding examples, for instance, the main verbs are *be* and *is.*

Verbs such as *appear, become, feel, grow, look, make, seem, smell, sound,* and *taste* are sometimes linking, depending on the sense of the sentence.

```
                    ┌── S ──┐┌── V ──┐┌ SC ┐
At the touch of love, everyone becomes a poet.
```

```
            ┌── S ──┐        ┌ V ┐┌ SC ┐
At first sight, original art often looks ugly.
```

When you suspect that a verb such as *becomes* or *looks* is linking, check to see if the word or words following it rename or describe the subject. In the sample sentences, *a poet* renames *everyone,* and *ugly* describes *art.*

Transitive verbs and direct objects

A transitive verb takes a direct object, a word or word group that names a receiver of the action.

```
┌──── S ────┐┌─ V ─┐┌────── DO ──────┐
The little snake studies the ways of the big serpent.
```

In such sentences, the subject and verb alone will seem incomplete. Once we have read "The little snake studies," for example, we want to know the rest: The little snake studies what? The answer to the question What? (or Whom?) is the complete direct object: *the ways of the big serpent.* The simple direct object is always a noun or pronoun, in this case *ways.* To find it, simply strip away all modifiers.

Transitive verbs usually appear in the active voice, with the subject doing the action and a direct object receiving the action. Active-voice sentences can be transformed into the passive voice, with the subject receiving the action instead. See 58c.

Transitive verbs, indirect objects,
and direct objects

The direct object of a transitive verb is sometimes preceded by an indirect object, a noun or pronoun telling to whom or for whom the action of the sentence is done.

```
S    V   IO ┌ DO ┐    S ┌─ V ─┐ IO ┌─ DO ┐
You show me a hero, and I will write you a tragedy.
```

The simple indirect object is always a noun or pronoun. To test for an indirect object, insert the word *to* or *for* before the word or word group in question. If the sentence makes sense, the word or word group is an indirect object.

You show [to] me a hero, and I will write [for] you a tragedy.

An indirect object may be turned into a prepositional phrase using *to* or *for: You show a hero to me, and I will write a tragedy for you.*

Only certain transitive verbs take indirect objects. Common examples are *give, ask, bring, find, get, hand, lend, offer, pay, pour, promise, read, send, show, teach, tell, throw,* and *write.*

Transitive verbs, direct objects, and object complements

The direct object of a transitive verb is sometimes followed by an object complement, a word or word group that completes the direct object's meaning by renaming or describing it.

```
  ┌─ S ─┐      ┌ V ┐┌─ DO ─┐┌───────────── OC ─────────────┐
```
People now call a spade an agricultural implement.

```
  ┌─ S ─┐┌─ V ─┐┌──── DO ────┐┌─ OC ─┐
```
Love makes all hard hearts gentle.

When the object complement renames the direct object, it is a noun or pronoun (such as *implement*). When it describes the direct object, it is an adjective (such as *gentle*).

Intransitive verbs

Intransitive verbs take no objects or complements. Their pattern is always subject/verb.

```
     S      V
```
Money talks.

```
  ┌───── S ─────┐      ┌V┐
```
Revolutions never go backward.

Nothing receives the actions of talking and going in these sentences, so the verbs are intransitive. Notice that such verbs may or may not be followed by adverbial modifiers. In the second sentence, *backward* is an adverb modifying *go*.

NOTE: The dictionary will tell you whether a verb is transitive or intransitive. Some verbs have both transitive and intransitive functions.

> **TRANSITIVE**   Sandra flew her Cessna over the canyon.
>
> **INTRANSITIVE**   A bald eagle flew overhead.

In the first example, *flew* has a direct object that receives the action: *her Cessna*. In the second example, the verb is followed by an adverb (*overhead*), not by a direct object.

EXERCISE 58–2

Label the subject complements, direct objects, indirect objects, and object complements in the following sentences. If an object or complement consists of more than one word, bracket and label all of it. Answers to lettered sentences appear in the back of the book. Example:

$$DO \quad \overset{OC}{\frown}$$

All work and no play make Jack a dull boy.

a. The best mind-altering drug is truth.　　　　— Lily Tomlin
b. No one tests the depth of a river with both feet.
　　　　　　　　　　　　　　　　　　— West African proverb
c. All looks yellow to a jaundiced eye.　　　　— Alexander Pope
d. Luck never made a man [or a woman] wise.
　　　　　　　　　　　　　　　　　　— Seneca the Younger
e. You show me a capitalist and I will show you a bloodsucker.
　　　　　　　　　　　　　　　　　　— Malcolm X

1. Accomplishments have no color.　　　　— Leontyne Price
2. Gardening is an exercise in optimism.　　　— Marina Schinz
3. The mob has many heads but no brains.　　— Thomas Fuller
4. I never promised you a rose garden.　　　— Hannah Green
5. Moral indignation is jealousy with a halo.　　— H. G. Wells

Sentence patterns

Subject / linking verb / subject complement

┌─── S ───┐ V ┌─── SC ───┐
Advertising is legalized lying. [*Legalized lying* renames *Advertising.*]

┌──── S ────┐ V ┌─ SC ─┐
Great intellects are skeptical. [*Skeptical* describes *Great intellects.*]

Subject / transitive verb / direct object

┌── S ──┐ ┌── V ──┐ ┌ DO ┐
A stumble may prevent a fall.

Subject / transitive verb / indirect object / direct object

S   V   IO ┌── DO ──┐
Fate gives us our relatives.

Subject / transitive verb / direct object / object complement

┌── S ──┐┌─ V ─┐DO   OC
Our fears do make us traitors. [*Traitors* renames *us.*]

┌─ S ─┐ V ┌── DO ──┐ OC
The pot calls the kettle black. [*Black* describes *the kettle.*]

Subject / intransitive verb

S   V
Time flies.

58c Pattern variations

Although most sentences follow one of the five patterns in the chart on this page, variations of these patterns commonly occur in questions, commands, sentences with delayed subjects, and passive transformations.

Questions and commands

Questions are sometimes patterned in normal word order, with the subject preceding the verb.

> S ⌐— V —⌐
> Who will take the first step?

Just as frequently, however, the pattern of a question is inverted, with the subject appearing between the helping and main verbs or after the verb.

> HV   S   MV
> Will you take the first step?

> V ⌐——— S ———⌐
> Why is the first step so difficult?

In commands, the subject of the sentence is an understood *you.*

> [You] Keep your mouth shut and your eyes open.

Sentences with delayed subjects

Writers sometimes choose to delay the subject of a sentence to achieve a special effect such as suspense or humor.

> V ⌐——— S ———⌐
> Behind the phony tinsel of Hollywood lies the real tinsel.

The subject of the sentence is also delayed in sentences opening with the expletives *There* or *It.* When used as expletives, the words *There* and *It* have no strict grammatical function; they serve merely to get the sentence started.

> V ⌐———————— S ————————⌐
> There are many paths to the top of the mountain.

```
V              ┌──────── S ────────┐
```
It is not good to wake a sleeping lion.

The subject in the second example is an infinitive phrase. (See 59c.)

Passive transformations

Transitive verbs, those that can take direct objects, usually appear in the active voice. In the active voice, the subject does the action and a direct object receives the action.

```
                      S              V  ┌──── DO ────┐
```
ACTIVE   The early *bird* sometimes *catches the early worm.*

Sentences in the active voice may be transformed into the passive voice, with the subject receiving the action instead.

```
          ┌──────── S ───────┐ HV        ┌─ MV ─┐
```
PASSIVE   *The early worm is* sometimes *caught* by the early
bird.

What was once the direct object (*the early worm*) has become the subject in the passive-voice transformation, and the original subject appears in a prepositional phrase beginning with *by.* The *by* phrase is frequently omitted in passive-voice constructions.

PASSIVE   The early worm is sometimes caught.

Verbs in the passive voice can be identified by their form alone. The main verb is always a past participle, such as *caught* (see 57c), preceded by a form of *be* (*be, am, is, are, was, were, being, been*): *is caught.* Sometimes adverbs intervene (*is* sometimes *caught*).

NOTE: Writers sometimes use the passive voice when the active voice would be more appropriate (see 14a). For a review of the uses of the active and the passive voice, see 28c.

59

Subordinate word groups

Subordinate word groups include prepositional phrases, subordinate clauses, verbal phrases, appositives, and absolutes. Not all of these word groups are subordinate in quite the same way. Some are subordinate because they are modifiers; others function as noun equivalents, not as modifiers.

59a Prepositional phrases

A prepositional phrase begins with a preposition such as *at, by, for, from, in, of, on, to,* or *with* (see 57f) and usually ends with a noun or noun equivalent: *on the table, for him, with great fanfare.* The noun or noun equivalent is known as the *object of the preposition.*

Prepositional phrases function either as adjectives modifying a noun or pronoun or as adverbs modifying a verb, an adjective, or another adverb. When functioning as an adjective, a prepositional phrase nearly always appears immediately following the noun or pronoun it modifies.

Variety is the spice *of life.*

Adjective phrases usually answer one or both of the questions Which one? and What kind of? If we ask Which spice? or What kind of spice? we get a sensible answer: the spice *of life.*

Adverbial prepositional phrases that modify the verb can appear nearly anywhere in a sentence.

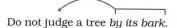

Do not judge a tree *by its bark*.

Tyranny will *in time* lead to revolution.

To the ant, a few drops of rain are a flood.

Adverbial word groups usually answer one of these questions: When? Where? How? Why? Under what conditions? To what degree?

> Do not judge a tree *how? By its bark*.
>
> Tyranny will lead to revolution *when? In time*.
>
> A few drops of rain are a flood *under what conditions? To the ant*.

If a prepositional phrase is movable, you can be certain that it is adverbial; adjectival prepositional phrases are wedded to the words they modify. At least some of the time, adverbials can be moved to other positions in the sentence.

> *By their fruits* you shall know them.
>
> You shall know them *by their fruits*.

In questions and subordinate clauses, a preposition may appear after its object.

> *What* are you afraid *of?*
>
> We avoided the clerk *whom* John had warned us *about*.

NOTE: The ability to recognize the object of a preposition will help you edit for problems with pronoun case (such as *I* versus *me*). (See 24.)

EXERCISE 59–1

Underline the prepositional phrases in the following sentences. Be prepared to explain the function of each phrase. Answers to lettered sentences appear in the back of the book. Example:

You can stroke people <u>with words</u>. *(Adverbial phrase modifying canstroke)*

a. Laughter is a tranquilizer with no side effects.
— Arnold Glasgow

b. Any mother could perform the job of several air traffic controllers with ease.
— Lisa Alther

c. She wears her morals like a loose garment.
— Langston Hughes

d. You can tell the ideals of a nation by its advertising.
— Norman Douglas

e. In prosperity, no altar smokes.
— Italian proverb

1. We know that the road to freedom has always been stalked by death.
— Angela Davis

2. A society of sheep produces a government of wolves.
— Bertrand de Jouvenal

3. Some people feel with their heads and think with their hearts.
— G. C. Lichtenberg

4. In love and war, all is fair.
— Francis Edward Smedley

5. On their side, the workers had only the Constitution. The other side had bayonets.
— Mother Jones

59b Subordinate clauses

Subordinate clauses are patterned like sentences, having subjects and verbs and sometimes objects or complements. But they function within sentences as adjectives, adverbs, or nouns. They cannot stand alone as complete sentences.

A subordinate clause usually begins with a subordinating conjunction or a relative pronoun.

SUBORDINATING CONJUNCTIONS

after	before	rather than	though	where
although	even though	since	unless	whether
as	if	so that	until	while
as if	how	than	when	why
because	in order that	that		

RELATIVE PRONOUNS

that	who	whom	whose	which

The chart on page 677 classifies these words according to the kinds of clauses (adjective, adverb, or noun) they introduce.

Adjective clauses

Like other word groups functioning as adjectives, adjective clauses modify nouns or pronouns. An adjective clause nearly always appears immediately following the noun or pronoun it modifies.

The arrow *that has left the bow* never returns.

Relatives are persons *who live too near and visit too often.*

To test whether a subordinate clause functions as an adjective, ask the adjective questions: Which one? What kind of? The answer should make sense. Which arrow? The arrow *that has left the bow.* What kind of persons? Persons *who live too near and visit too often.*

Most adjective clauses begin with a relative pronoun (*who, whom, whose, which,* or *that*), which marks them as grammatically subordinate. In addition to introducing the clause, the relative pronoun points back to the noun that the clause modifies.

The fur *that warms a monarch* once warmed a bear.

Relative pronouns are sometimes "understood."

> The things [*that*] we know best are the things [*that*] we haven't been taught.

Occasionally an adjective clause is introduced by a relative adverb, usually *when, where,* or *why.*

> Home is the place *where you slip in the tub and break your neck.*

The parts of an adjective clause are often arranged as in sentences (subject/verb/object or complement).

>   **S**   **V** **DO**
> We often forgive the people *who bore us.*

Frequently, however, the object or complement appears first, violating the normal order of subject/verb/object.

>   **DO** **S** **V**
> We rarely forgive those *whom we bore.*

To determine the subject of a clause, ask Who? or What? and insert the verb. Don't be surprised if the answer is an echo, as in the first adjective clause above: Who bore us? *Who.* To find any objects or complements, read the subject and the verb and then ask Who? Whom? or What? Again, be prepared for a possible echo, as in the second adjective clause: We bore whom? *Whom.*

NOTE: For punctuation of adjective clauses, see 32e and 33e. If English is not your native language, see 31c for a common problem with adjective clauses.

Adverb clauses

Adverb clauses usually modify verbs, in which case they may appear nearly anywhere in a sentence—at the beginning, at the end, or in the middle. Like other adverbial word groups, they tell when, where, why, under what conditions, or to what degree an action occurred or a situation existed.

When the well is dry, we know the worth of water.

Venice would be a fine city *if it were only drained.*

When do we know the worth of water? *When the well is dry.* Under what conditions would Venice be a fine city? *If it were only drained.*

Unlike adjective clauses, adverb clauses are frequently movable. In the preceding example sentences, for instance, the adverb clauses can be moved without affecting the meaning of the sentences.

We know the worth of water *when the well is dry.*

If it were only drained, Venice would be a fine city.

When an adverb clause modifies an adjective or an adverb, it is not movable; it must appear next to the word it modifies. In the following examples the *because* clause modifies the adjective *angry,* and the *than* clause modifies the adverb *faster.*

Angry *because the mayor had not kept his promises,* we worked for his defeat.

Joan can run faster *than I can bicycle.*

Adverb clauses always begin with a subordinating conjunction (see the chart on page 677 for a list). Subordinating conjunctions introduce clauses and express their relation to the rest of the sentence.

Adverb clauses are sometimes elliptical, with some of their words being "understood."

When [it is] painted, the room will look larger.

Noun clauses

Because they do not function as modifiers, noun clauses are not subordinate in the same sense as are adjective and adverb clauses. They are called subordinate only because they cannot stand alone: They must function within a sentence, always as nouns.

A noun clause functions just like a single-word noun, usually as a subject, subject complement, direct object, or object of a preposition.

┌————— **S** —————┐
Whoever gossips to you will gossip of you.

┌————— **DO** —————┐
We never forget *that we buried the hatchet.*

A noun clause usually begins with one of the following words: *how, that, which, who, whoever, whom, whomever, what, whatever, when, where, whether, whose, why* or with one of the following subordinating conjunctions: *how, when, where, whether, why.* The subordinating word may or may not play a significant role in the clause. In the preceding example sentences, *whoever* is the subject of its clause, but *that* does not perform a function in its clause.

As with adjective clauses, the parts of a noun clause may appear out of their normal order (subject/verb/object).

        DO   **S**   **V**
Talent is *what you possess.*

The parts of a noun clause may also appear in their normal order.

        S   **V**   **DO**
Genius is *what possesses you.*

Words that introduce
subordinate clauses

WORDS INTRODUCING ADVERB CLAUSES

Subordinating conjunctions: after, although, as, as if, because, before, even though, if, in order that, rather than, since, so that, than, that, though, unless, until, when, where, whether, while

WORDS INTRODUCING ADJECTIVE CLAUSES

Relative pronouns: that, which, who, whom, whose

Relative adverbs: when, where, why

WORDS INTRODUCING NOUN CLAUSES

Relative pronouns: that, who, whom, whose

Other pronouns: whoever, whomever, what, whatever, whichever

Subordinating conjunctions: how, if, when, whenever, where, wherever, whether, why

---

EXERCISE 59–2

Underline the subordinate clauses in the following sentences. Be prepared to explain the function of each clause. Answers to lettered sentences appear in the back of the book. Example:

Dig a well <u>before you are thirsty.</u> *(Adverbial clause modifying Dig)*

a. It is hard to fight an enemy who has outposts in your head.
— Sally Kempton

b. An idea that is not dangerous is unworthy to be called an idea at all.   — Elbert Hubbard

c. When I am an old woman, I shall wear purple. — Jenny Joseph

d. Dreams say what they mean, but they don't say it in daytime language.   — Gail Godwin

e. A fraud is not perfect unless it is practiced on clever persons.
    — Arab proverb

1. What history teaches us is that we have never learned anything from it.   — Georg Wilhelm Hegel

2. When a dog is drowning, everyone offers him a drink.
    — George Herbert

3. Whoever named it necking was a poor judge of anatomy.
    — Groucho Marx

4. Science commits suicide when it adopts a creed.
    — T. H. Huxley

5. He gave her a look that you could have poured on a waffle.
    — Ring Lardner

59c Verbal phrases

A verbal is a verb form that does not function as the verb of a clause. Verbals include infinitives (the word *to* plus the base form of the verb), present participles (the *-ing* form of the verb), and past participles (the verb form usually ending in *-d, -ed, -n, -en,* or *-t*). (See 27a and 57c.)

INFINITIVE	PRESENT PARTICIPLE	PAST PARTICIPLE
to dream	dreaming	dreamed
to choose	choosing	chosen
to build	building	built
to grow	growing	grown

Instead of functioning as the verb of a clause, a verbal or a verbal phrase functions as an adjective, a noun, or an adverb.

ADJECTIVE   *Stolen* grapes are especially sweet.

NOUN   Continual *dripping* wears away a stone.

ADVERB   Were we born *to suffer?*

Verbals can take objects, complements, and modifiers to form verbal phrases; the phrases usually lack subjects.

Living well is the best revenge.

Governments exist *to protect the rights of minorities.*

The verbal *Living* is followed by an adverb modifier, *well;* the verbal *to protect* is followed by a direct object, *the rights of minorities.*

Like single-word verbals, verbal phrases function as adjectives, nouns, or adverbs. In the sentences just given, for example, *living well* functions as a noun used as the subject of the sentence, and *to protect the rights of minorities* functions as an adverb, answering the question Why?

Verbal phrases are ordinarily classified as participles, gerunds, and infinitives. This classification is based partly on form (whether the verbal is a present participle, a past participle, or an infinitive) and partly on function (whether the whole phrase functions as an adjective, a noun, or an adverb).

NOTE: For advice on editing dangling verbal phrases, see 12e.

Participial phrases

Participial phrases always function as adjectives. Their verbals are either present participles, always ending in *-ing*, or past participles, frequently ending in *-d*, *-ed*, *-n*, *-en*, or *-t* (see 27a).

Participial phrases frequently appear immediately following the noun or pronoun they modify.

Congress shall make no law *abridging the freedom of speech or of the press.*

Truth *kept in the dark* will never save the world.

Unlike other adjectival word groups, however, which must always follow the noun or pronoun they modify, participial phrases are often movable. They can precede the word they modify.

Being weak, foxes are distinguished by superior tact.

They may also appear at some distance from the word they modify.

History is something that never happened, *written by someone who wasn't there.*

Gerund phrases

Gerund phrases are built around present participles (verb forms ending in *-ing*), and they always function as nouns: usually as subjects, subject complements, direct objects, or objects of a preposition.

— S —
Justifying a fault doubles it.

— SC —
The secret of education is *respecting the pupil.*

— DO —
Kleptomaniacs can't help *helping themselves.*

┌───── **OBJ OF PREP** ─────┐
The hen is an egg's way of *producing another egg.*

Infinitive phrases

Infinitive phrases, usually constructed around *to* plus the base form of the verb (*to call, to drink*), can function as nouns, as adjectives, or as adverbs.

When functioning as a noun, an infinitive phrase may appear in almost any noun slot in a sentence, usually as a subject, subject complement, or direct object.

┌─────── **S** ───────┐
To side with truth is noble.

┌──────────── **DO** ────────────┐
Never try *to leap a chasm in two jumps.*

Infinitive phrases functioning as adjectives usually appear immediately following the noun or pronoun they modify.

We do not have the right *to abandon the poor.*

The infinitive phrase modifies the noun *right.* Which right? *The right to abandon the poor.*

Adverbial infinitive phrases usually qualify the meaning of the verb, telling when, where, how, why, under what conditions, or to what degree an action occurred.

He cut off his nose *to spite his face.*

Why did he cut off his nose? *To spite his face.*

NOTE: In some constructions, the infinitive is unmarked; in other words, the *to* does not appear: *No one can make you* [*to*] *feel inferior without your consent.* (See 29c.)

EXERCISE 59–3

Underline the verbal phrases in the following sentences. Be prepared to explain the function of each phrase. Answers to lettered sentences appear in the back of the book. Example:

> Do you want <u>to be a writer?</u> Then write. *(Infinitive phrase used as direct object of Do want)*

a. The best substitute for experience is being sixteen.
  —Raymond Duncan

b. Fate tried to conceal him by naming him Smith.
  —Oliver Wendell Holmes, Jr.

c. Scandal is gossip made tedious by morality. —Oscar Wilde

d. Being a philosopher, I have a problem for every solution.
  —Robert Zend

e. For years I wanted to be older, and now I am.
  —Margaret Atwood

1. The thing generally raised on city land is taxes.
  —C. D. Warner

2. Do not use a hatchet to remove a fly from your friend's forehead.
  —Chinese proverb

3. He has the gall of a shoplifter returning an item for a refund.
  —W. I. E. Gates

4. I don't deserve any credit for turning the other cheek as my tongue is always in it.   —Flannery O'Connor

5. Concealing a disease is no way to cure it.
  —Ethiopian proverb

59d Appositive phrases

Though strictly speaking they are not subordinate word groups, appositive phrases function somewhat as adjectives do, to describe nouns or pronouns. Instead of modifying nouns or pronouns, however, appositive phrases rename them. In form they are nouns or noun equivalents.

Appositives are said to be "in apposition" to the nouns or pronouns they rename.

> Politicians, *acrobats at heart,* can sit on a fence and yet keep both ears to the ground.

Acrobats at heart is in apposition to the noun *politicians.*

59e Absolute phrases

An absolute phrase modifies a whole clause or sentence, not just one word, and it may appear nearly anywhere in the sentence. It consists of a noun or noun equivalent usually followed by a participial phrase.

> *His words dipped in honey,* the senator mesmerized the crowd.
>
> The senator mesmerized the crowd, *his words dipped in honey.*

60

Sentence types

Sentences are classified in two ways: according to their structure (simple, compound, complex, and compound-complex) and according to their purpose (declarative, imperative, interrogative, and exclamatory).

60a Sentence structures

Depending on the number and types of clauses they contain, sentences are classified as simple, compound, complex, or compound-complex.

Clauses come in two varieties: independent and subordinate. An independent clause is a full sentence pattern that does not function within another sentence pattern: It contains a subject and verb plus any objects, complements, and modifiers of that verb, and it either stands alone or could stand alone. A subordinate clause is a full sentence pattern that functions within a sentence as an adjective, an adverb, or a noun but that cannot stand alone as a complete sentence. (See 59b.)

Simple sentences

A simple sentence is one independent clause with no subordinate clauses.

┌─────────── **INDEPENDENT CLAUSE** ───────────┐
Without music, life would be a mistake.

This sentence contains a subject (*life*), a verb (*would be*), a complement (*a mistake*), and an adverbial modifier (*Without music*).

A simple sentence may contain compound elements — a compound subject, verb, or object, for example — but it does not contain more than one full sentence pattern. The following sentence is simple because its two verbs (*enters* and *spreads*) share a subject (*Evil*).

┌─────────── **INDEPENDENT CLAUSE** ───────────┐
Evil enters like a needle and spreads like an oak.

Compound sentences

A compound sentence is composed of two or more independent clauses with no subordinate clauses. The independent clauses are usually joined with a comma and a coordinating conjunction (*and, but, or, nor, for, so, yet*) or with a semicolon. (See 8.)

┌─ **INDEPENDENT CLAUSE** ─┐   ┌─── **INDEPENDENT CLAUSE** ───┐
One arrow is easily broken, but you can't break a bundle of ten.

┌──── **INDEPENDENT CLAUSE** ────┐ ┌─ **INDEPENDENT** ─
We are born brave, trusting, and greedy; most of us have
─ **CLAUSE** ───┐
remained greedy.

Complex sentences

A complex sentence is composed of one independent clause
with one or more subordinate clauses. (See 59b.)

SUBORDINATE
┌──── **CLAUSE** ───┐
ADJECTIVE They that sow in tears shall reap in joy.

SUBORDINATE
┌──── **CLAUSE** ───┐
ADVERB If you scatter thorns, don't go barefoot.

┌──────── **SUBORDINATE CLAUSE** ────────┐
NOUN What the scientists have in their briefcases is
terrifying.

Compound-complex sentences

A compound-complex sentence contains at least two independent clauses and at least one subordinate clause. The following sentence contains two full sentence patterns that can
stand alone.

┌ **INDEPENDENT CLAUSE** ┐   ┌─ **INDEPENDENT CLAUSE** ─┐
Tell me what you eat, and I will tell you what you are.

And each independent clause contains a subordinate clause,
making the sentence both compound and complex.

```
 ┌──────── IND CL ────────┐   ┌──────── IND CL ────────┐
 ┌ ┌─── SUB CL ──┐        ┌     ┌─── SUB CL ──┐
```
Tell me what you eat, and I will tell you what you are.

60b Sentence purposes

Writers use declarative sentences to make statements, imperative sentences to issue requests or commands, interrogative sentences to ask questions, and exclamatory sentences to make exclamations.

DECLARATIVE	The echo always has the last word.
IMPERATIVE	Love your neighbor.
INTERROGATIVE	Are second thoughts always wisest?
EXCLAMATORY	I want to wash the flag, not burn it!

EXERCISE 60–1

Identify the following sentences as simple, compound, complex, or compound-complex. Be prepared to identify the subordinate clauses and classify them according to their function: adjective, adverb, or noun. (See 59b.) Answers to lettered sentences appear in the back of the book. Example:

The frog in the well knows nothing of the ocean. *simple*

    a. A primitive artist is an amateur whose work sells.
                                        — Grandma Moses
    b. My folks didn't come over on the Mayflower; they were there to meet the boat.   — Will Rogers
    c. No pessimist ever discovered the secrets of the stars, or sailed to an uncharted land, or opened a new heaven to the human spirit.
                                      — Helen Keller
    d. If you don't go to other people's funerals, they won't go to yours.
                                      — Clarence Day

e. Tell us your phobias, and we will tell you what you are afraid of.
— Robert Benchley

1. Seek simplicity and distrust it.   — Alfred North Whitehead
2. Those who write clearly have readers; those who write obscurely have commentators.   — Albert Camus
3. The children are always the chief victims of social chaos.
— Agnes Meyer
4. Morality cannot be legislated, but behavior can be regulated.
— Martin Luther King, Jr.
5. When an elephant is in trouble, even a frog will kick him.
— Hindu proverb

Glossary of Usage

This glossary includes words commonly confused (such as *accept* and *except*), words commonly misused (such as *hopefully*), and words that are nonstandard (such as *hisself*). It also lists colloquialisms and jargon. Colloquialisms are expressions that may be appropriate in informal speech but are inappropriate in formal writing. Jargon is needlessly technical or pretentious language that is inappropriate in most contexts. If an item is not listed here, consult the index. For irregular verbs (such as *sing, sang, sung*), see 27a. For idiomatic use of prepositions, see 18d.

a, an Use *an* before a vowel sound, *a* before a consonant sound: *an apple, a peach.* Problems sometimes arise with words beginning with *h*. If the *h* is silent, the word begins with a vowel sound, so use *an: an hour, an heir, an honest senator, an honorable deed.* If the *h* is pronounced, the word begins with a consonant sound, so use *a: a hospital, a hymn, a historian, a hotel.*

accept, except *Accept* is a verb meaning "to receive." *Except* is usually a preposition meaning "excluding." *I will accept all the packages except that one. Except* is also a verb meaning "to exclude." *Please except that item from the list.*

adapt, adopt *Adapt* means "to adjust or become accustomed"; it is usually followed by *to. Adopt* means "to take as one's own." *Our family adopted a Vietnamese orphan, who quickly adapted to his new surroundings.*

adverse, averse   *Adverse* means "unfavorable." *Averse* means "opposed" or "reluctant"; it is usually followed by *to*. *I am averse to your proposal because it could have an adverse impact on the economy.*

advice, advise   *Advice* is a noun, *advise* a verb. *We advise you to follow John's advice.*

affect, effect   *Affect* is usually a verb meaning "to influence." *Effect* is usually a noun meaning "result." *The drug did not affect the disease, and it had several adverse side effects. Effect* can also be a verb meaning "to bring about." *Only the president can effect such a dramatic change.*

aggravate   *Aggravate* means "to make worse or more troublesome." *Overgrazing aggravated the soil erosion.* In formal writing, avoid the colloquial use of *aggravate* meaning "to annoy or irritate." *Her babbling annoyed* (not *aggravated*) *me.*

agree to, agree with   *Agree to* means "to give consent." *Agree with* means "to be in accord" or "to come to an understanding." *He agrees with me about the need for change, but he won't agree to my plan.*

ain't   *Ain't* is nonstandard. Use *am not, are not* (*aren't*), or *is not* (*isn't*). *I am not* (not *ain't*) *going home for spring break.*

all ready, already   *All ready* means "completely prepared." *Already* means "previously." *Susan was all ready for the concert, but her friends had already left.*

all right   *All right* is written as two words. *Alright* is nonstandard.

all together, altogether   *All together* means "everyone gathered." *Altogether* means "entirely." *We were not altogether certain that we could bring the family all together for the reunion.*

allude   To *allude* to something is to make an indirect reference to it. Do not use *allude* to mean "to refer directly." *In his lecture the professor referred* (not *alluded*) *to several pre-Socratic philosophers.*

allusion, illusion   An *allusion* is an indirect reference. An *illusion* is a misconception or false impression. *Did you catch my allusion to Shakespeare? Mirrors give the room an illusion of depth.*

a lot   *A lot* is two words. Do not write *alot. We have had a lot of rain this spring.* See also *lots, lots of.*

A.M., P.M., a.m., p.m.   Use these abbreviations with numerals: *6:00 P.M., 11:00 a.m.* Do not use them as substitutes for the words *morning* and *evening. I worked until late in the evening* (not *p.m.*) *yesterday.*

among, between   See *between, among.*

amoral, immoral   *Amoral* means "neither moral nor immoral"; it also means "not caring about moral judgments." *Immoral* means "morally wrong." *Until recently, most business courses were taught from an amoral perspective. Murder is immoral.*

amount, number   Use *amount* with quantities that cannot be counted; use *number* with those that can. *This recipe calls for a large amount of sugar. We have a large number of toads in our garden.*

an   See *a, an.*

and etc.   *Et cetera* (*etc.*) means "and so forth"; therefore, *and etc.* is redundant. See also *etc.*

and/or   Avoid the awkward construction *and/or* except in technical or legal documents.

angry at, angry with   To write that one is *angry at* another person is nonstandard. Use *angry with* instead.

ante-, anti-   The prefix *ante-* means "earlier" or "in front of"; the prefix *anti-* means "against" or "opposed to." *William Lloyd Garrison was one of the leaders of the antislavery movement during the antebellum period. Anti-* should be used with a hyphen when it is followed by a capital letter or a word beginning with *i.*

anxious   *Anxious* means "worried" or "apprehensive." In formal writing, avoid using *anxious* to mean "eager." *We are eager* (not *anxious*) *to see your new house.*

anybody, anyone   *Anybody* and *anyone* are singular. (See 21d and 22a.)

anymore   Reserve the adverb *anymore* for negative contexts, where it means "any longer." *Moviegoers are rarely shocked anymore by profanity.* Do not use *anymore* in positive contexts. Use *now* or *nowadays* instead. *Interest rates are so low nowadays* (not *anymore*) *that more people can afford to buy homes.*

anyone   See *anybody, anyone.*

anyone, any one   *Anyone*, an indefinite pronoun, means "any person at all." *Any one*, the pronoun *one* preceded by the adjective *any*, refers to a particular person or thing in a group. *Anyone from Chicago may choose any one of the games on display.*

anyplace   *Anyplace* is informal for *anywhere.* Avoid *anyplace* in formal writing.

anyways, anywheres *Anyways* and *anywheres* are nonstandard. Use *anyway* and *anywhere*.

as *As* is sometimes used to mean "because." But do not use it if there is any chance of ambiguity. *We canceled the picnic because* (not *as*) *it began raining. As* here could mean "because" or "when."

as, like See *like, as.*

averse See *adverse, averse.*

awful The adjective *awful* means "awe-inspiring." Colloquially it is used to mean "terrible" or "bad." The adverb *awfully* is sometimes used in conversation as an intensifier meaning "very." In formal writing, avoid these colloquial uses. *I was very* (not *awfully*) *upset last night. Susan had a terrible* (not *an awful*) *time calming her nerves.*

awhile, a while *Awhile* is an adverb; it can modify a verb, but it cannot be the object of a preposition such as *for.* The two-word form *a while* is a noun preceded by an article and therefore can be the object of a preposition. *Stay awhile. Stay for a while.*

bad, badly *Bad* is an adjective, *badly* an adverb. (See 26a and 26b.) *They felt bad about being early and ruining the surprise. Her arm hurt badly after she slid headfirst into second base.*

being as, being that *Being as* and *being that* are nonstandard expressions. Write *because* or *since* instead. *Because* (not *Being as*) *I slept late, I had to skip breakfast.*

beside, besides *Beside* is a preposition meaning "at the side of" or "next to." *Annie Oakley slept with her gun beside her bed. Besides* is a preposition meaning "except" or "in addition to." *No one besides Terrie can have that ice cream. Besides* is also an adverb meaning "in addition." *I'm not hungry; besides, I don't like ice cream.*

between, among Ordinarily, use *among* with three or more entities, *between* with two. *The prize was divided among several contestants. You have a choice between carrots and beans.*

bring, take Use *bring* when an object is being transported toward you, *take* when it is being moved away. *Please bring me a glass of water. Please take these flowers to Mr. Scott.*

burst, bursted; bust, busted *Burst* is an irregular verb meaning "to come open or fly apart suddenly or violently." Its principal parts are *burst, burst, burst.* The past-tense form *bursted* is nonstandard. *Bust* and *busted* are slang for *burst* and, along with *bursted,* should not be used in formal writing.

can, may The distinction between *can* and *may* is fading, but many careful writers still observe it in formal writing. *Can* is traditionally reserved for ability, *may* for permission. *Can you ski down the advanced slope without falling? May I help you?*

capital, capitol *Capital* refers to a city, *capitol* to a building where lawmakers meet. *Capital* also refers to wealth or resources. *The capitol has undergone extensive renovations. The residents of the state capital protested the development plans.*

censor, censure *Censor* means "to remove or suppress material considered objectionable." *Censure* means "to criticize severely." *The library's new policy of censoring controversial books has been censured by the media.*

cite, site *Cite* means "to quote as an authority or example." *Site* is usually a noun meaning "a particular place." *He cited the zoning law in his argument against the proposed site of the gas station.*

climactic, climatic *Climactic* is derived from *climax*, the point of greatest intensity in a series or progression of events. *Climatic* is derived from *climate* and refers to meteorological conditions. *The climactic period in the dinosaurs' reign was reached just before severe climatic conditions brought on an ice age.*

coarse, course *Coarse* means "crude" or "rough in texture." *The coarse weave of the wall hanging gave it a three-dimensional quality. Course* usually refers to a path, a playing field, or a unit of study; the expression *of course* means "certainly." *I plan to take a course in car repair this summer. Of course, you are welcome to join me.*

compare to, compare with *Compare to* means "to represent as similar." *She compared him to a wild stallion. Compare with* means "to examine the ways in which two things are similar." *The study compared the language ability of apes with that of dolphins.*

complement, compliment *Complement* is a verb meaning "to go with or complete" or a noun meaning "something that completes." *Compliment* as a verb means "to flatter"; as a noun it means "flattering remark." *Her skill at rushing the net complements his skill at volleying. Mother's flower arrangements receive many compliments.*

conscience, conscious *Conscience* is a noun meaning "moral principles." *Conscious* is an adjective meaning "aware or alert." *Let your conscience be your guide. Were you conscious of his love for you?*

contact Although the use of *contact* to mean "to get in touch with" is common in speech, it is not appropriate in formal writing. If possible, use a precise verb such as *write* or *telephone*. *We will telephone* (not *contact*) *you soon.*

continual, continuous *Continual* means "repeated regularly and frequently." *She grew weary of the continual telephone calls. Continuous* means "extended or prolonged without interruption." *The broken siren made a continuous wail.*

could care less *Could care less* is a nonstandard expression. Write *couldn't care less* instead. *He couldn't* (not *could*) *care less about his psychology final.*

could of *Could of* is nonstandard for *could have*. *We could have* (not *could of*) *had steak for dinner if we had been hungry.*

council, counsel A *council* is a deliberative body, and a *councilor* is a member of such a body. *Counsel* usually means "advice" and can also mean "lawyer"; *counselor* is one who gives advice or guidance. *The councilors met to draft the council's position paper. The pastor offered wise counsel to the troubled teenager.*

criteria *Criteria* is the plural of *criterion*, which means "a standard or rule or test on which a judgment or decision can be based." *The only criterion for the scholarship is ability.*

data *Data* is a plural noun technically meaning "facts or propositions." But *data* is increasingly being accepted as a singular noun. *The new data suggest* (or *suggests*) *that our theory is correct.* (The singular *datum* is rarely used.)

different from, different than Ordinarily, write *different from*. *Your sense of style is different from Jim's.* However, *different than* is acceptable to avoid an awkward construction. *Please let me know if your plans are different than* (to avoid *from what*) *they were six weeks ago.*

differ from, differ with *Differ from* means "to be unlike"; *differ with* means "to disagree." *She differed with me about the wording of the agreement. My approach to the problem differed from hers.*

disinterested, uninterested *Disinterested* means "impartial, objective"; *uninterested* means "not interested." *We sought the advice of a disinterested counselor to help us solve our problem. He was uninterested in anyone's opinion but his own.*

don't *Don't* is the contraction for *do not*. *I don't want any. Don't* should not be used as the contraction for *does not*, which is *doesn't*. *He doesn't* (not *don't*) *want any.* (See 27c.)

double negative Standard English allows two negatives only if a positive meaning is intended. *The runners were not unhappy with their performance.* Double negatives used to emphasize negation are nonstandard. *Jack doesn't have to answer to anybody* (not *nobody*).

due to *Due to* is an adjective phrase and should not be used as a preposition meaning "because of." *The trip was canceled because of* (not *due to*) *lack of interest. Due to* is acceptable as a subject complement and usually follows a form of the verb *be. His success was due to hard work.*

each *Each* is singular. (See 21d and 22a.)

effect See *affect, effect.*

e.g. In formal writing, replace the Latin abbreviation *e.g.* with its English equivalent: *for example* or *for instance.*

either *Either* is singular. (See 21d and 22a.) (For *either . . . or* constructions, see 21c and 22d.)

elicit, illicit *Elicit* is a verb meaning "to bring out" or "to evoke." *Illicit* is an adjective meaning "unlawful." *The reporter was unable to elicit any information from the police about illicit drug traffic.*

emigrate from, immigrate to *Emigrate* means "to leave one country or region to settle in another." *In 1900, my grandfather emigrated from Russia to escape the religious pogroms. Immigrate* means "to enter another country and reside there." *Many Mexicans immigrate to the United States to find work.*

eminent, imminent *Eminent* means "outstanding" or "distinguished." *We met an eminent professor of Greek history. Imminent* means "about to happen." *The announcement is imminent.*

enthused Many people object to the use of *enthused* as an adjective. Use *enthusiastic* instead. *The children were enthusiastic* (not *enthused*) *about going to the circus.*

-ess Many people find the *-ess* suffix demeaning. Write *poet,* not *poetess; Jew,* not *Jewess; author,* not *authoress.*

etc. Avoid ending a list with *etc.* It is more emphatic to end with an example, and in most contexts readers will understand that the list is not exhaustive. When you don't wish to end with an example, *and so on* is more graceful than *etc.* See also *and etc.*

eventually, ultimately Often used interchangeably, *eventually* is the better choice to mean "at an unspecified time in the future" and *ul-*

timately is better to mean "the furthest possible extent or greatest extreme." *He knew that eventually he would complete his degree. The existentialist considered suicide the ultimately rational act.*

everybody, everyone *Everybody* and *everyone* are singular. (See 21d and 22a.)

everyone, every one *Everyone* is an indefinite pronoun. *Every one,* the pronoun *one* preceded by the adjective *every,* means "each individual or thing in a particular group." *Every one* is usually followed by *of. Everyone wanted to go. Every one of the missing books was found.*

except See *accept, except.*

expect Avoid the colloquial use of *expect* meaning "to believe, think, or suppose." *I think* (not *expect*) *it will rain tonight.*

explicit, implicit *Explicit* means "expressed directly" or "clearly defined"; *implicit* means "implied, unstated." *I gave him explicit instructions not to go swimming. My mother's silence indicated her implicit approval.*

farther, further *Farther* usually describes distances. *Further* usually suggests quantity or degree. *Chicago is farther from Miami than I thought. You extended the curfew further than you should have.*

female, male The terms *female* and *male* are jargon for "woman" and "man." *Two women* (not *females*) *and one man* (not *male*) *applied for the position.*

fewer, less *Fewer* refers to items that can be counted; *less* refers to general amounts. *Fewer people are living in the city. Please put less sugar in my tea.*

finalize *Finalize* is jargon meaning "to make final or complete." Use ordinary English instead. *The architect prepared final drawings* (not *finalized the drawings*).

firstly *Firstly* sounds pretentious, and it leads to the ungainly series *firstly, secondly, thirdly, fourthly,* and so on. Write *first, second, third* instead.

folks *Folks* is an informal expression for "parents" or "relatives" or "people" in general. Use a more formal expression instead.

further See *farther, further.*

get *Get* has many colloquial uses. In writing, avoid using *get* to mean the following: "to evoke an emotional response" (*That music always* *gets to me*); "to annoy" (*After a while his sulking got to me*); "to take revenge on" (*I got back at him by leaving the room*); "to become" (*He got sick*); "to start or begin" (*Let's get going*). Avoid using *have got to* in place of *must*. *I must* (not *have got to*) *finish this paper tonight.*

good, well *Good* is an adjective, *well* an adverb. (See 26.) *He hasn't felt good about his game since he sprained his wrist last season. She performed well on the uneven parallel bars.*

hanged, hung *Hanged* is the past-tense and past-participle form of the verb *hang* meaning "to execute." *The prisoner was hanged at dawn. Hung* is the past-tense and past-participle form of the verb *hang* meaning "to fasten or suspend." *The stockings were hung by the chimney with care.*

hardly Avoid expressions such as *can't hardly* and *not hardly*, which are considered double negatives. *I can* (not *can't*) *hardly describe my elation at getting the job.*

has got, have got *Got* is unnecessary and awkward in such constructions. It should be dropped. *We have* (not *have got*) *three days to prepare for the opening.*

he At one time *he* was commonly used to mean "he or she." Today such usage is inappropriate. (See 17f and 22a for alternative constructions.)

he/she, his/her In formal writing, use *he or she* or *his or her*. For alternatives to these wordy constructions, see 17f and 22a.

hisself *Hisself* is nonstandard. Use *himself.*

hopefully *Hopefully* means "in a hopeful manner." *We looked hopefully to the future.* Do not use *hopefully* in constructions such as the following: *Hopefully, your daughter will recover soon.* Indicate who is doing the hoping: *I hope that your daughter will recover soon.*

hung See *hanged, hung.*

i.e. In formal writing, replace the Latin abbreviation *i.e.* with its English equivalent: *that is.*

if, whether Use *if* to express a condition and *whether* to express alternatives. *If you go on a trip, whether it be to Nebraska or New Jersey, remember to bring traveler's checks.*

illusion See *allusion, illusion.*

imminent See *eminent, imminent.*

immoral See *amoral, immoral.*

implement *Implement* is a pretentious way of saying "do," "carry out," or "accomplish." Use ordinary language instead. *We carried out* (not *implemented*) *the director's orders with some reluctance.*

imply, infer *Imply* means "to suggest or state indirectly"; *infer* means "to draw a conclusion." *John implied that he knew all about computers, but the interviewer inferred that John was inexperienced.*

in, into *In* indicates location or condition; *into* indicates movement or a change in condition. *They found the lost letters in a box after moving into the house.*

individual *Individual* is a pretentious substitute for *person*. *We invited several persons* (not *individuals*) *from the audience to participate in the experiment.*

ingenious, ingenuous *Ingenious* means "clever." *Sarah's solution to the problem was ingenious. Ingenuous* means "naive" or "frank." *For a successful manager, Ed is surprisingly ingenuous.*

in regards to *In regards to* confuses two different phrases: *in regard to* and *as regards*. Use one or the other. *In regard to* (or *As regards*) *the contract, ignore the first clause.*

irregardless *Irregardless* is nonstandard. Use *regardless*.

is when, is where These mixed constructions are often incorrectly used in definitions. *A run-off election is a second election held to break a tie* (not *is when a second election breaks a tie*). (See 11c.)

It is *It is* is nonstandard when used to mean "there is." *There is* (not *it is*) *a fly in my soup.*

its, it's *Its* is a possessive pronoun; *it's* is a contraction for *it is*. (See 36c and 36e.) *The dog licked its wound whenever its owner walked into the room. It's a perfect day to walk the twenty-mile trail.*

kind(s) *Kind* is singular and should be treated as such. Don't write *These kind of chairs are rare*. Write instead *This kind of chair is rare. Kinds* is plural and should be used only when you mean more than one kind. *These kinds of chairs are rare.*

kind of, sort of Avoid using *kind of* or *sort of* to mean "somewhat." *The movie was kind of boring*. Do not put *a* after either phrase. *That kind of* (not *kind of a*) *salesclerk annoys me.*

lead, led *Lead* is a noun referring to a metal. *Led* is the past tense of the verb *lead. He led me to the treasure.*

learn, teach *Learn* means "to gain knowledge"; *teach* means "to impart knowledge." *I must teach (not learn) my sister to read.*

leave, let *Leave* means "to exit." Avoid using it with the nonstandard meaning "to permit." *Let (not leave) me help you with the dishes.*

less See *fewer, less.*

let, leave See *leave, let.*

liable *Liable* means "obligated" or "responsible." Do not use it to mean "likely." *You're likely (not liable) to trip if you don't tie your shoelaces.*

lie, lay *Lie* is an intransitive verb meaning "to recline or rest on a surface." Its principal parts are *lie, lay, lain. Lay* is a transitive verb meaning "to put or place." Its principal parts are *lay, laid, laid.* (See 27b.)

like, as *Like* is a preposition, not a subordinating conjunction. It can be followed only by a noun or a noun phrase. *As* is a subordinating conjunction that introduces a subordinate clause. In casual speech you may say *She looks like she hasn't slept* or *You don't know her like I do.* But in formal writing, use *as. She looks as if she hasn't slept. You don't know her as I do.* (See prepositions and subordinating conjunctions, 57f and 57g.)

loose, lose *Loose* is an adjective meaning "not securely fastened." *Lose* is a verb meaning "to misplace" or "to not win." *Did you lose your only loose pair of work pants?*

lots, lots of *Lots* and *lots of* are colloquial substitutes for *many, much,* or *a lot.* Avoid using them in formal writing.

male, female See *female, male.*

mankind Avoid *mankind* whenever possible. It offends many readers because it excludes women. Use *humanity, humans, the human race,* or *humankind* instead.

may See *can, may.*

maybe, may be *Maybe* is an adverb meaning "possibly." *May be* is a verb phrase. *Maybe the sun will shine tomorrow. Tomorrow may be a brighter day.*

may of, might of *May of* and *might of* are nonstandard for *may have* and *might have. We may have (not may of) had too many cookies.*

media, medium   *Media* is the plural of *medium. Of all the media that cover the Olympics, television is the medium that best captures the spectacle of the events.*

most   *Most* is colloquial when used to mean "almost" and should be avoided. *Almost* (not *Most*) *everyone went to the parade.*

must of   See *may of.*

myself   *Myself* is a reflexive or intensive pronoun. Reflexive: *I cut myself.* Intensive: *I will drive you myself.* Do not use *myself* in place of *I* or *me. He gave the flowers to Melinda and me* (not *myself*). (See also 24.)

neither   *Neither* is singular. (See 21d and 22a.) For *neither . . . nor* constructions, see 21c and 22d.

none   *None* is usually singular. (See 21d.)

nowheres   *Nowheres* is nonstandard for *nowhere.*

number   See *amount, number.*

of   Use the verb *have,* not the preposition *of,* after the verbs *could, should, would, may, might,* and *must. They must have* (not *of*) *left early.*

off of   *Off* is sufficient. Omit *of. The ball rolled off* (not *off of*) *the table.*

OK, O.K., okay   All three spellings are acceptable, but in formal speech and writing avoid these colloquial expressions for consent or approval.

parameters   *Parameter* is a mathematical term that has become jargon for "fixed limit," "boundary," or "guideline." Use ordinary English instead. *The task force was asked to work within certain guidelines* (not *parameters*).

passed, past   *Passed* is the past tense of the verb *pass. Mother passed me another slice of cake. Past* usually means "belonging to a former time" or "beyond a time or place." *Our past president spoke until past midnight. The hotel is just past the next intersection.*

percent, per cent, percentage   *Percent* (also spelled *per cent*) is always used with a specific number. *Percentage* is used with a descriptive term such as *large* or *small,* not with a specific number. *The candidate won 80 percent of the primary vote. Only a small percentage of registered voters turned out for the election.*

phenomena   *Phenomena* is the plural of *phenomenon,* which means "an observable occurrence or fact." *Strange phenomena occur at all* *hours of the night in that house, but last night's phenomenon was the strangest of all.*

plus *Plus* should not be used to join independent clauses. *This raincoat is dirty; moreover* (not *plus*), *it has a hole in it.*

precede, proceed *Precede* means "to come before." *Proceed* means "to go forward." *As we proceeded up the mountain, we noticed fresh tracks in the mud, evidence that a group of hikers had preceded us.*

principal, principle *Principal* is a noun meaning "the head of a school or organization" or "a sum of money." It is also an adjective meaning "most important." *Principle* is a noun meaning "a basic truth or law." *The principal expelled her for three principal reasons. We believe in the principle of equal justice for all.*

proceed, precede See *precede, proceed.*

quote, quotation *Quote* is a verb; *quotation* is a noun. Avoid using *quote* as a shortened form of *quotation*. *Her quotations* (not *quotes*) *from Shakespeare intrigued us.*

raise, rise *Raise* is a transitive verb meaning "to move or cause to move upward." It takes a direct object. *I raised the shades. Rise* is an intransitive verb meaning "to go up." It does not take a direct object. *Heat rises.*

real, really *Real* is an adjective; *really* is an adverb. *Real* is sometimes used informally as an adverb, but avoid this use in formal writing. *She was really* (not *real*) *angry.* (See 26a.)

reason is because Use *that* instead of *because*. *The reason I'm late is that* (not *because*) *my car broke down.* (See 11c.)

reason why The expression *reason why* is redundant. *The reason* (not *The reason why*) *Jones lost the election is clear.*

relation, relationship *Relation* describes a connection between things. *Relationship* describes a connection between people. *There is a relation between poverty and infant mortality. Our business relationship has cooled over the years.*

respectfully, respectively *Respectfully* means "showing or marked by respect." *Respectively* means "each in the order given." *He respectfully submitted his opinion to the judge. John, Tom, and Larry were a butcher, a baker, and a lawyer, respectively.*

sensual, sensuous *Sensual* means "gratifying the physical senses," especially those associated with sexual pleasure. *Sensuous* means "pleasing to the senses," especially those involved in the experience of art, music, and nature. *The sensuous music and balmy air led the dancers to more sensual movements.*

set, sit   *Set* is a transitive verb meaning "to put" or "to place." Its principal parts are *set, set, set. Sit* is an intransitive verb meaning "to be seated." Its principal parts are *sit, sat, sat. She set the dough in a warm corner of the kitchen. The cat sat in the warmest part of the room.*

shall, will   *Shall* was once used as the helping verb with *I* or *we: I shall, we shall, you will, he/she/it will, they will.* Today, however, *will* is generally accepted even when the subject is *I* or *we.* The word *shall* occurs primarily in polite questions (*Shall I find you a pillow?*) and in legalistic sentences suggesting duty or obligation (*The applicant shall file form 1080 by December 31*).

should of   *Should of* is nonstandard for *should have. They should have* (not *should of*) *been home an hour ago.*

since   Do not use *since* to mean *because* if there is any chance of ambiguity. *Since we won the game, we have been celebrating with a pitcher of beer. Since* here could mean "because" or "from the time that."

sit   See *set, sit.*

site, cite   See *cite, site.*

somebody, someone   *Somebody* and *someone* are singular. (See 21d and 22a.)

something   *Something* is singular. (See 21d.)

sometime, some time, sometimes   *Sometime* is an adverb meaning "at an indefinite or unstated time." *Some time* is the adjective *some* modifying the noun *time* and is spelled as two words to mean "a period of time." *Sometimes* is an adverb meaning "at times, now and then." *I'll see you sometime soon. I haven't lived there for some time. Sometimes I run into him at the library.*

sure and   *Sure and* is nonstandard for *sure to. We were all taught to be sure to* (not *and*) *look both ways before crossing a street.*

take   See *bring, take.*

than, then   *Than* is a conjunction used in comparisons; *then* is an adverb denoting time. *That pizza is more than I can eat. Tom laughed, and then we recognized him.*

that   See *who, which, that.*

that, which Many writers reserve *that* for restrictive clauses, *which* for nonrestrictive clauses. (See 32e.)

theirselves *Theirselves* is nonstandard for *themselves. The two people were able to push the Volkswagen out of the way themselves* (not *theirselves*).

them The use of *them* in place of *those* is nonstandard. *Please send those* (not *them*) *flowers to the patient in room 220.*

there, their, they're *There* is an adverb specifying place; it is also an expletive. Adverb: *Sylvia is lying there unconscious.* Expletive: *There are two plums left. Their* is a possessive pronoun: *Fred and Jane finally washed their car. They're* is a contraction of *they are: They're later than usual today.*

they The use of *they* to indicate possession is nonstandard. Use *their* instead. *Cindy and Sam decided to sell their* (not *they*) *1975 Corvette.*

this kind See *kind(s).*

to, too, two *To* is a preposition; *too* is an adverb; *two* is a number. *Too many of your shots slice to the left, but the last two were right on the mark.*

toward, towards *Toward* and *towards* are generally interchangeable, although *toward* is preferred in American English.

try and *Try and* is nonstandard for *try to. The teacher asked us all to try to* (not *and*) *write an original haiku.*

ultimately, eventually See *eventually, ultimately.*

unique Avoid expressions such as *most unique, more straight, less perfect, very round.* Something either is unique or it isn't. It is illogical to suggest degrees of uniqueness. (See 26c.)

usage The noun *usage* should not be substituted for *use* when the meaning intended is "employment of." The *use* (not *usage*) *of computers dramatically increased the company's profits.*

use to, suppose to *Use to* and *suppose to* are nonstandard. Write *used to* and *supposed to* instead.

utilize *Utilize* means "to make use of." It often sounds pretentious; in most cases, *use* is sufficient. *I used* (not *utilized*) *the best workers to get the job done fast.*

wait for, wait on *Wait for* means "to be in readiness for" or "await." *Wait on* means "to serve." *We're only waiting for* (not *waiting on*) *Ruth to take us to the game.*

ways   *Ways* is colloquial when used to mean "distance." *The city is a long way* (not *ways*) *from here.*

weather, whether   The noun *weather* refers to the state of the atmosphere. *Whether* is a conjunction referring to a choice between alternatives. *We wondered whether the weather would clear up in time for our picnic.*

well, good   See *good, well.*

where   Do not use *where* in place of *that. I heard that* (not *where*) *the crime rate is increasing.*

which   See *that, which* and *who, which, that.*

while   Avoid using *while* to mean "although" or "whereas" if there is any chance of ambiguity. *Although* (not *While*) *Gloria lost money in the slot machine, Tom won it at roulette.* Here *While* could mean either "although" or "at the same time that."

who, which, that   Do not use *which* to refer to persons. Use *who* instead. *That,* though generally used to refer to things, may be used to refer to a group or class of people. *Fans wondered how an old man who* (not *that* or *which*) *walked with a limp could play football. The team that scores the most points in this game will win the tournament.*

who, whom   *Who* is used for subjects and subject complements; *whom* is used for objects. (See 25.)

who's, whose   *Who's* is a contraction of *who is; whose* is a possessive pronoun. *Who's ready for more popcorn? Whose coat is this?* (See 36c and 36e.)

will   See *shall, will.*

would of   *Would of* is nonstandard for *would have. She would have* (not *would of*) *had a chance to play if she had arrived on time.*

you   In formal writing, avoid *you* in an indefinite sense meaning "anyone." (See 23d.) *Any spectator* (not *You*) *could tell by the way John caught the ball that his throw would be too late.*

your, you're   *Your* is a possessive pronoun; *you're* is a contraction of *you are. Is that your new motorcycle? You're on the list of finalists.* (See 36c and 36e.)

Answers to Lettered Exercises

EXERCISE 8–2, page 124

Possible revisions:

a. My grandfather, who has dramatic mood swings, was diagnosed as manic-depressive.
b. The losing team was made up of superstars who acted as isolated individuals on the court.
c. Because we are concerned about the environment, we keep our use of insecticides, herbicides, and fungicides to a minimum.
d. The aides help the younger children with their weakest subjects, reading and math.
e. My first sky dive, from an altitude of 12,500 feet, was the most frightening experience of my life.

EXERCISE 8–3, page 127

Possible revisions:

a. During a routine morning at the clinic, an infant in cardiac arrest arrived by ambulance.
b. My 1969 Camaro, an original SS396, is no longer street legal.
c. When I presented the idea of job sharing to my supervisors, to my surprise they were delighted with the idea.
d. Although outsiders have forced changes on them, native Hawaiians try to preserve their ancestors' sacred customs.
e. Sophia's country kitchen, formerly a lean-to porch, overlooks a field where horses and cattle graze among old tombstones.

EXERCISE 9-1, page 133

Possible revisions:

a. The system has capabilities such as communicating with other computers, processing records, and performing mathematical functions.
b. The personnel officer told me that I would answer the phone, welcome visitors, distribute mail, and do some typing.
c. Nolan helped by cutting the grass, trimming shrubs, mulching flowerbeds, and raking leaves.
d. How ideal it seems to raise a family here in Winnebago instead of in the air-polluted suburbs.
e. Michiko told the judge that she had been pulled out of a line of fast-moving traffic and that she had a perfect driving record.

EXERCISE 10-1, page 139

Possible revisions:

a. Dip the paintbrush into the paint remover and spread a thick coat on a small section of the door.
b. Some say that Ella Fitzgerald's renditions of Cole Porter's songs are better than any other singer's.
c. SETI (the Search for Extraterrestrial Intelligence) has excited and will continue to excite interest among space buffs.
d. Samantha got along better with the chimpanzees than with Albert. [or . . . than Albert did.]
e. We were glad to see that Yellowstone National Park was recovering from the devastating forest fire.

EXERCISE 11-1, page 145

Possible revisions:

a. My instant reaction was anger and disappointment.
b. I brought a problem into the house that my mother wasn't sure how to handle.
c. It is through the misery of others that old Harvey has become rich.
d. A cloverleaf allows traffic on limited-access freeways to change direction.
e. Bowman established the format that future football card companies would emulate for years to come.

EXERCISE 12-1, page 150

Possible revisions:

a. He wanted to buy only three roses, not a dozen.
b. Within the next few years, orthodontists will be using as standard practice the technique Kurtz developed.
c. Cella received a flier from a Japanese nun about a workshop on making a kimono.

d. Jurors are encouraged to sift through the evidence carefully and thoroughly.
e. Each state would set into motion a program of recycling all reusable products.

EXERCISE 12–2, page 153

Possible revisions:

a. Reaching the heart, the surgeon performed a bypass on the severely blocked arteries.
b. When I was nestled in the cockpit, the pounding of the engine was muffled only slightly by my helmet.
c. While we dined at night, the lights along the Baja coastline created a romantic atmosphere perfect for our first anniversary.
d. While my sister was still a beginner at tennis, the coaches recruited her to train for the Olympics.
e. After Marcus Garvey returned to Jamaica, his "Back to Africa" movement slowly died.

EXERCISE 13–1, page 163

Possible revisions:

a. The young man who burglarized our house was sentenced to probation for one year, a small price to pay for robbing us of our personal possessions as well as our trust in other human beings.
b. After the count of three, Mikah and I placed the injured woman on the scoop stretcher. Then I took her vital signs.
c. Ministers often have a hard time because they have to please so many different people.
d. We drove for eight hours until we reached the South Dakota Badlands. We could hardly believe the eeriness of the landscape at dusk.
e. The question is whether ferrets bred in captivity have the instinct to prey on prairie dogs or whether this is a learned skill.

EXERCISE 14–1, page 167

Possible revisions:

a. Her letter acknowledged the students' participation in the literacy program.
b. Ahmed, the producer, manages the entire operation.
c. Emphatic and active; no change.
d. Players were fighting on both sides of the rink.
e. Emphatic and active; no change.

EXERCISE 16–1, page 187

Possible revisions:

a. The drawing room in the west wing is said to be haunted.
b. Dr. Santiti has seen problems like yours many times.

c. Bloom's race for the governorship is futile.
d. New fares must be reported to all of our transportation offices.
e. In the heart of Beijing lies the Forbidden City, an imperial palace built during the Ming dynasty.

EXERCISE 17–1, page 193

Possible revisions:

a. It is a widely held myth that middle-aged people can't change.
b. All work-study students must prove that they are enrolled.
c. In 1985 I bought a house in need of repair.
d. When Sal was laid off from his high-paying factory job, he learned what it was like to be poor.
e. Passengers should try to complete the customs declaration form before leaving the plane.

EXERCISE 17–3, page 201

Possible revisions:

a. Asha Purpura is the defense attorney appointed by the court. Al Jones has been assigned to work with her on the case.
b. A young graduate who is careful about investments can accumulate a significant sum in a relatively short period.
c. An elementary school teacher should understand the concept of nurturing if he or she intends to be a success.
d. Because Dr. Brown and Dr. Coombs were the senior professors in the department, they served as co-chairpersons of the promotion committee.
e. If we do not stop polluting our environment, we will perish.

EXERCISE 18–3, page 207

Possible revisions:

a. Many of us are not persistent enough to make a change for the better.
b. It is sometimes difficult to hear in church because the acoustics are so terrible.
c. Liu Kwan began his career as a lawyer, but now he is a real estate mogul.
d. When Robert Frost died at age eighty-eight, he left a legacy of poems that will make him immortal.
e. This patient is kept in isolation to prevent her from catching our germs.

EXERCISE 18–4, page 209

Possible revisions:

a. Queen Anne was so angry with Sarah Churchill that she refused to see her again.
b. Correct
c. Try to come up with the rough outline, and Marika will fill in the details.

d. For the frightened refugees, the dangerous trek across the mountains was preferable to life in a war zone.
e. The parade moved off the street and onto the beach.

EXERCISE 18–5, page 212

Possible revisions:

a. Juanita told Kyle that keeping secrets would be dangerous.
b. The president thought that the scientists were using science as a means of furthering their political goals.
c. Ours was a long courtship; we waited ten years before finally deciding to marry.
d. We ironed out the wrinkles in our relationship.
e. Sasha told us that he wasn't willing to take the chance.

EXERCISE 19–1, page 223

Possible revisions:

a. As I stood in front of the microwave, I recalled my grandmother bending over her old black stove and remembered what she taught me: that any food can have soul if you love the people you are cooking for.
b. It has been said that there are only three indigenous American art forms: jazz, musical comedy, and soap opera.
c. Correct
d. We need to stop believing myths about drinking — that strong black coffee will sober you up, for example, or that a cold shower will straighten you out.
e. As we walked up the path, we came upon the gun batteries, large gray concrete structures covered with ivy and weeds.

EXERCISE 20–1, page 233

Possible revisions:

a. The city had one public swimming pool that stayed packed with children all summer long.
b. The building is being renovated, so at times we have no heat, water, or electricity.
c. Why should we pay taxes to support public transportation? We prefer to save energy dollars by carpooling.
d. Suddenly there was a loud silence; the shelling had stopped.
e. In Garvey's time the caste system in the West Indies was simple: the lighter the skin tone, the higher the status.

EXERCISE 20–2, page 235

Possible revisions:

a. Because the trail up Mount Finegold was declared impassable, we decided to return to our hotel a day early.

b. Correct
c. The instructor never talked to the class; she just assigned busywork and sat at her desk reading the newspaper.
d. Researchers studying the fertility of Texas land tortoises X-rayed all the female tortoises to see how many eggs they had.
e. The suburbs seemed cold; they lacked the warmth and excitement of our Italian neighborhood.

EXERCISE 21–1, page 249

a. Subject: friendship and support; verb: have; b. Subject: rings; verb: are; c. Subject: Each; verb: was; d. Subject: source; verb: is; e. Subject: signs or traces; verb: were.

EXERCISE 21–2, page 250

a. High concentrations of carbon monoxide result in headaches, dizziness, unconsciousness, and even death.
b. Correct
c. Correct
d. Crystal chandeliers, polished floors, and a new oil painting have transformed Sandra's apartment.
e. Either Gertrude or Alice takes the dog out for its nightly walk.

EXERCISE 22–1, page 259

Possible revisions:

a. I can be standing in front of a Xerox machine, with parts scattered around my feet, and someone will ask me for permission to make a copy.
b. Correct
c. The instructor has asked everyone to bring his or her own tools to carpentry class.
d. An eighteenth-century architect was also a classical scholar who was often at the forefront of archeological research.
e. On the first day of class, Mr. Bhatti asked each of us why we wanted to stop smoking.

EXERCISE 23–1, page 267

Possible revisions:

a. The detective photographed the body after removing the blood-stained shawl.
b. In Professor Jamal's class, students are lucky to earn a C.
c. Please be patient with the elderly residents who have difficulty moving through the cafeteria line.
d. The Comanche braves lived violent lives; they gained respect for their skill as warriors.
e. All students can secure parking permits from the campus police office, which is open from 8 A.M. until 8 P.M.

EXERCISE 24–1, page 276

a. My Ethiopian neighbor was puzzled by the dedication of us joggers.
b. Correct
c. Sue's husband is ten years older than she.
d. Everyone laughed whenever Sandra described how her brother and she had seen the Lock Ness monster and fed it sandwiches.
e. Correct

EXERCISE 25–1, page 280

a. In his first production of *Hamlet,* whom did Laurence Olivier replace?
b. Correct
c. Correct
d. Some group leaders cannot handle the pressure; they give whoever makes the most noise most of their attention.
e. One of the women whom Martinez hired became the most successful lawyer in the agency.

EXERCISE 26–1, page 288

a. When Tina began breathing normally, we could relax.
b. All of us on the team felt bad about our performance.
c. Tim's friends cheered and clapped very loudly when he made it to the bottom of the beginners' slope.
d. Correct
e. Last Christmas was the most wonderful day of my life.

EXERCISE 27–1, page 295

a. Noticing that my roommate was shivering and looking pale, I rang for the nurse.
b. When I get the urge to exercise, I lie down until it passes.
c. Grandmother had driven our new jeep to the sunrise church service on Savage Mountain, so we were left with the station wagon.
d. I just heard on the news that Claudia Brandolini has broken the world record for the high jump.
e. Correct

EXERCISE 27–2, page 304

a. Correct
b. The museum visitors were not supposed to touch the exhibits.
c. Our church has all the latest technology, even a closed-circuit television.
d. We often don't know whether he is angry or just joking.
e. Staggered working hours have reduced traffic jams and saved motorists many gallons of gas.

EXERCISE 28–1, page 313

a. Correct
b. Watson and Crick discovered the mechanism that controls inheritance in all life: the workings of the DNA molecule.
c. In 1941 Hitler decided to kill the Jews. But Himmler and his SS were three years ahead of him; they had had mass murder in mind since 1938.
d. Toni could be an excellent student if she weren't so distracted by problems at home.
e. Correct

EXERCISE 28–2, page 315

Possible revisions:

a. Fra Angelico painted each bedroom in the monastery.
b. Scientists use carbon dating to determine the approximate age of an object.
c. As the patient undressed, we saw scars on his back, stomach, and thighs. We suspected child abuse.
d. We noted right away that the taxi driver had been exposed to Americans because he knew all the latest slang.
e. The painter patched and sanded the holes, primed the walls, and painted the ceiling.

EXERCISE 29–1, page 322

Answers:

a. We will make this a better country.
b. There is nothing in the world that TV has not touched on.
c. Did you understand my question?
d. A hard wind was blowing while we were climbing the mountain.
e. The child's innocent world has been taken away from him.

EXERCISE 29–2, page 325

Possible sentences:

a. He would have won the election if he had gone to the inner city to campaign.
b. If Martin Luther King, Jr., were alive today, he would be appalled by the violence in our inner cities.
c. Whenever my uncle comes to visit, he brings me an expensive present.
d. We will lose our largest client unless we update our computer system.
e. If Verena wins a fellowship, she will go to graduate school.

EXERCISE 29–3, page 328

Possible sentences:

a. I enjoy riding my motorcycle.
b. Will you help Samantha study for the test?
c. The team hopes to work hard and win the championship.
d. Ricardo and his brothers miss surfing during the winter.
e. The babysitter let Roger stay up until midnight.

EXERCISE 31-1, page 340

Answers:

a. The roses they brought home cost three dollars each.
b. There are two grocery stores on Elm Street.
c. The prime minister is the most popular leader in my country.
d. Pavel hasn't heard from the cousin he wrote to last month.
e. The king, who had served since the age of sixteen, was an old man when he died.

EXERCISE 31-2, page 343

Answers:

a. an attractive young Vietnamese woman
b. a dedicated Catholic priest
c. her old blue wool sweater
d. Joe's delicious Scandinavian bread
e. many beautiful antique bird cages

EXERCISE 31-3, page 345

Answers:

a. Having to listen to everyone's complaints was irritating.
b. The noise in the hall was distracting to me.
c. Correct
d. The violence in recent movies is often disgusting.
e. Correct

EXERCISE 31-4, page 347

Possible revisions:

a. We spent seven days in June at the beach and it rained every day.
b. Correct
c. Usually she met with her patients in the afternoon, but on that day she stayed at home to take care of her son.
d. The clock is hanging on the wall in the dining room.
e. In Germany it is difficult for foreigners to become citizens even if they've lived in the country for a long time.

EXERCISE 32-1, page 352

Answers:

a. Correct
b. The man at the next table complained loudly, and the waiter stomped off in disgust.
c. Instead of eating half a cake or two dozen cookies, I now grab a banana and an orange.
d. Nursing is physically and mentally demanding, yet the pay is low.
e. Uncle Sven's dulcimers disappeared as soon as he put them up for sale, but he always kept one for himself.

EXERCISE 32–2, page 355

Answers:

a. She wore a black silk cape, a rhinestone collar, satin gloves, and high tops.
b. There is no need to prune, weed, fertilize, or repot your air fern.
c. City Café is noted for its spicy vegetarian dishes and its friendly, efficient service.
d. Juan walked through the room with casual, elegant grace.
e. Correct

EXERCISE 32–3, page 359

Answers:

a. B. B. King and Lucille, his customized black Gibson, have electrified audiences all over the world.
b. The Scott Pack, which is a twenty-five-pound steel bottle of air, is designed to be worn on a firefighter's back.
c. Correct
d. Shakespeare's tragedy *King Lear* was given a splendid performance by the actor Laurence Olivier.
e. Correct

EXERCISE 32–4, page 365

Answers:

a. The whiskey stills, which were run mostly by farmers and fishermen, were about twenty miles from the nearest town.
b. At the sound of a starting pistol, the horses surged forward toward the first obstacle, a sharp incline three feet high.
c. Each morning the seventy-year-old woman cleans the barn, shovels manure, and spreads clean hay around the milking stalls.
d. The students of Highpoint are required to wear dull green polyester pleated skirts.
e. Beauty is in the eye of the beholder, but glamour is for anyone who can afford it.

EXERCISE 32–5, page 366

Answers:

a. April 13, 1995, is the final deadline for all applications.
b. The coach having bawled us out thoroughly, we left the locker room with his last, harsh words ringing in our ears.
c. Good technique does not guarantee, however, that the power you develop will be sufficient for Kyok Pa competition.
d. We all piled into Sadiq's car, which we affectionately referred to as the Blue Goose.
e. Please make the check payable to David Kerr, D.D.S., not David Kerr, M.D.

EXERCISE 33–1, page 375

Answers:

a. We'd rather spend our money on blue-chip stocks than speculate on pork-bellies.
b. Being prepared for the worst is one way to escape disappointment.
c. When he heard the groans, he opened the door and ran out.
d. My father said that he would move to California if I would agree to transfer to UCLA.
e. I quickly accepted the fact that I was literally in third-class quarters.

EXERCISE 34–1, page 380

Answers:

a. When a woman behaves like a man, why doesn't she behave like a nice man?
b. No amount of experimentation can ever prove me right; a single experiment can prove me wrong.
c. Don't talk about yourself; it will be done when you leave.
d. The only sensible ends of literature are first, the pleasurable toil of writing; second, the gratification of one's family and friends; and lastly, the solid cash.
e. When men talk about defense, they always claim to be protecting women and children, but they never ask the women and children what they think.

EXERCISE 34–2, page 381

Answers:

a. Many people believe that ferrets are vicious little rodents; in fact, ferrets are affectionate animals that tend to bite only out of fear.
b. America has been called a country of pragmatists, although the American devotion to ideals is legendary.
c. The first requirement is honesty; everything else follows.
d. I am not fond of opera; I must admit, however, that I was greatly moved by *Les Misérables.*
e. Correct

EXERCISE 35–1, page 384

Answers:

a. The second and most memorable week of survival school consisted of five stages: orientation, long treks, POW camp, escape and evasion, and return to civilization.
b. Among the canceled classes were calculus, physics, advanced biology, and English 101.
c. Correct
d. For example, Teddy Roosevelt once referred to the wolf as "the beast of waste and desolation."
e. Correct

EXERCISE 36–1, page 388

Answers:

a. In a democracy anyone's vote counts as much as mine.
b. Correct
c. The puppy's favorite activity was chasing its tail.
d. After we bought J.J. the latest style pants and shirts, he decided that last year's faded, ragged jeans were perfect for all occasions.
e. A crocodile's life span is about thirteen years.

EXERCISE 37–1, page 396

Answers:

a. Correct
b. As Emerson wrote in 1849, "I hate quotations. Tell me what you know."
c. Andrew Marvell's most famous poem, "To His Coy Mistress," is a tightly structured argument.
d. Correct
e. Historians Segal and Stineback tell us that the English settlers considered these epidemics "the hand of God making room for His followers in the 'New World.' "

EXERCISE 39–1, page 405

Answers:

a. We lived in Davenport, Iowa, during the early years of our marriage.
b. Every night after her jazzercise class, Elizaveta bragged about how invigorated she felt, but she always looked exhausted.
c. Correct
d. Every person there — from the youngest toddler to the oldest great-grandparent — was expected to sit through the three-hour sermon in respectful silence.
e. The class stood, faced the flag, placed hands over hearts, and raced through "I pledge allegiance . . . liberty and justice for all" in less than sixty seconds.

EXERCISE 40–1, page 411

Answers:

a. Correct
b. Denzil spent all night studying for his psychology exam.
c. Correct
d. The first discovery of America was definitely not in A.D. 1492.
e. Turning to page 195, Marion realized that she had finally reached the end of chapter 22.

EXERCISE 41–1, page 414

Answers:

a. We have ordered four azaleas, three rhododendrons, and two mountain laurels for the back area of the garden.

b.   Correct
c.   Correct
d.   We ordered three 4-door sedans for company executives.
e.   The Vietnam Veterans Memorial in Washington, D.C., had 58,132 names inscribed on it when it was dedicated in 1982.

EXERCISE 42–1, page 417

Answers:

a.   Howard Hughes commissioned the *Spruce Goose*, a beautifully built but thoroughly impractical wooden aircraft.
b.   Pulaski was so exhausted he could barely lift his foot the six inches to the elevator floor.
c.   Even though it is almost always hot in Mexico in the summer, you can usually find a cool spot on one of the park benches in the town's *zócalo*.
d.   Correct
e.   *The City and the Pillar* was an early novel by Gore Vidal.

EXERCISE 44–1, page 431

Answers:

a.   Correct
b.   The quietly purring cat cleaned first one paw and then the other before curling up under the stove.
c.   The Moche were a pre-Columbian people who established a sophisticated culture in ancient Peru.
d.   Your dog is well known in our neighborhood.
e.   Correct

EXERCISE 45–1, page 437

Answers:

a.   District Attorney Johnson was disgusted when the jurors turned in a verdict of not guilty after only one hour of deliberation.
b.   My mother has begun to research the history of her Indian ancestors in North Carolina.
c.   Correct
d.   Refugees from Central America are finding it more and more difficult to cross the Rio Grande into the United States.
e.   I want to take Environmental Biology 103, one other biology course, and one English course.

EXERCISE 52–1, page 587

Answers:

a. hasty generalization; b. false analogy; c. emotional appeal; d. faulty cause-and-effect reasoning; e. *either . . . or* fallacy

EXERCISE 57–1, page 643

Answers:

a. idea, words, freedom, movement; b. Pride, bottom, mistakes; c. trouble, rat (noun/adjective), race, rat; d. censorship, flick, dial; e. Figures, liars

EXERCISE 57–2, page 647

Answers:

a. Every (pronoun/adjective), its (pronoun/adjective), its (pronoun/adjective); b. those, who; c. I, some (pronoun/adjective), I, myself; d. I, You, He; e. I, it

EXERCISE 57–3, page 649

Answers:

a. have been; b. can be savored; c. does bring down; d. is, could rephrase; e. Do scald

EXERCISE 57–4, page 652

Answers:

a. Adjectives: General, wrong; adverb: generally; b. Adjectives: The (article), American, tolerant; adverb: wonderfully; c. Adjectives: a (article), rational; adverb: not; d. Adjectives: a (article), thin; adverb: very; e. Adjective: the (article); adverb: faster

EXERCISE 58–1, page 662

Answers:

a. Complete subject: A spoiled child; simple subject: child; b. Complete subject: all facts; simple subject: facts; c. Complete subject: (You); d. Complete subject: nothing except change; simple subject: nothing; e. Complete subject: The only difference between a rut and a grave; simple subject: difference

EXERCISE 58–2, page 666

Answers:

a. Subject complement: truth; b. Direct object: the depth of a river; c. Subject complement: yellow; d. Direct object: a man [or a woman]; object complement: wise; e. Indirect objects: me, you; direct objects: a capitalist, a bloodsucker

EXERCISE 59–1, page 672

Answers:

a. with no side effects (adjective phrase modifying *tranquilizer*); b. of several air traffic controllers (adjective phrase modifying *job*), with ease (adverbial phrase modifying *could perform*); c. like a loose garment (adverbial phrase modifying *wears*); d. of a nation (adjective phrase modifying *ideals*), by its advertising (adverbial phrase modifying *can tell*); e. In prosperity (adverbial phrase modifying *smokes*)

EXERCISE 59–2, page 677

Answers:

a. who has outposts in your head (adjective clause modifying *enemy*); b. that is not dangerous (adjective clause modifying *idea*); c. When I am an old woman (adverbial clause modifying *shall wear*); d. what they mean (noun clause used as the direct object of *say*); e. unless it is practiced on clever persons (adverb clause modifying *is*)

EXERCISE 59–3, page 682

Answers:

a. being sixteen (gerund phrase used as subject complement); b. to conceal him (infinitive phrase used as direct object of *tried*), naming him Smith (gerund phrase used as object of the preposition *by*); c. made tedious by morality (participial phrase modifying *gossip*); d. Being a philosopher (participial phrase modifying *I*); e. to be older (infinitive phrase used as direct object of *wanted*)

EXERCISE 60–1, page 686

Answers:

a. complex; whose work sells (adjective clause); b. compound; c. simple; d. complex; If you don't go to other people's funerals (adverb clause); e. compound-complex; what you are afraid of (noun clause)

(Continued from page iv)

Eugene Boe, from "Pioneers to Eternity: Norwegians on the Prairie" by Eugene Boe from *The Immigrant Experience,* edited by Thomas C. Wheeler. Copyright © 1971 by Thomas C. Wheeler. A Dial Press Book. Reprinted by permission of Doubleday & Company, Inc.

Jane Brody, from *Jane Brody's Nutrition Book.* Copyright © 1981 by Jane E. Brody. Reprinted by permission of W. W. Norton & Company, Inc.

Roger Caras, from "What's a Koala?" Copyright 1983 by Roger Caras. First appeared in *Geo* Magazine, May 1983. Reprinted by permission of Roberta Pryor, Inc.

Bruce Catton, from "Grant and Lee: A Study in Contrasts," *The American Story,* Earl Schenck Miers, editor. © 1956 by Broadcast Music, Inc. Reprinted by permission of the U.S. Capitol Historical Society.

Napoleon A. Chagnon, from *Yanomamo: The Fierce People.* Reprinted by permission of Holt, Rinehart and Winston, Publishers.

Barnaby Conrad III, from " 'Train of Kings, the King of Trains' Is Back on Track," *Smithsonian,* December 1983. Reprinted by permission of *Smithsonian.*

Earl Conrad, from *Harriet Tubman.* Reprinted by permission of Paul S. Erikson, Publisher.

James Underwood Crockett, Oliver E. Allen, and the Editors of Time-Life Books, from *The Time-Life Encyclopedia of Gardening.* © 1977 Time-Life Books, Inc. Reprinted by permission of Time-Life Books, Inc.

Emily Dickinson, from "The Snake." Reprinted by permission of the publishers and the Trustees of Amherst College from *The Poems of Emily Dickinson,* Thomas H. Johnson, Ed. Cambridge, Mass.: The Belknap Press of Harvard University Press, copyright 1951, © 1955, 1979, 1983 by the President and Fellows of Harvard College. "Opinion is a flitting Thing," from *Life and Letters of Emily Dickinson,* edited by Martha D. Bianchi. Copyright 1924 by Martha Dickinson Bianchi. Copyright renewed 1952 by Alfred Leete Hampson. Reprinted by permission of Houghton Mifflin Company.

Annie Dillard, from *Teaching a Stone to Talk.* Copyright © 1982 by Annie Dillard. Reprinted by permission of HarperCollins Publishers.

Erik Eckholm, from "Pygmy Chimp Readily Learns Language Skill," *The New York Times.* Copyright © 1985 by The New York Times Company. Reprinted by permission.

Jane Goodall, from *In the Shadow of Man.* Copyright © 1971 by Hugo and Jane van Lawick-Goodall. Reprinted by permission of Houghton Mifflin Company.

Ellen Goodman, from "Bad Samaritans," *The Washington Post,* March 10, 1984.

Stephen Jay Gould, from "Were Dinosaurs Dumb?" *The Panda's Thumb: More Reflections on Natural History.* Copyright © 1980 by Stephen Jay Gould. Reprinted by permission of W. W. Norton & Company, Inc.

Hillary Hauser, from "Exploring a Sunken Realm in Australia," *National Geographic,* January 1984. Reprinted by permission of the National Geographic Society.

Richard Hofstadter, from *America at 1750: A Social Portrait.* Copyright © 1971 by Beatrice K. Hofstadter, executrix of the estate of Richard Hofstadter. Reprinted by permission of Alfred A. Knopf, Inc.

Langston Hughes, "Ballad of the Landlord." Reprinted by permission of Harold Ober Associates Incorporated. Copyright 1951 by Langston Hughes. Copyright renewed 1979 by George Houston Bass.

Phillip Kopper, "How to Open an Oyster." Copyright © 1979 by Phillip Kopper. Reprinted by permission of Times Books, a division of Quadrangle/The New York Times Book Co., Inc., from *The Wild Edge: Life and Lore of the Great American Beaches* by Phillip Kopper.

William Least Heat Moon, from *Blue Highways*. Copyright © 1982 by William Least Heat Moon. Reprinted by permission of Little, Brown and Company.

Margaret Mead, from "New Superstitions for Old," *A Way of Seeing*. Reprinted by permission of William Morrow & Company, Inc.

Gloria Naylor, from *Linden Hills*. Copyright © 1985 by Gloria Naylor. Reprinted by permission of Houghton Mifflin Company.

Flannery O'Connor, from "The King of the Birds," *Mystery and Manners*. Copyright © 1969. Reprinted by permission of Farrar, Straus and Giroux, Inc.

Readers' Guide to Periodical Literature, March 1982–February 1983, from entries under "Animal Communications." Copyright © 1982, 1983 by The H. W. Wilson Company. Material reproduced by permission of the publisher.

Paul Reps, from "The Moon Cannot Be Stolen," *Zen Flesh, Zen Bones*. Reprinted by permission of Charles E. Tuttle Co., Inc., of Tokyo, Japan.

Richard Rodriguez, from "Aria: A Memoir of a Bilingual Childhood." Reprinted by permission of the author. Copyright © 1980 by Richard Rodriguez. First published in *The American Scholar*.

Arthur M. Schlesinger, Jr., from *The Age of Roosevelt: The Crisis of the Old Order*. Copyright © 1957 by Arthur M. Schlesinger, Jr. Reprinted by permission of Houghton Mifflin Company.

Julian Simon, "Immigration for a Stronger America," *The Washington Post*, September 1, 1990.

Lewis Thomas, from "On Societies as Organisms" and "Your Very Good Health," *The Lives of a Cell*. Copyright © 1974 by Lewis Thomas. From "Notes on Punctuation," *The Medusa and the Snail*. Copyright © 1979 by Lewis Thomas. All rights reserved. Reprinted by permission of Viking Penguin, Inc.

James Thurber, from "University Days," *My Life and Hard Times*. Copyright © 1933, 1961 by James Thurber. Published by Harper & Row, Publishers, Inc. Reprinted by permission.

Margaret Visser, from *Much Depends on Dinner* by Margaret Visser. Reprinted by permission of Grove Press and the Canadian publishers, McClelland & Stewart, Toronto.

Olivia Vlahos, from *Human Beginnings*. Published by Viking Penguin, Inc. Reprinted by permission of the author.

Alice Walker, from "In Search of Our Mothers' Gardens," *In Search of Our Mothers' Gardens*. Copyright 1967 by Alice Walker. Reprinted by permission of Harcourt Brace & Co.

E. B. White, from "Here is New York," from *Essays of E. B. White*. Copyright 1949 by E. B. White. Published by Harper & Row, Publishers, Inc. Reprinted by permission of HarperCollins Publishers.

Index

S

W

Y

A complete section on major ESL problems:

ESL notes in other sections:

A LIST OF CHARTS

A List of Charts (continued)

CORRECTION SYMBOLS

Boldface numbers refer to sections of the handbook.

abbr	faulty abbreviation **40**		num	error in use of numbers **41**
ad	misuse of adverb or adjective **26**		om	omitted word **10, 30, 31a**
agr	faulty agreement **21, 22**		p	error in punctuation
appr	inappropriate language **17**		⌃	comma **32**
art	article **30**		no ,	no comma **33**
awk	awkward		;	semicolon **34**
cap	capital letter **45**		:	colon **35**
case	error in case **24, 25**		⌄	apostrophe **36**
coh	coherence **7**		" "	quotation marks **37**
coord	faulty coordination **8b**		. ? !	period, question mark, exclamation point **38**
cs	comma splice **20**		— ( ) [ ] . . . /	dash, parentheses, brackets, ellipsis marks, slash **39**
dev	inadequate development **2, 6**			
dm	dangling modifier **12e**		par, ¶	new paragraph **6d**
-ed	error in -ed ending **27d**		pass	ineffective passive **14a, 28c**
emph	emphasis **14**		ref	error in pronoun reference **23**
ESL	English as a second language **29–31**		rev	revise **3, 4**
exact	inexact language **18**		-s	error in -s ending **27c, 21**
frag	sentence fragment **19**		shift	distracting shift **13**
fs	fused sentence **20**		sp	misspelled word **43**
gl/us	see Glossary of Usage		sub	faulty subordination **8c–d**
hyph	error in use of hyphen **44**		t	error in verb tense **28a**
inc	incomplete construction **10**		trans	transition needed **7e**
irreg	error in irregular verb **27a**		v	voice **14a, 28c**
ital	italics (underlining) **42**		var	lack of variety in sentence structure **8, 15**
lc	use lowercase letter **45**		vb	error in verb form **27**
mixed	mixed construction **11**		w	wordy **16**
mm	misplaced modifier **12a–e**		//	faulty parallelism **9**
mood	error in mood **28b**		∧	insert
ms	manuscript form **55**		x	obvious error
nonst	nonstandard usage **17d, 27**		#	insert space
			⌒	close up space